Simplicity's
Simply the Best
SEWING BOOK

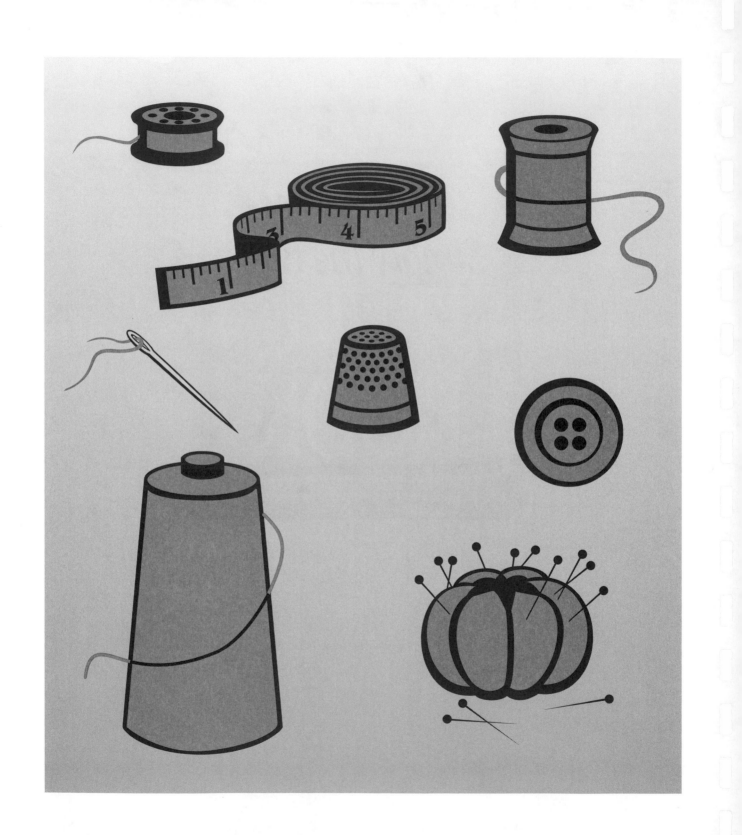

Simplicity's
Simply the Best
SEWING BOOK

REVISED EDITION

Edited by
Anne Marie Soto
and the
Staff of the Simplicity Pattern Company

Fashion Illustrations by Martha Vaughn

THE SIMPLICITY PATTERN CO. INC.

acknowledgements

In developing this revised edition of *Simplicity's® Simply the Best Sewing Book*, we drew on the creative talents, product expertise, sewing experience and enthusiasm of many people. We are especially grateful to the following individuals.

EDITOR: Anne Marie Soto

SENIOR VICE PRESIDENT, PRODUCT, SIMPLICITY PATTERNS: Judy Raymond

CONTRIBUTING WRITER: Janis Bullis

TECHNICAL ILLUSTRATIONS: Phoebe Gaughan, Angela Erenberg

FASHION ILLUSTRATIONS: Martha Vaughan

COPYEDITORS: Didi Charney, Rosalie Cooke

COVER AND INTERIOR DESIGN: Chris Swirnoff Design

PRODUCTION: Ripinsky & Company

LITERARY AGENT: Marlene Connor Lynch, Connor Literary Agency

TECHNICAL EXPERTISE:
The Staff of the Simplicity Pattern Company, especially Karen Burkhart, Richard Kite, Deborah Kreiling, Carol Tomassini, Dena Strong

The Staff of Simplicity Sewing Machines, especially Ann Regal, Rita West, Ann Macklin, Margo Morris, Paula Spoon, June Andres

In addition, this revised edition of *Simplicity's Simply the Best Sewing Book* owes a large debt of gratitude to those who contributed their time and talent to the original version. Their achievements provided the foundation for this updated version. We would like to particularly acknowledge the following people.

FOR THEIR SEWING AND SERGER EXPERTISE:
Grace McMahon-Johnson, Janice S. Saunders, Nancy Nix Rice, Betty Ann Pillsworth, Ann Marie Timinelli

FOR THE TECHNICAL ILLUSTRATIONS:
Terry Baldessari, Ada Cruz, Helen Pettee

SIMPLICITY'S SIMPLY THE BEST SEWING BOOK

FIRST REVISED EDITION

Exclusive paperback book club edition produced by arrangement with Bookspan, 1540 Broadway, New York , N.Y. 10036

ISBN 0-7394-2100-X

Designed by Christine Swirnoff

Library of Congress Cataloging-in Publication Data

Simplicity's simply the best sewing book/by the Simplicity Pattern Co. Inc.
Includes index.

1. Dressmaking.   2. Sewing.   1. Simplicity Pattern Co.
TT525.S995   1988

646.'304—dc19   87-24940

contents

chapter 5
The Universal Basics

chapter 6
Simply the Best Sewing Techniques

chapter 7
Sewing on Special Fabrics

chapter 8
Simply the Best Patternless Projects

Sized for grown-ups and kids.

There is a color section between pages 144-145

introduction
How this Book Evolved

When *Simplicity's® Simply the Best Sewing Book* was first published in 1988, the concept of teaching conventional and serger sewing step-by-step and side-by-side was "right on." As the years have progressed, and more and more consumers are discovering the joys of serger sewing, this concept has truly withstood the test of time.

Although the original version of this book has been a consistent best seller, we were motivated to create a revised edition. Our reasons were simple. First, today's consumers want to be sure that they have access to the latest techniques. Second, sewing interests are always changing and evolving—which is one reason why sewing is such a fascinating subject and such a rewarding pastime!

Throughout this revision, our goal was to address the concerns of contemporary sewers. We worked carefully with Simplicity's Consumer Relations Department which monitors consumer concerns about sewing in general and handles requests for specific information.

We were encouraged by the positive reactions the original book has received over the years from both consumers and retailers. They applauded the book's contents and its conversational tone…the feeling that someone is working with you as you read through the instructions, someone who cares that your sewing project be the best it can be. We made the commitment to retain everything consumers loved, while making the second version even better.

This book has been updated to reflect new developments in both conventional sewing machines and sergers. New sewing techniques and time-saving tips are introduced. Product information has been updated to reflect recent offerings in the marketplace. A new chapter—"Sewing on Special Fabrics"—contains helpful information to transform challenging fabrics into sewer-friendly fabrics. The patternless projects have been updated to reflect the fashion attitudes of the 21st century. New projects make kids' clothes an important part of this section.

The result is a book for today's sewers…one that is still the best, most comprehensive source for sewing information for new sewers and experienced sewers, as well as for those who are rediscovering the joys of this rewarding craft.

The Simplicity Pattern Company

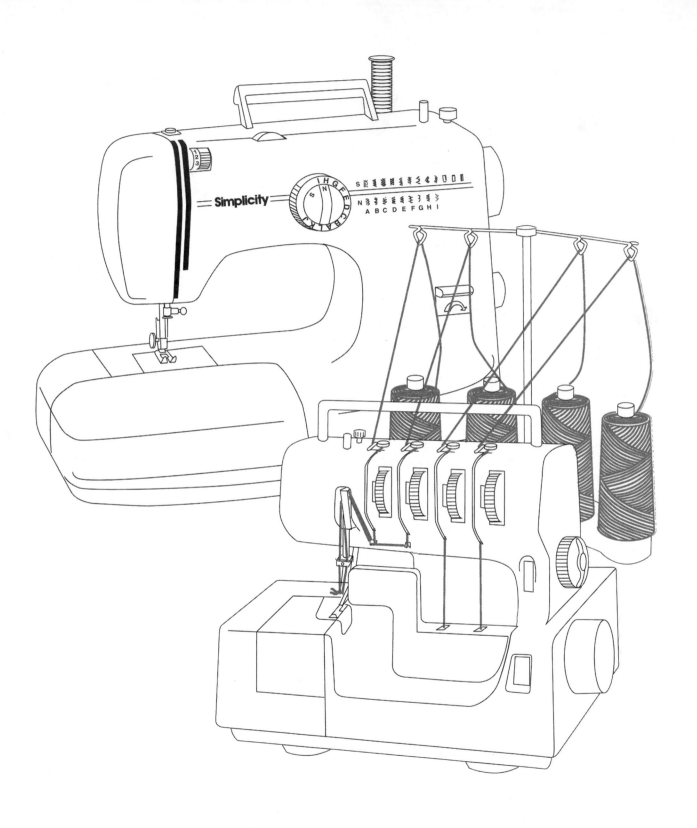

chapter 1

Sewing for Today

Not long ago, if you asked a group of people why they sewed, you would probably get one of two answers. The first would be "to save money." The second would be "because there is nothing suitable in the stores."

Ask that same question today, and you'll get a rainbow of answers.

> **" Sewing is a way to express myself. "**

In this age of advanced technology and mass production, sewing provides the means for expressing individuality. It doesn't matter if you shop in a department store, an expensive boutique or a discount chain...or if you shop at the high or low end of the line. When you buy ready-made clothes, you can always see someone else coming and going in "your" outfit. If you sew, however, you can say to yourself, "No, I'm not a dress designer. I could never design my own garment, but through fabric and pat-

tern, I can have a lot of fun and get a lot of satisfaction expressing myself as an individual."

> **" Sewing gives me time to unwind. "**

Sewing is the perfect antidote for stress—it offers the opportunity to escape, even if it's for only half an hour, from the cares and pressures of the day. An activity that occupies both your hands and your brain, sewing absorbs your complete attention. When sewing time is over, you can go back to the "real" world with a clearer head.

> **" The garments I sew are better made...in better fabric than the ones I could afford to buy. "**

Buttons fall off, seams aren't finished, hems come undone...even on the most expensive ready-to-

wear garments. If you invest that same amount of money in quality fabric and a flattering pattern, you'll end up with a garment that will look better and last longer than the one you would have bought. With today's easy sewing techniques, helpful notions and new sewing machine technology, anyone can turn out a professional-looking garment.

In fact, the more you sew, the more discriminating a buyer you will become. You'll be able to recognize quality construction when you see it...which means you'll ultimately get more for your ready-to-wear dollars, too.

> **" I have small children...and buying clothes for them is SO expensive. "**

Sewing children's clothes is a great way to save money—and a great way to create a pint-size wardrobe with irresistible appeal. Since children's clothes take relatively little fabric, you may be able to use the leftovers from the clothes you sew for yourself. Remnant tables, with yardages that are frequently insufficient for adult garments, provide countless bargains for children's sewing. Sewing children's garments is also a great way to experiment with new techniques—stitching details, appliqués, trims, etc. A small child won't notice, or even care, if the plaids don't match perfectly or the buttonholes aren't exactly straight.

> **" Sewing is fun…and now it's so easy!"**

If you learned to sew back in the days when finishing the seams on a garment was a real task, when making a jacket meant hours of laborious padstitching or when reading pattern instructions was like learning a foreign language, you're in for a pleasant surprise. "State-of-the-art" sewing has never been easier.

● *Computerized sewing machines* require no more than a light touch of the finger to change stitch length, width or configuration, allowing you to go from straight stitch to zigzag stitch to stretch stitch in a matter of seconds. As with all good computers, these sewing machines have a memory, making it possible to program the size, then duplicate the same buttonhole as many times as you wish; or to program a variety of decorative stitches in almost infinite combinations.

● *Serger (overlock) sewing machines*, once the exclusive property of the garment industry, are now widely available for home use. These magic machines are the perfect complement to the conventional sewing machine. They stitch, trim and overcast a seam— all in one operation. They can do narrow rolled hems on anything from linen napkins and tablecloths to lightweight silks and chiffons. They can clean-finish the edge of a garment, eliminating the need for facings, with a stitch that is both functional and decorative. And they perform all of these feats at a speed that's twice as fast as the fastest conventional machine. Chapters 5 and 6 are full of examples of how the serger can enhance your conventional sewing.

● *Sewing patterns* are easier to use than ever before, and now there are even special pattern groups, each identified by its own unique logo, which focus on the needs of the beginner, on overlock sewing, and on quick, easy sewing— among others. In addition, many patterns available today include specialized fitting information. Chapter 2 gives further details.

● *Fusible interfacings* that really stay fused through repeated washings or dry cleanings take the work out of shaping a garment. This holds true whether you are merely adding interfacing to the collar and cuffs of a blouse or constructing a tailored jacket.

● *Sewing aids and notions* have simplified sewing in ways that your grandmother couldn't have dreamed possible. Imagine basting thread that dissolves in the wash, disappearing marking pens that make it possible to mark directly on the right side of the fabric, a lightweight, sheer seam binding that automatically curls around the edge of the fabric as you apply it or a liquid that invisibly seals the raw edges of seams, trim, buttonholes and so on. The tips and techniques in Chapters 5, 6 and 7 include these—and many more— timesaving notions.

CHOOSING YOUR SEWING PHILOSOPHY

Who, in this busy world of ours, has time to sew everything she needs? With so many beautiful fabrics and patterns to choose from, it makes good sense to adopt a sewing philosophy to help you decide where your sewing priorities lie.

BUY HARD, SEW EASY

Sew simple, easy-fitting garments that don't have a lot of complicated details, in fabrics that don't require special handling. For example, you might make the top and the skirt— but buy the coordinating tailored jacket to complete the outfit. If you're short on time or experience, this may be the sewing philosophy for you.

BUY EASY, SEW HARD

Put your time and money into the luxury fabrics and special details that greatly increase the cost of a ready-to-wear garment. With this approach, you would buy the top and the pants, and use your sewing time to create the jacket.

SEW THE CLASSICS

Choose traditional styles that won't go out of fashion for several seasons. If you're sewing mostly for pleasure, it may not matter how soon the project is finished. Concentrate on seasonless fabrics (see Chapter 3) so that the garment can go straight into your wardrobe regardless of when it's finished.

SEW THE "FAD" STYLES

If you want to be the first with the newest fashions, keep up-to-date on all of the latest shortcut techniques. Because you sew a style for today with the understanding that tomorrow it may be passé, timesaving patterns and techniques are essential to making this sewing objective a success.

> **" When I sew, I get to be the designer, the one who picks the style, the fabric and the color for my garment. "**

SEW FOR SPECIAL OCCASIONS

If you love "dressing to the nines," you may want to devote your sewing time exclusively to the very satisfying sewing category of evening wear. Not only are the fabrics for formal clothes wonder-ful and inspiring to work with, but you can also save money by sewing the glamorous parts of your wardrobe.

SEW SIMPLY BECAUSE YOU LOVE TO

If you enjoy the opportunity to experiment with different types of fabrics and patterns, sewing anything that catches your eye, then you're someone who enjoys sewing for the pure pleasure of it. If you're not in this category now, with a little sewing experience you'll soon graduate to it!

FINDING WHAT FLATTERS

Regardless of why you sew or what sewing philosophy you adopt, how do you combine fabric, pattern and fit to achieve the most flattering wardrobe ever?

This is the question that challenges everyone who sews her own clothes. The answer, believe it or not, can be found in the clothes you already own. Open your closet and pull out the items you wear most often. If you're like most people, you wear only 10 percent of your clothes 90 percent of the time. While not immediately apparent, there are some very good reasons why this is so.

ANALYZING YOUR FAVORITE GARMENTS

Examine each garment carefully and try it on—you're going to analyze what it is that makes each one a favorite. Make lots of notes as you go.

● *Fabric.* Perhaps you like the look and feel of natural fibers… or the easy care of a synthetic. Do you wear this garment because it keeps you very warm or very cool? Does the fabric have some "give" (for example, is it a knit or is it cut on the bias) that enhances the fit and adds to the comfort?

● *Color.* If it's an outfit that brings you lots of compliments, it may just be the color. Even the simplest of garments in a flattering color will win rave reviews.

● *Style.* Do you like the garment because it makes you look taller, shorter or thinner? Because it camouflages wide hips, a thick waist, narrow shoulders, a large bust or a flat chest?

● *Fit.* You won't feel comfortable in a garment unless it fits well. Notice what features provide you with a good fit. Are the sleeves cut full in the upper arm? Is the dress a no-waistline or elasticized-waist style? Do the trousers have front pleats? Pay particular attention to the proportions. Do many of your favorite jackets and tops end at the waistline or high hipbone…or do you prefer styles that cover up the fullest part of your hips and derriére? What shirt lengths enhance your proportions and provide the most comfort?

● *Compatibility.* Do some garments get a lot of wear because they coordinate well with other things in your wardrobe?

As you go through this list, award the garment points for each category: two points if it's a success, one point if it's just okay, no points if it's a flop. Some of the garments in your 10 percent group will score high marks in all five categories. Others will have only one or two features that make them favorites, such as great fit and/or comfortable fabric, but a color that does nothing special for you. Pay closest attention to the garments that get the highest scores.

WHAT YOUR WARDROBE CAN TELL YOU

Now go back to your closet and take a look at the things that you seldom wear. As you compare the two sets of clothes, certain themes will begin to emerge. Notice how, when you shopped, you were attracted to a variety of styles, fabrics and colors. However, once you got those garments home, you only wore certain ones; the others were relegated to the far corners of your closet—a waste of time and money.

Analyzing the good and bad points of your current wardrobe gives you clues about where to concentrate your sewing efforts. If you focus on the clothes you love,

pinpointing fabric type, color, style and fit, you will have established valuable guidelines to use in choosing patterns, fabrics and sewing techniques.

Remember: The purpose of a wardrobe analysis is not to look for clothes to duplicate (although that's a fine idea if that's what you want to do) but rather to give you information about your best personal style. It will help you make wise choices about what you sew and avoid repeating the mistakes you found in the clothes you've purchased. Write down the good points and bad points you've discovered about the clothes from your closet. Keep the points handy as you read and act on the information in Chapters 2 and 3 on selecting patterns and fabric. Don't make the mistake of thinking your best personal style is fixed on one fashion category either. Loose-fitting, tailored, very casual or elegant—there's a wide range of style, fabric, color and fit combinations to be discovered—if you're open to them.

As you look over your favorite

clothes, don't be dissuaded by thoughts like "Oh, but I could never sew something like that!" Look more closely. Turn the garment inside out—see how it's constructed and think about what techniques were used. Browse through Chapters 6 and 7 to find similar construction techniques. Chances are that most garments, including the ones you love best, are well within your sewing abilities. If not, begin with something simpler. As your confidence builds, you'll be able to sew all of the styles you love.

> **❝ Sewing provides you with the opportunity to combine good fit, complimentary color, suitable fabric and flattering style all in one garment. When you sew, every garment in your closet can rate a '10'. ❞**

chapter 2
Pattern Savvy

Leafing through the pages of a pattern catalog is like being turned loose in a candy store. There are so many goodies to choose from!

FASHION INSPIRATION

The pattern catalog itself is one of your most valuable sources of inspiration. It's full of ideas for coordinating separates, combining colors and prints, and picking fabrics. By studying the photographs and sketches carefully, you'll also pick up some good ideas about how to accessorize your finished garment.

In addition to the pattern catalog that is carried in the fabric store, some pattern companies make their catalogs available to sewers on a subscription basis. In addition, catalogs may be available for viewing on-line. (Check out Simplicity's Web site: www.simplicity.com.) There, you can choose your sewing projects from a selection of the newest patterns—right in the comfort of your own home.

Also check your local newsstand for magazines devoted to sewing. These national publications include regular features on new patterns and fabrics.

A CLIPPING FILE

Of course, when it comes to fashion inspiration, you're not limited to pattern catalogs and pattern magazines. One of the advantages of sewing is that the ultimate choice of pattern-and-fabric combinations can be all your own. Magazines and newspapers are full of ideas to get your creative juices flowing. Why not start a fashion file? Clip and save anything that catches your eye. Here's one place where price is no object. You can be equally inspired by an inexpensive outfit as by one that costs thousands of dollars. Look for pleasing design lines, attractive color combinations, unusual fabric mixes, and interesting trims and details. It's fun once you tune in on the possibilities.

SELECTING A PATTERN

For some people, sifting through the pattern catalog with its wide range of choices is pure delight. For others, particularly beginners at sewing, the process of choosing a pattern seems a bit overwhelming. It's really very easy if you just keep three simple criteria in mind: Choose a style that you like. Choose design lines that are flattering to your figure. Look for design details that are compatible with your sewing skills.

A STYLE THAT YOU LIKE

Don't select a pattern just because the style is "in" or just because it's easy. How many people do you know who were turned off to sewing because they were required to make something way back in junior high school that they would never wear? Make sure you really like what you select. After all, half the fun of sewing is being able to show off what you have made.

A STYLE THAT FLATTERS

Be sure that the style you love is also a style that flatters. Use the knowledge you gained from analyzing your current wardrobe. If the style you're considering is a radical departure from anything you've ever worn, it might be wise to spend some time trying on a few similar ready-to-wear garments before you purchase your fabric and pattern.

A STYLE THAT MATCHES YOUR SEWING SKILLS

If you were learning to cook, you probably wouldn't begin by making a soufflé! Instead, you'd start with something basic and gradually work your way up to more complicated recipes. Learning to sew is much the same.

As you thumb through the catalog, notice how the patterns are grouped together in various ways. You'll find color bars printed along the bottom and side of each catalog page. These indicate garment or other categories, such as "Dresses," "Sportswear," "Evening, Prom, Bridal" or "Home Dec & Crafts," as well as special size and age ranges such as "Large Sizes," "Children" and "Junior." For easy reference, the entire color bar is printed on the extension of the back inside cover. It also appears on the inside front cover and first page of every Simplicity catalog, along with the page numbers that are assigned to each category. In addition, there are two other pattern categories, one based on fitting techniques and the other on sewing tech-

niques. They may have their own tabs or they may be found under the tabs for particular garment, size or age range categories.

● *Fit.* Patterns with logos such as FIT *for* PETITE™ are designed to help solve certain fitting dilemmas. (See Chapter 4 for more information.)

● *Sewing Level.* If you're just learning to sew, if you're experimenting with a difficult-to-handle fabric, or if you need to sew something fast, look at patterns with logos such as 1 HOUR™ or 2 HOUR™ (which indicate sewing time, not cutting and marking time) or EASY TO SEW™. Patterns marked OVERLOCK/SERGER include instructions for sewing on the serger as well as on the conventional machine. Although these are certainly not the only patterns you can use with a serger, they're a great help when you're just learning to use this fabulous machine.

Although the above examples are all from the Simplicity™ pattern catalog, every major pattern company has its own set of terms or logos to indicate its specialized patterns. As the sewing and fashion picture changes, new categories may be developed. If you're not sure what the terms mean, turn to the back of the pattern catalog. You'll usually find a page that includes an explanation of each category. If the category doesn't have its own section, you'll often find an index that includes a listing of the specialized patterns and their appropriate page numbers.

CREATIVE PATTERN SELECTION

Suppose you've fallen in love with a particular garment from your clipping file and you can't find a pattern that looks like it. Here are a few ideas:

● If it's a dress, see if you can find a skirt and blouse combination that will give you the same look. The bonus in having a two-piece dress is that you'll have two items that look smashing together or that can go their own separate ways in your wardrobe.

● If it's a jumpsuit, consider pants and a top of the same fabric. These will be easier to fit, as well as more versatile, than a one-piece garment.

● If you can find a blouse pattern that has the right lines, consider lengthening it to make a dress. Be sure to buy enough extra fabric to accommodate the longer length.

THE CATALOG PAGE

The catalog page is a treasure trove of information. If you know how to "read" it properly, you'll be able to pick the pattern that's just right for your needs.

Here's the information you will find, keyed here by number to its location on the sample catalog page at right.

❶ A *fashion photo* of one of the views shows how the pattern will look when it's all sewn up. The garment may have been altered slightly to fit the model's individual proportions, but no more so than for anyone else. Therefore,

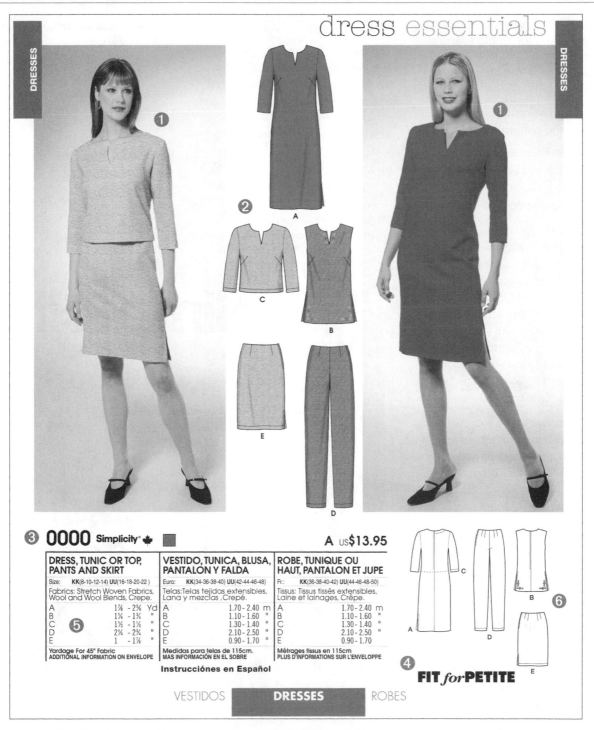

dress essentials

DRESSES

DRESSES

❸ **0000** Simplicity ❋

A US**$13.95**

DRESS, TUNIC OR TOP, PANTS AND SKIRT	VESTIDO, TUNICA, BLUSA, PANTALON Y FALDA	ROBE, TUNIQUE OU HAUT, PANTALON ET JUPE
Size: **KK**(8-10-12-14) **UU**(16-18-20-22)	Euro: **KK**(34-36-38-40) **UU**(42-44-46-48)	Fr.: **KK**(36-38-40-42) **UU**(44-46-48-50)
Fabrics: Stretch Woven Fabrics, Wool and Wool Blends, Crêpe.	Telas:Telas tejidas extensibles, Lana y mezclas ,Crepé.	Tissus: Tissus tissés extensibles, Laine et lainages, Crêpe.

A	1⅞ - 2⅜ Yd	A	1.70 - 2.40 m
B	1¼ - 1¾ "	B	1.10 - 1.60 "
C	1½ - 1½ "	C	1.30 - 1.40 "
D	2¼ - 2¾ "	D	2.10 - 2.50 "
E	1 - 1⅞ "	E	0.90 - 1.70 "

A	1.70 - 2.40 m
B	1.10 - 1.60 "
C	1.30 - 1.40 "
D	2.10 - 2.50 "
E	0.90 - 1.70

❺

Yardage For 45" Fabric
ADDITIONAL INFORMATION ON ENVELOPE

Medidas para telas de 115cm.
MAS INFORMACIÓN EN EL SOBRE

Métrages tissus en 115cm
PLUS D'INFORMATIONS SUR L'ENVELOPPE

Instrucciónes en Español

❹ **FIT** *for* **PETITE**

❻

VESTIDOS   **DRESSES**   ROBES

you can consider the photograph an accurate guide as to how the pattern should fit. It also provides

you with visual clues about what fabric weights and textures are suitable for the design.

❷ *Fashion drawings* show what other views or versions are included in the pattern. They're illustrated in different colors, prints or fabric types from the photo to inspire you with more fashion and fabric ideas that are compatible with the design.

❸ *Identification information* includes the pattern number and the price.

❹ A *logo* (such as *easy to sew*, *6 made easy!* or FIT *for* PETITE) identifies any special category for the pattern.

❺ A *chart* includes the sizes the pattern comes in, a brief list of suggested fabrics and the approximate amount of fabric needed for the size range. This chart is handy if you've come to the store for fabric and you've forgotten to bring your pattern…or if you're looking for a pattern to go with a piece of fabric you already own.

❻ *Back views* show you fashion details, such as zipper, pocket or button locations, seams and darts that are not visible from the front.

THE PATTERN ENVELOPE

The pattern envelope contains much the same information as the catalog page—but in greater detail.

THE ENVELOPE FRONT

The front of the envelope (right) includes the same sketches and photographs that were featured on the catalog page, as well as the pattern number, the price, the size range, any identifying logos for special pattern categories and the UPC bar code.

THE ENVELOPE BACK

The back of the envelope serves as a convenient shopping list for the fabric and notions you'll need to make the pattern. It repeats and expands on some of the information that was on the catalog page, such as the pattern identification number and the back views, as well as supplying some new information. The sample envelope back on page 17 includes numbers keyed to the following information.

❶ *Identification information* includes pattern number and the number of pattern pieces, and notes if the pattern includes French or Spanish translations. It also includes basic size category and style information, such as "Misses' Shirt."

❷ *Back views* help clarify how the garment looks and fits.

❸ *Suggested fabric list* expands on the information that is printed on the catalog page. This is your

0000
SIZE **KK** 8,10,12,14
EUR. 34-40
FR. 36-42
0 00000 00000 7

Simplicity®
dress essentials

A
B
C
D
E

tip

Patterns are not returnable, so make sure you've got the pattern you want in the size and figure type you need, before you pay for it.

guide to selecting the fabric that will give you the best results. See Chapter 3 for additional information.

❹ ***Notions*** are all of the extras, such as buttons, zippers, seam bindings and shoulder pads, that you'll need to complete the garment. To save time and to ensure a close color match, you'll probably want to purchase these at the same time as you buy your fabric.

❺ ***Standard body measurements*** were in the back of the pattern catalog to help you determine your correct pattern size. They're repeated on the envelope as a convenient reference guide for making pattern adjustments later on. For additional information, see Chapter 4.

❻ ***Yardage chart*** tells you how much fabric to buy for the size and view you want to make. Note that different yardage amounts are listed, depending on the width of the fabric and whether it is with or without nap. If a garment is made from 45" (115 cm) wide fabric, it usually requires more yardage than if it is made from 60" (150 cm) wide fabric. If the fabric has a texture or design that must go in one direction on the finished garment (a "with nap" fabric), you'll need more yardage than you would for a fabric without a nap. Note that on the chart, * indicates yardage for "without nap" fabrics; ** indicates yardage for "with nap" fabrics; *** means it doesn't matter if the fabric has a nap because the pattern layout will be the same for both types of fabric.

Yardage requirements for any lining, interfacing, elastic or trim are also included in this chart.

❼ ***Finished garment measurements*** will help you judge the length or fullness of the design. For example, "Skirt width" and "Skirt length" may be included on a dress or skirt pattern. "Finished

❶

0000

15 PIECES/PIEZAS

Métrages et instructions de couture en Français à l'intérieur de l'enveloppe.

❷

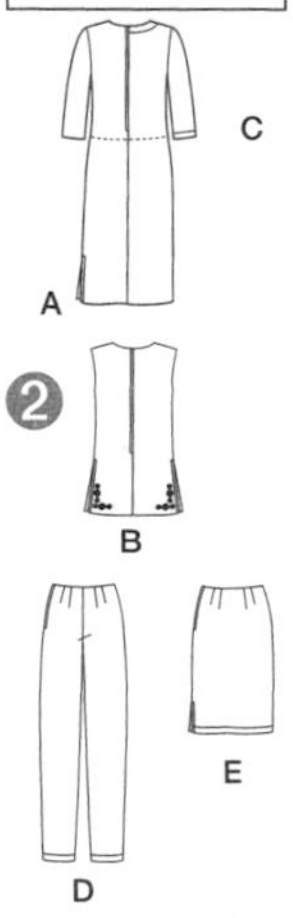

MISSES'/MISS PETITE DRESS, TUNIC OR TOP, PANTS AND SKIRT

Fabrics: Stretch Woven Fabrics, Lightweight Wool and Wool Blends, Crepe, Laundered Silks/Rayons, Lightweight Linen and Linen Blends, Pique, Poplin, Lightweight Denim, Shantung, Taffeta, Lightweight Double Knits, Lightweight Synthetic Leather, Lightweight Synthetic Suede. Extra fabric needed to match plaids, stripes or one-way design fabrics. ❸

Notions: Thread. **A, B, C**: one 16" zipper, hook and eye. **B**: embroidered appliques (opt.). **D, E** 7" zipper, hook and eye, one pkg. ⅜" wide cotton twill tape. Look for Simplicity notions. ❹

BODY MEASUREMENTS ❺										
Bust		31½	32½	34	36	38	40	42	44	In
Waist		24	25	26½	28	30	32	34	37	"
Hip-9" below waist		33½	34½	36	38	40	42	44	46	"
Back-neck to waist		15¾	16	16¼	16½	16¾	17	17¼	17⅜	"
Sizes		8	10	12	14	16	18	20	22	
Sizes-European		34	36	38	40	42	44	46	48	
A ❻	45"**	1⅞	1⅞	2¼	2½	2½	2½	2⅝	2⅝	Yd
	60"**	1¾	1⅞	1⅞	1⅞	1⅞	1⅞	1⅞	1⅞	"
B	45"**	1¼	1¼	1½	1½	1½	1¾	1¾	1¾	Yd
	60"**	1⅛	1⅛	1⅛	1⅛	1⅛	1⅛	1⅛	1¼	"
Interfacing- ⅝ yd. of 22" to 36" lightweight fusible or non fusible										
C	45"**	1½	1½	1½	1½	1½	1½	1½	1½	Yd
	60"**	1¼	1¼	1¼	1¼	1¼	1¼	1⅜	1⅜	"
A, C Interfacing- ⅜ yd. of 22" to 36" lightweight fusible or non fusible										
D	45"**	2¼	2⅜	2½	2½	2½	2¾	2¾	2¾	Yd
	60"**	1½	1½	1½	1⅝	1⅞	2¼	2¼	2¼	"
E	45"**	1	1	1	1⅞	1⅞	1⅞	1⅞	1⅞	Yd
	60"**	1	1	1	1	1	1	1	1	"
D, E Interfacing- ¼ yd. of 23" to 36" lightweight fusible or non fusible										
GARMENT MEASUREMENTS (Bust & Hip Printed on Pattern Tissue)										
A, B, C - Bust		36	37	38½	40½	42½	44½	46½	48½	In
D, E - Hip		37	38	39½	41½	43½	45½	47½	49½	"
Finished back length from base of neck:										
A		39¾	40	40¼	40½	40¾	41	41¼	41½	In
B ❼		25¾	26	26¼	26½	26¾	27	27¼	27½	"
A width		38	39	40½	42½	44½	46½	48½	50½	"
D side length		39¾	40	40¼	40½	40¾	41	41¼	41½	"
E length		24	24	24	24	24	24	24	24	"
E width		37	38	39½	41½	43½	45½	47½	49½	"

*without nap **with nap ***with or without nap

ROBE, TUNIQUE OU HAUT, PANTALON ET JUPE POUR JEUNE FEMME/PETITE JEUNE FEMME

Mercerie: Fil. **A, B, C**: une glissière de 40cm, une agrafe. **B**: applications brodées (facult.). **D, E**: une glissière de 18cm, une agrafe, un paquet de talonnette de coton de 1cm. Demandez la mercerie Simplicity.

VESTIDO, TUNICA O BLUSA, PANTALON Y FALDA PARA SEÑORITAS/SEÑORITAS PEQUEÑAS

Telas: telas tejidas extensibles, Lana y mezclas de lana ligera, Crepé, sedas/rayones lavadas, Tela de lino y similares, Piqué, Popelina fina, Dril ligero, Shantung, Tafetán, Mallas dobles ligeras, Cuero y gamuza sintéticos finos. Se necesita tela adicional para casar cuadros, rayas o telas estampadas en una dirección.

Mercería: Hilo. **A, B, C**: una cremallera de 40cm, un corchete. **B**: apliciones bordadas (opcional). **D, E**: una cremallera de 18cm, un corchete, un paquete de galón asargado de 1cm de ancho. Pida la mercería Simplicity.

MESURES NORMALISEES/MEDIDAS DEL CUERPO										
Poitrine/Busto		80	83	87	92	97	102	107	112	cm
Taille/Cintura		61	64	67	71	76	81	87	94	"
Hanches (23cm au-dessous de la taille)/Caderas (23cm abajo de la cintura)		85	88	92	97	102	107	112	117	"
Dos (encolure à taille)/Espalda (escote a cintura)		40	40.5	41.5	42	42.5	43	44	44	"
Tailles ❽		8	10	12	14	16	18	20	22	
Tailles Françaises		36	38	40	42	44	46	48	50	
Tallas Europeas		34	36	38	40	42	44	46	48	
A	115cm**	1.70	1.70	2.10	2.30	2.30	2.30	2.30	2.40	m
	150cm**	1.70	1.70	1.70	1.70	1.70	1.70	1.70	1.70	"
B	115cm**	1.10	1.20	1.30	1.40	1.40	1.60	1.60	1.60	m
	150cm**	1.00	1.00	1.00	1.00	1.00	1.00	1.00	1.10	"
Entoilage- 0.60m de 55cm à 90cm léger, thermocollant ou non/**Entretela-** 0.60m de 55cm a 90cm ligera, adhesiva o no.										
C	115cm**	1.30	1.30	1.30	1.40	1.40	1.40	1.40	1.40	m
	150cm**	1.10	1.10	1.10	1.20	1.20	1.20	1.20	1.20	"
A, C Entoilage- 0.30m de 55cm à 90cm léger, thermocollant ou non/**A, C Entretela-** 0.30m de 55cm a 90cm ligera, adhesiva o no.										
D	115cm**	2.10	2.10	2.30	2.30	2.30	2.50	2.50	2.50	m
	150cm**	1.40	1.40	1.40	1.40	1.70	2.10	2.10	2.10	"
E	115cm**	0.90	0.90	0.90	1.70	1.70	1.70	1.70	1.70	m
	150cm**	0.90	0.90	0.90	0.90	0.90	0.90	0.90	0.90	"
D, E Entoilage- 0.30m de 60cm à 90cm léger, thermocollant ou non/**D, E Entretela-** 0.30m de 60cm a 90cm ligera, adhesiva o no										

*sans sens **avec sens ***avec ou sans sens *sin pelusa **con pelusa ***con o sin pelusa

back length from base of neck" may be included on a dress or top pattern. "Pants leg width" or "Side length" may be included on trousers, shorts or culottes patterns. Depending on the type of garment, the circumference measurement at the bust and/or hip will also be included. It will be helpful if you take these measurements on several garments you already own, as shown above. Write them down and take them with you when you pick out your pattern. That way you'll have a meaningful reference point for comparison.

❽ *Metric equivalents* for the yardage and notion require-

ments, as well as Spanish and French translations of the lists of suggested fabrics and required notions, are provided on a separate chart, opposite the Imperial chart.

tip

Although your pattern view may not use every piece, the total number of pattern pieces is one way to evaluate the amount of time or sewing skill a pattern will require. Use it as a guide when you're trying to decide which of two similar designs is the easiest.

INSIDE THE ENVELOPE

Your pattern envelope contains two things: the pattern instruction sheet and all of the pattern pieces you need to make your garment.

THE PATTERN INSTRUCTION SHEET

The sheet of instructions inside the envelope guides your sewing every step of the way—from laying out and cutting the pattern to working at your sewing machine.

Before you purchase the pattern, you might want to pull out the instruction sheet and glance through it. Consider how many of the techniques are new to you... and how fast you want to complete this project. If you're sewing against a deadline, and the pattern has several new techniques, you might want to make another selection. If you are going to make another selection, please refold the instruction sheet and carefully return it to the pattern envelope. Because customers have been careless about the way they treat patterns they decide not to buy, some retailers will not permit their customers to open a pattern until they purchase it. Please be considerate of the retailer and of the next person who is interested in that pattern.

Once you get the pattern home, don't do any pinning or cutting until you've had time to carefully read the instruction sheet. If there is more than one instruction sheet, each page is numbered so that you know what order to follow. Make sure you understand all of the notations and that the sewing instructions make sense. Pay particular attention to any sewing technique that is new to you. Check out the index in the back of this book and review the sections that are pertinent to the technique.

A sample of the instruction sheet is reproduced on pages 20–22 and it includes numbers keyed to the following information. On the left-hand side of the first page of the instruction sheet you'll find:

❶ *Line drawings* are simplified sketches of all of the views or versions that are included in the pattern. These sketches clearly show all of the technical design details. In addition, because the layout and the sewing instructions may vary depending on the view, these drawings provide you with a convenient way to double-check which view you're following.

❷ The *pattern pieces section* contains simplified diagrams of each pattern piece. Each diagram is identified by a number. Look below the drawings to find out what each number stands for, as well as what view(s) each pattern piece is used for. Put a check mark next to each piece you will need for the view you are making.

❸ *Contact information* is provided so you can contact Simplicity via phone, e-mail or through our Web site if you have any questions or concerns about the pattern.

❹ The section labeled *"General Directions"* is positioned in either the upper right or the lower left

quadrant of the first page of the instruction sheet. "The Pattern" section explains the most common pattern symbols and how to make simple lengthen or shorten adjustments. The "Cutting/ Marking" section includes tips to make your cutting and marking easier, along with an explanation of the special cutting notes that may be included in "Cutting Layouts." The "Sewing" section defines some basic sewing procedures, including pinning, stitching, trimming and pressing a seam. For a more detailed explanation of any of these topics, turn to Chapter 5.

❺ *"Cutting Layouts"* shows you how to position the pattern pieces properly on your fabric with the least amount of waste. Layouts are given for different pattern sizes and various fabric widths. Find the diagram for your view, pattern size and fabric width, and then draw a circle around it. If you are new to sewing, or if you are using a "with nap" fabric, or if there is anything you don't understand about the cutting layout, it would be a good idea to review "The Cutting Layout" in Chapter 5. Note that the cutting layout may continue on the back of the instruction sheet.

❻ *"Sewing Directions,"* which starts on either the front or back of the instruction sheet, takes you step-by-step through the process of constructing the garment (see sample sheet on page 22). The instructions are organized by garment section so that all of the stitching and pressing is completed in one area, such as the bodice,

tip

In shopping for patterns and fabrics, it's a very good idea to analyze your wardrobe beforehand, especially the clothing that makes you feel most comfortable and good about yourself. The notes you take about the styles, the types of fabrics, and colors you like will make a useful buying guide.

before going on to another. This is the fastest, easiest system for most sewers to follow. However, as you become more experienced, you may find it faster to work on several sections simultaneously, sewing as far as you can on each one until you must stop and press. This method minimizes back-and-forth trips to the ironing board. If you are going to use this faster method, it's absolutely essential that you take the time to read through the sewing directions before you begin. Otherwise, in your enthusiasm, it's all too easy to sew too far or skip a step.

THE PATTERN PIECES

Each pattern piece contains written directions and symbols such as dots and arrows—a kind of shorthand that's easy to learn and speeds your sewing because it shows you which edges to match and where to position details.

❶ *General information* in English, French and Spanish includes the pattern number, the sizes included on this tissue, the name of the pattern

(text continues on page 23)

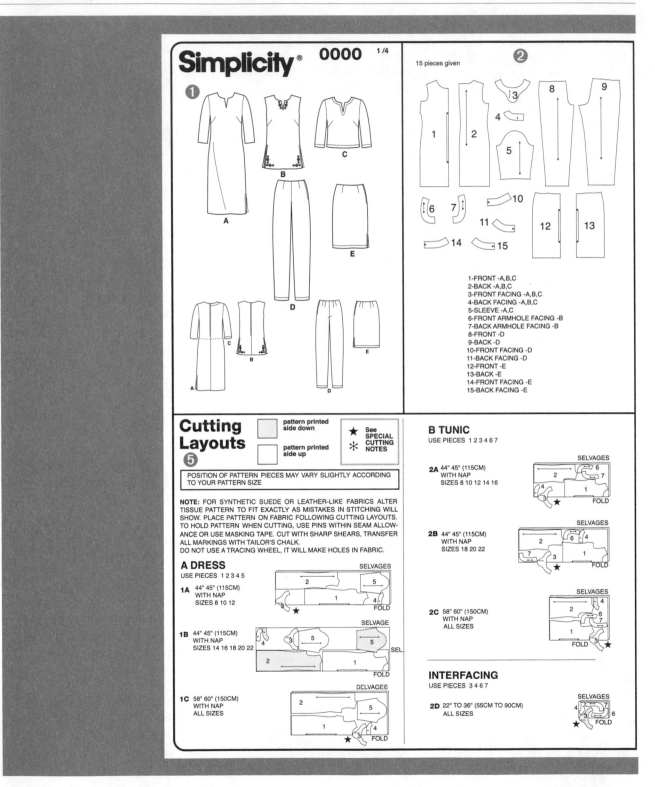

Simplicity® 0000 1/4

❶

❷ 15 pieces given

1-FRONT -A,B,C
2-BACK -A,B,C
3-FRONT FACING -A,B,C
4-BACK FACING -A,B,C
5-SLEEVE -A,C
6-FRONT ARMHOLE FACING -B
7-BACK ARMHOLE FACING -B
8-FRONT -D
9-BACK -D
10-FRONT FACING -D
11-BACK FACING -D
12-FRONT -E
13-BACK -E
14-FRONT FACING -E
15-BACK FACING -E

Cutting Layouts

❺

☐ pattern printed side down
☐ pattern printed side up
★ See SPECIAL CUTTING NOTES
✳

POSITION OF PATTERN PIECES MAY VARY SLIGHTLY ACCORDING TO YOUR PATTERN SIZE

NOTE: FOR SYNTHETIC SUEDE OR LEATHER-LIKE FABRICS ALTER TISSUE PATTERN TO FIT EXACTLY AS MISTAKES IN STITCHING WILL SHOW. PLACE PATTERN ON FABRIC FOLLOWING CUTTING LAYOUTS. TO HOLD PATTERN WHEN CUTTING, USE PINS WITHIN SEAM ALLOW-ANCE OR USE MASKING TAPE. CUT WITH SHARP SHEARS, TRANSFER ALL MARKINGS WITH TAILOR'S CHALK.
DO NOT USE A TRACING WHEEL, IT WILL MAKE HOLES IN FABRIC.

A DRESS
USE PIECES 1 2 3 4 5

1A 44" 45" (115CM) WITH NAP SIZES 8 10 12

1B 44" 45" (115CM) WITH NAP SIZES 14 16 18 20 22

1C 58" 60" (150CM) WITH NAP ALL SIZES

B TUNIC
USE PIECES 1 2 3 4 6 7

2A 44" 45" (115CM) WITH NAP SIZES 8 10 12 14 16

2B 44" 45" (115CM) WITH NAP SIZES 18 20 22

2C 58" 60" (150CM) WITH NAP ALL SIZES

INTERFACING
USE PIECES 3 4 6 7

2D 22" TO 36" (55CM TO 90CM) ALL SIZES

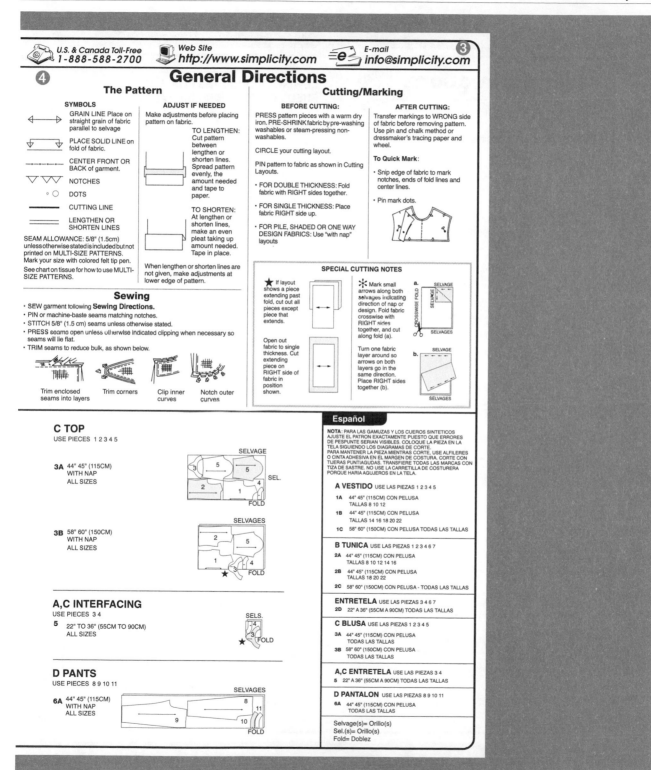

U.S. & Canada Toll-Free
1-888-588-2700

Web Site
http://www.simplicity.com

E-mail
info@simplicity.com

General Directions

The Pattern

SYMBOLS

⟷ GRAIN LINE Place on straight grain of fabric parallel to selvage

PLACE SOLID LINE on fold of fabric.

CENTER FRONT OR BACK of garment.

▽ ▽▽ NOTCHES

° ○ DOTS

— CUTTING LINE

LENGTHEN OR SHORTEN LINES

SEAM ALLOWANCE: 5/8" (1.5cm) unless otherwise stated is included but not printed on MULTI-SIZE PATTERNS. Mark your size with colored felt tip pen. See chart on tissue for how to use MULTI-SIZE PATTERNS.

ADJUST IF NEEDED

Make adjustments before placing pattern on fabric.

TO LENGTHEN: Cut pattern between lengthen or shorten lines. Spread pattern evenly, the amount needed and tape to paper.

TO SHORTEN: At lengthen or shorten lines, make an even pleat taking up amount needed. Tape in place.

When lengthen or shorten lines are not given, make adjustments at lower edge of pattern.

Sewing

- SEW garment following **Sewing Directions.**
- PIN or machine-baste seams matching notches.
- STITCH 5/8" (1.5 cm) seams unless otherwise stated.
- PRESS seams open unless otherwise indicated clipping when necessary so seams will lie flat.
- TRIM seams to reduce bulk, as shown below.

Trim enclosed seams into layers

Trim corners

Clip inner curves

Notch outer curves

Cutting/Marking

BEFORE CUTTING:

PRESS pattern pieces with a warm dry iron. PRE-SHRINK fabric by pre-washing washables or steam-pressing non-washables.

CIRCLE your cutting layout.

PIN pattern to fabric as shown in Cutting Layouts.

- FOR DOUBLE THICKNESS: Fold fabric with RIGHT sides together.
- FOR SINGLE THICKNESS: Place fabric RIGHT side up.
- FOR PILE, SHADED OR ONE WAY DESIGN FABRICS: Use "with nap" layouts

AFTER CUTTING:

Transfer markings to WRONG side of fabric before removing pattern. Use pin and chalk method or dressmaker's tracing paper and wheel.

To Quick Mark:

- Snip edge of fabric to mark notches, ends of fold lines and center lines.
- Pin mark dots.

SPECIAL CUTTING NOTES

★ If layout shows a piece extending past fold, cut out all pieces except piece that extends.

Open out fabric to single thickness. Cut extending piece on RIGHT side of fabric in position shown.

✂ Mark small arrows along both selvages indicating direction of nap or design. Fold fabric crosswise with RIGHT sides together, and cut along fold (a).

Turn one fabric layer around so arrows on both layers go in the same direction. Place RIGHT sides together (b).

a. SELVAGE / CROSSWISE FOLD / SELVAGE / SELVAGES

b. SELVAGE / SELVAGES

C TOP

USE PIECES 1 2 3 4 5

3A 44" 45" (115CM) WITH NAP ALL SIZES

SELVAGE / SEL. / FOLD

3B 58" 60" (150CM) WITH NAP ALL SIZES

SELVAGES / FOLD

A,C INTERFACING

USE PIECES 3 4

5 22" TO 36" (55CM TO 90CM) ALL SIZES

SELS. / FOLD

D PANTS

USE PIECES 8 9 10 11

6A 44" 45" (115CM) WITH NAP ALL SIZES

SELVAGES / FOLD

Español

NOTA: PARA LAS GAMUZAS Y LOS CUEROS SINTETICOS AJUSTE EL PATRON EXACTAMENTE PUESTO QUE ERRORES DE PESPUNTE SERIAN VISIBLES. COLOQUE LA PIEZA EN LA TELA SIGUIENDO LOS DIAGRAMAS DE CORTE. PARA MANTENER LA PIEZA MIENTRAS CORTE, USE ALFILERES O CINTA ADHESIVA EN EL MARGEN DE COSTURA. CORTE CON TIJERAS PUNTIAGUDAS. TRANSFIERE TODAS LAS MARCAS CON TIZA DE SASTRE. NO USE LA CARRETILLA DE COSTURERA PORQUE HARIA AGUJEROS EN LA TELA.

A VESTIDO USE LAS PIEZAS 1 2 3 4 5

1A 44" 45" (115CM) CON PELUSA
TALLAS 8 10 12

1B 44" 45" (115CM) CON PELUSA
TALLAS 14 16 18 20 22

1C 58" 60" (150CM) CON PELUSA TODAS LAS TALLAS

B TUNICA USE LAS PIEZAS 1 2 3 4 6 7

2A 44" 45" (115CM) CON PELUSA
TALLAS 8 10 12 14 16

2B 44" 45" (115CM) CON PELUSA
TALLAS 18 20 22

2C 58" 60" (150CM) CON PELUSA - TODAS LAS TALLAS

ENTRETELA USE LAS PIEZAS 3 4 6 7

2D 22" A 36" (55CM A 90CM) TODAS LAS TALLAS

C BLUSA USE LAS PIEZAS 1 2 3 4 5

3A 44" 45" (115CM) CON PELUSA
TODAS LAS TALLAS

3B 58" 60" (150CM) CON PELUSA
TODAS LAS TALLAS

A,C ENTRETELA USE LAS PIEZAS 3 4

5 22" A 36" (55CM A 90CM) TODAS LAS TALLAS

D PANTALON USE LAS PIEZAS 8 9 10 11

6A 44" 45" (115CM) CON PELUSA
TODAS LAS TALLAS

Selvage(s)= Orillo(s)
Sel.(s)= Orillo(s)
Fold= Doblez

Sewing Directions ⑥

FABRIC KEY	RIGHT SIDE	WRONG SIDE	INTERFACING	LINING

Read **General Directions** on page 1 before you begin.

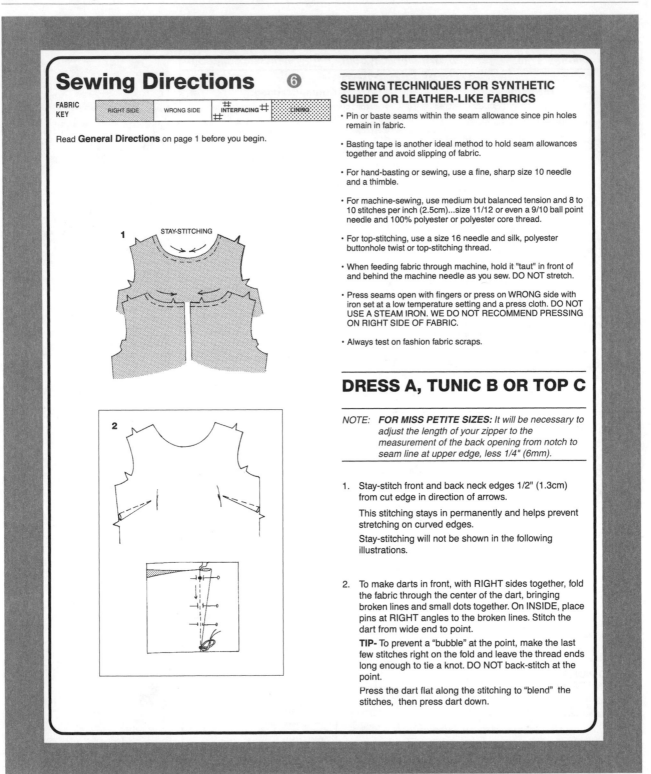

1 STAY-STITCHING

2

SEWING TECHNIQUES FOR SYNTHETIC SUEDE OR LEATHER-LIKE FABRICS

· Pin or baste seams within the seam allowance since pin holes remain in fabric.

· Basting tape is another ideal method to hold seam allowances together and avoid slipping of fabric.

· For hand-basting or sewing, use a fine, sharp size 10 needle and a thimble.

· For machine-sewing, use medium but balanced tension and 8 to 10 stitches per inch (2.5cm)...size 11/12 or even a 9/10 ball point needle and 100% polyester or polyester core thread.

· For top-stitching, use a size 16 needle and silk, polyester buttonhole twist or top-stitching thread.

· When feeding fabric through machine, hold it "taut" in front of and behind the machine needle as you sew. DO NOT stretch.

· Press seams open with fingers or press on WRONG side with iron set at a low temperature setting and a press cloth. DO NOT USE A STEAM IRON. WE DO NOT RECOMMEND PRESSING ON RIGHT SIDE OF FABRIC.

· Always test on fashion fabric scraps.

DRESS A, TUNIC B OR TOP C

NOTE: **FOR MISS PETITE SIZES:** *It will be necessary to adjust the length of your zipper to the measurement of the back opening from notch to seam line at upper edge, less 1/4" (6mm).*

1. Stay-stitch front and back neck edges 1/2" (1.3cm) from cut edge in direction of arrows.

   This stitching stays in permanently and helps prevent stretching on curved edges.

   Stay-stitching will not be shown in the following illustrations.

2. To make darts in front, with RIGHT sides together, fold the fabric through the center of the dart, bringing broken lines and small dots together. On INSIDE, place pins at RIGHT angles to the broken lines. Stitch the dart from wide end to point.

   TIP- To prevent a "bubble" at the point, make the last few stitches right on the fold and leave the thread ends long enough to tie a knot. DO NOT back-stitch at the point.

   Press the dart flat along the stitching to "blend" the stitches, then press dart down.

piece and simple cutting directions, such as "Cut 2." An identification number is included so you can quickly tell one piece from the other. The top of the number always points to the top of the pattern piece. These numbers correspond to the ones used on the instruction sheet's diagrams and cutting layout.

2 *Notches* are triangular symbols extending from the cutting line into the seam allowance. To mark notches, cut triangles or snip into the seam allowances along notch lines. If you think you may have to let out a seam after stitching, mark notches by cutting triangular shapes that extend out from the cutting lines.

3 *Solid lines** show where buttonholes are positioned, indicate the location of the bustline, waistline and hipline, and show where to fold the fabric.

4 *Center line** is a dot-dash line that appears on some pattern pieces.

5 *Grainline arrow* is used for positioning the pattern piece on the correct fabric grain.

A straight grainline arrow indicates a pattern piece that must be placed parallel to the selvage edge of your fabric.

A squared-off grainline arrow indicates a pattern piece that is placed along a folded fabric edge.

*The symbols with an asterisk (*) eventually get transferred onto your fabric; you'll learn more about this in Chapter 5.

6 *Cutting lines* are solid lines along the outer edge. Multi-Size patterns have multiple sets of lines—one for each size. Follow the cutting line that corresponds to your desired size when you cut your fabric.

7 *Finished garment measurements* are printed at the bustline, waistline and hipline on the appropriate pattern pieces. You'll learn how to use this information as a fitting tool in Chapter 4.

8 *Dots** are circles that mark points to be matched before stitching. They also mark the placement of details such as darts, tabs and belt loops.

9 *Hem* tells you how much fabric to turn up for the hem.

10 *Darts** are shown as V-shaped broken lines with dots. To sew, match the dots, folding fabric with right sides together, and stitch along the broken line. Darts shape

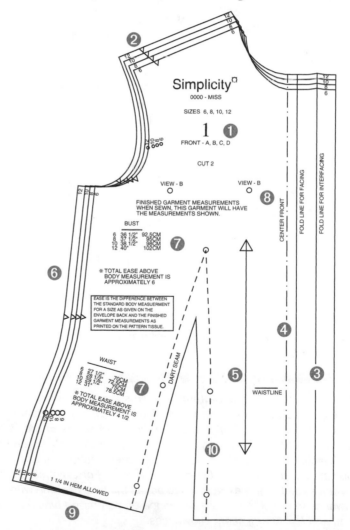

fabric to fit over your body curves—bust, hips, shoulders.

⓫ *Lengthen or Shorten Lines* are two parallel lines that indicate where to make the pattern piece longer or shorter so the finished length will be correct without distorting the garment shape. If the pattern is adjustable for petite sizes, a broken line above the lengthen or shorten line indicates where and how much to shorten the pattern.

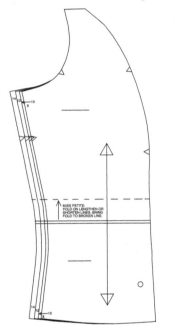

⓬ *Tucks* are shown as broken lines with the word "tuck" in between. To sew, match the broken lines, folding the fabric with right sides together, and stitch along lines.

⓭ *Pleats* are shown as broken and solid lines with directional arrows in between, at the end of each pleat. To make a pleat, fold your fabric on the solid line and bring the fold to the broken line. Press. Baste across top of pleat.

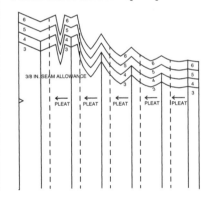

*The symbols with an asterisk (*) eventually get transferred onto your fabric; you'll learn more about this in Chapter 5.

---

tip

Before the advent of Multi-Size patterns, patterns came with one size per envelope and seamlines were marked on the pattern piece with broken lines. As Multi-Size patterns became more popular, pattern companies discontinued marking the seamlines. All of those cutting lines and seamlines were just too confusing! Today, it is understood that, for most fashion sewing, seamlines are usually 5/8" (1.5 cm) from the cutting line. Simplicity tells you this in the "General Directions" section of the pattern instruction sheet. If a different seam allowance is used, it will be indicated in the "Sewing Directions" section. For example, a tight-fitting bodice might have 1" (2.5cm) seam allowances so there is extra room to adjust the fit; a neckline with a narrow binding might have a 1/4" (6mm) seam allowance to match the seam allowance on purchased binding; home dec and craft projects generally use 1/2" (1.3cm) and 1/4" (6mm) seam allowances.

chapter 3
A Buyer's Guide to Fabrics, Notions and Sewing Machines

One of the most exciting things about sewing is being able to put fabric and pattern together to create a garment that is uniquely you…one that expresses your creativity, your wardrobe needs, your color preferences and your fashion style.

Many sewers, especially beginners, are so afraid of making a mistake that they spend hours looking for the exact fabric featured in the pattern catalog. If it's a fabric that suits your needs, that's fine. However, if you always let someone else's taste in fabrics dictate your selection, you're missing out on half the fun of sewing.

CLUES TO FABRIC SELECTION

Begin by studying the fashion photograph and fashion sketches on the catalog page and pattern envelope. Notice how the fabric falls in relation to the model's figure. It might be relaxed and flowing, gently accentuating the curves of the body. It might hug the figure closely, imitating the body's contours. It might be stiff and structured, creating a silhouette that is fuller or more architectural than the body that's underneath.

Next, read the list of fabric suggestions printed on the catalog page and on the back of the pattern envelope. Because there are so many fabric blends on the market today, the suggestion list often starts by indicating the type of fabric to look for, such as "silk and silk types" or "cotton and cotton blends."

Some garments require soft, drapable fabrics such as jersey, crepe de chine, charmeuse, challis or handkerchief linen. Other garments call for crisper, more structured fabrics such as corduroy, gabardine, suiting weight linens, taffeta, brocade or tweed. Sometimes the list of fabric suggestions may include both fabrics that are crisp, such as taffeta, and fabrics that are soft, such as dotted swiss. Because the silhouette is versatile enough for either type of fabric, the choice depends on the fashion mood you desire.

WHEN ONLY A KNIT WILL DO

Many patterns are suitable both for wovens and for knits with a small amount of stretch, such as double knit or jersey.

However, some patterns are designed exclusively for stretch knit fabrics. Most swimwear, sweatshirts and exercise wear, as well as many body-hugging silhouettes are "knits-only" fashions. If you tried to use a woven fabric or a knit that did not have enough stretch, the garment would be much too tight. In fact, since many of these garments are pull-on-over-the-head or pull-up-over-the-hips styles, you probably couldn't even get them on.

On Simplicity patterns, if it is a "knits-only" style, a caution under fabric suggestions will say "sized for

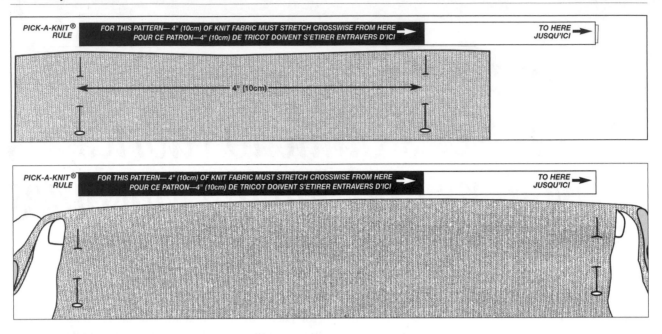

stretch knits only." Then, printed on the back of the pattern envelope, you'll find the Pick-a-Knit® Rule, which is designed to tell you if the knit you want to use has the right amount of stretch. To use this rule, fold the knit fabric crosswise and hold it against the left end of the rule. Pull on the knit to see if the indicated amount of fabric (usually 4" or 10cm) will easily stretch to the end of the rule. Now let go of the fabric; it should relax to its original size and shape. If the fabric doesn't have the proper stretch and recovery, it's not the right knit for that pattern.

THE EFFECTS OF TEXTURE AND SCALE

The next time you get a chance to people-watch, observe the fabrics they are wearing, paying careful attention to texture and scale. Note how your eye is automatically drawn to garments that feature:

- lighter or brighter colors
- bold or large-scale prints
- bulky fabrics, such as tweed, mohair and fake fur
- fabrics that cling, such as jersey and any fabric cut on the bias
- fabrics that attract the light, such as satins and metallics

Use what you learn from observing other people to select fabric for yourself. Your goal is to emphasize your good features, while minimizing your less-than-perfect ones. For example, if you're large busted, use eye-catching fabrics for a skirt or pants, not for a top or jacket.

GETTING THE BEST VALUE

There's no doubt about it: Shopping for fabric is fun and exciting. But before you are dazzled by a particular fabric's color, texture or print—or even its

great price—there are some other things you should think about before you part with your money.

Examine the information printed on the end of the cardboard bolt or on the attached hangtag. Besides telling you the width and the price per yard, it will also provide you with information about fiber content, special finishes and care requirements.

tip

You can tell a lot about a fabric just by handling it. Drape it over your arm. Does it lay smoothly against your skin or does it seem to have a shape of its own? Scrunch it up to create fullness. Does it fall into soft gathers or does it stand away from you? When you release the fabric, is it smooth or wrinkled?

FIBER CONTENT

Fibers are divided into two categories. Natural fibers, such as cotton, linen, silk and wool, come from plants and animals. Synthetic fibers, such as acrylic, polyester and nylon, are man-made.

Fabrics made from 100 percent natural fibers are generally more comfortable, more durable and more absorbent than those made from 100 percent synthetics. Natural fibers are easier to handle during sewing. Ripples and puckers are less of a problem. When they do occur, they can often be "erased" with the gentle touch of a steam iron.

On the other hand, synthetic fibers are usually much easier to care for—a particularly important factor for active sportswear and children's play clothes. Most can be either hand or machine washed. Usually, they are wrinkle resistant. Once sewn, the garment rarely has to be pressed between cleanings. However, during sewing, this same characteristic sometimes makes it difficult to get synthetics to hold a crease or retain a sharp edge. You can't rely on a steam iron to do all of the work. Instead, you must use topstitching or edgestitching to hold the edges flat.

Blends combine the best features of naturals and synthetics. As a rule, the fiber that is present in the highest percentage dominates the characteristics of the fabric. The chart (below) tells you what performance characteristics to expect from various types of fibers. To make this chart more meaningful to you, examine the labels in your favorite ready-to-wear garments. Note their fiber content and care requirements. Which ones seem to dominate your wardrobe? These are the ones to

Fiber Facts

	FIBER AND TRADENAMES	COMMON FABRIC TYPES	SPECIAL PROPERTIES		TYPICAL CARE
			ADVANTAGES	DISADVANTAGES	
NATURALS	COTTON	Batiste, broadcloth, corduroy, denim, flannel, seersucker, sheeting, terry, velveteen	Absorbent, cool, strong	Wrinkles and shrinks (unless treated, it is weakened by mildew)	Machine wash, tumble dry; can be bleached; iron while damp
	LINEN	Damask, handkerchief, lawn, fabrics with nubby textures	Absorbent, cool, strong	Wrinkles, shrinks; weakened by mildew	Dry clean to retain crispness, or wash to soften; iron while damp
	SILK	Broadcloth, charmeuse, chiffon, crepe de chine, linen, organza, raw silk, satin	Absorbent, warm, lustrous; drapes beautifully	Weakened by sunlight and perspiration	Dry clean, although some can be hand washed; iron on wrong side at low temperature
	WOOL	Challis, crepe, flannel, gabardine, jersey, melton, tweed	Absorbent, warm; flame and wrinkle resistant; good insulation	Shrinks; attracts moths; knits tend to stretch during wear	Dry clean, although some can be machine washed; press with steam iron and press cloth on right side
SYNTHETICS	ACETATE Celebrate® Estron® Chromspon®	Satin, silk-like fabrics, taffeta, twill	Silk-like luster; drapes well; dries quickly; low cost	Fades; relatively weak; exhibits static cling; wrinkles	Dry clean or gently machine wash, tumble dry (low); iron low temperature
	ACRYLIC Acrilan® Biokryl® Creslan® MicroSupreme® Orlon® Zefram®	Double knits, fleece, pile fabrics, wool-like fabrics	Warm; resists wrinkles, mildew, moths and oily stains	Sensitive to heat; pills; has static cling	Machine wash, tumble dry; needs no ironing

(FIBER FACTS continued on next page)

Fiber Facts (continued)				
FIBER AND TRADENAMES	**COMMON FABRIC TYPES**	**SPECIAL PROPERTIES**		**TYPICAL CARE**
		ADVANTAGES	DISADVANTAGES	
NYLON Anso IV® Antron® Caprolan® Softglow® Tactel®	Illusion, net, tricot, two-way stretch knits (swimwear) wet-look ciré	Strong, warm, light-weight; resists moths, wrinkles and mildew	Has static cling; pills; holds body heat	Hand or machine wash, tumble dry; iron at low temperature
POLYESTER Avlin® Dacron® EcoSpun® Encron® Fortrel® Hollofil® Kodel® Micromatique® Trevira®	Cotton-, silk- and wool-like fabrics, crepe, double and single knits, fleece, georgette, jersey, panne velvet, satin, taffeta	Strong, warm; very wrinkle-resistant; holds shape and a pressed crease; resists moths and mildew	Has static cling; pills; stains are hard to remove; holds body heat	Machine wash, tumble dry; needs little or no ironing
RAYON Avril® Modal® Polynosic® Zantrel®	Challis, crepe, faille, linen-like fabrics, matte jersey, velvet	Absorbent	Relatively fragile; holds body heat; wrinkles; shrinks	Dry clean or gently machine wash; iron at moderate temperature; can be bleached
SPANDEX Byrene® Cleerspan® Glospan® Lycra® Spandelle®	Stretch wovens; two-way stretch knits (swimwear, activewear fabrics)	Excellent stretch properties; good durability; no pilling or static cling	White fabrics may become yellow from prolonged exposure to air	Wash or dry clean; iron quickly on low temperature setting
BLENDS	Combination of two or more fibers	Meant to bring out the best properties of each fiber included		Care determined by most sensitive fiber

(SYNTHETICS — vertical label spanning NYLON through SPANDEX rows)

keep in mind as you select your fabric.

FABRIC FINISHES

Fabrics are often treated with special finishes that improve or alter their basic characteristics. The following are some of the most common fabric finishes. If the fabric is treated with one of these, it will be mentioned on the hangtag.

● *Flame-retardant:* Resists spread of flames, required by law on children's sleepwear and home furnishings fabrics.

● *Permanent press:* Sheds wrinkles after wearing or washing; needs little pressing. Cottons treated with a permanent press finish retain the look and feel of cotton without the wrinkling. However, when you sew a permanent press cotton, it will handle like a synthetic. You won't be able to use your iron to steam out any puckers. Instead, you can keep the puckers away by carefully holding the fabric taut, with one hand in front and one hand behind the presser foot as you stitch.

● *Preshrunk or shrink-resistant:* Keeps later (residual) shrinkage to a minimum. However, have you ever noticed how some ready-to-wear garments labeled preshrunk develop small puckers along the stitching lines after the first wash-

tip

Can't find the fabric of your dreams in your local stores? Consider mail order. For names, addresses, Web sites and specific details, consult the advertising pages of your favorite sewing magazine.

"Sizing" is a starch or resin added to the fabric for extra body. Because it's usually a temporary finish, you won't find it mentioned on the fabric label. Unbranded, "bargain" fabrics may be sized to make them look and feel like their more costly counterparts. But the first time these fabrics are washed, the sizing disappears, leaving you with a limp piece of goods— another excellent reason for pretreating your fabric. Examine the fabric carefully: If the weave is loose, but the fabric feels firm and crisp, it's a result of the sizing.

ing? Even a small amount of residual shrinkage can cause this. To keep it from happening to the garments you sew, make it a practice to pretreat your fabrics according to their care labels, regardless of the finish, before cutting out your pattern. Chapter 5 includes more information on pretreating your fabric.

● **Wash and wear:** Requires little or no ironing after laundering.

● **Waterproof:** Fabric treated so no moisture or air can penetrate it. Garments made of waterproof fabric may keep you dry but can make you feel clammy.

● **Water-repellent/water-resistant:** Resists absorption of liquids; they will bead on the surface. However, because air can penetrate the spaces between the yarns, fabrics with this type of finish make comfortable rainwear and running suits.

CARE REQUIREMENTS

Think before you buy! Now's the time to find out how to take care of that fabric. Otherwise, you might be in for some unpleasant surprises later on!

First, read the care label. Next, crush a corner of the fabric in your hand, release it and observe how much it wrinkles. If it wrinkles a lot, will you have the time to iron the garment before every wearing? If not, a knit or a wrinkle-resistant woven might be a better choice.

If frequent dry-cleaning bills on a white silk blouse are more than your budget can bear, a silk-like polyester

Don't make the mistake of buying a shoddy fabric "to practice on." You'll hate working on it— and end up with a garment that you'll probably never wear. Choose a quality fabric that's worthy of your sewing time. Even if your stitching is less than perfect, the fabric will still be lovely to look at and the resulting garment will be a pleasure to wear.

might be a better choice. Note that some silks can be washed. However, ironing freshly laundered silk can be

RATING A FABRIC'S SEWABILITY: When it comes to easy sewing, not all fabrics are equal. If you're just learning to sew, or if speed sewing is your goal, here are some fabrics you may want to avoid:

● *Slippery fabrics. They're hard to handle as you cut and stitch. For best results, cut them out single thickness and baste whenever necessary before machine stitching.*
● *Loosely woven fabrics. Because they ravel easily, special seam finishes are required. However, if you own a serger machine, finishing the raw edges is a breeze.*
● *Sheer fabrics. Because you can see through them, the inside of the garment must look as nice as the outside. This requires extra time and care...unless you own a serger. Then, you can stitch narrow, finished seams in one operation.*
● *Thick, bulky fabrics. They're hard to pin, sew and press.*
● *Fabrics with a one-way design unless your pattern features a "with nap" layout.*
● *Pile fabrics, such as corduroy, velvet or velveteen. In addition to requiring a "with nap" layout, these fabrics also call for special techniques to keep the layers from shifting as you pin and stitch, and—in the case of velvet—to keep the pile from being flattened as you press.*
● *Stripes and plaids. It takes extra time and thought to lay out the pattern pieces so that the color bars are attractively placed and accurately matched on the finished garment. For information on matching plaids and stripes, see "Special Layouts" in Chapter 5. For more information on sewing special fabrics, see Chapter 7.*

extremely time-consuming, usually with less than satisfactory results, unless you've selected a simple pattern. A T-top or dress with minimal details would be an excellent choice if you want to be able to wash your silk garment.

In-home dry-cleaning products may mean that you can bypass the professional cleaners by using your dryer. However, if the cleaned garment needs a crisp look, thorough pressing is still required. More time on garment care means less time to sew!

QUALITY FACTORS

Before the salesperson cuts your fabric, ask him or her to unroll it so you can examine the full length.

● Be sure the color is even throughout the piece, with no streaks or faded spots.

● If the fabric has a brushed surface, make sure there are no pills. If it pills on the bolt, you can be sure the problem will get even worse on your body.

● On knits, check for snags and pulls.

● If the fabric was folded, then rolled onto the bolt, check the fold line to make sure there are no permanent signs of wear. This is a particular problem with knits. If necessary, purchase extra fabric so you can work around the fold as you lay out the pattern pieces.

NOTIONS

At the same time that you're shopping for fabric, you'll want to purchase the other supplies necessary to complete your project. Review the information on the back of the pattern envelope. Look at the yardage requirements for your particular view. Note how many yards of interfacing, lining and/or trim you need to buy. Look at the "Notions" section. Note if, and how much, you'll need of items such as seam tape, elastic, shoulder pads, buttons, hooks and eyes, snaps, zippers, etc.

As you purchase these extras, keep your fashion fabric selection in mind…and check the labels for care requirements. Some cautions:

● Don't buy a dry-clean-only trim for a garment that you intend to wash.

● If you're buying elastic for a swimsuit, make sure it is labeled safe for swimwear. Some elastics lose their stretch when wet. Others lose their stretch or turn yellow when they come in contact with chlorine.

● Check buttons for care requirements. Some are dry-clean only. A few very special ones may be too fragile to risk even dry cleaning. Are you willing to remove them every time the garment is cleaned?

● Don't buy a trim that's too heavy for your fabric. For example, if you tried to trim a delicate chiffon with a heavy, beaded trim, puckers and a sagging hemline would be your reward.

● Select an interfacing that's compatible in weight and care with your fashion fabric. For a review of interfacing types and techniques, see the section in Chapter 6 on interfacings.

● If your pattern calls for lining, make sure you're purchasing a fabric that's suitable. Since a lining is designed to protect the inside of a garment and make it easier to get the garment on and off, the fabric should have a smooth, slippery surface. Silk types and satins are good lining choices. Because it is weakened by perspiration, 100 percent silk is a luxurious but not necessarily practical choice. If you can't find the right color match, don't despair. Linings don't have to match exactly. For a vivid effect, use a contrasting color; for a more subtle effect, choose a neutral, such as gray, black, beige, white or navy, that blends with the fashion fabric.

STITCHING TOOLS

Pins, needles and thread are integral parts of any project. The time to stock up is when you're in the store buying your fabric.

STRAIGHT PINS

All-purpose or dressmaker pins, in rust-proof stainless steel or brass, are good for all general pinning. Pins come with regular (flat) or round heads. Many sewers prefer round heads because they are easier to see and handle. If you have a choice between glass and plastic heads, choose the glass ones— they won't melt under the heat of your iron.

tip

Be sure to start every new project with a new needle. A worn, dull or damaged needle may appear fine to the naked eye but can cause stitch problems. All too often, the sewing machine is blamed when the problem is easily fixed by changing the needle.

NEEDLES

Don't spend too much time belaboring what size machine needle to buy. The smartest sewers keep packets of several different sizes on hand so they'll always have the right size needle for their project.

How do you know if you're using the right size needle? If the needle breaks (and you didn't sew over a pin), it's too small. If the seam draws up or if your machine skips stitches, the needle is too large.

Consult your sewing machine manual for its recommendations. It's also a good idea to check with your sewing machine dealer to see what brands he or she recommends. If a certain brand or type of needle isn't compatible with your machine, this knowledge will save you hours of frustration.

THREAD

The most important thing to remember when purchasing thread is to buy quality thread. How do you recognize quality thread? The next time you're shopping, pick up a spool of "promotional" thread (the type that's offered at a price too good to be true) and compare it to a spool of more expensive, branded thread. Notice the "fuzzies" on the cheaper thread. They're a sure sign that the thread is made inexpensively from short fibers. This type of thread will fray and break as you try to stitch with it. It will also deposit little bits of lint that will eventually clog up your sewing machine. Bargain threads are no bargain!

● Polyester or cotton-covered polyester thread is the universal recommendation for all fabrics. It's a must if you're sewing on synthetics. Use regular for general sewing; extrafine for lightweight fabrics, such as chiffon, organdy, organza and tricot knit, as well as for machine embroidery.

● Mercerized cotton thread is used on fabrics with little or no stretch.

● Silk thread is used on silk, wool and silk-like synthetic fabrics. Because it is expensive, sometimes hard to find and only available in a limited color range, many sewers prefer to use polyester or cotton-covered polyester.

tip

If you can't find the right color thread, pick one that's a shade darker than the fabric. Thread usually looks lighter when sewn.

● Special purpose or decorative threads, such as elastic, metallic and woolly nylon threads, all have an important place in your sewing. In Chapter 6, you'll learn how to use these threads, as well as thicker "threads" such as yarn, crochet cotton or narrow knitting ribbon, to achieve special effects with both your serger and conventional machine.

CUTTING TOOLS

These are the basic cutting tools to get you started. As your sewing skills develop, you may want to invest in other specialty scissors and cutting tools.

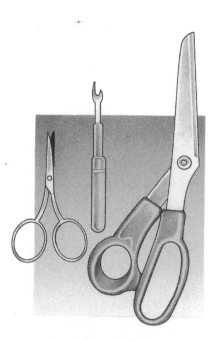

● *Bent-handle dressmaking shears:* These shears have 7" or 8"(18cm or 20.5cm) blades and two differently shaped handles that accommodate the configuration of your fingers for better control. The handles are bent up so that the fabric stays flat on the table as you cut out your pattern.

● *Seam ripper:* Even the most experienced seamstress makes mistakes. This pencil-thin tool with a curved blade makes it easy to remove stitches without harming the fabric.

● *Embroidery scissors:* These small scissors are used for detail work and for clipping threads.

MEASURING TOOLS

● *Tape measure:* A flexible 60" (153cm) synthetic or fiberglass tape measure will be your constant companion throughout the sewing process.

● *Yardstick or meter stick:* This 36" (1m) wooden ruler is particularly handy during pattern layout

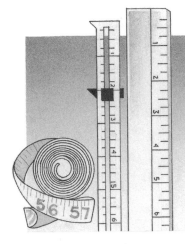

to check the grainline position (see Chapter 5). It's also useful anytime you need a long, straight, firm edge.

● *Seam gauge:* This small metal ruler with a sliding marker is useful for marking or checking measurements during construction. A short 6" (15cm) plastic ruler is a good substitute.

For information on fitting tools, see Chapter 4. For information on marking tools and pressing tools, see "Marking" and "Sewing With Your Iron" in Chapter 5.

A SEWING MACHINE

Although there is no one "perfect" machine, your skill level, sewing style and sewing interests will affect your final decision. If you are a beginning sewer, you may be in the market for a new or used machine. If you already own a machine, it may be time to trade in your old one for a newer model. Before you start any serious shopping, ask yourself the following questions:

● *What is my sewing expertise?* If you're just getting started, you probably won't want to invest in

the fanciest machine on the block. Most budget to midprice machines are mechanical machines, which means that you manually adjust the stitch width, stitch length and tension. A mechanical machine is driven by a single motor. A computerized machine contains multiple electronic motors synchronized by a computer. The result is a seemingly endless variety of built-in stitching options, including the ability to program and store customized stitch sequences. Top-of-the-line computerized machines, often referred to as embroidery machines, have a separate embroidery unit attached to the machine bed. Manufacturers also offer a variety of accessories for these machines, which allow them to interface with your home computer to create customized embroidery designs.

Although many articles are written about the fancier computerized machines, the basic mechanical machine is still the one most people own. If you are a returning sewer, you might want to upgrade to a more advanced model. The key is to be realistic so that you do not end up with more machine than you need.

tip

Your sewing machine's manual is key to getting the best performance from your machine. In fact, sewing machine manufacturers estimate that 80 percent of all expensive repairs could be avoided if owners would read and follow the guidelines in the manual. If your manual is among the missing, contact the manufacturer for a new one. To ensure that you get the right manual, include the model number of your machine with your request. This number is usually stamped on a small metal plate secured to the machine. On a free-arm machine, the plate is located to the back of the machine; on a flatbed machine, it's located on the front.

tip

When shopping for a machine, consumers are sometimes confused by the terms "built-in stitches" and "stitch functions." "Built-in stitches" refers to the actual stitches that are a permanent part of your machine. "Stitch functions" refers to how many different things you can do with these stitches. For example, the zigzag stitch is a built-in stitch. It can be used for many stitch functions, including overedge stitches to finish a raw edge, bartacks to reinforce pocket corners and belt loops and to attach flat buttons by machine, satin stitches to sew around the edges of appliqués, and zigzag stitches to sew flexible seams in knits. The blind hem is a built-in stitch that can be used for many functions, including hemming, folk art appliqué and applying decorative braid.

● *How do I rate my current machine?* Have you been pleased with its performance? Is it easy to use? What features do you wish it had? Do you want to replace it with a newer machine, one with similar features but with state-of-the-art electronics? If you have friends who sew, interview them about their machines.

● *What are my sewing interests?* If everyday sewing and mending are all you expect to do, a basic mechanical machine that does a simple buttonhole and comes with a few basic attachments, such as an all-purpose presser foot, a zipper foot, a buttonhole foot and a button sewing foot, will serve you well. But if you are interested in garment construction, home dec sewing and quilting (even if these are on your "someday" list), you'll want a machine with a greater variety of features, such as a free arm, more stitch options and more specialized presser feet.

● *What are my customer service expectations?* Although today's

machines are far superior to the ones our grandmothers used, there is always a possibility that your sewing machine, like any other household appliance, could break down. Conventional wisdom says to shop for a sewing machine dealer as carefully as you shop for the machine itself so that you will have a place to go for questions and lessons, as well as for repairs. Although this is still the ideal situation, our society is increasingly mobile. The best buy may not be the one closest to home…or "home" may change to another town or state. In addition, there are now many other ways to purchase a machine, including via mail order, the Web and television shopping networks. So it's a good idea to check with the manufacturer before you make a final decision. Some sewing machine manufacturers will refer you to a local dealer for service regardless of where you bought the machine; others will make arrangements for you to return the machine directly to their

service center. In the case of the latter, it is important that you hold on to the machine's original carton and packing materials. If you no longer have them, ask the manufacturer about proper packing materials before sending off your machine. And never return a machine directly to the manufacturer without checking first. These days it's easy to locate the address and phone number. Most manufacturers advertise regularly in the sewing magazines…or you can surf the Internet to locate their Web sites.

● *What is my price range?* Whatever your budget, there is a machine that will give you hours of sewing satisfaction. You can always start out with a modest machine and trade up as your sewing skills improve.

If you have your heart set on a particular machine but can't afford the newest version, check out the classified ads, as well as estate and garage sales, for bargains on a used machine. Be familiar with the machine before you shop so you will know if there are missing parts or feet. Take a variety of fabric swatches with you so you can test-sew before you buy.

THE ANATOMY OF A SEWING MACHINE

Knowing the names of the parts of your sewing machine will help you maximize its performance.

The actual location and configuration of some of these features will vary, depending on the make and model of your machine.

THE ANATOMY OF A SEWING MACHINE

FRONT VIEW

1–*Face cover:* Flips open to provide access to the lightbulb and the presser foot pressure regulator.

2–*Bobbin winding tension disc:* Upper thread goes through this disc when you are threading the machine to wind the bobbin.

3–*Thread tension dial:* Controls the upper thread for proper stitch formation.

4–*Stitch width dial:* Sets the width of your stitch.

5–*Stitch selector dial:* Use this dial to select your machine's built-in stitches.

6–*Bobbin winder spindle:* Holds the empty bobbin so you can fill it up to thread the lower (bobbin) part of your machine.

7–*Hand wheel:* Turning the hand wheel raises and lowers the needle.

8–*Reverse lever or button:* Allows you to sew in reverse.

9–*Stitch length dial:* Lets you adjust the length of your stitches.

10–*Free-arm cover:* Provides a flat surface for most sewing. With the cover removed, it is easier to access some parts of a garment when mending, as well as to sew "round" seams, such as armholes and necklines.

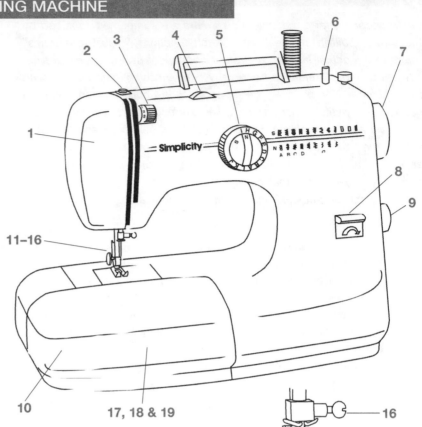

11–*Feed teeth:* The metal teeth under the needle plate, which push or feed the fabric through the machine. This area is sometimes referred to as the feed dog.

12–*Presser foot:* Holds the fabric firmly against the feed teeth so that the stitches form properly.

13–*Presser foot holder:* Holds the snap-on presser feet in sewing position. When you use a screw-on presser foot, the presser foot holder is attached to the foot.

14–*Needle plate:* This flat, metal plate covers the area where the bobbin is inserted and supports the fabric during sewing. Common seam allowances are permanently marked on the plate to guide you in sewing accurately.

15–*Presser foot thumb screw:* Secures the presser foot holder

THE ANATOMY OF A SEWING MACHINE *(continued)*

to the presser foot bar. You will need to loosen this thumb screw before changing to another screw-on presser foot, and then tighten it once the new foot is in place.

16–*Needle clamp screw:* Loosen to remove a needle; tighten to secure a needle in position.

LOWER THREAD AREA

17–*Bobbin:* A metal or clear plastic spool that holds the lower thread. Depending on the make and model of your machine, the bobbin holder may be located under a cover on the front, side or back of the machine, and it can be positioned so that the bobbin is inserted horizontally or vertically.

18–*Bobbin case:* If the bobbin is inserted horizontally, the bobbin case will be built in. If the bobbin is inserted vertically, it is necessary to remove the bobbin case before inserting the bobbin.

19–*Shuttle area:* This is where the mechanisms that move the bobbin are housed. Dust and loose threads can build up in this area so check it regularly and brush it clean following the instructions in your machine's manual.

BACK VIEW

20–*Carry handle:* For convenient carrying when you need to move the machine.

21–*Presser foot lever:* Lift it to raise the presser foot and release the thread tension; lower it to lower the presser foot and engage the thread tension.

22–*Thread cutter:* A convenient way to cut the threads after completing a seam.

23–*Power cord receptacle:* Connect the power cord's three-prong plug here.

24–*Main switch:* Turns the power and the machine's built-in sewing light on or off.

25–*Retractable spool pins:* These hold the upper thread. If your machine is capable of twin needle sewing, there will be two spool pins. Be sure that they are fully extended for sewing.

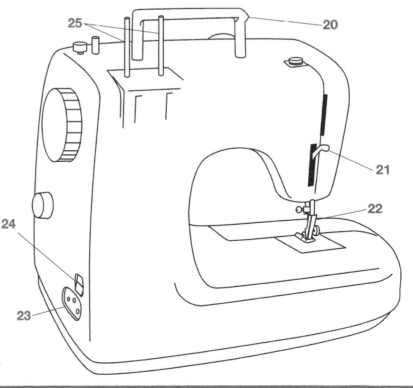

A PLACE TO SEW

Everyone needs a place to sew. However, your workspace need not be as fancy or as elaborate as sometimes suggested. The pictures are often that way in the hopes that you'll buy the products shown! And while it might be nice to dream about having a whole room devoted to sewing projects, where you can leave everything "in progress" and just close the door, it shouldn't hold you back from sewing if you don't have that kind of space.

All you really need to get started is a cleared-off surface for your sewing machine and a good light (an adjustable lamp is best). If possible, set up your iron and ironing board nearby. It cuts down on tedious trips back and forth between the sewing machine and the ironing board.

Your sewing notions should be stored somewhere in easy reach. Put them in a sewing box, in a wicker basket, in a rolling cart with wire baskets or in a set of plastic organizers. If your sewing area is permanent, hang the notions you use most often from a pegboard or mug rack above your sewing machine.

You'll also need a place to store all of the pieces of your project between sewing sessions. Consider an empty drawer, a large wicker basket, a large dress box or an empty suitcase.

One final piece of equipment is a full-length mirror. If you can, put it in the same room as your sewing machine. You'll need it for the fit-as-you-go techniques you'll learn in the next chapter.

chapter 4
The Easy Way to a Perfect Fit

Somewhere in the history of sewing, people got the idea that there were only two ways to end up with a well-fitting garment: Either start with a perfect body *or* spend hours fussing with a fitting muslin, making complicated adjustments on the pattern tissue and attending every fitting seminar in town. Fortunately for today's sewer, this simply isn't true.

The path to a perfect fit is an easy one. It begins with something so basic that you might think it's obvious—the right size pattern. Too many people purchase a pattern by their ready-to-wear size, without ever looking at, or analyzing, the measurements provided in the pattern catalog.

Most people think that they know what size they are. Suppose that you "know" you're a size 12. Think honestly about the last time you went shopping for clothes. Did *every* size 12 dress, skirt or pair of pants fit you? Of course not! Each ready-to-wear manufacturer has its own set of standard measurements. That's why you might be a size 12

in some clothes, but a size smaller or larger in others.

To choose the right size pattern, you'll need to clear your head of any preconceived notions about what size you wear. Then follow these simple steps:

1. Take your measurements.

2. Determine your figure type.

3. Select the size within your figure type. You will probably—*but not necessarily*—end up with a pattern size that corresponds to your ready-to-wear size. You might even end up with a different size pattern for tops and bottoms. This is one of the reasons Multi-Size patterns are so popular.

MEASURING YOUR BODY

You won't know where to begin to choose figure type and pattern size unless you have some body measurements to guide you. Using the accompanying Personal Measurement Chart, record your measurements in column 1.

Height and back waist length will

be used to determine your correct figure type. Bust, waist and hips will be used to determine your correct pattern size. The other measurements will help you fine-tune the fit of your pattern.

The procedures for determining figure type and pattern size are the same for everyone, male or female, adult or child. Basically, the same measurements are needed. The exceptions are the high bust and the shoulder-to-bust measurements (for females only) and the neck measurement (for males only). If you're sewing for a child, regardless of sex, these measurements are not necessary.

HOW TO MEASURE

● Don't try to take your measurements by yourself. Only a contortionist could do that successfully! Enlist the aid of a friend.

● For women and girls, take the measurements over undergarments or a leotard. For men and boys, take them over a T-shirt and shorts or unbelted, lightweight slacks.

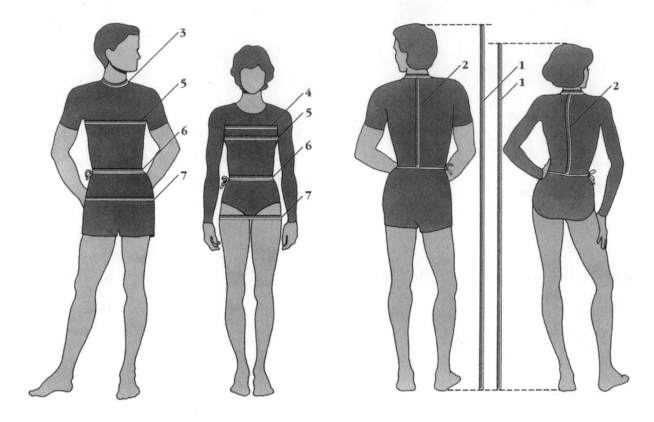

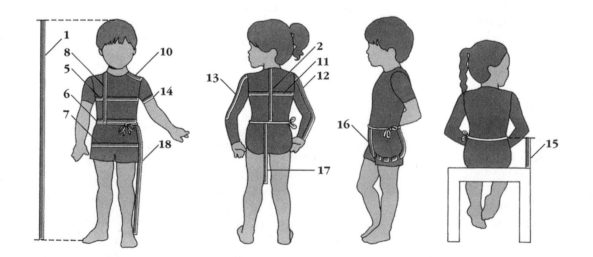

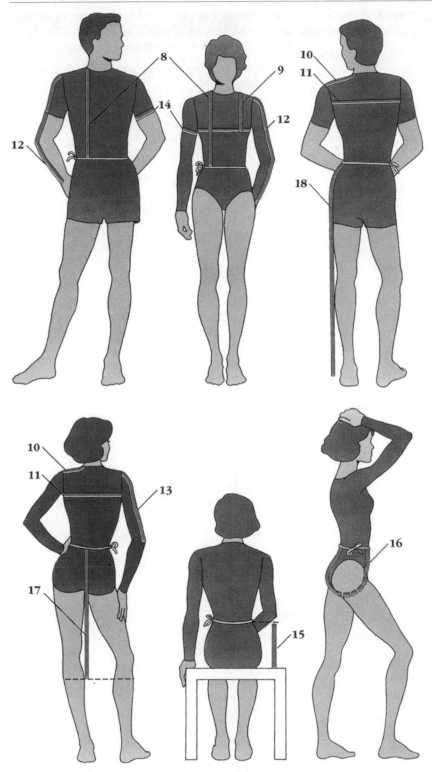

- Stand in a relaxed, normal position and look straight ahead.

- To locate the natural waistline, tie a string snugly around the waist. If the waist is hard to find (a common problem on men and children), have the person bend sideways. The crease that forms is at the natural waistline.

- To find the shoulder point, raise the arm to shoulder level. A dimple will form at the shoulder bone—that's the shoulder point.

- To find the back neck bone, bend the head forward so you can feel the first neck bone, or vertebra.

- To locate the base of the neck in front, shrug your shoulders so that a hollow forms at the neck base.

- For the "around" measurements, keep the tape measure parallel to the floor. The tape should be snug, but not tight, against the body.

- Retake these measurements every six months, just in case the figure has changed enough to require another size pattern or different adjustments. With rapidly growing children, you will probably need to remeasure more often.

HOW TO DETERMINE YOUR FIGURE TYPE

Your height and back waist length (measurements 1 and 2), along with your body proportions, are the keys to determining your figure type.

To find your figure type, examine the Figure Types/Pattern Body Measurements charts on pages 41-45. Read the figure type descriptions, study the sketches and locate

(text continued on page 46)

Personal Measurement Chart

WHAT TO MEASURE	BODY MEASUREMENTS		ADJUSTMENT
	YOURS	SIMPLICITY STANDARDS *(See charts on pages 41-45.)*	(+ or −)
1. **HEIGHT** (without shoes)			
2. **BACK WAIST LENGTH** from prominent bone at back neck base to waist			
3. **NECK** (males only) at the Adam's apple. Add 1/2" (1.3cm) to neck body measurement. This measurement is now the same as the ready-to-wear collar size.			
4. **HIGH BUST** (females only) directly under the arms, above the bust and around the back			
5. **BUST/CHEST** around the fullest part			
6. **WAIST** over the string			
7. **HIPS/SEAT*** around the fullest part. See note (*) below for information pertinent to the various figure types.			
8. **FRONT WAIST LENGTH** from shoulder at neck base to waist (over bust point on females)			
9. **SHOULDER TO BUST** (females only) from shoulder at neck base to bust point			
10. **SHOULDER LENGTH** from neck base to shoulder bone			
11. **BACK WIDTH**** across the midback. See note (**) below for information pertinent to the various figure types.			
12. **ARM LENGTH** from shoulder bone to wristbone over a slightly bent elbow			
13. **SHOULDER TO ELBOW** (females only) from end of shoulder to middle of a slightly bent elbow			
14. **UPPER ARM** around arm at fullest part between shoulder and elbow			
15. **CROTCH DEPTH.** Measure from side waist to chair. Sit on a hard, flat chair and use a straightedge ruler.		See page 55.	
16. **CROTCH LENGTH.** Measure from center back waist, between legs, to center front waist		See page 56.	
17. **BACK SKIRT LENGTH.** (females only) Measure from center back at waist to desired length		Measure pattern piece	
18. **PANTS SIDE LENGTH.** Measure from side waistline to desired length along outside of leg		Measure pattern piece	

* To determine the HIP measurement, measure around the body at these distances below waist:
    MISSES' & WOMEN'S—9" (23cm)
    MISS PETITE, WOMEN'S PETITE, JUNIORS' & TEEN-BOYS—7"(18cm)
    GIRLS' & GIRLS' PLUS—5" to 7" (14cm to 18cm)
    BOYS'—6" (15cm)
    CHILD'S—4" to 5⅝" (11.5cm to 14.3cm)
    TODDLERS'—3" to 4" (9cm to 11.5cm)

** To determine the BACK WIDTH measurement, measure across the back at these distances below the neck base:
    MISSES', MISS PETITE, WOMEN'S, WOMEN'S PETITE & JUNIORS'—5"(12.5cm)
    MEN—6" (15cm)
    TEEN-BOYS'—4" (11.5cm)
    GIRLS', GIRLS' PLUS & BOYS'—4" (10cm)
    CHILD'S—3" (7.5cm)
    TODDLERS'—2" (7cm)

FEMALES: Figure Types and Pattern Body Measurements

Misses'/Miss Petite—For well-proportioned, developed figures.
Misses' about 5'5" (1.65m) to 5'6" (1.68m) tall without shoes. Miss Petite under 5'4" (1.63m) tall without shoes.

Inches													Centimeters											
4	6	8	10	12	14	16	18	20	22	24	26	Sizes	4	6	8	10	12	14	16	18	20	22	24	26
30	32	34	36	38	40	42	44	46	48	50	52	European	30	32	34	36	38	40	42	44	46	48	50	52
29½	30½	31½	32½	34	36	38	40	42	44	46	48	Bust	75	78	80	83	87	92	97	102	107	112	117	122
22	23	24	25	26½	28	30	32	34	37	39	41½	Waist	56	58	61	64	67	71	76	81	87	94	99	106
31½	32½	33½	34½	36	38	40	42	44	46	48	50	Hip-9" (23cm) Below Waist	80	83	85	88	92	97	102	107	112	117	122	127
15¼	15½	15¾	16	16¼	16½	16¾	17	17¼	17⅜	17½	17¾	Back Waist Length	38.5	39.5	40	40.5	41.5	42	42.5	43	44	44	44.5	45
14¼	14½	14¾	15	15¼	15½	15¾	16	16¼	16⅜	16½	16⅝	Petite-Back Waist Length	36	37	37.5	38	38.5	39.5	40	40.5	41.5	41.5	42	42
16⅜	16¾	17	17⅜	17¾	18	18⅜	18⅝	19	19¼	19⅞	20⅜	Front Waist Length	41.5	42.5	43	44	45	45.5	46.5	47.5	48.5	49	50	51.5
15⅜	15⅞	16⅛	16½	16¾	17⅛	17¼	17¾	18⅛	18⅜	18¾	19⅛	Petite- Front Waist Length	38.5	40	40.5	42	42.5	43	44	45	45.5	46.5	47.5	48.5
8⅞	9⅛	9⅜	9⅝	9⅞	10⅛	10⅜	10⅝	10⅞	11⅛	11⅜	11⅝	Shoulder to Bust	22	23	23.5	24.5	25	25.5	26	26.5	27.5	28	28.5	29.5
4½	4⅝	4¾	4⅞	5	5⅛	5¼	5⅜	5½	5⅝	5¾	5⅞	Shoulder Length	11.5	11.5	12	12	12.5	12.5	13.5	13.5	14	14	14.5	15
13½	13¾	14	14¼	14⅝	15⅛	15⅜	16	16½	16⅞	17⅛	17⅝	Back Width	34.5	35	35.5	36	37	38	39.5	40.5	42	42.5	43.5	44.5
22	22¾	23	23¼	23½	23¾	24	24¼	24½	24¾	25	25¼	Arm Length	56	58	58.5	59	59.5	60.5	61	61.5	62	63	63.5	64
13⅜	13½	13⅝	13¾	13⅞	14	14⅛	14¼	14⅜	14½	14⅝	14¾	Shoulder to Elbow	34	34.5	34.5	35	35.5	35.5	36	36	36.5	36.5	37	37
8¾	9¼	9¾	10¼	10¾	11¼	11¾	12¼	12¾	13¼	13¾	14¼	Upper Arm	22	23.5	25	26	27.5	28.5	30	31	32.5	33.5	35	36

Women's/Women's Petite—For the larger, more fully mature figures. Women's about 5'5" (1.65m) to 5'6" (1.68m)tall without shoes. Women's Petite under 5'4" (1.63m) tall without shoes.

Inches									Centimeters							
18W	20W	22W	24W	26W	28W	30W	32W	Sizes	18W	20W	22W	24W	26W	28W	30W	32W
44	46	48	50	52	54	56	58	European	44	46	48	50	52	54	56	58
40	42	44	46	48	50	52	54	Bust	102	107	112	117	122	127	132	137
33	35	37	39	41½	44	46½	49	Waist	84	89	94	99	105	112	118	124
42	44	46	48	50	52	54	56	Hip-9" (23cm) Below Waist	107	112	117	122	127	132	137	142
17⅛	17¼	17⅜	17½	17⅝	17¾	17⅞	18	Back Waist Length	43	44	44	44.5	45	45	45.5	46
16⅛	16¼	16⅜	16½	16⅝	16¾	16⅞	17	Petite-Back Waist Length	40.5	41.5	41.5	42	42	42.5	42.5	43
19⅜	19⅝	19⅞	20⅛	20⅜	20⅝	20⅞	21⅜	Front Waist Length	49	49.5	51	51.5	52	52.5	53	54
18⅝	18¾	19	19¼	19½	19¾	20	20½	Petite-Front Waist Length	47	47.5	48.5	49	49.5	50	51	52
11¾	12	12¼	12½	12¾	13	13¼	13½	Shoulder to Bust	30	30.5	31	32	32.5	33	33.5	34.5
4⅞	5	5	5⅛	5⅛	5¼	5⅜	5⅜	Shoulder Length	12	12.5	12.5	13	13	13.5	13.5	14
15¾	16¼	16¾	17¼	17¾	18¼	18¾	19¼	Back Width	40	41.5	42.5	44	45	46.5	47.5	49
23½	23¾	24	24¼	24½	24¾	25	25¼	Arm Length	59.5	60.5	61	61.5	62	63	63.5	64
14¼	14⅜	14½	14⅝	14¾	14⅞	15	15⅛	Shoulder to Elbow	36	36.5	37	37	37.5	37.5	38	38
13	13½	14	14½	15	15½	16	16½	Upper Arm	33	34.5	35.5	37	38	39.5	40.5	42

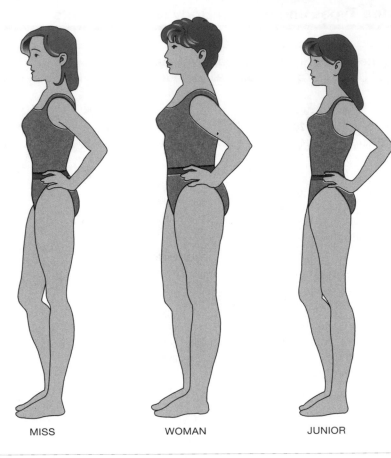

MISS   WOMAN   JUNIOR

JUNIORS'—A developing figure, slightly shorter than a Miss, about 5'3" (1.60m) to 5'5" (1.65m) tall, with a shorter waist length than the Miss.

Inches											Sizes	Centimeters										
3/4	5/6	7/8	9/10	11/12	13/14	15/16	17/18	19/20	21/22	23/24		3/4	5/6	7/8	9/10	11/12	13/14	15/16	17/18	19/20	21/22	23/24
28	29	30½	32	33½	35	36½	38½	40½	42½	44½	Bust	71	73.5	77.5	81.5	85	89	92.5	98	103	108	113
22	23	24	25	26	27	28	29½	31	33½	35½	Waist	56	58.5	61	63.5	66	68.5	71	75	78.5	85	90
31	32	33½	35	36½	38	39½	41½	43½	45½	47½	Hip-7"(18cm) Below Waist	78.5	81.5	85	89	92.5	96.5	100.5	106	111	116	121
13½	14	14½	15	15⅜	15¾	16⅛	16⅜	16⅝	16⅞	17⅛	Back Waist Length	34.5	35.5	37	38	39	40	41	42	42.5	43	43.5
14¾	15¼	15⅞	16⅜	17	17½	18⅛	18⅝	19⅛	19⅝	20⅛	Front Waist Length	37.5	38.5	40	42	43	44.5	45.5	47	48.5	49.5	51
8½	8¾	9⅛	9½	9¾	10	10¼	10½	10¾	11	11¼	Shoulder to Bust	21.5	22	23	24	25	25.5	26	26.5	27.5	28	28.5
4	4⅛	4¼	4⅜	4½	4⅝	4¾	4⅞	5	5⅛	5¼	Shoulder Length	10.5	10.5	11	11.5	11.5	12	12	12.5	12.5	13	13.5
12½	12¾	13⅛	13½	13⅞	14¼	14⅞	15¼	15⅞	16¼	16⅞	Back Width	32	32.5	33	34.5	35	36	37.5	38.5	40	41.5	42.5
21¼	21¾	22⅛	22⅝	23	23⅜	23¾	24⅛	24½	24⅞	25¼	Arm Length	54	55	56	57	58.5	59.5	60.5	61	62	63	63.5
11¾	12	12⅜	12¾	13	13⅜	13¾	14⅛	14½	14⅞	15¼	Shoulder to Elbow	30	30.5	32	32.5	33	33.5	35	36	37	38	38.5
8⅞	9⅜	9⅞	10⅜	10⅞	11⅜	11¾	12⅛	12⅝	13	13⅜	Upper Arm	22.5	23.5	25	26	27.5	28.5	30	30.5	32	33	34

CHILDREN: Figure Types and Pattern Body Measurements

TODDLERS'- For figures that are taller then Babies but shorter than Children. Pants have a diaper allowance and often apply to both boys and girls; dresses are shorter than Children's sizes.

Inches						Centimeters				
½	1	2	3	4	Sizes	½	1	2	3	4
19	20	21	22	23	Chest	48	51	53	56	58
19	19½	20	20½	21	Waist	48	50	51	52	53
20	21	22	23	24	Hip	51	53.5	56	58.5	61
7½	8	8½	9	9½	Back Waist Length	19	20.5	21.5	23	24
8⅜	8⅞	9⅜	9⅞	10⅜	Front Waist Length	21.5	22.5	24	25	26.5
2⅜	2½	2⅝	2¾	2⅞	Shoulder Length	6	6.5	6.5	7	7.5
7¾	8	8¼	8½	8¾	Back Width	19.5	20.5	21	21.5	22.5
10	10¾	11½	12¼	13	Arm Length	25.5	27.5	29.5	31	33
6½	6⅞	7¼	7⅝	8	Shoulder to Elbow	16.5	17.5	18.5	19.5	20.5
6¼	6½	6¾	7	7¼	Upper Arm	16	16.5	17	18	18.5
28	31	34	37	40	Approx. Height	71	79	87	94	102

CHILD'S—The younger child has the same chest and waist measurements as Toddlers' but is taller with wider shoulders and back. In many instances, designs are suitable for both boys and girls.

Inches								Centimeters							
2	3	4	5	6	6X	7	8	Sizes	2	3	4	5	6	6X	7	8
21	22	23	24	25	25½	26	27	Chest	53	56	58	61	64	65	66	69
20	20½	21	21½	22	22½	23	23½	Waist	51	52	53	55	56	57	58	60
—	—	24	25	26	26½	27	28	Hip	—	—	61	64	66	67	69	71
8½	9	9½	10	10½	10¾	11½	12	Back Waist Length	22	23	24	25.5	27	27.5	29.5	31
9⅜	9⅞	10⅜	10⅞	11⅜	11⅝	12⅝	13⅛	Front Waist Length	23.5	25	26.5	27.5	29	29.5	32	33
2⅞	3	3⅛	3¼	3⅜	3½	3⅝	3¾	Shoulder Length	7.5	7.5	8	8.5	8.5	9	9.5	10
9½	9¾	10	10¼	10½	10⅝	11½	11⅞	Back Width	24	24.5	25.5	26	26.5	27	29	30.5
12¾	13½	14¼	15	15¾	16⅛	17½	18¼	Arm Length	32.5	34.5	36	38	40	41	44.5	46.5
7¾	8⅛	8⅝	9	9½	9⅞	10⅜	10⅞	Shoulder to Elbow	20	21	22	23	24	25	26.5	28
6¾	7	7¼	7½	7¾	7⅞	8¼	8½	Upper Arm	17	18	18.5	19	19.5	20	21	21.5
35	38	41	44	47	48	50	52	Approx. Height	89	97	104	112	119	122	127	132

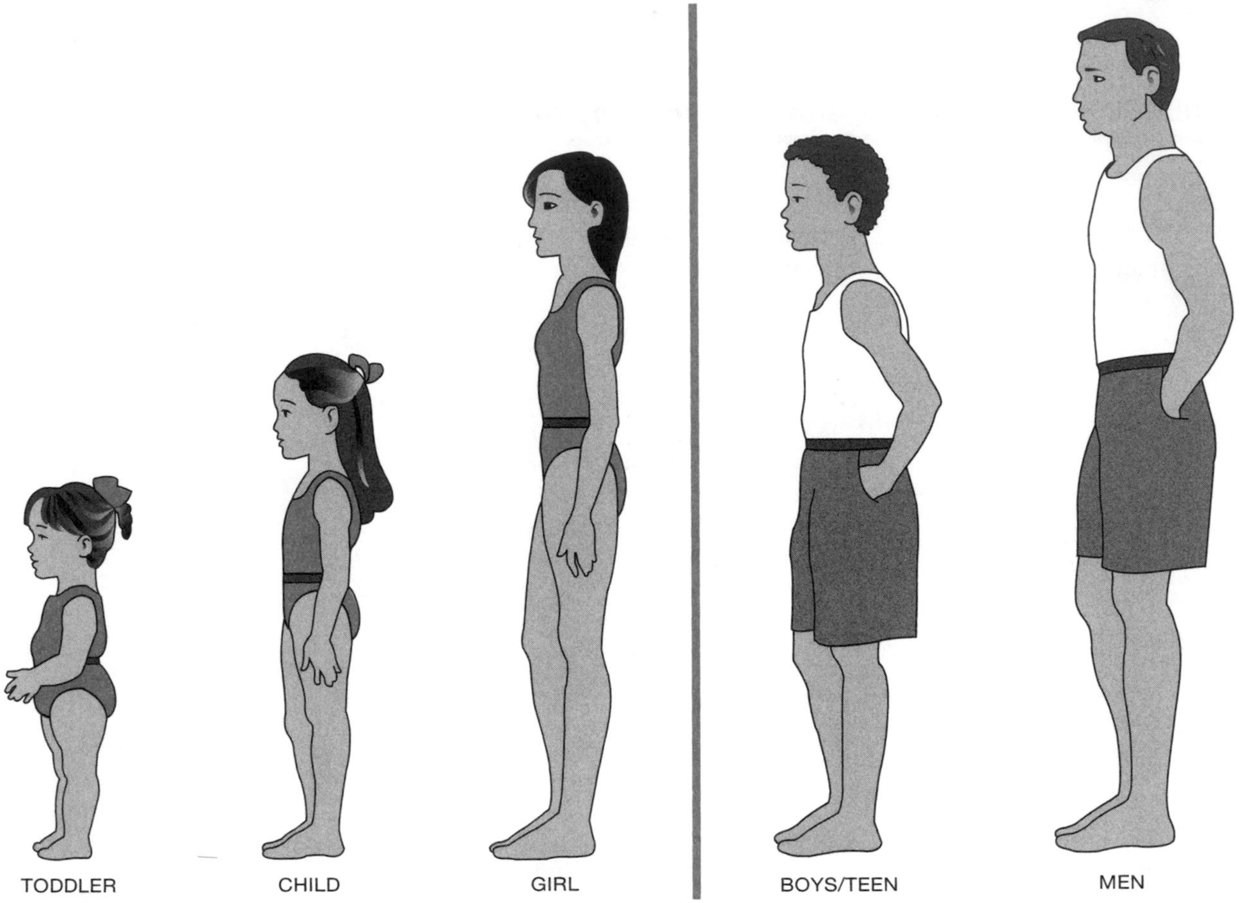
TODDLER
CHILD
GIRL
BOYS/TEEN
MEN

GIRLS'/GIRLS' PLUS—For the growing girl who has not yet begun to mature. Girls' Plus are designed for girls over the average weight for their age and height.

Girls						Girls' Plus						Girls						Girls' Plus				
Inches												Centimeters										
7	8	10	12	14	16	8 ½	10 ½	12 ½	14 ½	16 ½	Sizes	7	8	10	12	14	16	8 ½	10 ½	12 ½	14 ½	16 ½
26	27	28½	30	32	34	30	31½	33	34½	36	**Chest**	66	69	73	76	81	87	76	80	84	88	92
23	23½	24½	25½	26½	27½	28	29	30	31	32	**Waist**	58	60	62	65	67	70	71	74	76	79	81
27	28	30	32	34	36	33	34½	36	37½	39	**Hip**	69	71	76	81	87	92	84	88	92	96	96
11½	12	12¾	13½	14¼	15	12½	13¼	14	14¾	15½	**Back Waist Length**	29.5	31	32.5	34.5	36	38	32	34	35.5	37.5	39.5
12⅜	13	13 ⅞	14¾	15⅝	16½	12½	13¼	14	14¾	15½	**Front Waist Length**	31.5	33	35.5	37.5	39.5	42	32	33.5	35.5	37.5	39.5
6¾	6 7/8	7¼	7⅝	8	8⅜	7⅜	7¾	8⅛	8½	8 ⅞	**Shoulder to Chest**	17	17.5	18.5	19.5	20.5	21.5	18.5	19	20.5	21.5	22.5
3⅝	3¾	4	4¼	4⅜	4½	4 ⅛	4¼	4½	4¾	5	**Shoulder Length**	9.5	9.5	10.5	10.5	11	11.5	10.5	11	11.5	12	12.5
11¾	12	12½	13	13½	14	12⅜	13	13⅝	14¼	14 ⅞	**Back Width**	30	30.5	31.5	33	34.5	35.5	32	33	34	36	37.5
17 ⅞	18½	19¾	21	21½	22	19	20½	22	23½	24	**Arm Length**	45.5	47	50.5	53.5	54.5	56	48.5	52	56	59.5	61
10⅝	11	11⅝	12¼	12⅜	12⅝	10¾	11⅛	12¼	13	13¼	**Shoulder to Elbow**	27	28	29.5	31	31.5	32	27.5	28	31	33	33.5
8¼	8½	9	9½	10	10½	9½	10	10½	11	11½	**Upper Arm**	21	21.5	23	24	25.5	26.5	24	25.5	26.5	28	29
50	52	56	58½	61	61½	52	56	58½	61	63½	**Approx. Height**	127	132	142	149	155	156	132	142	149	155	161

MALES: Figure Types and Pattern Body Measurements

BOYS' & TEEN BOYS'—For growing boys and young men who have not reached full adult stature.

Inches									Centimeters							
7	8	10	12	14	16	18	20	Sizes	7	8	10	12	14	16	18	20
26	27	28	30	32	33½	35	36½	**Chest**	66	69	71	76	81	85	89	93
23	24	25	26	27	28	29	30	**Waist**	58	61	64	66	69	71	74	75
27	28	29½	31	32½	34¼	35½	37	**Hip**	69	71	75	79	83	87	90	94
11⅜	11¾	12½	13¼	14	14¾	15½	16¼	**Back Waist Length**	29	30	32	33.5	35.5	37.5	39	41
12⅜	12¾	13½	14¼	14⅝	15⅜	16⅛	16⅞	**Front Waist Length**	31	32	34.5	36	37	39	41	43
4	4⅛	4¼	4½	4¾	5	5¼	5½	**Shoulder Length**	10	10.5	11	11.5	12	12.5	13	14
11½	11¾	12⅛	12¾	13⅞	14½	15⅛	15¾	**Back Width**	29	30	31	32	35	37	38.5	41
16⅝	17¼	18½	19¾	21⅞	22½	23⅛	23¾	**Arm Length**	42	44	47	50	55.5	57	59	60.5
8	8¼	8¾	9¼	9¾	10¼	10¾	11¼	**Upper Arm**	20.5	21	22	23.5	25	26	27.5	28.5
11¼	11½	12	12½	13	13½	14	14½	**Neck**	28.5	29.5	30.5	32	33	34.5	35.5	36.5
11¾	12	12½	13	13½	14	14½	15	**Neck Band**	30	31	32	33	34.5	35.5	37	38
22⅜	23¼	25	26¾	29	30	31	32	**Shirtsleeve**	57	59	64	68	74	76	79	81
48	50	54	58	61	64	66	68	**Approx. Height**	122	127	137	147	155	163	168	173

MEN'S—For men of average build about 5' 10" (1.78m) tall without shoes.

Inches												Centimeters										
32	34	36	38	40	42	44	46	48	50	52	Sizes	32	34	36	38	40	42	44	46	48	50	52
42	44	46	48	50	52	54	56	58	60	62	Sizes-Eur/Fr	42	44	46	48	50	52	54	56	58	60	62
32	34	36	38	40	42	44	46	48	50	52	**Chest**	82	87	92	97	102	107	112	117	122	127	132
27	28	30	32	34	36	39	42	44	46	48	**Waist**	66	71	76	81	87	92	99	107	112	117	122
34	35	37	39	41	43	45	47	49	51	53	**Hip**	84	89	94	99	104	109	114	119	124	130	135
17¼	17½	17¾	18	18¼	18½	18¾	19	19¼	19½	19¾	**Back Waist Length**	44	44.5	45	45.5	46.5	47	47.5	48.5	49	49.5	50.5
17½	17¾	18	18¼	18½	18¾	19	19¼	19½	19¾	20	**Front Waist Length**	44.5	45	45.5	46.5	47	47.5	48.5	49	49.5	50.5	51
6	6⅛	6¼	6⅜	6½	6⅝	6¾	6⅞	7	7⅛	7¼	**Shoulder Length**	15	15.5	15.5	16	16.5	16.5	17	17.5	17.5	18	18.5
15½	16	16½	17	17½	18	18½	19	19½	20	20½	**Back Width**	39.5	40.5	42	43.5	44.5	45.5	47	48.5	49.5	50.5	52
23⅜	23⅝	23⅞	24⅛	24⅜	24⅝	24⅞	25⅛	25⅜	25⅝	25⅞	**Arm Length**	59	60	60.5	61.5	62	62.5	63.5	64	64.5	65	65.5
10	10½	11	11½	12	12½	13	13½	14	14½	15	**Upper Arm**	25.5	26.5	28	29	30.5	32	33	34.5	35.5	37	38
13	13½	14	14½	15	15½	16	16½	17	17½	18	**Neck**	33	34	35.5	36.5	38	39.5	40.5	42	43.5	44.5	46
13½	14	14½	15	15½	16	16½	17	17½	18	18½	**Neck Band**	34.5	35.5	37	38	39.5	40.5	42	43	44.5	45.5	47
31	32	32	33	33	34	34	35	35	36	36	**Shirtsleeve**	78.5	81	81	84	84	87	87	89	89	91.5	91.5

UNISEX: Figure Types and Pattern Body Measurements

UNISEX—For figures within Misses', Men's, Teen-Boys', Boys'and Girls' size ranges.

Inches								Centimeters						
XXS	XS	S	M	L	XL	XXL	Sizes	XXS	XS	S	M	L	XL	XXL
28-29	30-32	34-36	38-40	42-44	46-48	50-52	**Chest/Bust**	71-74	76-81	87-92	97-102	107-112	117-122	127-132
29-30	31-32½	35-37	39-41	43-45	47-49	51-53	**Hip**	74-76	79-83	89-94	99-104	109-114	119-124	130-135

the back waist length measurements. If you find two figures with similar bust, waist and hip measurements, choose the one with the back waist length that is closest to your own.

SELECTING THE PROPER SIZE

Compare your bust, waist and hip measurements to the ones listed for your figure type. If you're a perfect match, lucky you! You can always buy the same size pattern, regardless of what you're making. However, if you're like most people, you're not an exact match. Therefore, when you select your pattern size, you may need to consider the type of garment. By varying the size according to the type of garment, you'll be able to achieve the best possible fit with the fewest adjustments or alterations.

SOME COMMON QUESTIONS ABOUT PATTERN SIZE

● *How do I know what size maternity pattern to buy?* Purchase the same size as before pregnancy or use your bust measurement. Don't buy a larger size— maternity patterns already include the required additional ease.

● *What if I fall between sizes?* Choose the smaller size if you're small boned, want a closer fit or are using a knit. Choose the larger size if you're large boned, want a looser fit or are using a woven fabric.

● *Why do you recommend buying most patterns by the bust size?* Sewing should be easy—and

Key Measurements for Pattern Selection	
TYPE OF GARMENT	**KEY MEASUREMENT TO USE FOR PATTERN SELECTIONS**
1. Dress, blouse, shirt, jumpsuit, coordinated separates pattern	**Bust** for adult females. However, if there is a 2¹/₂" (6.3cm) or more difference between your bust and your high bust, use your **high bust** measurement. **Breast** for young females. **Chest** or ready-to-wear **neck band** (collar) size for males.
2. Suits, coats and jackets	Use same guidelines as for dress, blouse, skirt and jumpsuit. These patterns are designed with enough ease to fit over other garments.
3. Pants and slim skirts	Use your hip measurement.
4. Fuller skirts	Use your waist measurement.

pattern adjustments are much easier to make in the waist and hip areas.

● *Are there any shortcuts to adjusting a pattern if I'm a different size on top and on the bottom?* Multi-Size patterns are printed with several sizes on the same pattern tissue, which means you can use one set of cutting lines for the upper portion of your garment and another set for the lower portion.

● *What size bra cup are patterns designed for...and why do I need to take my high bust measurement?* Patterns are drafted for the B-cup figure. If your bra cup size is larger than a B, it will affect the way the pattern fits. To determine your cup size, subtract your high bust measurement from your bust measurement. If the difference is less than 2¹/₂" (6.3cm), you're an A or B cup. If the difference is 2¹/₂" to 3" (6.3cm to 7.5cm), you're a C cup. If it's 3¹/₂" to 4" (9cm to 10cm), you're a D cup. If you are a B cup or smaller, purchase your pattern according to your bust measurement. If you are a C cup or larger, determine

your pattern size by matching your high bust measurement to the bust measurement on the Standard Body Measurement Chart. This will ensure good fit in those hard-to-adjust areas— shoulders, neckline, chest and upper back. Follow the directions starting on page 50 to adjust the cup size.

● *I'm confused about the difference between Toddlers' and Child's sizes. How do I know what figure type to look at when sewing for little ones?* Toddlers' patterns include a built-in "diaper allowance." Children's patterns do not. The Child's figure type is also slightly taller than the Toddlers'.

● *If I'm a Petite, why can't I just shorten the pattern at the hemline?* The Miss Petite and Women's Petite figures all have shorter back waist lengths and a shorter distance between waistline and hipline than the Misses' or Women's figures. Patterns with the FIT *for* PETITE™ logo have special, easy-to-follow instructions for adjusting the lengthwise proportions of the pattern to suit the Petite figure.

● *How do I determine my size in Small, Medium, Large Size patterns? What about Unisex patterns?* Patterns sized small, medium and large are cut for the largest size in each designation. Unisex patterns, because they are designed to fit both men and women, use the man's chest measurement to determine the size range. For these patterns, match your bust measurement to the chest measurement.

PATTERN ADJUSTMENTS

Once upon a sewing time, making a muslin fitting shell was the recommended—and time-consuming—way to find out if you needed to make any pattern adjustments. Today's smart sewer can say goodbye to that tedious method and turn to her tape measure instead.

The "basic five" measurements (bust, waist, hip, height and back waist length) are used to determine your figure type and pattern size. If you take a careful look at the Figure Types/Pattern Body Measurements charts on pages 41-45, you'll note that they include additional measurements. These extra pattern fitting measurements are the ones you need to fine-tune your fit.

tip

Don't be confused by the terms adjustment and alteration. Adjustment refers to a change made on the pattern tissue before the garment is cut out; alteration refers to a change made on the actual garment.

Using these charts, locate the Simplicity® standard measurements for your pattern size. Record these standards in column 3 of the Personal Measurement Chart. To determine if you will need any adjustments, compare your personal measurements (column 2) with the Simplicity® standard (column 3). Record any differences in column 4.

PATTERN EASE

Don't make the mistake of thinking it's easier and more efficient to determine adjustments by comparing your measurements with the actual pattern piece measurements. Sewers who do that may find themselves in big trouble because of something called ease.

Ease, or the fullness included in a pattern design, determines how the fashion will fit and look. Patterns are designed with two types of ease—wearing ease and design ease.

The finished garment measurements that appear on the pattern tissue and the back of the pattern envelope are the sum total of three elements:

STANDARD BODY MEASUREMENTS
+ WEARING EASE + DESIGN EASE
= FINISHED GARMENT MEASUREMENTS

Wearing ease is the amount of "wiggle room" built into a garment. Without it, your garment would be skintight. Because this extra fullness is added to the standard body measurements when the pattern is designed, the actual pattern pieces will measure more than the standard body measurements. All garments, except swimwear and some exercise wear, contain some wearing ease. Patterns designed for knits only include less wearing ease because the fabric itself stretches to provide the necessary fit, comfort and mobility. In fact, some of these patterns will actually measure less than the standard body measurement to accommodate for the stretch factor of the recommended knit fabric.

Design ease is fashion ease; it's the extra fullness, over and above wearing ease, that determines the garment's silhouette. In today's fashion world, there is no one contemporary silhouette. Garments that hug the body are just as fashionable as those that are loose and billowy.

STOP AND THINK: IS THIS ADJUSTMENT REALLY NECESSARY?

As you review the entries you made in column 4 of the Personal Measurement Chart (page 40), don't get discouraged if it looks like everything needs to be adjusted. That's highly unlikely! In fact, many people have a tendency to overfit.

To analyze whether or not the adjustment is necessary, keep three things in mind:

- the amount of the adjustment
- its location on the garment
- the style of the garment

Lengthwise measurements are critical to the fit and proportion of a garment.

● Crotch depth and crotch length: If either of these varies 1/8" (3mm) or more from the pattern tissue measurement, you should always make the adjustment (see pages 55–56).

● Back waist length and front waist length: Examine the silhouette and analyze the amount of the adjustment. If it's 1/8" (3mm) or less, and the garment has no waistline seam and no design features below the waist, you can omit the adjustment and simply cut the hem a little bit longer. However, if the garment has any type of defined waistline, and the difference in the back waist length measurement is more than 1/8" (3mm), you'll need to adjust the pattern (see pages 48–49).

The basic circumference adjustments—bust, waist and hip—may or may not be necessary, depending on the amount of the difference and the silhouette of the garment. Loose-fitting silhouettes will require fewer adjustments than close-fitting ones. Adjustments of 1/2" (1.3cm) or less can usually be accommodated for by simply stitching narrower seam allowances.

On long-sleeved garments, arm length is critical. On fitted garments with set-in sleeves, shoulder length is also important. If your shoulders are narrow, an alternative to pattern adjustment is to add, or use thicker, shoulder pads. If you have broad shoulders, you might want to avoid the issue altogether by choosing patterns with dropped or extended shoulders, or raglan or kimono-style sleeves.

ADJUSTING FOR LENGTH

Special lines printed on the pattern piece indicate where to shorten or lengthen it. Sometimes you can also change the length at the lower edge.

To Shorten

● *Along the shorten/lengthen line:*
● Measure up from the printed shorten/lengthen line the amount needed; draw a new line straight across the pattern at that point.

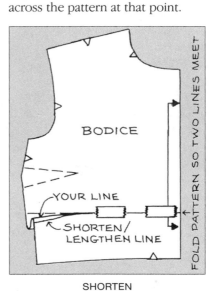

SHORTEN

● Fold the pattern along the printed line, bring the fold to the drawn line and pin or tape the fold in place.

● Re-draw the affected cutting and stitching lines, including any darts.

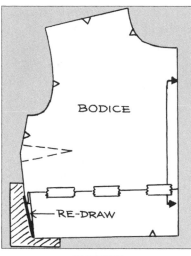

SHORTEN

● *At the lower edge:*

Measure and mark the change; then cut off the excess pattern tissue.

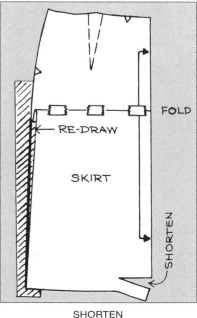

SHORTEN

To Lengthen
● *Along the shorten/lengthen line:*
● Cut the pattern piece apart on the printed shorten/lengthen line. Place one portion of the pattern piece on top of a piece of paper

and pin or tape in place along the printed line.

● Measure down from the printed line the amount needed; draw a line straight across the paper at that point.

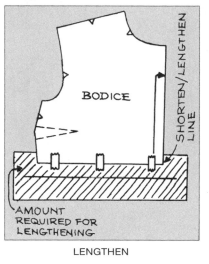

LENGTHEN

● Using a ruler to keep the grain-line or fold line aligned, position the printed line of the remaining pattern piece along the drawn line; pin or tape in place to the paper.

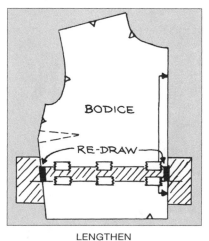

LENGTHEN

● Connect the affected cutting and stitching lines, including any darts.

tip

Remember to make adjustments on all corresponding pattern pieces. For example, if you adjusted the waistline on a skirt, you must also adjust the waistband a corresponding amount.

● *At the lower edge:*
● Pin or tape paper in place underneath the pattern.

● Extend the cutting lines evenly and re-draw the lower edge.

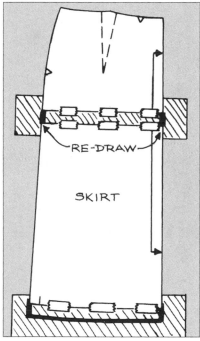

LENGTHEN

ADJUSTING FOR WIDTH
When you're adding to the pattern, you may need to pin or tape extra paper underneath the pieces.

Waist and Hip Adjustments
● *To adjust up to 2" (5cm)*, add or subtract one-quarter of the total amount at the side waist (for a

waist adjustment) or the side seam (for a hip adjustment). Do this on both the front and back pattern pieces. Taper the new cutting line back to meet the original cutting line.

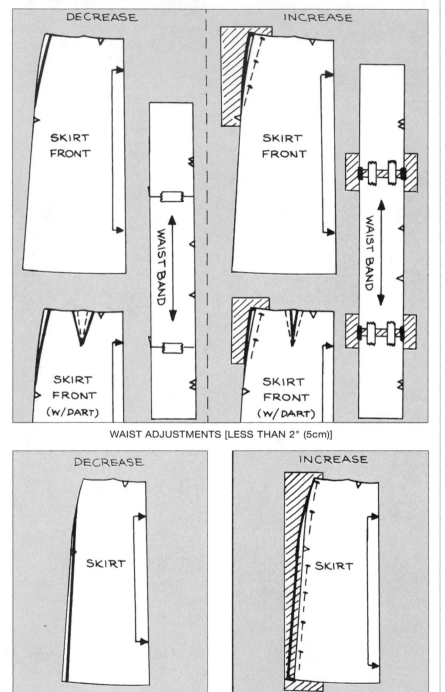

WAIST ADJUSTMENTS [LESS THAN 2" (5cm)]

HIP ADJUSTMENT [LESS THAN 2" (5CM)]

● *To adjust more than 2" (5cm)*, do one of the following:

● Check your pattern size again—you may need a larger or smaller size.

● Analyze the style of the garment. Adding more than 2" (5cm) at the sides may distort the design lines. If this is the case, you will be better off adjusting the pattern by slashing and spreading the front and back pattern pieces one-quarter of the total amount.

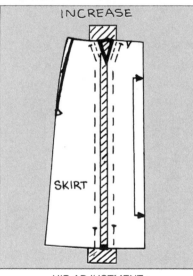

HIP ADJUSTMENT
[MORE THAN 2" (5CM)]

Bust Adjustments

● *To increase or decrease up to 1" (2.5cm)*: Small adjustments [up to 1" (2.5cm)] may be required if you are an A cup or if you are a B-cup figure with a bust measurement that is up to 1" (2.5cm) larger than the one listed for your pattern size.

● Mark half of the amount of increase or decrease at the side seam along the bustline. (For an increase, place paper under the side edges.)

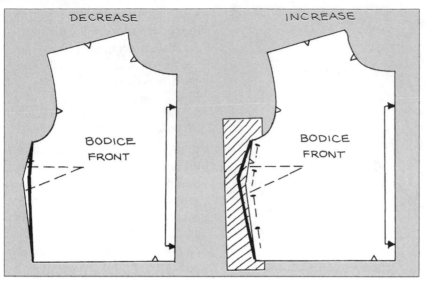

DECREASE   INCREASE

BODICE FRONT   BODICE FRONT

BUST ADJUSTMENT [UP TO 1" (2.5CM)]

tip
If you have narrow or uneven shoulders, or a large bust, adding shoulder pads to your garment may eliminate the need for any pattern adjustments. See "Shoulder Pads," pages 172-175.

● Draw a new cutting line, tapering up to the original line at the armhole and down to the original line at the waistline.

● *To increase more than 1" (2.5cm):* If you require a larger cup (C or D), your clothes may pull across the front and perhaps across the back, too. They may ride up at the front waistline where more length is needed. Since adding 1" (2.5cm) or more at the side seams will distort the fit of the garment, a different remedy is required.

The first step is to create the adjustment lines on your pattern:

● The bust point is located approximately 1/2" (1.3cm) from the end of the bust dart. The bust point may already be marked on your pattern or you may need to do this yourself. Once it is marked, reinforce the bust point with a piece of transparent tape.

● Draw a line parallel to the center front, from the lower edge through the bust point (a). (See page 52.) Extend the line diagonally up to the armhole notch (b).

● Draw a line from the bust point through the center of the existing underarm dart (c).

To increase the cup size:

● Cut along lines (a) and (b) from the bottom edge of the pattern, stopping just short of the armhole seamline. Now cut along line (c) from the side, stopping just short of the bust point.

● Place tissue paper under the cut edges of the pattern tissue and pin between the center front and the cut edge. Spread the pattern at the bust point, keeping the cut edges parallel below the bust point:

For a C cup, spread 1/2" (1.3cm).

For a D cup, spread 3/4" (2cm).

For larger than a D cup, spread 1 1/4" (3.2cm).

● Pin or tape all the cut edges in place. Re-draw the center front edge, as shown.

DECREASE BUST AREA IF FABRIC PUCKERS.

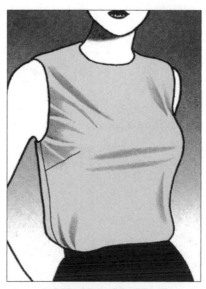

INCREASE BUST AREA IF FABRIC PULLS.

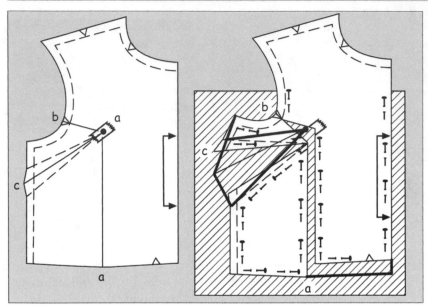

INCREASE BUST SIZE

• Mark a new bust point at the same level as the original one, but 1" to 1¼" (2.5cm to 3.2cm) closer to the side seam. Draw new dart lines from the side seam to the new bust point.

• To re-draw the side cutting lines, pin the new dart together and fold it down. Draw over the dart, connecting the original cutting lines and, if necessary, tapering up to the armhole. Unpin the dart and re-draw the remaining cutting lines.

Bust Dart Position

If your shoulder-to-bust measurement is longer or shorter than the measurement indicated for your pattern size, you may need to change the position of the pattern's bust darts. This difference may be a function of body proportion, because of an aging figure or simply the result of a poor choice of undergarments. If the latter is not the culprit, here's what to do:

• Subtract your shoulder-to-bust measurement from the pattern's standard measurement. This will tell you how much you need to raise or lower the dart.

• Trace the original dart area, including the bust point, from the pattern tissue onto another piece of tissue.

• Tape the traced dart in place on the pattern tissue at the appropriate level, keeping the old and new bust points aligned vertically. Re-draw the side cutting lines, as appropriate.

Shoulder Length

To adjust up to ¼"(6mm), mark the amount inside (to shorten) or outside (to lengthen) the shoulder seam at the armhole. Draw a new cutting line, tapering to the original line at the armhole notch. Do this on both the front and back pattern pieces.

  Because this adjustment may affect the way the sleeve hangs on the finished garment, baste the sleeve in place first and try on the garment. If necessary, pull out the basting stitches and reposition the sleeve until it hangs properly; then permanently stitch it in place.

Back Width

To adjust up to 1" (2.5cm), mark half of the amount needed inside

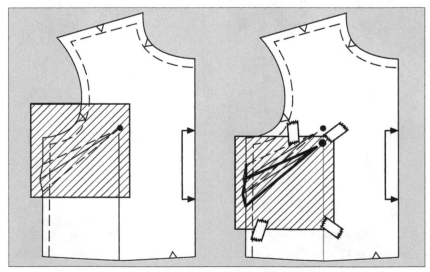

CHANGE BUST DART POSITION

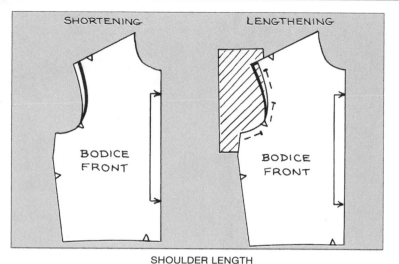

SHOULDER LENGTH

(to decrease) or outside (to increase) the armhole cutting line. Do this above the notch on the back pattern piece only. Do not adjust the front. Draw a new cutting line, starting at the mark and tapering up to the shoulder and down to the underarm.

This adjustment may affect the hang of the sleeve. Be sure to baste in the sleeve and try on the garment before permanently stitching the sleeve in place.

Rounded Back and Dowager's Hump

Whether the cause is poor posture or body changes that occur over time, a rounded back can cause your garment to wrinkle across the back shoulders and ride up at the back waistline. If the problem is severe, you may also have a noticeable bump at the back of your neck, which is called a dowager's hump. If this is the case, the garment's neckline will stand away from the body.

The adjustment is similar for both the rounded back and the dowager's hump. Begin by drawing in the seamlines on the bodice back pattern piece (see page 54). Then:

● At the point where your back curve is most prominent, draw a horizontal line that extends from the center back just to the armhole seam and is at right angles to the grainline. Mark the midpoint on this line.

● *For a rounded back:* Draw a diagonal line from the middle of the shoulder to the midpoint mark. (If there is a shoulder dart, draw the line through the dart.)

● *For a dowager's hump:* Draw a diagonal line from the middle of the neckline to the midpoint.

● *For both adjustments:* Slash along the horizontal line just to, but not through, the armhole seamline. Slash along the diagonal line just to, but not through, the horizontal line.

Place paper under the pattern. Keeping the center back aligned, spread along the horizontal slash until you have added the indicated amount. The pattern will automatically open along the diagonal slash to create a new or deeper dart. Pin or tape the cut edges in place. Clip the armhole seam allowance, if necessary, to make the pattern lie flat. Draw new stitching lines in the dart area and new cutting lines.

Full Upper Arm

If you need more width in the upper sleeve:

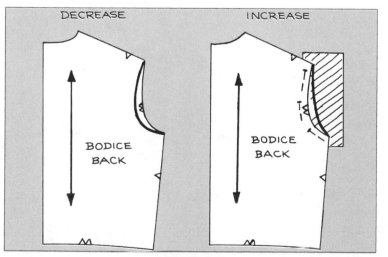

BACK WIDTH UP TO 1" (2.5 CM)

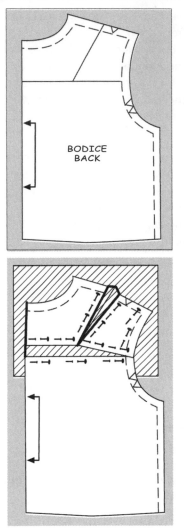

ROUNDED BACK

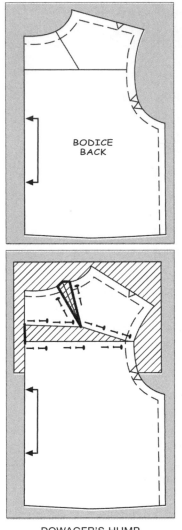

DOWAGER'S HUMP

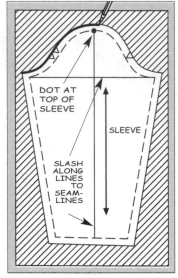

FULL UPPER ARM

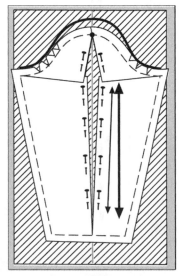

FULL UPPER ARM

• Draw in the seamlines and hemline on the sleeve pattern piece.

• On the sleeve pattern piece, draw a horizontal line that extends across the bottom of the sleeve cap, between the seamlines, and is at right angles to the grainline. Draw a vertical line that extends from the black dot at the top of the sleeve to the hemline and is parallel to the grainline.

• Slash along both lines just to,

but not through, the seamlines and hemline.

• Place the sleeve pattern on top of a large sheet of tissue paper and trace around the sleeve cap cutting line.

• At the point where the slashes intersect, spread the pattern until the bicep area is at least equal to your upper arm measurement plus 2" (5cm) for wearing ease. Clip the seam allowances at the cap and

underarm seams, as necessary, to make the cap lie flat as the horizontal slashed lines overlap. Pin or tape the cut edges in place.

• Draw a vertical line from the dot at the top of the sleeve cap to the slash line at the hemline. Draw a new grainline parallel to this line.

• Use the traced sleeve cap as the new cutting line.

SOME PANTS ADJUSTMENTS

Pants should fit smoothly and comfortably with enough room to move, bend and sit easily. The crotch depth and crotch length must be the correct ones for your body—or else the pants will bind or sag.

The way your ready-to-wear pants fit provides clues to the type of adjustments you may have to make. If yours smile when you're standing—meaning that there are wrinkles that point up from the crotch area—they're too tight in the crotch area. If they frown, they're too loose. Smiles or frowns can occur in the front or the back, depending on your figure.

Take another look at the Figure Types/Pattern Body Measurements charts. Note that the standards for crotch depth and length are not included. Now, remember the earlier rule about never measuring the actual pattern pieces? Well, here's the exception: For an accu-rate fit, you *must* compare your body measurements with the actual pattern pieces.

Crotch Depth

Important: Check and adjust the crotch depth first, **before** checking and adjusting the crotch length. Otherwise, it's a sure bet that your pants won't fit properly!

To check the crotch depth on your pattern, measure from the crotch line up to the waistline seam. Your measurement line should be close to the side seam, but parallel to the grainline, as shown on page 56. This measurement should be equal to your crotch depth (page 40), plus 1/2" or 1.3cm of ease for hips up to 36" (91.5cm) wide. Larger sizes may need to include up to 1 1/4" (3.2cm) of ease.

To lengthen or shorten the crotch depth, use the shorten/lengthen line on the pattern piece. Follow the procedures described under "Adjusting for Length" (page 48),

tip

Remember that stitching lines are not marked on Multi-Size patterns. In order to make accurate adjustments, you may need the stitching lines as a reference point. To create stitching lines on your pattern, measure and mark 5/8" (1.5cm) in from the appropriate cutting lines, as indicated in the illustrations for each adjustment.

slashing and spreading the pattern pieces to lengthen, or lapping them to shorten.

Crotch Length

Once you've checked and made any changes in the crotch depth, stand a tape measure or flexible ruler on end and measure along the stitching line of the center front and center back seams of your pants pattern. Measure from the waistline seam to the inner leg seam on both the front and back

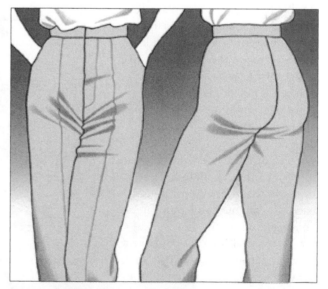

WHEN WRINKLES POINT DOWN, CROTCH IS TOO LOOSE

WHEN WRINKLES POINT UP, CROTCH AREA IS TOO TIGHT.

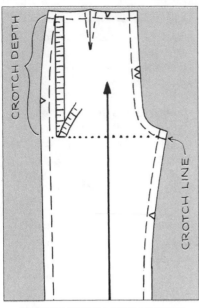

CROTCH DEPTH MEASUREMENT

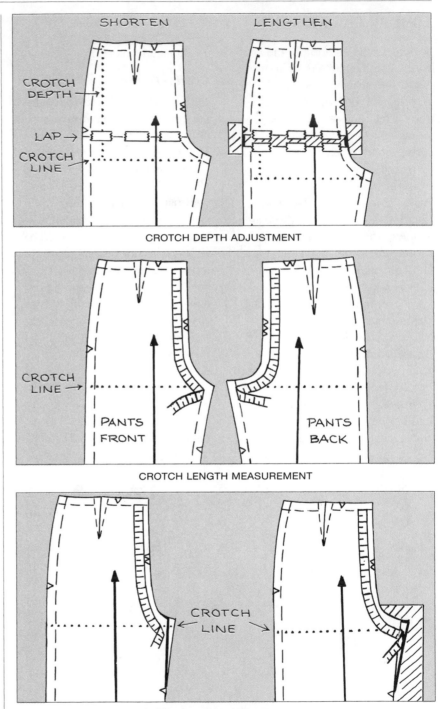

CROTCH DEPTH ADJUSTMENT

CROTCH LENGTH MEASUREMENT

CROTCH LENGTH ADJUSTMENT

pattern pieces. Add these two measurements together to get the pattern's crotch length.

The pattern's crotch length should be equal to your crotch length measurement plus 1½" to 2" (3.8cm to 5cm). This extra amount is the ease you need to be able to sit down.

Before you make any adjustments on the pattern tissue, stand sideways and take a look at your figure in the mirror. You can divide the difference in half and make an equal adjustment on the front and the back of the pants. However, depending on your shape, you can also divide it unevenly between the front and back. In fact, if you're round in the front and flat in the back, you might want to add the entire amount to the front; if you're "normal" in front but have a very flat derriere, you might want to subtract the entire amount from the back. Experience, and your

own good judgment, are your best guides.

Lengthen or shorten the crotch by

adding or subtracting half of the adjustment amount at the inner leg seam, as shown.

FITTING AS YOU SEW

Because fabric is not the same as tissue paper, you can't be guaranteed of a good fit simply by making the indicated adjustments on your pattern tissue.

As you sew, stop at least twice and try on the garment. The best time for the first fitting is right after the major garment seams are sewn. Be sure to wear the undergarments that you plan to wear with the finished product. Otherwise, you might be unpleasantly surprised at how a change of bra can alter the fit of a garment. If the pattern calls for shoulder pads, be sure to have a set available for your fittings. In fact, have several sets in different thicknesses. The right thickness of shoulder pad can solve many a fitting dilemma.

If the garment is a fitted or semi-fitted style, it might be a good idea to try it on with the major garment seams only basted together. Then, if alterations are required, you won't have to rip out any permanent stitching.

If you anticipate fitting problems in the sleeve area, baste them in first. Try the garment on a second time before permanently setting in the sleeves:

● If the sleeve cap twists toward the back, reset the sleeve, moving the center forward of the shoulder seam and redistributing the ease until the sleeve cap hangs smoothly.

● If the sleeve cap twists toward the front, reset the sleeve, moving the center behind the shoulder seam and redistributing the ease until the sleeve cap hangs smoothly.

● If there is excess fullness in the sleeve cap, reset the sleeve, taking a deeper seam allowance in the sleeve cap.

The final fitting should be to check the length before the garment is hemmed. Be sure to wear the same height heel, if not the same shoes, as you plan to wear with the finished garment. It's the smartest way to ensure pleasing lengthwise proportions.

FITTING TOOLS

In addition to your ever-present tape measure, these fitting tools will come in handy:

● *Gridded ruler:* A wide, clear plastic, straightedge ruler with vertical and horizontal markings is particularly helpful when you need to keep the cut edges of the pattern parallel. It can also do double duty as a T-square. Choose one that is at least 4" (10cm) wide and 14" (35cm) long.

● *French curve:* Sometimes called a styling curve, it is used to re-draw shaped or curved areas, such as armholes, necklines and princess seams.

● *Tape:* Clear cellophane tape will work just fine. Some sewers like to use a special pattern tape because it can be lifted and repositioned easily without tearing the pattern.

● *Paper:* Tissue paper (the type used for gift wrapping) is probably the most common paper for pattern adjustments.

chapter 5
The Universal Basics

No matter what style pattern you choose, what fabric catches your eye, or what your level of sewing skill, there are certain "universal basics" that are common to almost any project you make.

Much of what you'll learn in the following chapters will challenge some of traditional sewing's hard-and-fast rules. Fortunately, today's sewer can have it both ways—easy techniques *and* professional results—by combining serger sewing with conventional sewing.

So dust off your conventional sewing machine, take your serger out of the box and get ready to break some rules!

FABRIC PRELIMINARIES

Have you ever purchased a ready-to-wear garment that turned into a total disaster after its first laundering or dry cleaning? When you sew, it's easy to prevent these unpleasant (and expensive!) surprises.

PRESHRINKING

The first step, before you even think about cutting out your gar-

ment, is to preshrink the fabric.

The simplest preshrinking method is to put washable fabrics in the washing machine and take dry-clean-only fabrics to the dry cleaner. Pay attention to each manufacturer's recommendations for water temperature, drying cycle or dry cleaning solvents.

If the fabric is marked "sponged" or "preshrunk," or if the label says it will shrink less than 1 percent, you may be tempted to omit this step. However, shrinkage control is not the only reason you should pretreat your fabric. By preshrinking it, you can discover the fabric's true character.

● Some fabrics contain special finishes or sizings that dissolve the first time the fabric is cleaned. Consequently, your once-crisp garment may come out soft and limp.

tip

If you're a fabric collector, get into the habit of preshrinking your yardage before you put it away. Then it's always "needle ready."

● Some knits contain sizings that will cause your sewing machine to skip stitches. Preshrinking removes these sizings—eliminating the problem before it ever starts.

A GLOSSARY OF FABRIC TERMS

● *Selvage:* One of two finished lengthwise edges on a piece of fabric. These edges, which will not ravel, are usually a little stiffer and firmer than the crosswise, cut edges of the fabric.

● *Straight, or lengthwise, grain:* Refers to the threads (in a woven) or the ribs (in a knit) that are parallel to the selvages. Pattern pieces are usually laid out along the lengthwise grain because it has the least stretch and is the most stable.

● *Crosswise grain:* Refers to the threads that run across the fabric between the two selvages, perpendicular to the lengthwise threads or ribs. Fabric stretches more on the crosswise than on the lengthwise grain.

● *Bias:* Any diagonal direction.

● *True bias:* The diagonal edge formed when fabric is folded so

tip

Notions such as tapes, braids, zippers, linings and interfacings may require preshrinking, too. Read the labels and check the fiber content. Trims, braids and zipper tape made from 100 percent polyester do not *need to be preshrunk. Although most interfacings should be preshrunk, many fusibles do not require it. Check each manufacturer's information.*

that the lengthwise and crosswise grains match. Fabric has the greatest amount of stretch along the true bias.

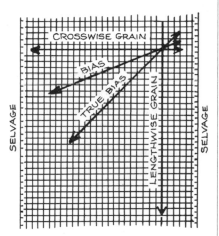

STRAIGHTENING

The ideal fabric is "on-grain," with lengthwise and crosswise yarns that are exactly perpendicular to one another.

One of the recurring myths of sewing is that every fabric should be straightened so that it is perfectly on-grain before the pattern pieces are cut out. Otherwise, the theory goes, the finished garment will have out-of-kilter seams and a drooping hem—the result of yarn's natural tendency to hang perpendicular to the floor. This was true before the advent of knits, modern synthetics and wonder finishes. When many of these newest fabrics are pulled off-grain during the manufacturing process, the fabric acquires a permanent memory that can't be altered, no matter how hard you try.

Truing the Fabric

Truing the fabric is today's smart substitute for straightening.

● If the fabric has a crosswise design: Fold it so that the design matches across the width of the fabric.

● If the fabric does not have a crosswise design: Draw a line at

one end of the fabric that is at right angles to a selvage edge. This crosswise line will function as your crosswise grainline. Fold the fabric so that this crosswise line matches at the selvage.

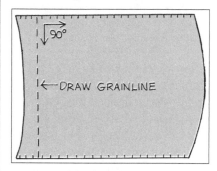

It's possible that the selvages won't match along the length of the fabric. If this is the case, use the lengthwise fold, not the selvage edge, as your reference point when you lay out the pattern pieces.

Straightening with Steam

A few fabrics, particularly those made of 100 percent natural fibers such as cotton, wool or linen, do not have a permanent memory. These fabrics usually can, and should, be straightened.

Begin by raveling a few crosswise threads until you can pull one thread off across the entire width of the fabric. Trim off the resulting fringe. Repeat at the other end of the fabric.

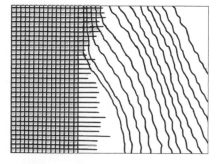

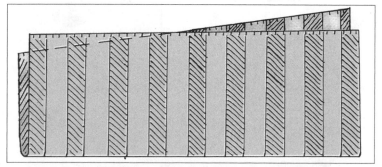

TRUING FABRIC WITH A CROSSWISE DESIGN

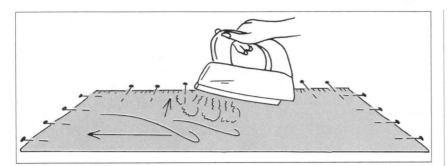

Spread the fabric out on a large, flat surface and fold it in half lengthwise, matching the selvages and the cut, crosswise ends. If the fabric bubbles, or if it ripples along the lengthwise fold, it is off-grain.

To straighten, steam-press until the bubbles or ripples disappear. As you press, move the iron in the lengthwise and crosswise direction only. Never move it diagonally, as this will further distort the fabric.

Don't attempt to pull or force any fabric into shape. Fabrics that require more than a gentle steam treatment are probably permanently and forever off-grain. If this is the case, use the truing method described earlier.

THE CUTTING LAYOUT

Open up your pattern envelope and pull out the instruction sheet. On the first page, you'll find a variety of *cutting diagrams*, or *layouts*. To locate the one you need, look for:

● The pattern view you're making

● The fabric width which is the same as yours

● Your pattern size

Once you've found the right layout, circle it so it's easy to locate as you refer back and forth from instruction sheet to fabric.

FOLD THE FABRIC

Make careful note of how the fabric is folded in your chosen layout. The most common way of folding fabric for cutting is in half lengthwise, with the selvage edges matching (A).

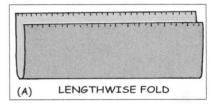

(A) LENGTHWISE FOLD

However, because pattern layouts are designed to make the most efficient use of the fabric, this is not the only way the fabric can be folded. Other layouts include:

● *Crosswise fold* (B). This is used only for fabrics that do not have a nap or one-way design.

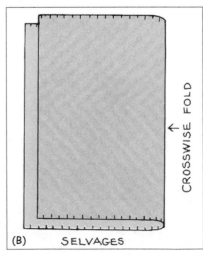

(B) SELVAGES

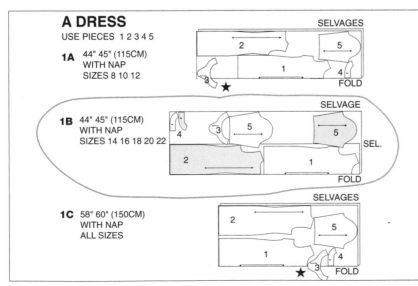

A DRESS
USE PIECES 1 2 3 4 5

1A 44" 45" (115CM)
WITH NAP
SIZES 8 10 12

SELVAGES
2   5
1   4
3   FOLD

1B 44" 45" (115CM)
WITH NAP
SIZES 14 16 18 20 22

SELVAGE
4 3 5   5
SEL.
2   1
FOLD

1C 58" 60" (150CM)
WITH NAP
ALL SIZES

SELVAGES
2   5
1   4
3 FOLD

● *Crosswise cut* (C). This type of "fold" is used for fabrics that have a nap, such as velvet or corduroy, and for fabrics that have a one-way design. The fabric is folded in half along the crosswise grain, and then cut along the fold. Next, the top layer is turned around so that the nap is running in the same direction on both layers.

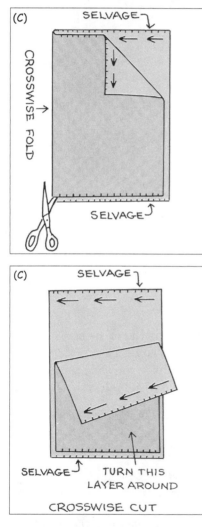

● *Single thickness* (D). Fabric is placed right side up.

● *Combination of lengthwise fold and single thickness* (E). The fabric is folded along a lengthwise grain so that the selvages are parallel to each other but not matching.

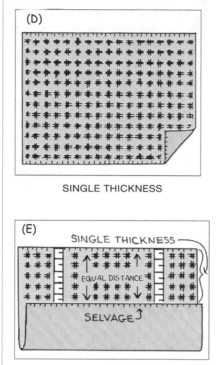

SINGLE THICKNESS

COMBINATION FOLD

● *Two lengthwise folds* (F). The fabric is folded so that the selvages meet in the center.

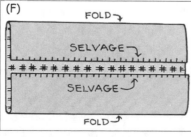

TWO LENGTHWISE FOLDS

Although fabric can be folded with either the right or the wrong sides together, most sewers prefer to fold it right sides together because:

● It makes it easier to transfer the pattern markings to the fabric; and

● Center seams are automatically matched and ready to sew once the pattern tissue is removed.

However, if your fabric has a bold design or one that requires matching, it's easier to fold it wrong sides together so you can readily see the design as you pin and cut. If the fabric has a thick nap, you may prefer to cut it out single thickness. Otherwise, the layers might shift as you pin and cut. For additional information, refer to "Special Layouts" (page 63) and to Chapter 7.

SECURE THE SELVAGES

Your pattern layout will be more accurate if you pin the selvages in place. This keeps the fabric from shifting as you pin and cut. Depending on how your fabric is folded, pin the two selvages together or pin one selvage in place along the length of the fabric.

tip

To make sure you don't miss any important information as you lay out and cut your pattern pieces, look over the pattern instruction sheet before you begin. Start at the upper left-hand corner and, reading each section completely, work your way from left to right. This may sound too obvious to have to mention, but you'd be surprised at how many people just let their eyes wander over the instruction sheet, reading sections at random. Then they wonder why their garments don't turn out right!

LAY OUT THE PATTERN PIECES

Check to make sure you have all of the pattern pieces you need for the view you are making. You'll find them listed at the beginning of each view's cutting layout. If you followed the guidelines in Chapter 4, you've already identified the cutting lines for your size and adjusted these pattern pieces to give you the best possible fit.

Before laying out your pattern, it's a good idea to press the pieces with a warm, dry iron to remove any creases or wrinkles. This will help make sure that your garment sections are accurate in size and shape.

The cutting layout not only shows you how to fold your fabric, but also shows you where to place the pattern pieces.

● Position the larger pieces first, beginning with those that should be placed on the fabric fold.

● Position all other pattern pieces so that the grainline arrow is parallel to the selvages or to the lengthwise fold. To be sure each piece is parallel, measure from each tip of the grainline marking to the selvage or the fold. Both

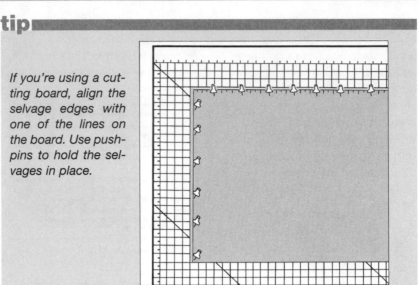

measurements should be the same. If they don't match, shift the pattern piece a bit until the measurements are equal.

● Once a pattern piece is properly positioned, pin it in place at each end of the arrow so it won't shift off-grain.

● As you work, don't let the fabric hang over the edge of the table or it might stretch out of shape. Instead, loosely roll up the excess fabric and leave it on the end of the table. Unroll it as you work your way along the cutting layout.

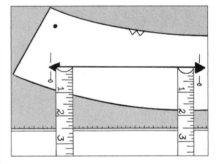

PINNING

Pin through all of the layers of pattern and fabric. First, position the pattern piece on-grain, anchoring it with pins at both ends of the grainline arrow. Next, pin diagonally at the corners, smoothing the pattern out from the grainline arrow as you go. Then add pins around the edge of the pattern. These pins should be placed parallel to the cutting line, at 2" to 3" (5cm to 7.5cm) intervals. Don't let the pins extend beyond the cutting line.

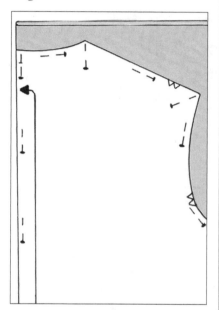

Depending on the size of your cutting surface, you may want to position all of the pattern pieces on-grain first. Once they are all positioned, you can go back and finish pinning each piece. If your cutting surface is small, you may have to work in sections. As you pin, check to make sure none of your cutting lines overlap. And unless you're following a special layout or your layout requires several different folds, don't do any cutting until all of your pattern pieces are in place. Cutting as you go means any miscalculations in your layout are permanent.

SPECIAL LAYOUTS

With most fabrics, you can confidently follow the layouts printed on the pattern instruction sheet. However, there are a few fabrics that require some special planning. Some need to be laid out so that all of the pattern pieces run in the same direction; others must be laid out so that the design either matches at the seamline or is attractively spaced on the body.

If your fabric requires a special layout, it will be easier to plan if you choose a simple pattern with a limited number of seams.

WITH NAP LAYOUT

Some fabrics will change the way they look depending on which way you hold them. Sometimes the difference is very obvious, as in the case of one-way designs. At other

tip

For fast, "pinless" pinning, use pattern weights. If you don't own pattern weights, tuna fish cans make a great substitute.

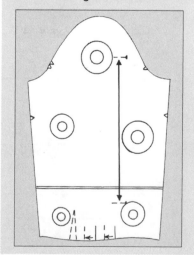

tip

Keep a magnetic pincushion close by as you pin and cut. It's a fast tool for "sweeping up" all those loose pins from the floor and the cutting surface.

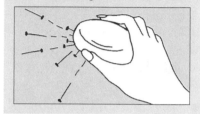

times, the difference might be a very subtle variation in color. For layout purposes, these are called "with nap" fabrics and include:

● *Pile fabrics*, such as velvet, velveteen, velour and corduroy. If you hold the fabric with the nap going down, it feels smoother and the color is lighter. If the nap runs up, the color is darker. For deeper color, the nap should go up; for better wear, the nap should go down.

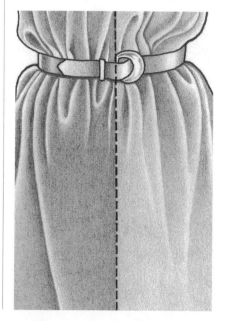

● *Fuzzy-surfaced fabrics*, such as brushed flannel and fake fur. Cut with the nap running down.

● *Shiny fabrics*, such as satin and damask, *and knits*. These reflect the light differently, depending on which way you hold them. It doesn't matter which direction you choose, as long as all of the pattern pieces run in the same direction.

● *Plaids and stripes with an uneven repeat*. In addition to following the "with nap" layout, you'll need to plan the placement of the pattern pieces so that the color bars match.

● *Printed or woven motifs with a "this end up" look*. For example, all of the flowers should "grow" in the same direction on every part of your garment.

Take another look at your pattern instruction sheet and at the example on pages 20-21. Note that the words "with nap" or "without nap" are printed next to each cutting layout. If your fabric falls into one of the categories listed above or if you are unsure about whether it has a nap, follow the "with nap" layout.

Sometimes, because of space limitations on the instruction sheet, the pattern doesn't include a "with nap" layout. If this is the case, you'll need to develop your own. Use the "without nap" layout as a guide, reversing the position of the pattern pieces as necessary so that the tops of all of the pattern pieces are pointed in the same direction. To accommodate this new layout, you'll probably need to purchase

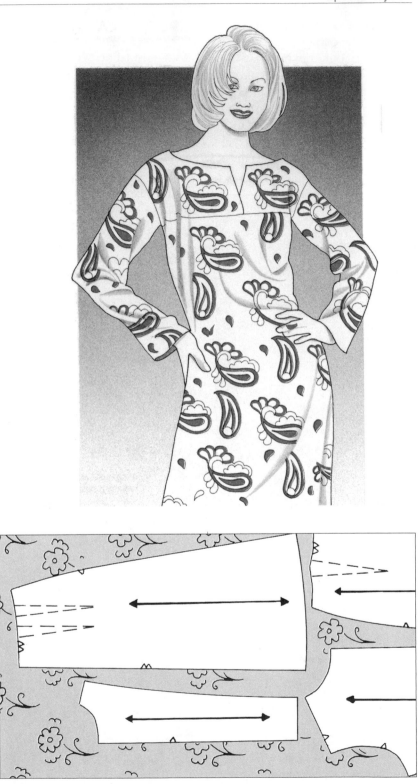

more fabric than the pattern enve-lope recommends.

DESIGNS THAT MUST BE MATCHED

Garments made from plaids, bold stripes, big and medium-size checks, border prints and large design motifs must match at the seams. To accomplish this, you must first mark the seamlines on your pattern tissue. Unless other-wise indicated on the pattern tissue or instruction sheet, seamlines are $5/8$" (1.5cm) in from the cutting line. Next, you'll have to make some adjustments to the cutting layout provided on your instruction sheet. In general, you'll find it easier to work with the fabric folded right side out or on a single thickness with the right side facing up.

Extra yardage is required to allow for this matching. How much extra depends on the size of the motif and the frequency of the repeat. Small, even plaids and stripes require about $1/4$ to $1/2$ yard (.30m

to .50m) extra; large, even designs require about $1/2$ to 1 yard (.50m to 1m) extra.

Positioning Bars or Motifs

Think about where you want the most prominent bar or motif to fall on your body. Beginning with the main front section, position the pat-tern pieces on the fabric so that:

● Prominent vertical bars and large squares or motifs fall at the center front and back of the garment, and at the center of sleeves, yokes and collars.

● Dominant horizontal bars fall at straight or slightly curved hem-lines. As you do this, observe what will happen on the rest of the gar-ment—you may not want a repeat of the dominant bar or motif to fall at the fullest part of the bust, abdomen or hips.

● In the case of a border print or large motif, the hemline falls just below the lower edge of the design.

● Where possible, motifs should not be chopped off at the seam-lines, creating an unattractive effect.

● The design matches vertically as well as horizontally—i.e., center back of collar to center back of garment.

As you lay out the first piece, be sure the grainline arrow is parallel to the selvages or to the bars of the design. Then position the remaining pattern pieces so that the adjoining pieces match at the seams. To match adjoining pieces:

● Trace the design of the fabric onto the pattern at the notch and indicate colors.

● Place the pattern piece to be joined on top of the first piece, lapping seamlines and matching notches. Trace the design onto the second piece.

● Place the second pattern piece on the fabric so that the traced design matches the fabric (top left on page 66.)

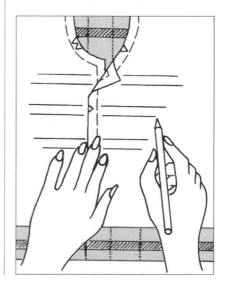

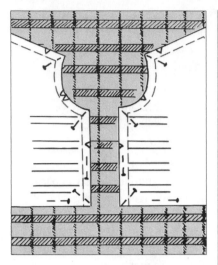

Some details can't be matched, no matter how hard you try. These include raglan seams, shoulder seams, darts, the area above a bust dart on princess seams, the back of the armhole seam, gathered or eased seams, and circle skirts. Half-circle skirts will chevron at the seams.

For more about working with plaids and stripes, see Chapter 7.

CUTTING

Use a pair of sharp, bent-handled dressmaking shears. The ones with the 7" or 8" (18cm or 20.5cm) blades are the most popular. Use your free hand to hold the edge of the pattern flat as you cut.

Do not use pinking shears to cut out your garment. They won't give you the sharp, straight cutting line that is the necessary guideline for accurate stitching. Pinking shears are meant to be used for finishing seams (see page 81).

The notches are printed on the pattern tissue as triangles within the seam allowances. Do not cut

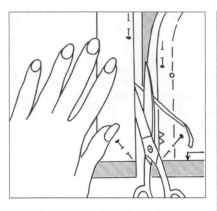

into these triangles. This will weaken your seam allowances. Instead, using the tip of your scissors, cut outward triangles at the notch locations. Another solution is to ignore them completely until you transfer the other markings. Then, using the tip of your scissors, make a small clip in the seam allowance at the center of each notch.

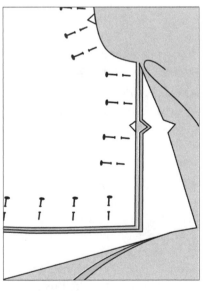

MARKING

As you learned in Chapter 2, a variety of notations, or symbols, are printed on the pattern tissue.

Many of these symbols serve as guidelines for matching up garment sections and for sewing details such as darts, pleats, zippers and tucks. In addition to the notches (which you may have already marked as you cut out your pattern), always mark the following:

● *Dots,* including those that indicate dart stitching lines.

● *Solid lines* that indicate fold-lines, as well as position lines for details such as pockets and buttonholes. Do not mark the solid line that indicates the grainline arrow.

● *Center front* and *center back,* as indicated by a broken line or a foldline, unless these are located on seamlines.

● *Stitching lines* that occur within the body of the garment section, such as for pleats, tucks or fly-front zipper openings.

MARKING METHODS

Use the method, or combination of methods, that suits your needs and your fabric.

● *Fabric marking pens* are one of the fastest and easiest ways to mark. These pens contain a disappearing ink that makes it possible to mark on either the right or wrong side of the fabric.

There are two types of disappearing ink pens:

● *Water-soluble marking pens* contain a blue ink that disappears when the marks are treated with plain water.

● *Evaporating,* or *air-soluble,*

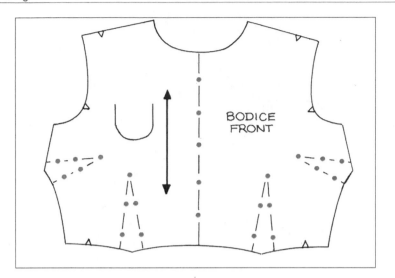

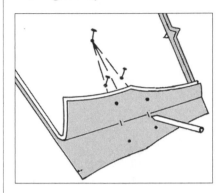

marking pens contain a purple ink that simply evaporates from the fabric, usually in less than 48 hours. To guarantee that your markings will still be visible when you need them, don't use these pens until just before you're ready to sew.

No matter which type of marking pen you choose, be sure to test for removability on a scrap of your fashion fabric. If your fabric water-spots or is dry-clean-only, then the water-soluble pen is not a good

choice. If the evaporating ink leaves an oily residue on the fabric, it's not a good choice, either.

To mark with either of these pens, stick pins straight through the pattern tissue and both fabric layers at all marking points.

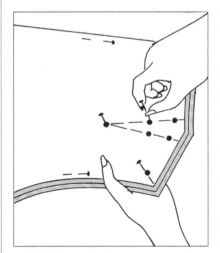

Starting from the outside edges of the pattern piece, carefully separate the layers of tissue and fabric just enough to place an ink dot where the pin is inserted. Mark both layers of fabric; then remove the pin. As you work your way from the outer cut edges of the

pattern to the center or center fold, continue separating and marking the layers.

● ***Dressmaker's marking pencils*** are available in two styles. The first contains a lead-like substance that can be washed out of the garment. The second contains a soft, chalk-like substance. The chalk pencils have a stiff brush on one end to "erase" the markings once the garment is completed. Test first on a scrap of your fabric to determine if you can use the chalk on the right side of the fabric. Mark as for the disappearing pens, using straight pins to locate the position of the symbols. Mark on the right or wrong side of the fashion fabric, as appropriate.

● ***Tracing paper*** (sometimes called dressmaker's carbon) and a ***tracing wheel*** are a good choice for marking smooth, flat-surfaced fabrics. On textured or bulky fabrics, the markings may be hard to see.

Traditionally, tracing paper markings were permanent. This meant that you couldn't use this method for sheers or for marking on the right side of the fabric. The introduction of "disappearing" tracing paper has changed all that. The markings can be sponged off with clear water. If you use one of these new tracing papers, read the manufacturer's directions carefully. Test first on a scrap of your fashion fabric. The heat of your iron may permanently set some of these formulas. If this is the case, sponge off the markings before you press that area of the garment.

You can usually save time by marking two layers at once. However, heavyweight fabrics must be marked one layer at a time so that the markings are clearly visible.

There are three types of tracing wheels to choose from: smooth edge, blunt edge teeth or sharp (pinpoint) teeth. If you are using one with sharp teeth, mark on a protected surface, such as a cutting board, or slip a magazine or piece of cardboard underneath the fabric and pattern.

To mark, remove any pins that are in your way and position the tracing paper between the layers of fabric and pattern. For standard tracing paper, the carbon sides should face the wrong sides of the fabric; for disappearing tracing paper, the carbon can face either the right or the wrong sides of the fabric. Roll the tracing wheel over any symbols to be marked. Use a ruler as a guide when tracing straight lines. Mark dots with an **X** so that one of the bars of the **X** is on the stitching line, as shown at center right.

● *Hand or machine basting* is a way to transfer markings from the wrong side to the right side of the fabric. It's particularly useful for indicating placement lines, such as

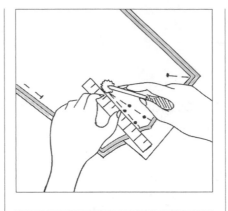

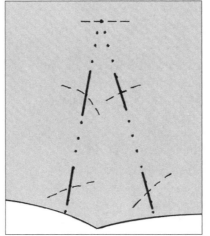

those for pockets or buttonholes, for marking center front and center back along the full length of the pattern piece, and for marking pleat foldlines and placement lines.

Use any appropriate method to mark on the wrong side of the fabric. Then separate the layers of fabric and hand- or machine-baste along the marking points. Now the

tip

Think before you snip-mark. This is not a suitable technique to use if there's any possibility that you'll need to let out the seams later on.

markings are visible on the inside and outside of the garment.

● *Snip marking* is a fast way to mark the ends of darts, foldlines, pleats and tucks, as well as center fronts and center backs. It's also an alternative way to mark notches. Just make a small clip ($1/8$" or 3mm deep) in the seam allowance at the marking point.

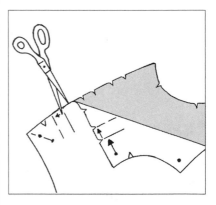

● *Press marking* is used in conjunction with snip marking to mark foldlines for details such as extended facings, folded casings, pleats and tucks.

● Make a tiny clip in the seam allowance at each end of the foldline. If pleats or tucks do not extend the length of the pattern piece, use one of the methods described earlier to mark the end of the foldline.

● Unpin and remove the pattern tissue so you can press-mark each fabric layer separately.

● Fold the fabric wrong sides together, using the clip marks as guides, and press the fold.

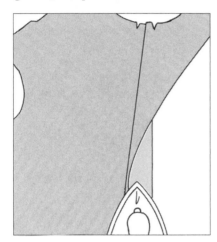

CONVENTIONAL MACHINE STITCHING

Whether your conventional sewing machine is a basic straight-stitch variety, a space-age computerized model or something in between, it's the most valuable and useful piece of sewing equipment you own.

Because features and capabilities vary among models and manufacturers, the best advice anyone can give you is to study the manual that comes with your sewing machine. Among other things, you'll learn important information about how to keep the machine in good working order, including:

● How to keep it clean and lint-free;

● Whether or not it requires oiling and lubricating—and how often this should be done;

● Recommended types and sizes of needles;

● Instructions for adjusting tension, pressure and stitch length—in short, all the things that contribute to good quality stitching.

THE PERFECT STITCH

If you follow the recommendations in the manual and keep your sewing machine in good working order, you can expect it to reward you with good-quality stitching. Then you'll be able to make the simple adjustments that fine-tune the stitch quality to match your fabric.

Before you sew even one seam on your garment, test-stitch on scraps of your fashion fabric.

Thread Tension

Tension refers to the amount of drag, or tautness, exerted on both the needle thread and the bobbin thread as they move through the sewing machine. When the tension is correctly set, the stitches should be perfectly balanced; the two threads interlock in the center of the fabric so that the stitches look the same on both sides of the fabric.

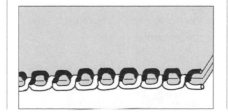

tip

If you don't understand how to operate some of the attachments or special features, stop in at a local dealer and ask about a few lessons. It will be time well spent!

If the tension is not balanced, your manual will tell you how to correct it by adjusting the dial or button that controls the needle tension. Most tension problems can be solved by adjusting the needle tension to match the bobbin tension. Although some machines have a screw on the bobbin case that controls the bobbin tension, most manufacturers do not recommend adjusting this screw. If a bobbin adjustment is required, you'll be better off leaving that to a skilled repairperson.

To test for balanced tension, take a scrap of the fashion fabric and fold it along the bias. Put a row of stitching about $1/2$" (1.3cm) from the fold. Then pull the fabric until a thread breaks.

● If both the bobbin and the needle thread break, then the tension is fine.

tip

Your sewing machine accessories may include small, round felt cushions with center holes. These are designed to fit over the spool pin before you add the thread. They will stabilize the spool, which prevents the thread from wrapping around the pin and also results in smoother stitching.

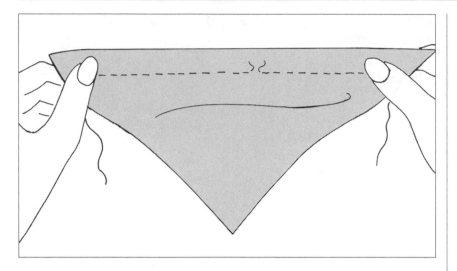

● If only the bobbin thread breaks, that means that the bobbin tension is tighter than the needle tension. Solution: Tighten the needle tension to match the bobbin.

● If only the needle thread breaks, that means that the needle tension is tighter than the bobbin tension. Solution: Loosen the needle tension to match the bobbin, as shown above.

Presser Foot Pressure

Pressure refers to the force the presser foot exerts on the fabric as it moves between the presser foot and the feed dog. The amount of pressure needed can be affected by the fabric's weight, bulk, texture or finishes. If the pressure is correctly set for the fabric, both layers will move through the machine at the same rate.

On most machines, the amount of pressure is regulated by a knob or dial. Check your manual to be sure. Your manual will also suggest suitable settings for various fabrics and sewing situations.

Stitch Length

Depending on the make and model of your machine, you will be able to adjust the stitch length by pushing a button or moving a lever or dial. These will all have numbers that correspond to various stitch lengths. On some machines, these numbers represent the number of stitches per inch; on other machines, they indicate, in millimeters, the length of each individual stitch. Consult your manual for information.

The following is a guide to the most commonly used stitch lengths.

● **Regulation:** 10 to 15 stitches per inch (per 2.5cm), or 2mm to 2.5mm long, is the length used for most general sewing, including stitching seams.

● **Basting:** the longest stitch on your machine, usually 6 to 8 stitches per inch (per 2.5cm) or 3mm to 4mm long. Since this is temporary stitching, the longer stitch is easier to remove.

● **Reinforcing:** the shortest stitch length, usually 18 to 20 stitches per inch (per 2.5cm) or 1mm to 1.5mm long.

● **Easing** or **Gathering:** 8 to 10 stitches per inch (per 2.5cm) or 2.5mm to 3mm long.

STITCHING TECHNIQUES

The guidelines for good stitching are so easy to follow that they soon become automatic.

1. Get a good start.

This technique guarantees that your beginning stitches will be smooth and that the thread won't get jammed up in the throat plate hole!

● Grasp the needle and bobbin threads with one hand and pull them under, and then behind, or to the side of, the presser foot.

• Place the fabric under the presser foot so that the right edge is aligned with the desired marking on the throat plate. The bulk of the fabric should be to the left of the presser foot.

• Turn the wheel to lower the needle into the fabric near the beginning of the seamline.

• While still holding the thread tails, lower the presser foot and begin stitching with a slow, even speed. Continue to hold on to the thread tails until you have stitched for about 1" (2.5cm).

• Release the thread tails and continue stitching.

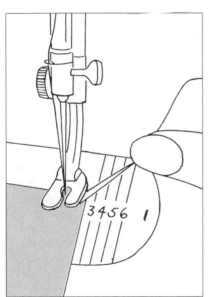

2. *Guide the fabric.*

Rest one hand on the fabric in front of the presser foot and the other hand behind the presser foot. Use both hands to gently guide the fabric through the machine as you stitch. At the same time, keep your eye on the cut edge of the fabric, rather than on

the needle. This helps you keep the stitching straight.

3. *Keep it accurate.*

The easiest way to maintain accurate stitching is to align the right edge of the fabric with one of the following stitching guides:

• The lines permanently etched on the throat plate of many sewing machines. These are placed at 1/8" (3mm) intervals.

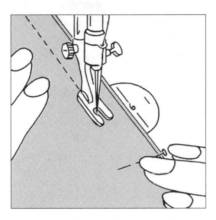

• A piece of tape placed on the throat plate at the desired distance from the needle hole.

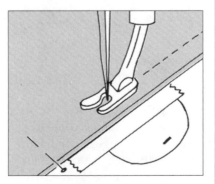

• A screw-on or magnetic seam guide placed the desired distance from the needle hole. Place it parallel to the presser foot for straight edges or at an angle for curves, shown at top of next column.

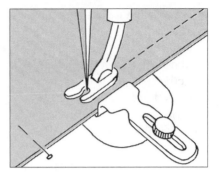

• A quilting foot attachment. This is particularly useful for curved edges and edges up to 2" (5cm) away from the needle.

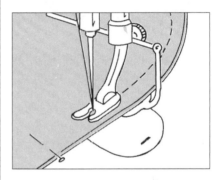

• The toe of the presser foot. This is particularly useful when stitching close to an edge or 1/4" (6mm) away from it.

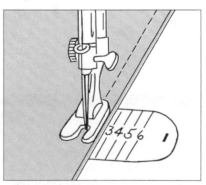

4. *Prevent slipping and shifting*

If you're working with two or more layers of fabric, you'll want to pin or baste them together

to keep them from slipping as you sew.

Match seam edges, markings and notches; then baste them together using one of the techniques described on pages 75-76. As you become more proficient, you may find that simple, straight seams will require only one or two pins unless the fabric is very slippery.

5. *Secure the thread ends.*

To prevent the stitching from coming undone at the beginning and end of the seam, use one of these techniques:

● *Backstitch.* Insert the needle a little bit in from the start of the seam, set the machine to stitch in reverse and backstitch (a). Set the machine to stitch forward and complete the seam (b). Slow down near the end of the seam and backstitch again (c).

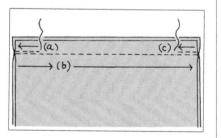

tip

If your fabric is still being swallowed up into the throat plate opening at the beginning of each seam, try using a smaller size needle. If the problem persists, use a scrap of nonwoven, tear-away stabilizer, such as Stitch-n-Tear™ or Trace Erase™ as a seam starter.

tip

If the seamline or stitching line will ultimately be intersected by another row of stitching, there's no need to secure the ends. The second row of stitching will "lock" the first row in place.

● *Tie the threads.* This technique is useful if the line of stitching ends before you reach the edge of the fabric, such as on a patch pocket, or if your machine doesn't stitch in reverse. Leave at least 4" (10cm) long thread tails at the beginning and end of the stitching.

Before tying the threads, it may be necessary to bring both tails of thread to the same side of the fabric. To do this, tug gently on one thread until the loop of the other thread appears; then insert a pin through the loop and draw it up.

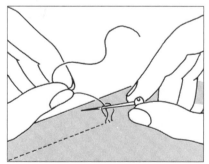

To tie the threads, hold the threads in the left hand and form a loop. With the right hand, bring the tails through the loop. Then insert a pin into the loop so that the tip of the pin is at the end of the line of stitching. Pull the thread ends until the loop forms a knot at the tip of the pin. Remove the pin and clip the thread tails, as shown at top right.

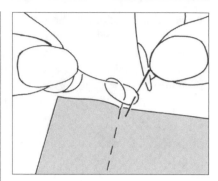

GLOSSARY OF STITCHING TERMS

Easestitching

This technique is used when you are joining a longer garment edge to a slightly shorter one. Although the technique is similar to one

tip

If only a small amount of easing is required, try ease-plus stitching—a quick method that crowds the fabric, distributing the fullness. Using a regulation stitch length, stitch between the ease markings. As you do this, press your index finger against the back of the presser foot crowding the fabric. Stitch for several inches (centimeters), letting the fabric pile up between your finger and the presser foot. Release the fabric and repeat.

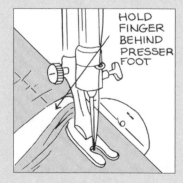

HOLD FINGER BEHIND PRESSER FOOT

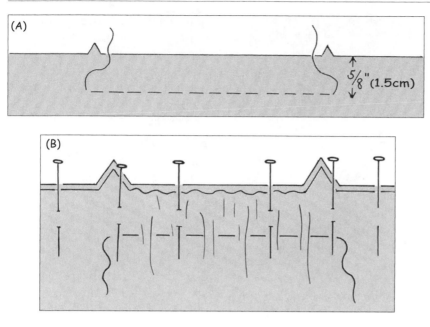

(A)

5/8" (1.5cm)

(B)

used for gathering, there shouldn't be any folds or gathers visible on the outside of the garment once the seam is stitched.

• Loosen the needle tension slightly and adjust the machine to sew with a longer (3mm or 8 to 10 stitches per inch) stitch.

• Stitch just next to the seamline, within the seam allowance. Stitch slightly beyond the markings on your pattern tissue that indicate the area to be eased (A). If desired, add a second row of stitches 1/4" (6mm) inside the seam allowance.

• Pin the eased section to the adjoining section, matching notches and markings. Draw the fabric up along the bobbin thread and distribute the fullness evenly (B). Stitch with the eased section up.

Edgestitching

This extra row of regulation-length stitches appears on the outside of a garment. It's placed approximately 1/8" (3mm) or less away from a seamline or foldline, or close to a finished edge. Although it is similar to topstitching, edgestitching is less noticeable because it is closer to the edge and is always done in matching thread.

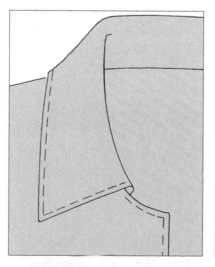

Reinforcement Stitching

This technique strengthens the stitching in areas that will be closely trimmed, such as corners, or along deep curves that will be clipped or notched at frequent intervals. The basic premise is simple—just sew with a shorter stitch length.

At inside and outside corners, reduce the stitch length for about 1" (2.5cm) on either side of the corner.

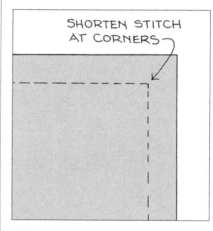

SHORTEN STITCH AT CORNERS

When joining an inside corner to an outside corner, first reinforce the inside corner with small stitches, and then clip just to the stitching.

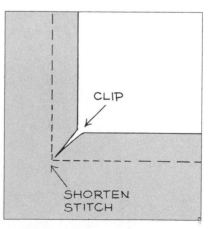

CLIP

SHORTEN STITCH

Staystitching

This line of regulation-length stitching prevents curved or bias edges, such as necklines, shoulders and waistlines, from stretching out of shape as they are handled. If your garment section requires it, staystitching should be the very first type of stitching you do.

To staystitch, stitch with a regulation-length stitch 1/2" (1.3cm) from the cut edge of the fabric. On deep curves, shorten the stitch length so the staystitching doubles as reinforcement stitching.

To keep the edge of the fabric from stretching as you staystitch, stitch in the same direction as the fabric grain. As a guideline, you may find arrows printed on the instruction sheet illustrations to indicate stitching direction, as shown below. If there are no arrows to direct you, you can determine which way to stitch by "stroking the cat." Run your finger along the cut edge of the fabric. The yarns will curl smoothly in one direction, just the way a cat's fur does. Stitch in that direction.

Stitch-in-the-Ditch

This technique is a quick way to hold layers of fabric in place at the

seams. It's an effective way to secure neckline, armhole or waistband facings, as well as fold-up cuffs.

On the outside of the garment, stitch in the groove formed by the seam. Be sure to catch all of the underneath layers in your stitching.

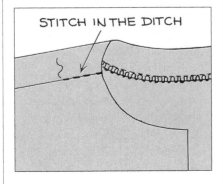

STITCH IN THE DITCH

Topstitching

This is an extra row of stitching on the outside of the garment along

or near a finished edge. Although topstitching is usually added as decoration, it can also be functional. For example, it can be used to attach a patch pocket or to help keep seam allowances flat on hard-to-press fabrics.

● Use a matching or contrasting color thread, depending on how noticeable you want the stitching to be.

● Stitch with a slightly longer stitch (3mm, or 8 to 10 stitches per inch).

● To keep your stitching straight, use one of the stitching guides as described on page 71.

● Before topstitching on your garment, test-stitch using the same number of layers (fashion fabric, interfacing, facing, lining, seam allowances, etc.) as your garment has. To make each stitch more pronounced, you may want to slightly loosen the needle thread tension. You may also need to adjust the presser foot pressure to accommodate the extra layers.

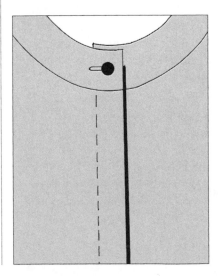

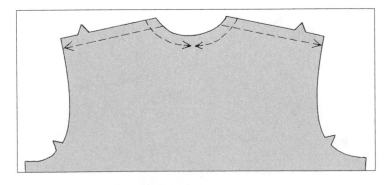

Understitching

This row of stitching prevents an inside layer of fabric, usually a facing, from rolling to the outside of the garment.

Understitching is done after the seam allowances are trimmed, graded and clipped or notched. (See "Sewing with Your Scissors," page 81.) Then:

• Press the seam allowances toward the facing.

• On the right side of the garment, stitch $1/8$" (3mm) from the seamline, through the facing and the seam allowances only.

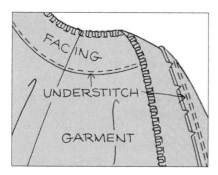

BASTING

Basting refers to any of several methods that can be used to temporarily join layers of fabric until they're permanently stitched on the machine.

• **Pin basting** is the most common method. Place pins perpendicular to the seamline, 1" to 3" (2.5cm to 7.5cm) apart. Insert the pins so you take small bites of fabric right at the seamline. The heads should be to the right of the presser foot so they can be efficiently removed as you stitch.

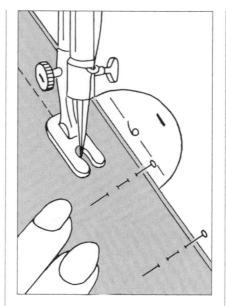

If your machine has a hinged presser foot, it is possible to sew right over the pins—but only if your manual describes this feature. Otherwise, don't experiment. The sad result will be a damaged sewing machine needle, which can cause all sorts of stitching problems.

tip

Fasten a strip of magnetic tape to the bed of your sewing machine or keep a magnetic pincushion (see page 63) close by. Use it to catch the pins as you remove them.

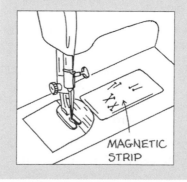

MAGNETIC STRIP

• Paper clips are a quick substitute for pins on bulky, hard-to-pin fabrics, such as fake fur. They're also useful for fabrics where pins would leave permanent holes, such as leather and vinyl. Never, never try to stitch over a paper clip!

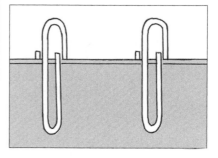

• **Fuse basting** is a fast way to hold fabric layers in place for hand finishing or topstitching. Cut a strip of fusible web the desired length. Sandwich it between the two fabric layers and fuse, holding the iron in place for only a few seconds. Follow the manufacturer's recommendations for heat and steam.

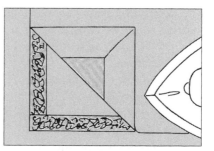

• **Machine basting** is most often used to temporarily sew a garment together in order to check the fit.

• Pin-baste the fabric layers together, matching the markings.

• Loosen the needle thread tension, adjust the stitch setting to the longest length and stitch.

tip

If you're doing a lot of machine basting, use different color threads in the bobbin and the needle. Later on, it will be easy to know which thread to clip and which one to pull.

Don't bother to secure the stitching at the ends of the seams.

To remove the basting easily, clip the needle thread every 1" (2.5cm) or so; then pull out the bobbin thread.

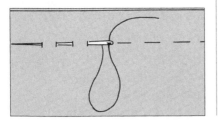

● *Hand basting* is a very secure method of basting. It is frequently used in detail areas where pin basting would not be accurate or secure enough and where machine basting would be difficult to do. It can also be used on sheer or very slippery fabrics.

For the firmest holding power, weave the needle in and out of the fabric so that the stitches and the spaces between them are all the same size—approximately 1/4" (6mm) long (see below).

For areas that don't need to be as

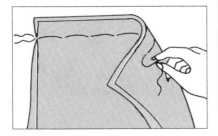

secure, make the stitches 1/4" (6mm) long and the spaces between them 1/2" to 3/4" (1.3cm to 2cm) long.

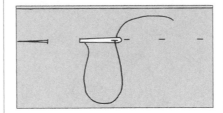

● *Double-faced basting tape* is a valuable aid when you need to be sure that stripes or plaids match at the seamline, or for positioning detail areas such as zippers and pockets. The water-soluble version will disappear when your garment is washed.

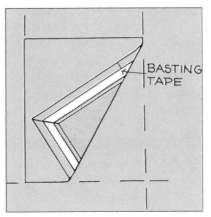

BASTING TAPE

To match a stripe or plaid along a seamline:

● Press one seam allowance under at the seamline.

● Position the basting tape so that the sticky side is against the right side of the seam allowance, about 1/8" (3mm) from the fold.

● Remove the protective covering from the tape. Lap the pressed seam allowance over the

unpressed one, matching both the seamline and fabric design.

● Turn the garment sections to the wrong side, open out the folded seam allowance and stitch along the crease line. *Do not* stitch through the tape, as it will gum up your needle.

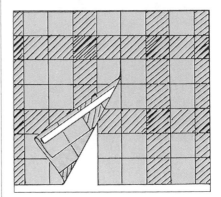

● *Glue stick* can be used instead of basting tape. Unlike basting tape, you can stitch right through the glue without harming your needle. Just be sure you've allowed a few minutes for the glue to dry thoroughly before stitching.

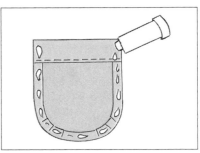

● *Liquid basting glue* comes in a squeeze bottle with a nozzle applicator. It is particularly useful to hold small details, such as appliqués and trims, in place for permanent stitching. Be sure the glue is dry before stitching through it.

SEAMS AND SEAM FINISHES

Seams are the backbone of your sewing. Happily, there's nothing to learn about seams that's difficult to grasp. Once you know the techniques, you're on your way to wonderful sewing results.

A seam is basically a line of stitching that joins two or more layers of fabric. Seams are stitched on the seamline. The seam allowance is the distance between the seamline and the cut edge. Unless your pattern instructions tell you otherwise, the standard seam allowance is ⅝" (1.5cm) wide.

SEAM TECHNIQUES

Some seams require special handling. Here are some terms and techniques you should be familiar with:

Directional Stitching

This means to stitch in the direction of the fabric grain. Directional stitching helps keep fabrics, especially knits and napped fabrics, from stretching out of shape or curling. Always use directional stitching when you staystitch. For more information, see "Staystitching," page 74.

Many sewing books will tell you to use directional stitching throughout your garment. In theory, this is a great idea. In fact, it isn't always practical when stitching seams. With some techniques and situations, you may not be able to clearly see what you're doing, or you may end up with too much fabric in the smaller

working space that's to the right of the machine needle. So...use directional stitching wherever it's practical.

Intersecting Seams

When one seam or dart will be crossed by another—for example, side seams crossed by a waist seam or the inside corners of a waistband—diagonally trim the ends of the first seam allowance or dart to reduce bulk.

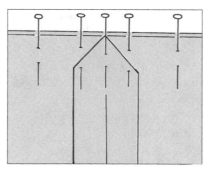

Trimming and Grading

Enclosed seams—those that end up sandwiched in between two layers of fabric—must be trimmed and graded to reduce bulk, or thickness. Enclosed seams are frequently found at the outer edges of collars and cuffs, as well as along any faced edges. See "Sewing with Your Scissors," page 81, for more about trimming and grading techniques.

Gathered or Eased Seams

Always stitch with the gathered side up. (This is a good example of where directional stitching may not be possible!) Guide the fabric with your hands to prevent unwanted tucks or puckers from forming.

Bias Seams

To join two bias edges, such as the side seam of a bias-cut skirt, hold the fabric in front and in back of the presser foot and stretch it gently as you stitch. Although this allows the seam to "give" as you stitch, it will also relax into a smooth seam when you are finished.

Corners

To strengthen seams at corners, shorten the stitch length for about 1" (2.5cm) on either side of the corner. This reinforcement stitching helps prevent the corner from fraying after it is trimmed and turned right side out.

For outward corners, trim diagonally.

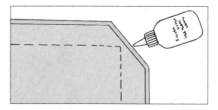

For sharp outward corners, for example, on a collar point, take one or two diagonal stitches across it instead of stitching right up to the point. Trim across the point first and then trim diagonally on either side.

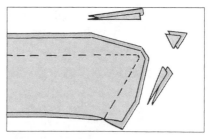

For inward corners, clip almost to the stitching.

To join an inward corner to an outward corner, for example, on a yoke, do the following:

• Reinforce the inward corner with small stitches and clip just to the stitching.

• Pin the two sections together, matching seamlines and markings, with the clipped section on top.

• Stitch to the corner, leave the needle in the fabric, raise the presser foot and pivot the fabric so that the clipped edge spreads apart and the cut edges of the fabric match.

• Lower the presser foot and continue stitching.

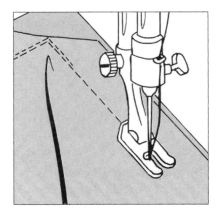

TYPES OF SEAMS

Although the plain seam is the one that you'll use most often, there are other choices. You might want a specific decorative look or you might be using a fabric that

tip

Machine basting and hand basting are also ways to transfer markings to the right side of the fabric. See page 68 for more information.

tip

If your fabric frays a lot, seal the corner with a dot of liquid seam sealant after you've trimmed it.

requires some special handling. The plain seam usually requires a seam finish. However, many of the other seams highlighted here incorporate the seam finish into the seam technique.

Remember: Your pattern instructions will probably utilize a plain seam but you have the option of changing that. Consult Chapter 7 for some suggestions for special fabrics. Be sure to make a sample seam in some scraps of your fabric before you begin.

Plain Seam

• With right sides together, stitch along the seamline, which is usually ⅝" (1.5cm) from the cut edge, with a regulation-length stitch. For knits, stretch the fabric slightly as you sew.

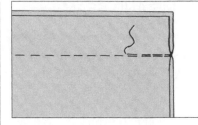

• Press the seam flat and then open, and finish the seam allowances with the appropriate finish.

Double-Stitched Seam

This is a combination seam-and-edge finish that creates a narrow seam especially good for sheers and knits. To prevent the fabric from raveling, it's stitched twice.

• Stitch a plain seam.

• Stitch again, ⅛" (3mm) away, within the seam allowance, using a straight or zigzag stitch.

• Trim close to the second row of stitching. (See next page, top left).

• Press the seam flat to set the stitches, and then press to one side.

tip

The trick to perfect corners is knowing just where to pivot the fabric. The easiest way to do this is to make a mark, using chalk or a disappearing marking pencil, at the point the two seamlines intersect.

• Stop the machine when you come within a few stitches of the mark. Then use the hand wheel to form the next few stitches until the needle is exactly at the mark.

• With the needle still in the fabric, raise the presser foot. Pivot the fabric to bring it into the correct position for stitching the seam on the second side of the corner, lower the presser foot and continue stitching.

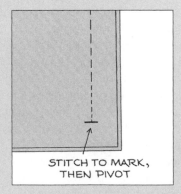

STITCH TO MARK, THEN PIVOT

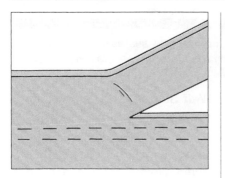

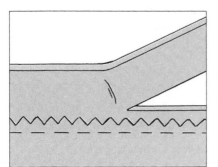

Stretch Knit Seams

Stretch knits need seams that are supple enough to "give" with the fabric. You can sew them with straight stitches, zigzag stitches or one of the stretch stitches built in to many conventional machines, or on your serger.

Here are some variations utilizing the straight stitch and the zigzag stitch:

● Stitch a plain seam, stretching the fabric slightly as you sew.

● For extra strength, stitch a double-stitched seam.

● For even greater strength, straight-stitch along the seamline or use a narrow, medium-length zigzag stitch. Then zigzag 1/4" (6mm) away, within the seam allowance, and trim close to the last stitching.

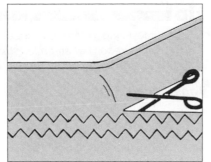

If your machine has a built-in stretch stitch, consult your owner's manual for instructions. Usually, the seam allowance must be trimmed before stitching.

Stabilizing Knit Seams

Seams at the neckline, shoulders and waistlines should not stretch. If they do, the knit garment will lose its shape. Stabilize these seams by stitching seam binding or twill tape into the seams…or use Stay-Tape™, a lightweight stabilized nylon tape that works well on lightweight knits and curved edges.

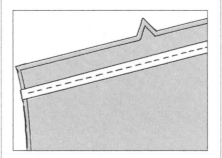

Flat-Fell Seam

The flat-fell seam is frequently used on sportswear, menswear and reversible garments.

● With the *wrong* sides of the fabric together, stitch a plain seam and press the seam allowances to one side.

● Trim the underneath seam allowance to 1/8" (3mm).

● Turn under 1/4"(6mm) of the top seam allowance and baste it in place over the trimmed edge. (For quick sewing, use pins or glue stick.)

● Edgestitch close to the fold.

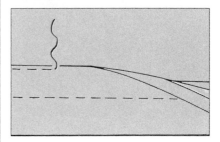

French Seam

This seam adds a couture look to the inside of garments made from sheers and lightweight silks. The finished seam, which should be very narrow, completely encloses the raw edges of the seam allowances.

● With the *wrong* sides together, stitch a 3/8" (1cm) seam.

● Trim the seam allowances to a scant 1/8" (3mm) and then press them open.

● Fold the fabric right sides together along the stitching line; then press.

tip

If you're using a machine zigzag, overcast or overlock stitch to finish your plain seams, plan ahead. Finish all of the seam allowances at one time, before stitching the seams.

• Stitch ¹/₄" (6mm) from the fold. Press the seam allowances flat and then to one side.

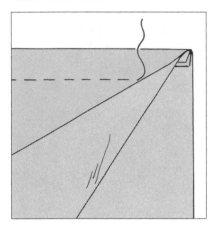

Lapped Seam

This type of seam is frequently used on nonwoven fabrics, such as synthetic suede and leather, as well as real suede and leather, because their edges do not fray.

• Trim away the seam allowance on the upper (overlap) section.

• Lap the edge over the under-neath section, placing the trimmed edge along the seamline; hold it in place with double-faced basting tape, glue stick or fuse basting.

• Edgestitch along the trimmed edge. Topstitch on the overlap ¹/₄" (6mm) away from the first stitching.

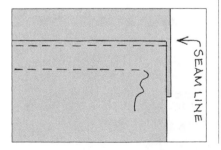

Topstitched Seam

This treatment accents the seam-lines. It also helps keep the seam allowances flat—a great benefit when you're working with crease-resistant fabrics.

• Stitch a plain seam and press it open.

• Working on the outside of the garment, topstitch on both sides of the seam ¹/₈" to ¹/₄"(3mm to 6mm) from the seamline.

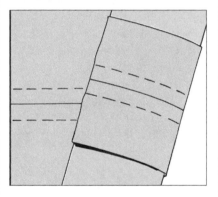

As an alternative, stitch a plain seam, press the seam allowances to one side and topstitch ¹/₈" to ¹/₄" (3mm to 6mm) from the seam, through all of the layers.

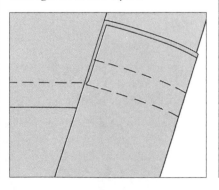

Welt Seam

This type of seam is a good way to reduce bulk and hold seam allowances flat on heavyweight fabrics. From the outside, it looks like a topstitched seam; the double-welt version looks like a flat-fell seam.

• Stitch a plain seam and press the seam allowances to one side.

• Trim the underneath seam allowance to a scant ¹/₄" (6mm).

• On the outside, topstitch ¹/₄" (6mm) from the seam, catching the untrimmed seam allowance.

• For a double-welt seam, also edgestitch close to the seamline.

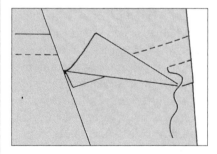

SEAM FINISHES

To prevent raveling and add durability, plain seams usually require some type of seam finish. However, if the garment is going to be lined, or if the fabric is very tightly woven, no seam finish is required.

Here are some easy-to-do seam finishes. They can also be used as an edge finish on facings and hems.

Stitch and Pink

This is the quickest method for finishing fabrics that do not ravel easily.

● Stitch 1/4" (6mm) from each seam allowance edge.

● Trim close to the stitching with pinking shears.

Zigzag

This is a good choice for most fabrics, including heavyweight ones that ravel. Experiment with the stitch width, using a smaller stitch width for lightweight fabrics and a larger one for heavyweights.

● Zigzag over, or as close as possible to, each raw edge, shown below.

● If your machine has an overcast stitch, you can use it in place of the zigzag stitch.

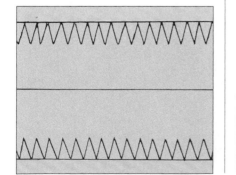

Straight Stitch

Use this finish on knits that curl, including swimwear fabrics, jersey and stretch terry. To minimize curling, finish the seams *before* stitching them.

● Stitch 1/4" (6mm) from the raw edges.

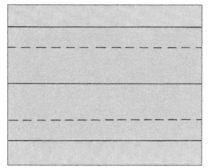

Tricot Bound

This is a custom finish that's suitable for any fabric. However, if the fabric ravels a great deal, bind the seam allowances before stitching the seams. Use a sheer, lightweight tricot seam binding, such as Seams Great®, or Seams Saver™. To make sure you are applying it so the binding automatically curls around the seam allowance, hold the tricot up and tug on the ends.

● Position the binding so it curls around the seam allowance and secure it at the beginning with a pin.

● Take one or two machine stitches, remove the pin and con-

tip

Don't use pinking shears on knit fabrics. It's unnecessary work— and may cause the fabric to curl.

tinue to stitch, gently stretching the tape so it encases the fabric. As you stitch, you'll be sewing through both edges of tape at once. You can use a straight stitch, but for best results, particularly on fabrics that ravel, use a narrow zigzag stitch.

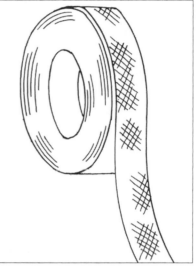

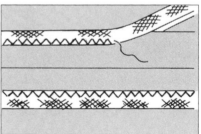

SEWING WITH YOUR SCISSORS

Not all good sewing techniques are centered around the sewing machine. Your scissors are an invaluable aid to professional results. Thanks to them, your garment can have crisper corners, flatter edges, and smoother curves and seams.

● *Trimming* simply means to cut away some of the seam allowance. Do this:

● in areas such as the underarm section of an armhole seam, where the wider seam allowance would interfere with the fit.

● when a special seam technique, such as French seams or welt seams, requires it.

● on enclosed seams as a preliminary step to grading.

● to eliminate excess fabric at the seam allowances of corners and points. That way, they will be smooth and flat once they're turned right side out.

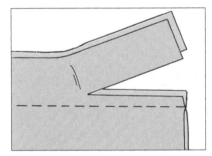

● *Grading* refers to the process of trimming each seam allowance to a different width so that the layers won't create ridges on the outside of the garment. This technique is most commonly used on enclosed seams, such as those sometimes found along collar, cuff, pocket and faced edges. If the fabric is lightweight, grading is usually not necessary—trimming is enough. However, if the fabric is medium to heavy weight, all enclosed seams must be trimmed and graded. Corners require special treatment (see page 77).

To grade, trim the seam allowance

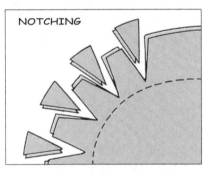

that will end up closest to the inside of the garment to $1/8$" (3mm); trim the seam allowance that will be closest to the outside of the garment to $1/4$" (6mm). The wider seam allowance acts as a cushion for the narrower one, as shown above.

● *Clipping and notching* are techniques used to make curved seams lie flat.

● On inside, or concave, curves, make little slits, or snips, in the seam allowance just to, but not through, the stitching.

● On outward, or convex, curves, cut wedge-shaped notches from the seam allowance to eliminate excess fullness when the seam is pressed open.

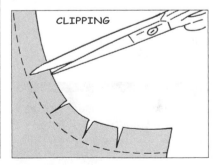

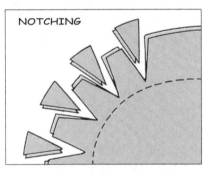

NOTCHING

tip

For a stronger seam, or when joining an inward curve to an outward curve, staystitch each curve a scant $1/4$" (3mm) inside the seamline. Pin or baste the garment sections together and stitch the seam. Then, being careful not to cut through the staystitching, clip one seam allowance to release the fabric and notch the other to eliminate excess fullness.

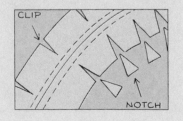

SEWING WITH A SERGER

Whether you call it a serger or an overlock, this wonderful sewing machine stitches the seam, trims off the excess fabric and overcasts the raw edges, all at the same time. Seams on the serger come out so narrow that they don't need to be trimmed and graded; shallow curves lie flat without any notching or clipping.

To get the most out of your serger, you'll want to use it hand in hand with your conventional machine. You can't entirely replace one machine with the other...but together there is almost no commercial sewing technique that you can't duplicate.

Like the other general sewing information included in this chapter, what follows here are the basics you need to know about operating your serger. Chapter 6 will show you how serger techniques can be used in place of conventional techniques. In addition, the next chapter will show you how to combine serger techniques with conventional techniques so you get the best of both sewing worlds.

SERGER BASICS

As you explore the world of serger sewing, you'll have to learn some new terminology. Take a look at the illustration on page 84. It will help you identify the various parts of this wonderful machine. As you review it, note that:

● Instead of bobbins, there are loopers. The two threads that

---

Discover the fabulous world of serger sewing!

FAST...sews a seam or finishes an edge at twice the speed of the fastest conventional home sewing machine.

EFFICIENT...stitches, trims and overcasts a seam in one simple step.

PROFESSIONAL...provides a true ready-to-wear look.

DECORATIVE...an easy way to create special effects on seams and edges.

FLEXIBLE...from sportswear to evening wear, perfect for knits, silks, synthetics, heavy coatings and actionwear fabrics.

VERSATILE...the best of all sewing worlds; use the serger alone or as a supplement to your conventional machine.

---

come up from underneath the needle plate are called the lower looper thread and the upper looper thread. Each looper has its own tension adjustment.

● Each needle thread has its own tension adjustment.

● On the right of the needle, there are blades that cut off the excess fabric.

The key to choosing a serger is to understand what each stitch function can do, then select the serger model that offers the functions that are most important to you.

Two-Thread Functions

There are two basic types of two-thread stitch functions.

The *two-thread serger or overlock stitch* uses one needle and one looper. The two threads interlock at the fabric edge. On the underside of the fabric, the needle thread forms a V.

Because the two-thread stitch uses only two threads, the result is a flat, economical stitch that's ideal for a seam finish. It also creates a stitch called a *flatlock*, which be used for decorative outside

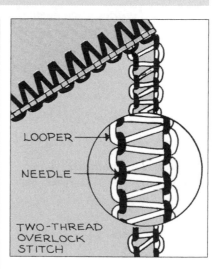

LOOPER

NEEDLE

TWO-THREAD OVERLOCK STITCH

seaming and to reduce bulk in specialty fabrics such as fake fur and sweater knits. The flatlock stitch can be done so that the "ladders" appear on the inside or outside of the garment.

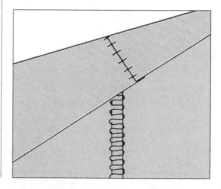

THE ANATOMY OF A SERGER

1–*Spool pins:* Spindles that hold the thread spools or cones in place.

2–*Extension bar:* Be sure it is fully extended so that the thread flows smoothly off the spool.

3–*Thread guide hanger:* Should be positioned so that its thread guides are right above the spool pins.

4–*Thread guides:* Each needle and each looper has its own set of thread guides.

5–*Lower looper tension disc**

6–*Upper looper tension disc**

7–*Right needle tension disc**

8–*Left needle tension disc**

9–*Pressure regulator:* Preset for serging on medium–weight fabric. Pressure can be decreased for lightweight fabrics, increased for heavyweight fabrics.

10–*Presser foot lifter:* Raises the presser foot. You will need to do this when you are changing the foot or for special techniques, such as serging around a corner.

11–*Presser foot releasing lever:* Disengages the presser foot when you want to change to another foot.

12–*Presser foot:* Most presser feet have markings on the front of the foot that line up with the

*For easy threading, each tension disc and corresponding set of threading points are color coded.

left and right needles so that you can position your serger stitches accurately.

13–*Needle plate:* Some sergers come with two needle plates— a general purpose plate and a rolled hem plate. Other sergers have a built–in rolled hem feature that does not require changing the plate.

14–*Extension table:* Provides a flat surface for most serging.

15–*Extension table lock/release lever:* Allows you to remove the outer part of the table. The result is a free–arm surface that provides easier access when serging "round" seams, such as armholes, cuffs and necklines.

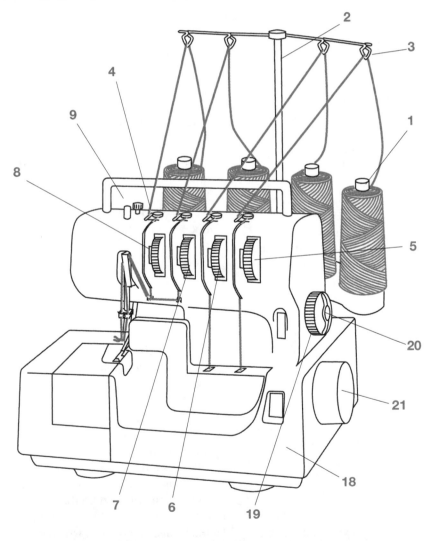

16–*Needles:* Use the type of needles recommended in your serger's manual.

17–*Blades:* There is an upper and a lower blade. The upper (or moving) blade can be disengaged when you want to serge without trimming the fabric.

18–*Front cover:* Folds down to expose threading points for the upper and lower loopers.

19–*Stitch length regulator:* Lets you adjust the length of your serger stitches.

20–*Differential feed regulator:* Can be adjusted to prevent waving seams on stretch fabrics and to ensure pucker–free seams in lightweight fabrics.

21–*Hand wheel:* Turning the hand wheel raises and lowers the needles.

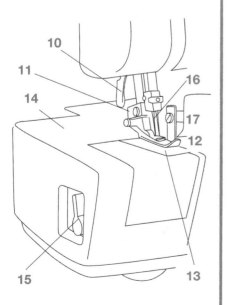

This two-thread serger stitch can also be used to create a *blind hem*.

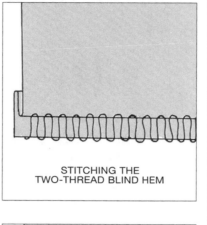

STITCHING THE
TWO-THREAD BLIND HEM

FINISHED
TWO-THREAD BLIND HEM

The *chain stitch* uses one needle and one looper to create a single line of stitches. This stitch is occasionally used alone as a replacement for the straight stitch on the conventional machine. Use it only for wovens; it is not flexible enough for knits. With the blade disengaged, the chain stitch can be used to create interesting, decorative topstitching. Most often, however, it is used in conjunction with the two-thread or three-thread serger stitch, particularly where extra stretch or security is desired. Five-thread sergers can create the chain stitch and the three-thread serger stitch simultaneously.

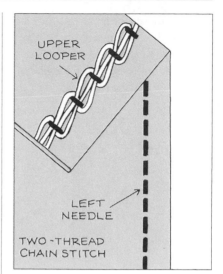

UPPER LOOPER

LEFT NEEDLE

TWO-THREAD CHAIN STITCH

Three-Thread Functions

The *three-thread serger stitch* uses one needle and two loopers. All three threads interlock at the fabric edge.

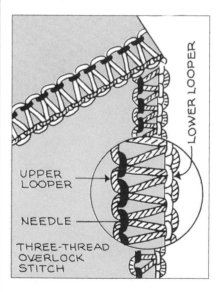

LOWER LOOPER

UPPER LOOPER

NEEDLE

THREE-THREAD OVERLOCK STITCH

The three-thread stitch can be used by itself to join and overcast a seam or as an edge finish for a seam stitched on a conventional machine. It can also be used to create a mock flatlock seam, a blind hem (although not as nice as the two-thread version) and a narrow hem. In addition, the three-thread stitch is the most popular choice for decorative work.

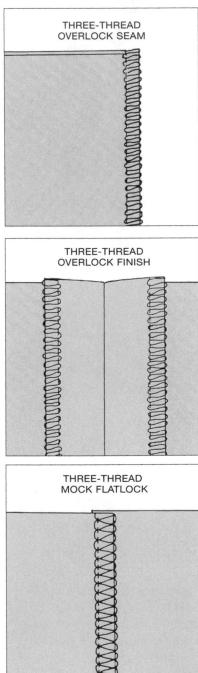

THREE-THREAD
OVERLOCK SEAM

THREE-THREAD
OVERLOCK FINISH

THREE-THREAD
MOCK FLATLOCK

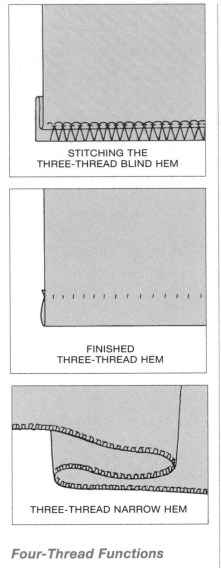

STITCHING THE
THREE-THREAD BLIND HEM

FINISHED
THREE-THREAD HEM

THREE-THREAD NARROW HEM

Four-Thread Functions

There are three types of four-thread serger stitches.

The *four-thread safety stitch* is a combination chain stitch and two-thread serger stitch. It uses two needles and two loopers. One needle and one looper create a two-thread safety chain stitch; the remaining needle and looper create a two-thread serger stitch.

This stitch is suitable for stable or woven fabrics. Because the chain

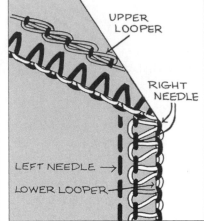

FOUR-THREAD SAFTEY STITCH

isn't a flexible, stretchable stitch, this stitch is not recommended for knits. The chain will "pop" when the fabric is stretched.

On machines that have this function, you can use the serger and chain stitches together or separately, as described in "Two-Thread Functions," page 83.

The *four-thread serger or overlock stitch* and the *four-thread mock safety stitch* use two needles and two loopers. The looper threads interlock with the needle threads at the left and with one another at the fabric edges. Although these functions were designed specifically with knits in mind, they can also be used on wovens. The extra row of straight stitching that runs down the middle of the overlock stitch configuration adds stability.

Narrow Rolled Edge Function

This is a variation of the three-thread stitch. It's used to create a fine edge finish on a wide variety

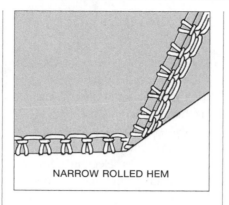

FOUR-THREAD OVERLOCK STITCH

RIGHT NEEDLE

UPPER LOOPER

LEFT NEEDLE

LOWER LOOPER

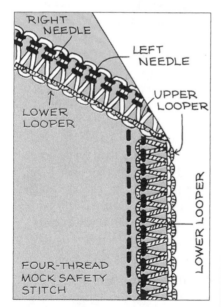

RIGHT NEEDLE

LEFT NEEDLE

LOWER LOOPER

UPPER LOOPER

LOWER LOOPER

FOUR-THREAD MOCK SAFETY STITCH

NARROW ROLLED HEM

Cover Stitch Function

The *cover stitch* uses one looper and two or three needles. The result is two or three parallel rows of stitching on one side of the fabric. The other side has one set of loops that interlock between the needle threads. Because this stitch is done away from the edge of the fabric, the upper blade must be disengaged.

This stitch can be used for decorative hemming or topstitching, with either the looper threads or the needle threads on the outside of the garment. Because the cover stitch has some "give," it is a good choice for stretch fabrics.

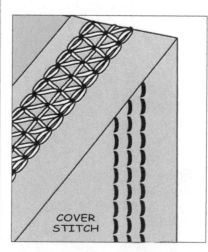

COVER STITCH

of items such as ruffles, scarves, napkins, tablecloths and garment hems.

The *narrow rolled hem* uses one needle and two loopers. The lower looper tension is tightened so that the upper looper thread rolls the fabric edge and encases it.

Differential Feed Function

Sergers that are equipped with a *differential feed* have two feed dogs, one in the front and one in the back. When the differential feed is set at "N" (normal), the front feed dog will move the fabric along at the same rate as the back feed dog.

When the differential feed is set at 1.3 to 2, the front feed dog will move the fabric at a faster rate than the back feed dog. As a result, the fabric will be gathered. Differential feed settings from 1.3 to 2 are used for gathering and easing, as well as to compensate for stretch distortion on knit fabrics.

When the differential feed is set at 0.6 to 0.8, the front feed dog moves the fabric at a slower rate than the back feed dog. This feature is useful for eliminating puckering on woven fabrics and for stretching knit fabrics for a lettuce-leaf effect.

MAINTENANCE

Not all sergers can create every type of overlock stitch. Some machines perform only one or two functions or stitch configurations, while others can perform several.

You'll hear them described as two-thread, three-thread, three/four-thread, four-thread, four-thread mock safety and even five- or eight-thread machines. While no serger uses all eight threads at the same time, more thread paths offer the flexibility to perform more thread functions.

No matter what type of serger you choose, the best advice anyone can give you is to read the manual carefully and familiarize yourself with the machine. Sergers are extremely easy to operate. Once you've learned how to thread the machine, and which tension dials control which thread, you've just about learned it all!

As you sew, the cutting action will create a great deal of lint. For good performance, it's important to keep your serger clean. Make it a practice to clean out the lint every time you sit down to sew. Open the front and side covers to expose the loopers. Using the small brush that comes with your machine, get rid of all of the lint that has accumulated. To keep it super-clean, apply a few squirts of compressed air.

SELECTING THE RIGHT THREAD

When it comes to choosing thread for your serger, the same basic rule applies as for your conventional machine: good-quality thread equals better stitch quality and fewer problems with thread breakage. This means selecting a thread that is made from long, continuous fibers.

One way to tell if it's a quality thread is to examine it carefully for the "fuzzies." These indicate that the thread is made up of lots of short fibers, resulting in a weaker thread that will break easily. The fuzzier the thread, the poorer the quality.

Because the serger sews fast—from 1200 to 1800 stitches per minute—the thread should be strong enough to withstand the speed, yet fine enough to create a soft, supple seam finish. One of the best all-purpose threads for conventional sewing is cotton thread with a polyester core. Although it is possible to use this same thread in your serger, you'll be happier with the results if you use a thread especially designed for the serger.

● *Cotton-wrapped or 100 percent polyester serger thread:* These threads are similar to, but finer than, conventional sewing threads. They're available on large (1,000 yards or more) cones.

● *Nylon serger thread:* This is very strong and is recommended for knit swimwear, lingerie and active sportswear, including leotards or other clothing made with Lycra® or elasticized fabric. It also works well for rolled hems when threaded through the upper looper. (See Chapter 6, page 155).

● *Woolly nylon thread:* This is a texturized (unspun) thread with a slightly kinked surface. As with nylon serger thread, it is recommended for knit swimwear, lingerie and leotards, as well as Lycra® or elasticized fabric. Because these garments have seams that come in direct contact with the body, you may prefer woolly nylon to 100 percent nylon serger thread because it's softer. It also lies flatter than many other threads. For a narrow rolled hem, this thread is a great choice for the upper looper. It will roll smoothly over the edge of the fabric and, because of its texturized surface, it will fill the edge with color.

● *100 percent silk thread:* This is the same silk thread that you use in your conventional machine. It has a luster, shine and color range difficult to find in other threads. However, it is expensive and may not be readily available. Save your silk thread and use it where it has the greatest value—for rolled hems. Because silk is very resilient

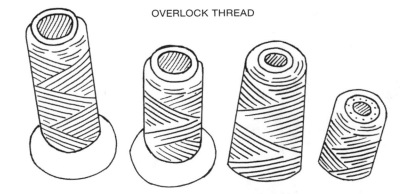

OVERLOCK THREAD

tip

If you're using conventional thread, place it on the spool pin with the notched end down and use a spool cap. This way, as the thread rapidly unwinds, it won't get caught in the spool's rough edges.

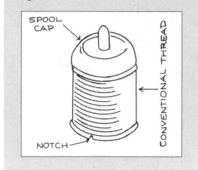

and lustrous, it will create a tighter, richer-looking edge.

● *100 percent cotton serger thread:* This type of thread isn't quite as strong as other threads. Use it only on woven fabrics…or use it in the loopers, with polyester or nylon thread in the needle(s).

● *Conventional sewing thread:* Sometimes this is the only thread you can find in the color you want. If that is the case, use the matching conventional thread in the needle(s) and use serger thread in the loopers. The serger thread should be in a color that "blends" with your fashion fabric. For example, try gray for medium to dark fabrics, white or ecru on pastels, brown on rust, navy on purple, etc.

● *Decorative threads:* Because a serger's loopers have large eyes that can accommodate heavier threads, you can use a wider range

of decorative threads on it than on the conventional sewing machine. Experiment! You'll probably prefer to use the decorative threads in the loopers only. Try baby yarn, metallic or silk thread, #8 pearl cotton, $1/16$" (2mm) wide silk or rayon ribbon, machine embroidery thread, shiny rayon thread, candlewicking thread, crochet cotton or even embroidery floss (two, three or six strands).

Some ideas:

● Thread the upper looper with baby yarn and serge the edges of a placemat, coat or jacket. It's a great substitute for fold-over braid or bias tape. (See Chapter 6, page 120.)

● Use metallic or silk thread in the upper looper for a beautiful rolled hem. (See Chapter 6, page 155.)

● Use variegated #8 pearl cotton in the looper and flatlock your

seams, using the two-thread stitch configuration. With a three-thread stitch configuration, try a mock flatlock seam, with the pearl cotton in the upper looper. (See Chapter 6, page 155.)

SOLVING YOUR STITCH PROBLEMS

Threading your serger in the proper sequence is key to achieving a balanced stitch. The usual sequence is upper looper first, then lower looper, then right needle and, finally, left needle. This may change depending on the brand and model of your serger. Check your machine's instruction manual to be sure.

Your serger manual also provides information on how to adjust your tension settings to achieve a well-balanced stitch. Sometimes, however, you may have stitching prob-

tip

Instead of rethreading the machine manually each time you change colors, try this:

● *Cut off the old thread just above the spool.*

● *Replace the old spool with the new thread and tie the ends together in a knot.*

● *Pull the threads through the machine in the following sequence—upper looper, lower looper, right needle, left needle. When the knot reaches the eye of the needle, cut it off and rethread the needle.*

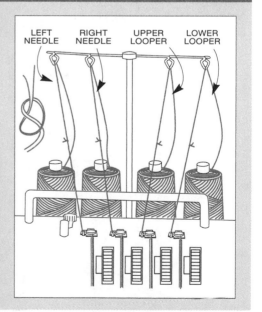

lems that no amount of fiddling with the tension will correct. For causes of, and solutions to, these problems see page 91.

PINNING AND BASTING

Safety First, Then Serge

Did you ever break a pin by sewing over it? Even if your conventional machine is designed to sew over pins, it's a bad habit to get into—particularly if you're joining the enthusiastic ranks of those who use a serger.

Sergers have both stationary and movable cutters, or blades. As you serge, they are constantly moving, cutting off the excess seam allowances or ragged fabric edges. If a pin happens to be in the way, it will be cut off, dulling the blades and sending pin fragments through the air. Flying pins can cut your face or damage your eyes. If they miss you and get into the inner workings of your machine, the result is a serviceperson's nightmare!

This doesn't mean you have to forgo pin basting altogether.

● Pull out the pins before the knife reaches them. A Grabbit® magnetic pincushion next to your machine provides the pins with a nice home.

● Place the pins at least 1" (2.5cm) from the cut edge, parallel to the seamline. This method is good for long seams but not for detail areas.

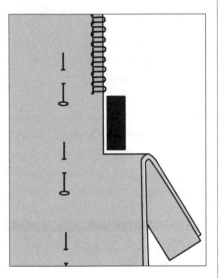

GETTING STARTED

With a conventional sewing machine, you must always remember to lower the presser foot before stitching and raise it again when you're finished—or else your machine won't form the stitches properly. With a serger, you can leave the presser foot in the "down" position all the time. For a smooth start, serge a 2" to 3" (5cm to 7.5cm) thread chain; then gently feed the fabric under the foot. If you're sewing on very thick fabric or through many layers, you may want to serge a chain and use your thumb to lift the front of the foot onto the fabric.

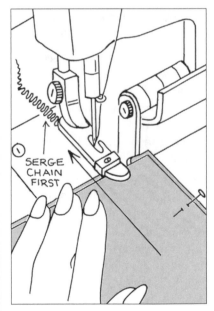

SERGE CHAIN FIRST

FINISHING UP

If you're using your serger to finish the seams, or if the seams will be intersected by other seams, you don't need to bother securing the thread ends. To simply end your stitching, here's what to do:

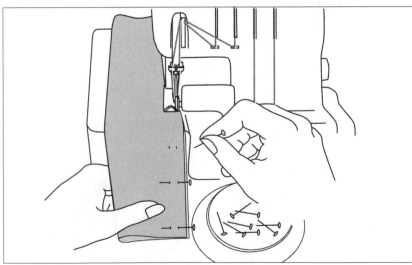

SOLVING YOUR STITCH PROBLEMS

PROBLEM:	POSSIBLE CAUSE:	SOLUTION:
Skipped stitches	Needle may be too heavy for the fabric.	Change to a finer needle.
	The upper looper tension may be too tight.	Loosen it slightly.
	The needle may be dull or bent.	Change to a new needle.
	The machine may be threaded incorrectly.	Rethread and check all of the threading points.
	The needle may not be the right type.	Use a new, sharp needle—size 11 or 14, designed for your serger. (Not all serger needles can be used with all machines. Check the needle package and your manual.)
	Needle tension may be too loose.	Tighten it slightly.
Stitches pull through to the right side of the fabric	Incorrect needle plate or wrong stitch width for weight of fabric.	Use a 3mm to 4mm needle plate or the widest stitch width.
	The thread is not fully lodged between the tension discs.	Hold the thread securely above the tension dial and pull the thread firmly below the knob, sliding it between the discs.
	Thread has slipped out of thread guides.	Same as above.
	Needle is dull, bent or burred.	Change the needle.
	Blade is not set correctly.	Consult the instruction manual or your dealer.
Threads break	Incorrect threading.	Rethread machine. Check your manual for the proper sequence. You may also need to loosen tensions to "0" before rethreading.
	Incorrect threading sequence.	If looper thread is breaking, remove the thread(s) from the eye of the needle(s) before rethreading the loopers.
	Thread pole isn't completely extended	Check and correct.
	Tension is too tight.	Reduce the tension slightly on the looper or needle thread that is breaking.
	Thread is caught on spool or wrapped around spool pin.	Check and correct.
	Needle is dull, bent or burred.	Change the needle. You'll need a new one every 60 to 100 hours of sewing time.
	Thread is old, brittle or coarse.	Try a different thread.
Loops form at the edge of the fabric	Thread is not lodged fully between tension discs.	Check to see that the thread is lodged inside the tension discs.
	Looper threads are too loose.	Increase tension on upper and lower loopers.
	Thread has slipped out of take-up lever or thread guides.	Recheck threading points.
	Blade is cutting too much fabric.	Check that the blade is aligned evenly with the needle plate. Consult the instruction manual or your dealer.
Machine is jamming	Presser foot pressure is too heavy for your fabric.	Consult the instruction manual to decrease pressure.
	Fabric has been inserted behind the blade.	Insert fabric from the front of the machine. Since the blade is in front of the needle, the fabric must be trimmed before it reaches the needle.
	Thread is caught under the presser foot.	After completing a row of stitching, continue stitching so that you "chain off" a 2" to 3" (5cm to 7.5cm) tail behind the presser foot.

tip

As a substitute for pin basting, try a glue stick or double-faced basting tape. Place the tape next to the cut edge of the fabric so you don't gum up your machine by stitching or cutting through it.

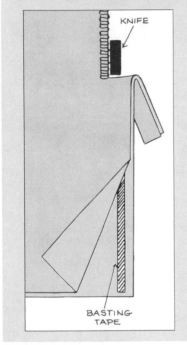

KNIFE

BASTING TAPE

• Serge off the fabric for about 5" to 6" (12.5cm to15cm).

• Without raising the presser foot, bring the chain and fabric around so the chain crosses in front of the blade. Stitch for a few more seconds so that the blades automatically cut the thread chain off for you.

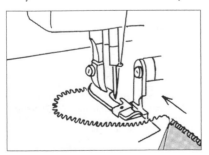

This method cuts the thread but doesn't secure the ends. To do that, use one of the following methods:

Backstitching

Your conventional machine usually has a backstitch button or knob that allows you to sew two or three stitches back over themselves. Although this isn't possible with a serger, it is possible to stitch back over a serged seam or thread chain.

●*At the beginning of the seam:*

• Serge a 2" (5cm) thread chain.

• Lift the tip of the presser foot with your thumb, place the garment underneath and take four or five stitches, leaving the needle in the fabric.

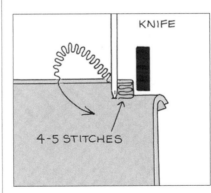

KNIFE

4-5 STITCHES

• Raise the presser foot. Swinging the chain around to the front from the left of the needle, place it within the seam allowance, between the needle and the knife (see top right.)

tip

Remember: If the serged seam is crossed by another seam, there is no need to backstitich.

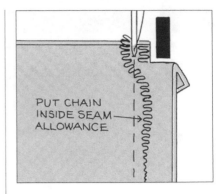

PUT CHAIN INSIDE SEAM ALLOWANCE

• Lower the presser foot and serge, encasing the thread chain in the seam allowance.

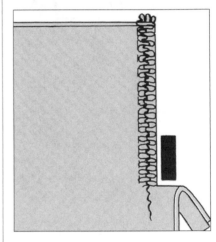

●*At the end of a seam:*

• Serge to the end of the seam, one stitch past the edge of the fabric. Stop with the needle up, out of the fabric.

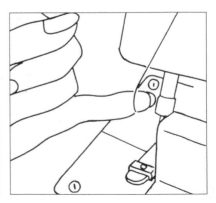

• Raise the presser foot. Then gently pull on the needle thread just above the needle to create slack.

• Pull the last stitch off the stitch fingers. Flip the fabric over and bring it around to the front of the needle.

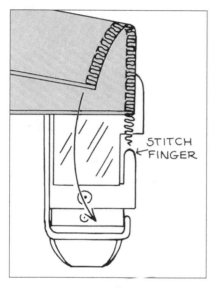

• Lower the presser foot and eliminate the slack by pulling on the needle thread just above the tension dial. Serge over the previous stitching for about 1" (2.5cm); then serge off the edge.

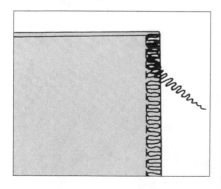

Tying Off

You may prefer to tie off the threads. There are two ways to

do this. The first method is quick but a little bulky. The second method results in an almost invisible knot.

• *Method 1:* Gently run your fingertips along the thread chain to smooth it out. Then tie the threads as described on page 72 for securing conventional machine stitching.

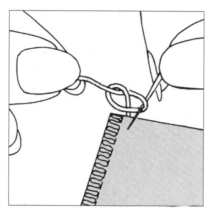

• *Method 2:* Hold the project and thread chain in one hand. With the other hand, use a pin (an extralong quilting pin works very well) to loosen the needle thread. Pull the needle thread out of the chain. Now all of the threads are free and can be tied in a small knot.

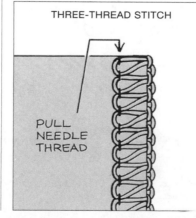

THREE-THREAD STITCH

PULL NEEDLE THREAD

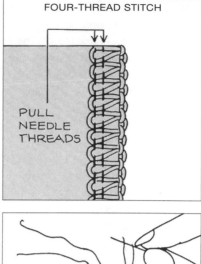

FOUR-THREAD STITCH

PULL NEEDLE THREADS

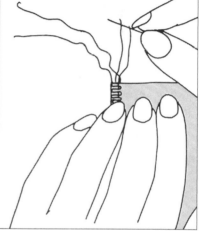

Burying the Threads

Thread the chain onto a large-eyed craft needle and then tunnel it back along the seam allowance, between the fabric and the stitches.

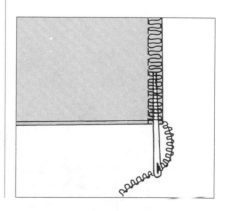

Liquid Seam Sealant

Apply a drop of liquid seam sealant, such as Fray Check™, to the last stitches. Let it dry and then clip off the threads. For extra security, tie off the thread ends first.

SEAMS

Your serger can be used as a finishing machine for seams that will eventually be sewn on a conventional sewing machine…or it can be used to simultaneously finish and stitch a seam.

When sewing on a conventional machine, the top layer of fabric always feeds slightly faster than the bottom layer. As a result, the rule is to stitch with the grain whenever possible and practical.

With your serger, this is a rule that you can happily break. Because the presser foot has a firmer pressure and the loopers

"knit" the threads across the fabric, as well as along its length, shifting is virtually eliminated. As a result, you can stitch your seams in any direction you please.

Continuous Overcasting

If you plan to stitch your seams on a conventional machine, you can use your serger, and the continuous overcasting technique, to speed up the mundane task of finishing the raw edges.

Depending on what type of serger you own, use either a two-thread or three-thread stitch to overcast, or serge, the edges. As you serge, the blade should skim the edge of the fabric so nothing is trimmed off the seam allowance except a few loose threads.

For continuous overcasting, you will need to line up all the garment sections so that the stitching is not broken as you move from the edge

of one section to the edge of another. Once the overcasting is finished, the thread chains are clipped and the garment sections are separated.

For example, suppose you are making a simple top and matching pair of shorts. Here's how you would line up the pattern pieces and feed them into the serger:

• Begin by overcasting all of the hem edges, cutting the threads in between.

• On the bodice front (as shown in the stitching diagram), begin at the hemline and overcast one side seam (A), the two shoulder seams (B and C) and then the other side seam (D).

• Without snipping the thread, and without raising the presser foot, move on to the bodice back. Overcast in the same sequence as for the bodice front (E, F, G and H).

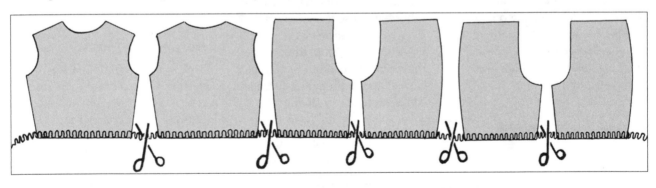

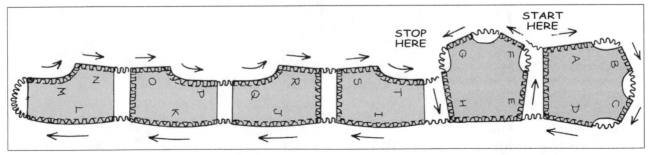

- Without snipping the threads, overcast the outside legs of the shorts front and shorts back (I, J, K and L). Your work will begin to resemble an oddly shaped kite tail!

- When you are finished with the outside legs, turn everything around and overcast the inside legs (M, N, O, P, Q, R , S and T).

- To separate the garment sections, simply snip the connecting thread chains.

Speed Seaming

This technique for joining the seams of a garment is similar to the sequence for continuous overcasting.

  Suppose you are making a simple top and want to join and finish the seams using only the serger.

- Overcast the bottom hem edges; then cut the threads in between.

- Pin the garment together at the side and shoulder seams.

- Starting at the hemline, serge up one side seam (A). Chain off but do not cut the threads.

- Serge the first shoulder seam (B), from armhole to neck edge, and chain off. Again, do not cut the threads.

- Serge the second shoulder seam from neck edge to armhole and then chain off (C).

- Serge the remaining side seam (D) from armhole to hemline.

- Snip the threads between the seams. Press the seams, and you're ready to go on to the finishing details, such as facing, bands and hems.

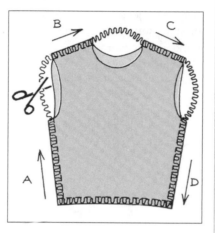

Staystitching

Fabrics that require special handling on a conventional machine are a breeze to sew on the serger. Stretchy sweater knits, stretch terrycloth and velour, slippery crepe de chine, jersey and nylon tricot are a few of the difficult fabrics that your serger will handle just like a piece of crisply woven cotton.

  One of the reasons that many sewers have avoided these "special" fabrics is their tendency to stretch out of shape, during both handling and sewing. Staystitching is the time-honored way to prevent fabric distortion. On a serger, it's really easy!

To staystitch, place a strand of 1/4" (6mm) twill tape, knitting ribbon or baby yarn so that it goes under the presser foot and over the finger guard, and serge slightly to the right of the seamline. If your machine has a presser foot with a hole for inserting cording, thread the tape, ribbon or yarn through the hole first; then pull it under the back of the foot and serge.

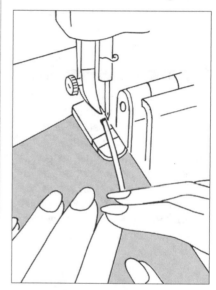

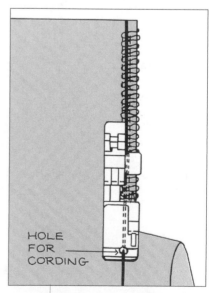

HOLE FOR CORDING

When you are ready to serge your garment together, remember that the blade on your serger has trimmed away the excess seam allowance. Sections that are staystitched will now have $1/4$" (6mm) seam allowances.

SPECIAL TECHNIQUES

Serging Outside Corners

Because of the way a serger creates the stitches, going around an outside corner calls for some (very

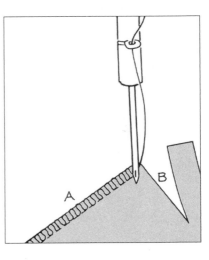

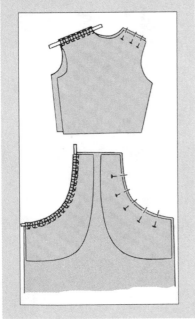

easy) special treatment. But if you don't use the following procedure, one of two things will happen: Either a small, untidy cloverleaf of thread will form at the corner or you won't be able to pivot the fabric to get a sharp point.

● Starting at one edge of the outside corner, make a 2" (5cm) long slash, parallel to and $3/8$" (9mm) in from the edge of the fabric. Note: If your project has a $1/4$" (6mm) hem allowance, you won't be trimming as you overcast so you can skip this step.

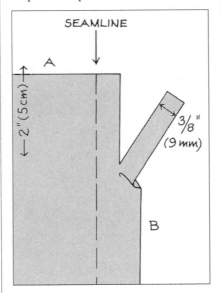

● Beginning on side A, serge to the corner, going just one stitch past the edge of the fabric (shown at top of next column.)

● Lift the presser foot and gently pull on the needle thread to create a little bit of slack.

● Carefully pull the last stitch off the stitch finger(s) and pivot the fabric, positioning it so that the new stitches will butt up against the previous stitches.

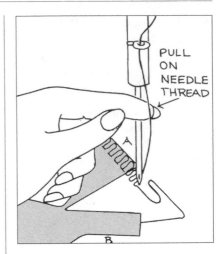

PULL ON NEEDLE THREAD

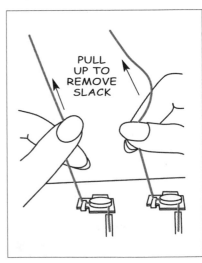

PULL UP TO REMOVE SLACK

- Pull the needle thread back up above the tension control to remove the slack; then serge side B. The result is a neat, clean corner.

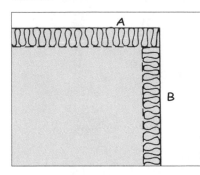

Serging Inside Corners

On rare occasions, you may want to serge an edge that includes an inside corner. This technique takes practice, so try it out first on some scraps of fabric until you're comfortable with the results.

- Using a disappearing marking pen, mark the corner at the intersection of the $5/8$" (1.5cm) seamlines. If your fabric is soft, staystitch the inside corner on your conventional sewing machine.

- Clip the corner, ending the clip $1/8$" (3mm) from the corner mark.

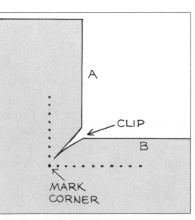

- Starting at the clip, and working on side B of the corner, trim the seam allowance to $1/8$" (3mm) for approximately 1" (2.5cm).

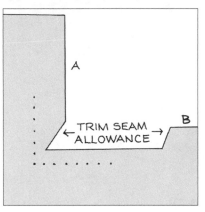

- Beginning at side A, serge until side B is just in front of the knife. Spread the fabric open so that the cut edge of side B is even with the edge of the blade. (Note: A small pleat will appear in the fabric when you do this.) Continue serging side B.

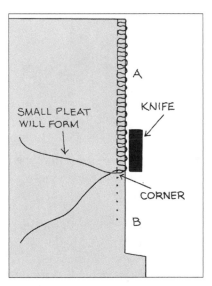

Serging in a Circle

Because serger stitches must always begin and end at the edge

of the fabric, and because a serger cannot backstitch, sewing in a circle requires some special—but easy—techniques. Suppose you want to attach a circular band to a neckline...or a circular cuff to the edge of a sleeve...or finish the edges of an oval placemat or round tablecloth. Here are two techniques:

- *Serge on/serge off:* Since this is the fastest—but not the neatest—method, it is usually used when the seam will be hidden inside the garment. All of the intersecting seams are serged before the circular seam is stitched.

- With right sides together, pin the two garment sections together.

- At some point along the seamline (usually the center back), make a 2" (5cm) long mark along the $5/8$" (1.5cm) seam allowance with a disappearing marking pen.

- Serge, starting just before the mark and angling the fabric until you are stitching along the mark.

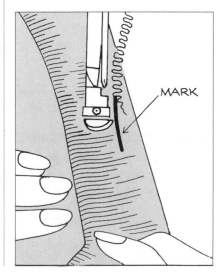

● Serge around the circular area until the stitches meet at the mark. Serge off the fabric.

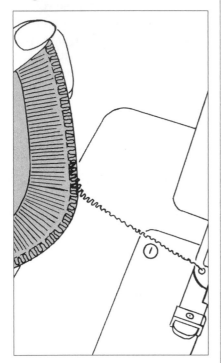

● *Clip method:* Use this method when you are finishing a continuous edge, such as the neckline or hemline of a garment, or hemming an item such as an oval placemat or round tablecloth.

● If you have a seam or hem allowance that is deeper than $1/4$" (6mm), make two parallel clips in the seam allowance 2" (5cm) apart. Trim the seam allowance away

tip

To prevent any "bumps" or distortion that might occur when serging over bulky, intersecting seams, press the seam allowances so that they will face in opposite directions when you serge.

between the clips. If the project has a $1/4$" (6mm) seam allowance, skip this step.

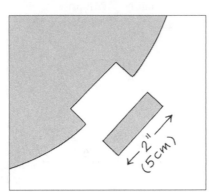

● Raise the presser foot and place the fabric so that the trimmed edge is next to the knife and the needle is at the top of the clipped area. Carefully lower the presser foot onto the fabric.

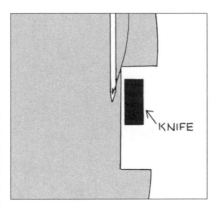

KNIFE

● Serge around the edge until the stitches meet and overlap for two or three stitches.

● Pull the thread through the needles by hand to create about 3" (7.5cm) of slack. Lift the presser foot and pull the fabric toward the back so the stitches come off the stitch fingers. Separate the thread chain and tie off the threads (see page 93).

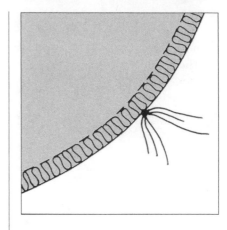

REMOVING STITCHES

"As she sews, so shall she rip!" Let's face it: Everyone, even the most experienced sewer, makes mistakes now and then.

Believe it or not, ripping out serger stitching is often easier than ripping out conventional stitching. However, when you go to restitch, remember that the blade has already trimmed the seam allowance.

● *For the two-, three- or four-thread serger or overlock stitches:* Simply run a seam ripper along the edge of the fabric, under the upper looper threads, cutting them as you go.

● *For a four-thread safety stitch:* To remove the "chain" part of the stitch, work from the underneath side of the serged stitches and start ripping at the end of the chain. If you can locate the looper thread, pull it. The chain will come undone like ready-to-wear stitches often do. To remove the overedge stitches, turn the fabric to the wrong side and cut along the V created by the needle threads.

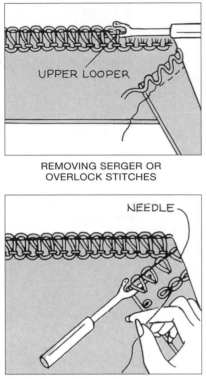

REMOVING SERGER OR
OVERLOCK STITCHES

REMOVING SAFETY STITCHES

SEWING WITH YOUR IRON

Careful pressing is as important as accurate stitching. In fact, if you want professional results, you can't have one without the other! Note that the term press—rather than iron—is used in sewing. The difference? To press means to move the iron across the fabric by lifting it

up and putting it back down in an overlapping pattern. To iron means to slide the iron across the fabric with a back-and-forth motion. Ironing may distort the shape of the garment; pressing won't.

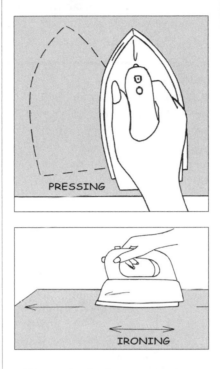

The cardinal rule in sewing is "press as you go." This means that you should never, ever cross one seam with another without first pressing the original seam.

This doesn't mean that you must constantly be hopping back and forth from ironing board to sewing machine. There are two easy solutions:

● Organize your sewing so that you are working on several different sections of the garment at the same time. Sew as far as you can on each section; then take them all to the ironing board and press everything that needs it.

● Keep your iron and a tabletop ironing board or a sturdy sleeve board within arm's reach of your sewing machine. That way, you can do small detail pressing without getting up.

Although some sewing procedures require special pressing techniques (see Chapter 6), there are three universal steps for achieving good results:

1. Press flat along the stitching line to blend the stitches.

2. Press the seam allowances open or to one side, as indicated in the pattern instructions, or to one side if the seam is serged.

3. Press the seam or detail area from the right side. If necessary, protect the fabric with a press cloth.

As a rule, it's best to use light pressure, without resting the full weight of the iron on the fabric. Some delicate fabrics or fabrics with a texture that could be flattened, such as velvet or fake furs, can be finger pressed. To do this, hold the iron above the fabric and apply a generous amount of steam. Then use your fingers, not the iron, to press seams, darts and edges.

PRESS-AS-YOU-SEW GUIDE

The chart on the opposite page is a useful guide to pressing today's common fibers and textures.

PRESSING EQUIPMENT

In addition to your iron and ironing board, there's a wide range of pressing equipment available. Pressing aids are designed to:

● Provide a shaped pressing surface that simulates the curves of the body.

● Allow you to press detail areas without putting creases into the rest of the garment.

Don't think you have to run out and buy all of the equipment listed. Start with a seam roll (or our no-cost substitute) and some press cloths. Add to your collection as your sewing skills develop.

GUIDE TO PRESSING EQUIPMENT

● *Seam roll:* Useful for pressing seams open on long, cylindrical garment sections, such as sleeves and pants legs. If you press the seams open using the tip of your iron, the curved surface prevents the seam allowances from creating imprints on the outside of the garment.

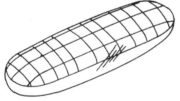

● *Press cloths:* These prevent scorch marks and iron shine. Use any of the following: specially treated press cloths, muslin in several different weights, a piece of your fashion fabric or a man's handkerchief.

● *Tailor's ham:* Useful for pressing curved areas such as darts, princess seams and sleeve caps.

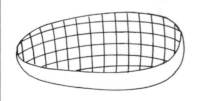

● *Paper strips:* Slip them underneath the seam allowances as the seams are pressed open. Then you won't have any seam allowance imprints on the outside of your garment. Cut strips from brown bags, use number 10 envelopes or rolls of adding machine tape.

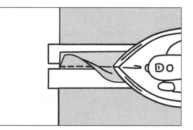

● *Point presser or tailor's board:* A multi-edged surface that makes it possible to press seams open on detail areas such as collars, cuffs and facings.

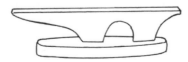

● *Sleeve board:* Great for pressing narrow garment sections that won't fit over the regular ironing board.

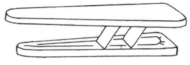

● *Needle board:* A good investment if you plan to sew with lots of velvets, velveteens or corduroys. Place the fabric facedown on the board and press. The short, dense needles keep the pile from being flattened.

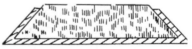

tips

● *As a quick substitute for a seam roll, place a magazine on top of a piece of muslin, roll it up tightly and secure with a few rubber bands.*

● *A fluffy terry cloth towel or a scrap of self-fabric provides a cushioned surface that can substitute for a needle board.*

PRESS-AS-YOU-SEW GUIDE

FIBER	PRESSURE	HEAT	MOISTURE	SPECIAL INSTRUCTIONS
Acetate	Light	Very low	Dry iron	Use press cloth on right side.
Acrylic	Light	Moderate	Dry iron	Same as acetate.
Cotton	Light to moderate	Moderate to high	Dry or steam iron	Press with steam iron. For more moisture, dampen fabric and press with dry iron. To avoid shine on dark colors, press from wrong side or use press cloth on right side.
Linen	Light to heavy	High	Dry or steam iron	Same as cotton.
Nylon	Light	Low to moderate	Dry or steam iron	Little or no ironing required.
Polyester	Moderate	Low to moderate	Dry or steam iron	May need press cloth on right side; test first.
Rayon	Light	Low to moderate	Dry or steam iron	Use press cloth to prevent shine and water spots.
Silk	Light	Low to moderate	Dry or steam iron	Press light to medium weights with dry iron. For heavy weights, use steam iron and dry press cloth to avoid water spots.
Wool	Light to moderate	Moderate	Dry or steam iron	Press with steam iron. For more moisture, press with dry iron and slightly damp press cloth. Use press cloth on right side to prevent shine. Press crepe with dry iron.
Blends	Press according to requirements of the most delicate fiber.			
TEXTURE				
Crepe	Light	Low to moderate	Dry iron	Use press cloth on right side.
Deep Pile	Finger-press	Moderate	Steam iron	Experiment on scraps to determine amount of pressure.
Glossy	Light	Low	Dry iron	Same as crepe.
Nap, Pile	Light or finger press	Low to moderate	Dry or steam iron	Press fabric over needle board, using light pressure or finger press.

IRON-ONS, FUSIBLES AND FUSIBLE WEBS

There are certain areas of sewing where you can put your sewing machine aside and "sew" with a wide range of heat-sensitive, iron-on sewing aids. Timesaving and easy to use, these fusibles, iron-ons and fusible webs are a fundamental part of today's sewing—provided you know how to use them. You'll find techniques for using these products throughout Chapter 6. But first—the basics:

● An *iron-on* is applied using heat and pressure only—no steam. Mending tape, mending patches and some hem tapes are today's most common iron-ons. However, as technology improves, more iron-on products are available. For quick glamour, there are embroidered appliqués and sequin trims that can be applied with the touch of your iron.

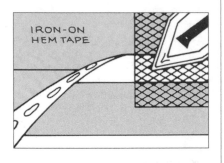

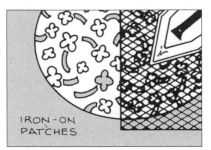

● A *fusible* is applied using a combination of heat, steam and pressure. Fusible products include interfacings and fusible web.

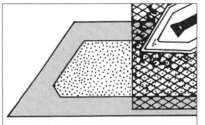

Both fusible and iron-on products come with instructions. Be sure to follow them carefully. To be on the safe side, always use a press cloth to protect your fabric.

● *Fusible web* is an adhesive web that "glues" two layers of fabric together. Don't confuse fusible web with fusible interfacing. Fusible web will not shape, support or reinforce your fabric the way fusible interfacing will. In fact, if you examine fusible web carefully, you'll see that it's not a fabric at all. It's a network of fibers. When the prescribed combination of heat, steam and pressure is applied, these fibers melt and "disappear," causing the two layers of fabric to adhere to one another.

● Use it as a substitute for hand tacking to keep facings, etc., from rolling to the outside of the garment.

● Fuse-baste with fusible web. Position the web between the two layers of fabric, cover with a damp press cloth and press lightly for two to three seconds. This basting method is great for preventing ribbons, trims, etc., from rippling and

tip

Some fusible webs, such as Wonder-Under™ from Pellon®, come with a paper backing that provides the stability needed to cut the web into any shape, no matter how small or detailed. With a light touch of your iron, and following the manufacturer's directions, you can transfer the web to fabric, peel away the paper and then fuse.

shifting as they are stitched. It's also a useful technique when sewing lapped seams on fabrics that can't be pinned, such as synthetic suede.

● Hems on casual clothes and children's garments can be fused in place instead of sewing. For more information, see "Hems," page 150.

● Design your own appliqués and fuse them in place with fusible web. Draw the shape directly on the right side of the fabric. Place the fabric, right side up, over the fusible web; then cut out both layers at the same time. This is a great way to cover tears and worn spots in children's garments!

HAND SEWING

Although most of your sewing will be done at the machine, there are times when only a hand stitch will do. The following stitches are the ones you'll use most frequently:

● *Basting:* Useful for transferring marking to the right side of the garment and for temporarily holding the garment together. For more information, see "Hand Basting," page 76.

● *Blindstitch:* This stitch is useful for hemming knits and bulky fabrics. It will help prevent a ridge from forming at the hemline on the outside of the garment.

● Fold back the garment slightly below the hem edge and hold it with your thumb.

● Fasten the thread in the hem edge and, working from right to left, take a tiny stitch about 1/4" (6mm) to the left in the garment.

● Take the next stitch 1/4" (6mm) away in the hem edge.

● Continue, alternating from garment to hem and keeping the stitches evenly spaced.

● *Catchstitch:* This stitch has some built-in stretch which makes it an especially good choice for hemming knits and for holding edges, such as facings, in place.

● Fasten the thread to the wrong side of the hem or facing.

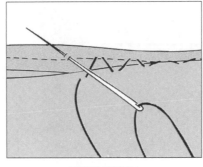

BLINDSTITCH

● Work from left to right, with the needle pointing to the left. Take a tiny stitch in the garment 1/4" (6mm) to the right, close to the hem or facing edge.

● Take the next stitch 1/4" (6mm) to the right in the hem or facing, so that the stitches form an **X**.

● Continue, alternating from garment to hem or facing, keeping the stitches fairly loose.

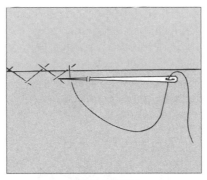

CATCHSTITCH

● *Hemming Stitch:* Use this stitch if the hem allowance is finished with seam binding.

● Begin at a seam, fastening the thread in the seam allowance.

● Take a tiny stitch through the garment, picking up a single thread.

● Insert the needle between the seam binding and the garment, and bring it out through the seam binding, about 1/4"(6mm) to the left of the first stitch.

● Take another stitch in the garment, 1/4"(6mm) to the left of the second stitch.

● Continue, alternating from seam binding to garment, and taking several stitches on the needle before drawing the thread through the fabric.

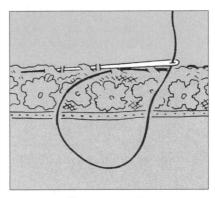

HEMMING STITCH

● *Pickstitch:* This stitch, also called a half-backstitch, is a good one to know if you are inserting a zipper in a fragile or hard-to-handle fabric, such as those used in bridal or evening wear. Use it in place of the final topstitching. To ensure a straight line of pickstitches, add a row of hand basting stitches as a guideline.

● Starting from the bottom of the zipper, fasten the thread on the underside of the zipper and bring the needle up through the zipper tape and garment layers.

● Insert the needle back down through all of the layers, a thread

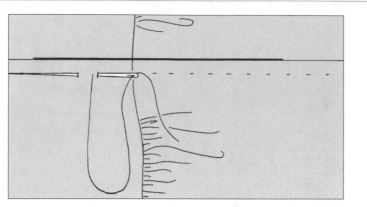

PICKSTITCH

or two behind the point where it first emerged.

- Bring the needle up again about ¹/₄"(6mm) ahead of the first stitch.

- Continue along the length of the zipper.

- *Slipstitch:* This is a good choice for securing turned-under edges because the stitches are invisible on both the inside and outside of the garment.

- Fasten the thread in the fold of the fabric. Working from right to left, pick up a single fabric thread just below the folded edge.

- Insert the needle into the fold directly above the first stitch and bring it out ¹/₄"(6mm) away.

- Pick up another single thread in the garment directly below the point where the needle emerged.

- Continue, alternating between garment and fold.

tip

The tacking stitch is useful for permanently attaching snaps or hooks and eyes. For more information, see "Closures" in Chapter 6, page 127.

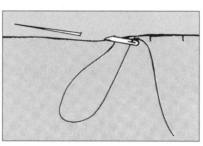

SLIPSTITCH

- *Tacking:* This stitch helps keep facings in place at the seams. Holding the edge of the facing and the seam allowance together, take three or four short stitches in one place through both layers. Do not sew through the garment fabric. Repeat on the other seam allowance.

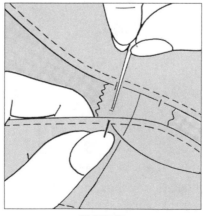

TACKING

HAND SEWING TIPS

- *For tangle-free sewing:*

- Cut the thread in lengths no longer than 18" (45.5cm).

- Draw the thread through beeswax. This will also make the thread stronger.

- *For easy needle threading:*

- Cut the thread diagonally by holding your scissors at a slant.

- Hold the needle up against a white background so you can see the eye clearly.

- Use a needle threader. Push the wire through the eye of the needle; then insert the thread through the wire (A). Pull the wire back out of the needle, drawing the thread through the eye (B).

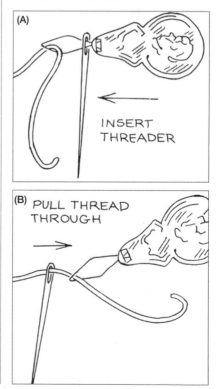

(A) INSERT THREADER

(B) PULL THREAD THROUGH

- Use a calyx-eyed needle. These are designed with a tiny opening at the top for easy threading.

- *To knot the thread:*

- Insert the thread through the eye of the needle and then cut it off at the desired length.

- Working with the end you just cut off the spool, hold the thread between your thumb and index finger, and then wrap the thread around your index finger (A).

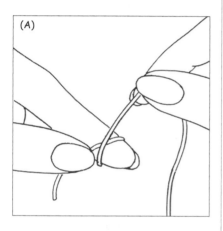

- While holding the thread taut, slide your index finger back along your thumb until the thread ends twist into a loop (B).

- Continue sliding your index finger back until the loop slides off your finger (C).

- Bring your middle finger down to hold the open loop; then pull on the thread to form a knot (D).

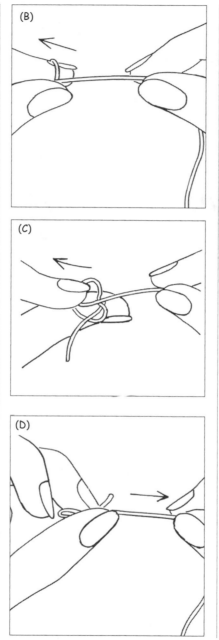

(B)

(C)

(D)

tip

Stitch-in-the-ditch (see page 74) is the quick machine alternative to hand tacking a facing in place.

- *To secure the stitching:*

- Form a thread loop by taking a very small backstitch at the point where the needle last emerged.

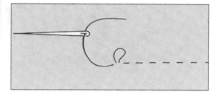

- Take a second small backstitch on top of the first. As you complete the stitch, bring the needle and thread through the loop.

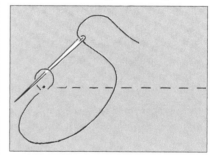

- Pull on the thread, drawing up the loop and making both stitches taut.

- If the stitching is subject to a great deal of strain, repeat to form a second "knot."

- Cut the thread.

chapter 6

Simply the Best Sewing Techniques

You may wonder why this section is devoted to many of the same techniques included on your pattern's instruction sheet. After all, the instruction sheet contains carefully sketched and expertly written step-by-step directions for putting the project together. However there are times when you may want more information than the pattern is able to give.

● Pattern companies usually select the techniques that are suitable for the broadest range of fabrics. But suppose your choice of fabric creates a special sewing situation. For example, it might be very sheer, or have a nap, or be quite bulky. In that case, you might want to vary the sewing techniques to suit your fabric.

● If a technique is confusing to you, reading "how to do it" in slightly different words, or looking at a sketch with a different perspective, might clarify it for you.

● As your sewing skills progress, you'll want to look for patterns with design details that expand your sewing knowledge. Use this section as a guide to deciding what techniques you want to focus on with each new pattern purchase.

● You may want to customize the look of your pattern by adding details not originally included in the pattern, such as appliqués, trims, ruffles, tucks or decorative edgings. This section contains many interesting options for you to use.

● Although many patterns are identified as containing special serger instructions, almost every pattern can benefit from blending serger and conventional sewing techniques. You will find your options in this section.

● For quick reference, an **S** will alert you every time a technique uses the serger. In some instances it makes no difference whether you use the conventional machine or serger, but the symbol appears because you may not have thought to use the serger for that technique.

HOW TO USE THE SERGER CHARTS

Many of the serger techniques in this section include a chart with

Technique			
TYPE OF SERGER STITCH:	**3**	**4**	**MINE**
Stitch length:	4mm-5mm	4mm-5mm	
Stitch width:	Widest	Widest	
Tensions—Needle:	Tight	Tight	
Right needle:	N/A	Normal	
Upper looper:	Normal	Normal	
Lower looper:	Normal	Normal	

recommended settings for two-, three-, or four-thread serger stitch settings, as appropriate. Because every serger, like every conventional machine, has its own "personality," there's also a space for you to record the appropriate settings for your machine. A sample of the serger stitch chart appears on the previous page. In each chart you will find the following four pieces of information.

TYPE OF SERGER STITCH

This identifies the serger settings for a two-, three- or four-thread stitch. If you don't know what type(s) your serger can make, check your owner's manual. The spaces under the third column, "mine," have been left blank for you to record the settings that are appropriate for your machine.

STITCH LENGTH

When serging seams on a woven fabric, a shorter stitch length provides greater durability. You might also want to shorten your stitch for some decorative effects or when making a narrow rolled hem. Where durability is not an issue, such as when overcasting the raw edges of a conventional seam, lengthen the stitch to save thread.

The stitch-length adjustment is usually located on the bottom left of the serger. It's turned either by hand or by using a screwdriver and a lock screw. The stitch length is calibrated on the metric system and ranges from slightly shorter than 1mm to about 5mm.

STITCH WIDTH

When serging on a woven fabric, you might want to widen your stitch so that your seam allowances will be deeper, resulting in seams that are more durable. When serging on knits, where raveling isn't a problem, a narrower width will give you a daintier seam. On sheer fabrics that do not ravel excessively, a narrow width creates a neater look, both inside and out.

Stitch width is generally determined by the throat plate and presser foot, or by whether you use the right or left needle. However, instead of changing throat plates, some machines use a dial-type width adjustment for both three-thread and four-thread serging.

● *On a three-thread serger:*

● Use a throat plate with a narrow stitch finger for a narrow width (approximately 1mm to 2mm).

● Use a throat plate with a wider stitch finger for the widest setting (usually 4mm to 5mm, although some new machines go as wide as 7.5mm).

● *On a four-thread serger:*

● Use the right needle to create a three-thread stitch with a narrow width (approximately 1mm to 2mm). To fine-tune the width, use a throat plate with a narrow stitch finger.

● Use the left needle for the widest stitch (approximately 4mm to 5mm). To fine-tune the width, use a throat plate with a wide stitch finger.

Note: Some sergers have adjustable stitch fingers that move in and out so you don't have to change the throat plate. Check your owner's manual for specifics.

TENSIONS

Thread Paths

● *Needle and right needle:*

● The three-thread serger stitch uses only one needle, so follow the guidelines for "needle" tensions.

● The four-thread serger has a left and a right needle. Follow the "needle" guidelines for the left needle and the "right needle" guidelines for the right needle.

● When "N/A" ("not applicable") appears next to the word "right needle," it means that you do not use the right needle for this type of stitch.

● *Upper looper:* This identifies how to set the tension on the upper looper. Thread suggestions may also be included.

● *Lower looper:* This identifies how to set the tensions on the lower looper.

Tension Settings

Thread tension dials are usually numbered or calibrated to indicate the tension settings.

● *Normal:* When the tension is "normal," the looper threads are smooth on both sides of the fabric and lock together evenly along the fabric edge. When a seam with normal tension is pressed to one side, you won't see any puckering or threads pulled to the surface on the right side of the fabric.

tip

S *Once you have established what the "normal" setting is for your serger, write it on a piece of masking tape and stick it to your machine for future reference.*

● *Very loose:* Set the appropriate tension dial approximately ⅓ of the way between "0," or no tension, and your "normal" setting.

● *Tight:* Set the appropriate tension dial approximately ⅓ to half of the way between your "normal" setting and the tightest possible tension setting for your serger.

● *Very tight:* Set the appropriate tension dial almost as tight as it can be adjusted.

APPLIQUÉS

Appliqués add pizzazz to any type of garment. They are particularly popular for children's garments and are often included as a design feature on their patterns. But adult clothes, too, are great places for appliqué. Depending on the choice of fabrics and colors, they can add a playful touch to casual garments, such as sweatshirts and T-shirts, or a sophisticated accent to tailored garments and evening apparel. Playful or sophisticated, they can create wearable art.

The easiest way to attach an appliqué is by machine.

PURCHASED APPLIQUÉS

Purchased appliqués usually are finished with a tight overcast edge. (Think Scout badges!) Apply them with a zigzag stitch all around the edges, or with a straight stitch that is positioned along the inside edge of the overcast stitches.

CUSTOM APPLIQUÉS

You can use a pattern or create your own appliqués. If you're not an artist, inspiration is all around you. Coloring books, wallpaper, wrapping paper, greeting cards, stencils and computer clip art are just some of the sources. Printed fabrics often have motifs that can be cut out and used as appliqués.

Basting

For successful results, the appliqué must be secured to the background fabric so that it won't shift during stitching. The two best methods are to use a glue stick or fusible web. (See "Iron-ons, Fusibles and Fusible Webs," page 101.)

Stitching Basics

● Set your machine for a narrow to medium-width zigzag stitch and a short stitch length. Position your project so that the appliqué is just to the left of the needle when the needle is in the right-hand position. Stitch slowly—it's the *only* way to achieve smooth edges and good control.

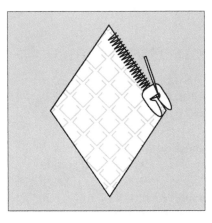

● For *outside curves*, stop stitching with the needle at the right-hand position so that it is in the background fabric. Raise the presser foot, pivot the fabric slightly, lower the foot and continue stitching.

● For *inside curves*, stop stitching with the needle in the left-hand position so that it is in the appliqué. Raise the presser foot, pivot the fabric slightly, lower the foot and continue stitching.

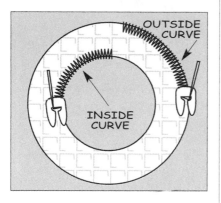

● For *deep curves*, stop and pivot at more frequent intervals than for shallow curves.

● For *outside corners*, stitch all the way to the end of the appliqué edge. Stop stitching with the needle in the right-hand position so that it is in the background fabric. Raise the presser foot, pivot the

tip

For best results, use your machine's satin stitch foot for machine appliqué. This foot is designed with a wide groove on the bottom so that it will glide smoothly over the build-up of thread that is created by the short zigzag stitch.

fabric, lower the foot and continue stitching along the next edge.

● For *inside corners*, stitch past the corner into the appliqué for a distance equal to the width of your zigzag stitch. Stop stitching with the needle in the left-hand position. Raise the presser foot, pivot the fabric, lower the foot and continue stitching along the next edge.

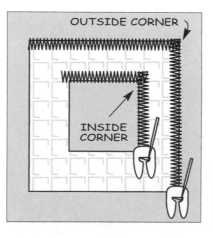

BANDS AND RIBBING

Bands are a neat, decorative way to finish necklines, armholes and front closings.

LAPPED V-NECK BAND

This type of band is particularly popular on knit garments that pull on over the head. It can be made from matching or contrasting fabric.

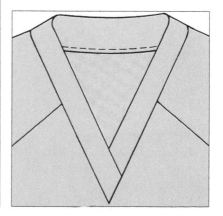

• With wrong sides together, fold the band in half lengthwise; pin or baste the raw edges together.

• On the garment front, reinforce the V at the tip of the neckline with a row of small machine stitches placed just inside the ⅝" (1.5cm) seamline.

• With right sides together, and beginning on one side of the garment, pin the band to the neck edge. For a smooth, accurate fit, carefully match the band markings. Leave the end of the band free on side B.

• Begin stitching at the first marking on side A of the band, as shown. (This marking should be matched exactly to the tip of the V.) Stop stitching when you reach the next-to-the-last marking on side B of the band. Tie the thread ends.

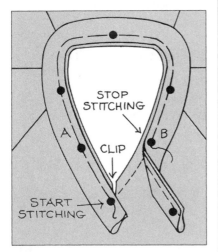

• Clip the garment seam allowance only at the tip of the V, just to, but not through, the reinforcement stitching. (Be careful—don't clip the band!) This will make it easier

to fold the seam allowances to the inside and finish the band.

• Turn the band up and tuck the ends inside the garment.

• On the inside of the garment, lap the free end of the band (side B) over the stitched end (side A), carefully matching all of the markings at the tip of the V. Hand-baste the ends of the bands together at the V.

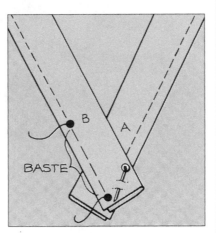

• Turn the seam allowances up and finish stitching the seam along side B of the neckline. End the stitching at the point of the V and tie off the threads.

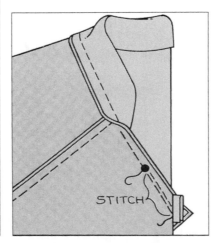

• To secure the loose end of the band, turn the seam allowances up along side A of the neckline V and stitch between the markings, right on top of the previous stitching.

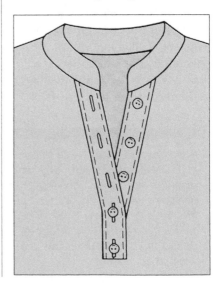

PLACKET BAND

This classic band is often used at the necklines of tailored dresses, shirts, tops and blouses. Traditionally tailored shirts or shirt jackets may feature a variation of this band as a finishing technique on the sleeve opening.

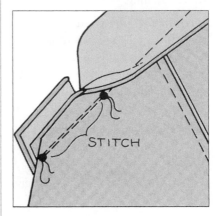

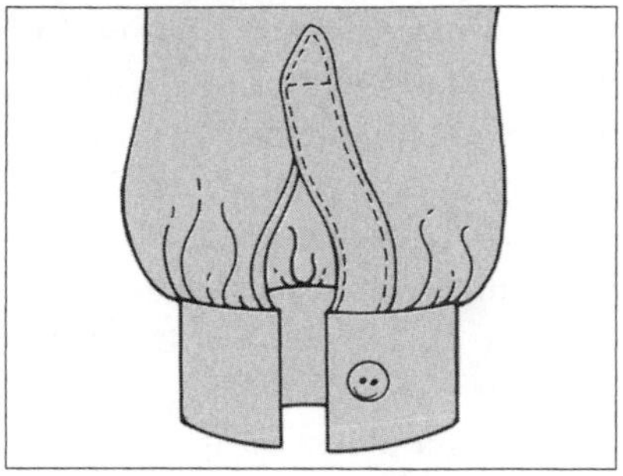

Before you begin, make sure you have transferred all of the markings, including stitching lines and fold lines, to the garment front and the band sections.

Note: The following directions will result in a classic women's right-over-left closing. However, your pattern may feature a menswear left-over-right closing.

- On the garment front, machine-stitch along the marked stitching lines. This will reinforce the corners, as well as provide you with a stitching guide when you attach the band sections.
- Slash the garment apart exactly in the middle of the two stitching lines. Make a small flap at the bottom by taking diagonal clips just to the corners of the stitching line. Be careful—don't clip through the stitches!

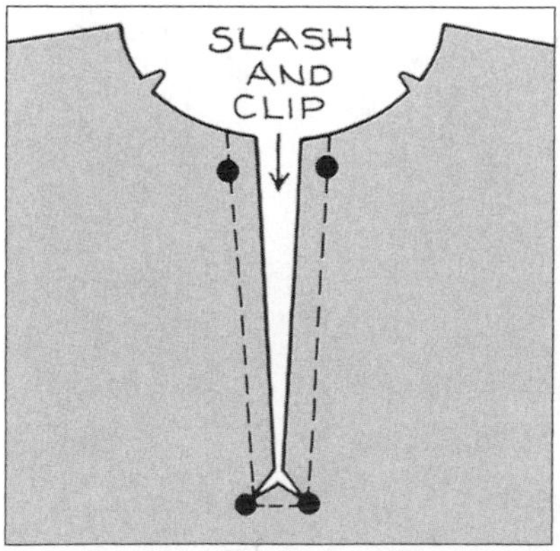

tip

If your fabric has a tendency to fray, treat the edges of the flap with a bit of liquid seam sealant, such as Fray Check™.

- Interface the band sections according to your pattern instructions.
- Press the seam allowance under on one long edge of the band section and trim to ¼" (6mm).
- With right sides together, pin the other long edge of the band to the garment front, matching markings.
- Machine-stitch along the stitching line, ending the stitching exactly at the bottom marking.
- Trim and grade the seam allowances, then press them toward the band.

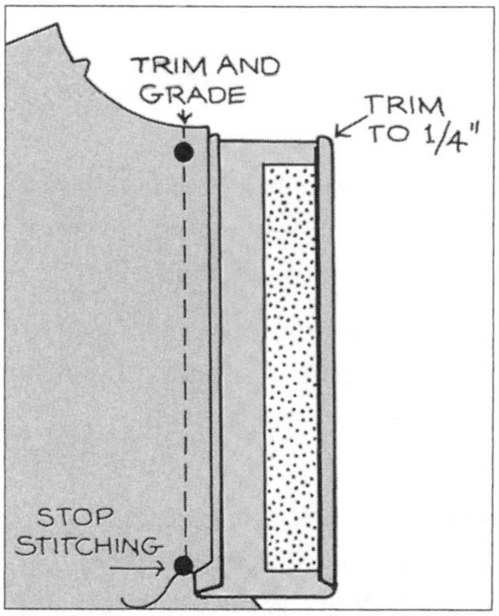

- Fold the band to the outside of the garment, and pin the pressed edge in place along the stitching line.
- Edgestitch close to both long edges of the band, ending the stitching at the lower marking.

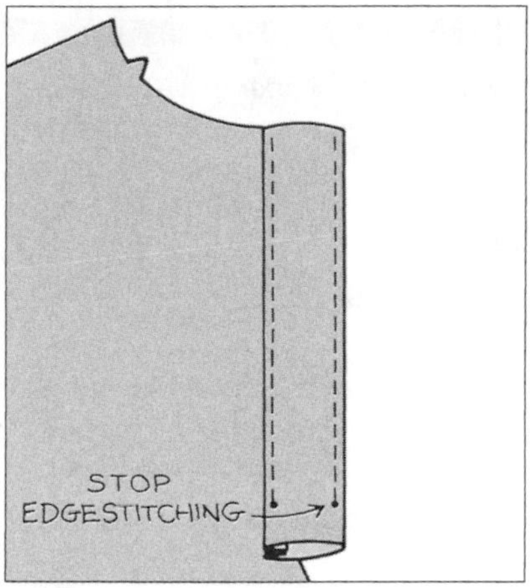

- Repeat, attaching the remaining band to the other side of the slashed opening.
- Slip the ends of the bands through to the inside of the garment. On the inside, lap the left band over the right. (For a menswear closing, lap the right over the left.) Pin, as shown, above the lower markings.

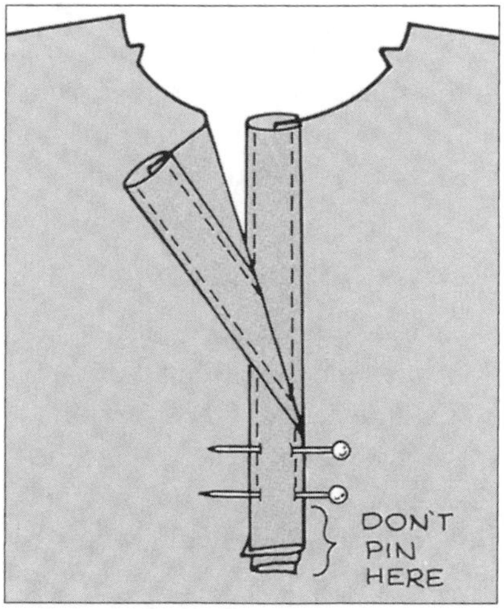

- Working with the wrong side of the garment face down, fold the lower portion of the garment up to expose the flap at the bottom of the opening. Baste the flap and the bands together along the

tip

● *If you're working with a slippery or stretchy fabric, you may want to interface the entire band. To keep it from becoming too stiff, use a lightweight or sheer weight fusible interfacing.*

stitching line, then machine-stitch as basted, keeping the garment free. Finish according to the pattern instructions.

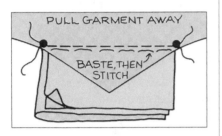

PULL GARMENT AWAY

BASTE, THEN STITCH

RIBBED BANDS

This type of band can be found at the neckline or the wrists, at the lower edge of a sweater-style top or at the ankles of a pair of sweatpants.

Use either rib-knit trim or by-the-yard tubular sweater-knit fabric.

Measuring and Cutting

Sometimes the hardest part of sewing ribbing is cutting it out. It slides and curls as you try to pin that long, narrow pattern piece to the fabric. This measuring and cutting technique does not require a pattern piece. It works equally well whether you're sewing ribbing on a conventional machine or a serger.

● *Width:*

● Decide on a finished width. If you have a pattern piece for ribbing, use it as a guide. Double the

finished width and then add 1¼" (3.2cm) for seam allowances.

● Fold the ribbing lengthwise into two to four thicknesses, mark the width, and cut out the band. Be sure to position the band crosswise with the ribs running up and down so that the greatest amount of stretch goes around the body.

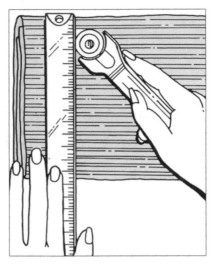

● *Length:*

Now that your band is the desired width, the next step is to determine how long it should be.

● Using your pattern pieces as a guide, measure the garment opening, eliminating any seam allowances.

● For a crew neck, the length of the band should equal two-thirds the length of the neckline opening.

● For a **V**-neck, **U**-neck, waistband or cuff, the length of the band should equal three-quarters the length of the garment opening.

● Before you actually cut the ribbing into what you've determined to be the correct length, check

your calculations by pin fitting. To do this, mark off the length, pin the ribbing together, slide it over the appropriate part of the body and analyze the fit. Ankle bands must slide over the widest part of the foot, neckbands over the head, and waistbands must slide down over the shoulders or up over the hips.

● Now add 1¼" (3.2cm) to the pin-fit length measurement to allow for the two ⅝" (1.5cm) seam allowances.

● Cut the band to the correct length.

The Flat Method

Since it's easiest to apply rib knit trim while the garment is still flat, leave one side seam, shoulder seam, leg seam or the sleeve seam unstitched.

● With wrong sides together, fold the band in half lengthwise and baste the edges together.

● Use pin markers to divide the garment into sections. Repeat on the band. Pin the band to the garment, matching the pin markings.

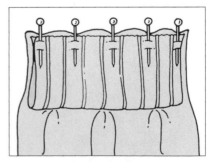

● With the band side up, machine-stitch the ⅝" (1.5cm) seam, stretching the ribbing to fit

tip

If you own a rotary cutter, use it to cut the ribbing. It will do a better job than scissors, especially through several thicknesses. To maintain an even cut, use a straight-edge ruler as a guide.

between the markings. Stitch again within the seam allowance, ¼" (6mm) from the first stitching, using a straight stitch or a zigzag stitch. Trim close to the stitching. *Or* serge on your serger.

● Press the seam allowance toward the garment.

● Stitch the garment seam allowance, beginning at the folded edge of the band. Stitch again within the seam allowance, ¼" (6mm) from the first stitching. Trim the seam allowance close to the stitching. *Or*, using your serger, chain for 2" (5cm) and then lift the presser foot. Slide the folded edge of the band under it and serge the seam.

● Press.

STITCH GARMENT SEAM SECOND

JOIN GARMENT TO RIBBING FIRST

S *The Round Method*

Many sewers shy away from sewing with sweater knits, stretch terrycloth or stretch velour because they think that the ribbing will be difficult to work with. You'll be delighted at how easy it is to attach it with your serger.

● With right sides together, serge the side seam to form a circle.

● Fold the band in half, wrong sides together, so the raw edges meet, and pin. If the ribbing curls, baste the edges together with a long, wide zigzag stitch on your conventional machine.

● Mark the band into quarters with pins or a marking pen. Do the same for the garment opening.

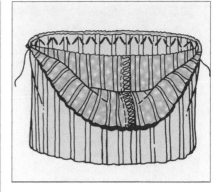

● With right sides together, pin the band to the garment opening, matching markings. Position the seam in the band so it matches a garment seam. With the band side up, serge, stretching the ribbing to fit the opening. Press the seam allowance toward the garment, as shown below.

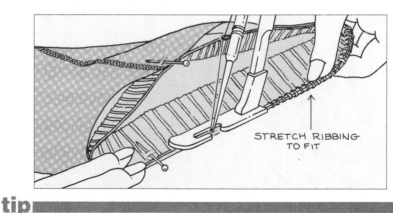

STRETCH RIBBING TO FIT

tip

S *Incorporate elastic thread into the seam when attaching ribbing to a garment. As you serge, the seam won't stretch out...and when you wear the garment it will maintain its elasticity. You may have a special hole in the presser foot of your serger to assist you in guiding the elastic. If not, guide the elastic by hand over the presser foot so it is caught in the chain as you serge. Do not stretch the elastic as you sew or the seam will pucker. The feed system of your serger will ease the ribbing for you.*
● *Pin the ribbing to the garment edge. Working with the ribbing side up, hold the ribbing up against the toe of your presser foot with your right hand. As you serge, catch the elastic thread in the seam.*
● *Serge the remaining garment seam, catching and securing the elastic in the stitching.*

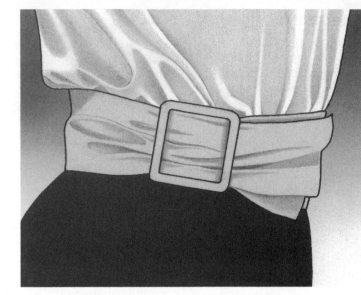

tip

Because heat and steam can distort the ribbing, press it carefully. To press a seam, hold the iron above it and apply steam until any ripples disappear from the seam allowances and the ribbing returns to its unstretched state. Gently press the seam allowances toward the garment by lifting the iron up and putting it back down. Let the ribbing dry thoroughly before you handle it again.

● For the ready-to-wear-look, use your conventional machine and a twin needle to topstitch on both sides of the seamline.

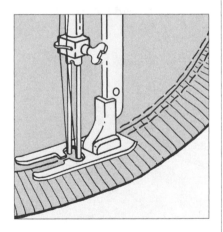

BELTS AND BELT LOOPS

Belts add the finishing touch to many ensembles. In fact, your local fabric store is probably a wonderful source for a wide array of gorgeous buckles.

COVERED BELTS

If you're going to make your own covered belt, check your fabric store for the stiffening material that is specifically designed to use inside belts. It's available in several widths and has the right blend of rigidity and flexibility necessary for a belt that is comfortable but won't curl. Don't be tempted to substitute several layers of interfacing. You'll end up with a belt that collapses into folds after several wearings. The stiffening material is sold by the yard or in kits with an accompanying buckle to cover. If it's your first belt, buy the kit and follow its directions to cover the belting.

SOFT BELTS

Done on either the conventional machine or serger, this simple stitched-and-turned method can be used to make a fabric sash or a soft, crushed belt that's attached to a slip-through buckle.

The Conventional Method

● Cut a lengthwise strip of fabric that's equal to the desired length plus 1¼" (3.2cm) and twice the desired width plus 1¼" (3.2cm).

● With right sides together, fold the belt in half lengthwise.

● Stitch along the ⅝" (1.5cm) seamline, leaving an opening at the center back for turning. To secure the stitching, backstitch at the corners and at either end of the opening.

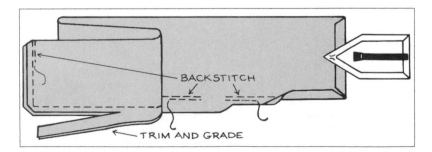

BACKSTITCH

TRIM AND GRADE

tip

Use a ruler to turn the belt right side out. Push one end toward, and out through, the opening. Repeat for the other end.

- Trim the seams and corners. If possible, press the seam allowances open. Otherwise, press the top seam allowance toward the body of the sash. This ensures that your finished sash will have crisp edges.

- Turn the belt right side out, press and slipstitch the opening closed.

S *The Serger Method*

- Cut a lengthwise strip of fabric that's equal to the desired length plus 1¼" (3.2cm) and twice the desired width plus 1¼" (3.2cm).

- With wrong sides together, fold the belt in half lengthwise.

- Serge around the outside edges as shown below. For fine fabrics, use all-purpose thread and a rolled hem. For heavy fabrics, try pearl cotton or ¹⁄₁₆" (2mm) silk or rayon ribbon in the upper looper.

STRETCH BELTS

Stretch belting and elasticized trims are available by the yard in a wide range of widths and styles, from solid colors to simple patterning to elaborately embellished surfaces. For the most gala evenings, there's even sequined or beaded stretch trim.

Purchase enough stretch belting or trim to fit comfortably around your waist, plus 2" (5cm). Buy a clasp buckle or interlocking buckle that fits the width of your trim.

- To keep the ends of the belting from raveling, seal them with Fray Check™, finish them on the serger or trim them with pinking shears.

- Slip the ends of the belting through each half of the buckle and fold back 1" (2.5cm).

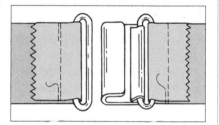

- Pin and stitch the edges in place, backstitching to secure. If your stretch belting is sequined or beaded, stitch by hand.

BELT LOOPS

No matter what type of belt you choose to make or buy, belt loops will help it stay put when you wear your garment. On a garment without a waistline seam they'll serve as anchors to keep the hemline from shifting and dipping as you stand up and sit down.

Placement

A pattern that calls for fabric loops will include a pattern piece and markings for placement. If you're adding loops, center them over the waistline. Plan on at least three loops—one at center back and one at each side seam. If your belt has a heavy buckle, you might want to add them to the front. Depending on the style of buckle, position one slightly off center, so that it's hidden from view when the buckle is fastened, or add two, each one midway between the side seam and the center front.

Fabric Loops

If you want fabric loops, and the instructions aren't included in your pattern, do the following:

- Cut a strip of fabric along the selvage, three times the width of the finished loop. To determine how long this strip should be, add ¾"

tip

Many sewers—even those with a great deal of experience—find it difficult to achieve the same crisp look that they admire on ready-to-wear covered belts. The solution is to get a professional to do it for you. Ask at your favorite fabric store or look in your local Yellow Pages. If you can't find a hometown source, there are mail-order companies that will do it for you. Look in the advertising section of your favorite sewing publication.

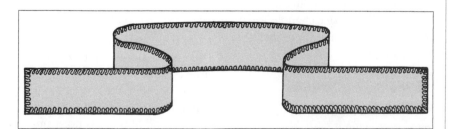

(2cm) to the width of the belt and then multiply by the number of loops.

● Fold the strip lengthwise in thirds with the selvage on top. Edgestitch along both folded edges.

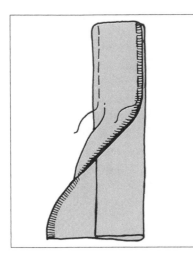

● Cut apart into the desired number of loops.

● To attach the loops to the garment, press the short ends under ¼" (6mm). Position one loop at each marking. Topstitch it to the garment by machine or slipstitch in place by hand.

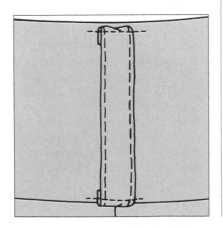

S *If your serger can do a narrow rolled hem, you can also use that stitch setting to create a thread chain suitable for loops. Set the machine for a narrow rolled edge and serge, without feeding fabric through the machine.*

Machine Thread Loops

On many ready-to-wear garments, fine thread chains are used as belt loops or button loops at the cuffs or neckline. They're not bulky and they're almost invisible.

The Conventional Method

● Take two or three lengths of fine cording, such as buttonhole twist, crochet cotton or tatting thread, and twist them tightly together.

● Stitch over them twice using a close, narrow zigzag stitch.

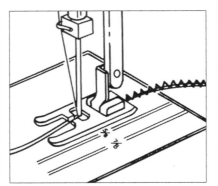

● Cut the thread chain into loops. To make them easy to handle, each loop should be three times its finished length.

S The Serger Method

● Thread the machine with all-purpose sewing thread that

matches the garment fabric. Set the tensions for general serging and shorten the stitch length so that the stitches lock into a tight chain.

● Serge a chain that is three times the finished length of each loop. As you serge, pull tightly on the thread tails so that the chain comes off the stitch fingers smoothly.

● Cut the chain apart into the desired number of lengths.

● Attaching the Chains:

Once you have made the chains, either by the conventional or serger method, you will need to attach them to the garment. Do one of the following

● Make the belt loops first; then catch them in the seamline as the garment is sewn together.

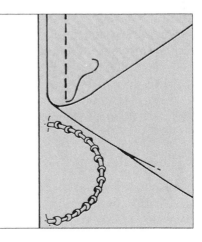

Or

● Sew the garment together first. Then, thread the loop through the large eye of a needle. Insert the needle between the stitches in a seamline or between the threads of the fabric (if there is no seamline) and gently pull the tail of the thread chain to the wrong side of the garment. Knot to secure. Repeat for the other end of the loop.

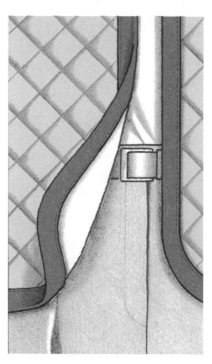

BINDINGS

Bindings are a clever way to decorate and finish a raw edge at the same time. Some patterns already include bindings as a design detail. Don't, however, feel you're limited to putting binding on only these patterns.

● Used at necklines, armholes, even hemline edges, bindings are an alternative to facings.

● Made in a contrasting color, bindings are a great way to liven up a simple garment, particularly for children's clothes.

● On sheers, narrow, self-fabric (i.e., cut from your fashion fabric) bindings eliminate unsightly facing show-through. The drawing on page 146 illustrates the use of this technique.

● Bindings are an easy way to finish the edges of a reversible garment, such as a jacket or vest.

● Bindings are a popular way to add emphasis to home decorating items such as placemats, napkins, tablecloths and curtain edges.

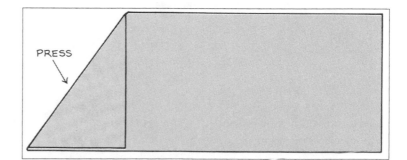

If your pattern calls for binding, check the back of the pattern envelope to determine the recommended binding width. Most patterns are designed for a ¼" (6mm) or ½"(1.3cm) finished width. You can make your own bias binding, or purchase double-fold bias tape or foldover braid.

MAKING CUSTOM BINDING

To provide give and flexibility, cut binding on the bias.

The continuous bias method is an easy way to mark and join make-your-own bias strips.

● Cut a rectangle of fashion fabric. The longer side of the rectangle can follow either the lengthwise or the crosswise grain of your fabric. Trim each side of the rectangle so that it exactly follows a thread of fabric.

● Fold one corner of the rectangle so that the crosswise and the lengthwise edges meet, and press; then open out the rectangle. (This crease is the true bias.)

● Cut a cardboard template the width required for your bias strips. Each strip should be four times the width of the finished binding.

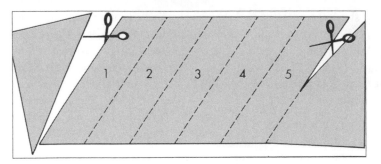

For example, for ¼" (6mm) finished binding width, mark 1" (2.5cm) wide strips; for ½" (1.3cm) binding, mark 2" (5cm) wide strips. Using the crease as your starting point and the cardboard template as your guide, pencil-mark parallel lines across the width of the fabric until you reach a corner.

● Cut off the triangles of un-marked fabric at either end of the rectangle.

● With right sides together, fold the fabric into a tube. Match the pencil lines so that one width of binding extends beyond the edge on each side. Sew a ¼" (6mm) seam and press open.

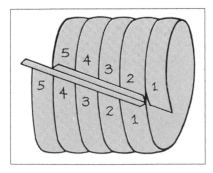

● Starting at one end cut along the pencil line, working your way around the tube until you've sepa-rated it into one long, continuous strip.

PIECING INDIVIDUAL STRIPS

You may not have enough fabric left over after cutting out your project to make a rectangle large enough to construct one long continuous strip…or you may need to piece strips of purchased binding. In either case, here's the professional-looking way to join them:

● Using bias-cut strips of the required width and with right sides together, pin the ends of the strips so they form a right (90°) angle. Stitch a ¼" (6mm) seam.

tips

● *If you're adding binding to a pattern that doesn't call for it, trim off the seam allowances on the garment edge(s) that will be encased in the binding. To determine how much binding you will need, measure the cut edges and then add at least ¹/4 yd. (23cm) for piecing and seam allowances.*

● *If your fabric is 45" (115cm) wide, a 5" x 45" (12.5cm x 115cm) rectangle will yield approxi-mately 2½ yds. (2.3m) of ½" (1.3cm) finished width binding or 5 yds. (4.6m) of ¹/4" (6mm) finished width binding.*

● Press the seam open and trim away the points that extend beyond the edge of the binding.

TWO-STEP APPLICATION METHOD FOR CUSTOM BINDING OR DOUBLE-FOLD BIAS TAPE

Because it's the fastest method, most patterns tell you to apply the binding entirely by machine. However, many sewers find it diffi-cult to achieve professional results using this method. The following combination of machine and hand sewing may take you a few minutes longer, but that extra time will pay off in great results!

● When applying 1" (2.5cm) bias strips, use ¼" (6mm) seams.

● When applying 2" (5cm) bias strips, use ½" (1.3cm) seams.

● When applying double-fold bias tape, unfold it and follow the creases for your seam widths.
   On binding that you've made yourself, fold and press under one long edge before you begin. The fold should be equal to one-fourth of the width of the binding. This will give you the folded edge you need for **Step 2**.

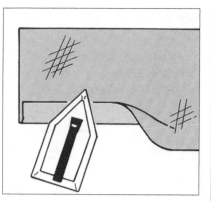

Step 1: With right sides together, machine stitch the binding to the garment edge. Press the seam toward the binding.

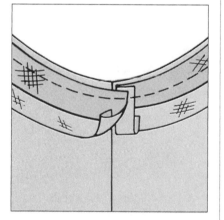

Step 2: Turn the folded edges of the binding to the inside so that it encases the raw edge and just covers the stitching line. Slip-stitch in place.

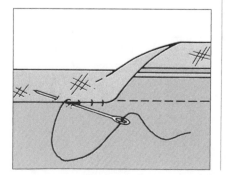

tip

*Begin and end the binding at an inconspicuous seam, such as the center back or underarms. Press under one short end of the binding. As you machine-stitch for **Step 1**, lap the unpressed end over the pressed end. (On the outside, the pressed end will be on top and visible.)*

At an Outside Corner:

Before you begin, use a fabric marking pen or dressmaker's pencil to mark where the seam allowances intersect at the corner.

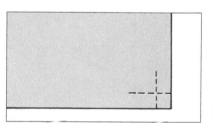

- Follow **Step 1**, ending your stitching where the seamlines intersect at the corner. Backstitch one or two stitches and cut the thread.

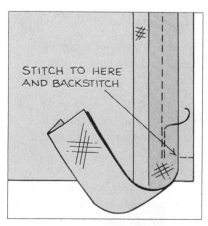

STITCH TO HERE AND BACKSTITCH

- Fold the binding back on itself to create a diagonal crease at the cor-

ner. Now fold the binding back again so that this new fold is even with the edge of the binding on side A and the seamlines of binding and garment match on side B.

- Insert the needle exactly at the corner marking and continue stitching.

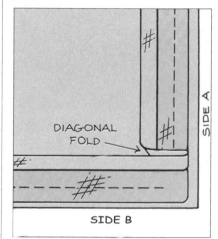

DIAGONAL FOLD

SIDE A

SIDE B

- Finish as in **Step 2**, making a diagonal fold at the corner and slipstitching the binding in place. If desired, slipstitch the corner folds also.

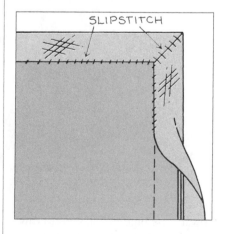

SLIPSTITCH

At an Inside Corner:

- Reinforce the corner with small stitches along the seamline. Clip the corner just to the stitches.

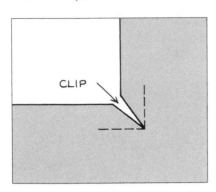

- Following **Step 1**, stitch binding to one fabric edge. Stop stitching when you reach the corner.

- Keeping the needle in the fabric, raise the presser foot and spread the fabric open at the clip so that it lines up with the edge of the binding. Lower the presser foot and continue stitching.

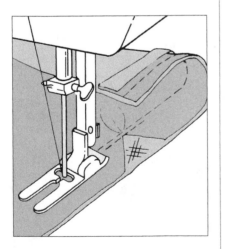

- Press the seam allowances toward the binding. As you do this, a diagonal fold will form at the corner, as shown at the top of the next column.

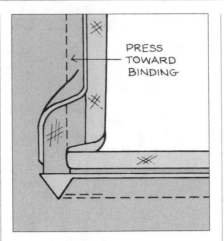

- Finish as in **Step 2**, forming another diagonal fold at the corner. If desired, slipstitch the corner folds.

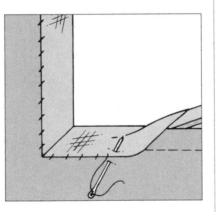

EDGESTITCHED APPLICATION

Use this method with purchased double-fold bias tape or foldover braid.

- Slip the binding over the raw garment edge and pin or baste in place. Note that these tapes and braids are folded so that one side is slightly wider than the other. Always sandwich your fabric between the folds with the wider side of the tape on the bottom. Then, working on the right side of the fabric, edgestitch the tape in place.

At an Outside Corner:

- Edgestitch the binding all the way to the perpendicular edge of the fabric. Remove the fabric from the machine and cut the threads.

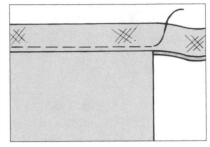

- Turn the binding around the corner and down the next side. Pin.

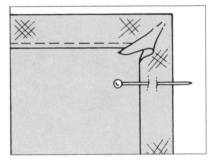

- Make a diagonal fold in the binding on both sides of the corner; press.

- Beginning just below the diagonal fold, backstitch to fold; then edgestitch along the binding. If desired, slipstitch the corner folds.

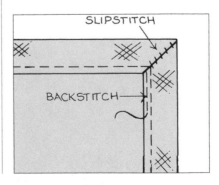

tips

● *To begin and end the binding, press under one short end. As you apply the binding, lap the pressed end over the unpressed end. Do this at an inconspicuous place on the garment, such as the center back or underarm.*

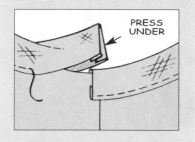

PRESS UNDER

● *To keep the binding from shifting as you sew, apply glue stick to the inside of the binding and then press it into position. Let the glue dry; then edge-stitch.*

At an Inside Corner

● Reinforce the corner with small machine stitches. Clip the corner just to the stitches.

● Edgestitch the binding to the garment, stopping when you reach the corner.

STOP HERE AND RAISE PRESSER FOOT

REINFORCE CORNER

● Keeping the needle in the fabric, raise the presser foot and spread the fabric to transform the corner into a straight edge. Slip the binding back over the fabric, lower the presser foot, and continue edgestitching.

INSIDE CORNER

● Press the binding at the corner so that a diagonal fold forms on both sides of the garment. If desired, slipstitch the corner folds to keep them in place.

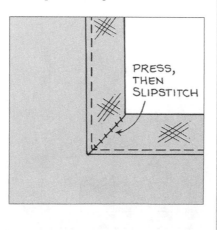

PRESS, THEN SLIPSTITCH

tip

Be careful not to stretch the binding as you sew, particularly when you are working on a curved edge. You may find it helpful to use steam to preshape the binding before you apply it. Pin the binding to your ironing board in a curve that matches the shape of the garment edge. Using a generous amount of steam, shrink out the excess full-ness, let the binding dry, and then attach it to the garment.

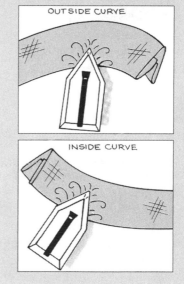

OUTSIDE CURVE

INSIDE CURVE

CASINGS AND ELASTIC

When elastic or a drawstring is used to control fullness in a garment, it is often inserted into a tunnel of fabric called a casing. However, with some techniques, the casing is created at the same time the elastic is applied. This is called the direct application method. Elastic can also be applied directly to a garment edge with no casing at all. These exposed applications are commonly used on lingerie.

tip

S*To reduce bulk on a folded casing, finish the raw edge on your serger instead of turning it under ¼" (6mm). Knits and firmly woven fabrics do not have to be pressed under and they don't have to be machine-finished either.*

TUNNEL CASINGS

There are three common types of tunnel casings:

● A *folded casing* (A) can be found at waistline, sleeve and pants leg edges. The pattern is designed with an extended garment edge that is pressed under ¼" (6mm), pressed under again along the foldline and then edgestitched along both folds.

● An *applied casing* (B) is a bias strip that is sewn to the edge of the garment, then folded to the inside and stitched close to both edges of the casing. When you're done, it looks like a folded casing from the outside of the garment. This technique is used in place of a folded casing if the garment edge is shaped or curved.

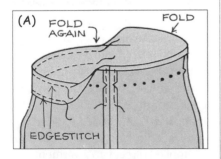

(A) FOLD AGAIN FOLD
EDGESTITCH

● A *bias casing* (C) is created by applying single fold bias tape or a strip of bias fabric a specified dis-

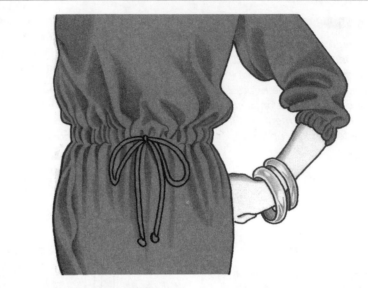

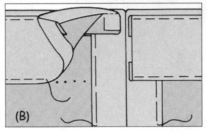

(B)

tance from a garment edge. Bias casings are often used on the inside of a one-piece dress, a tunic or a jacket to create waistline defintion. If the bias casing is placed a short distance in from a garment edge, a heading or ruffle forms at that edge once the elastic is inserted.

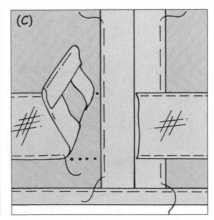

(C)

tip

Use a sheer tricot seam binding, such as Seams Great®, or Seam Saver™, as a lightweight substitute for bias tape. No need to turn the raw edges under as they will not fray.

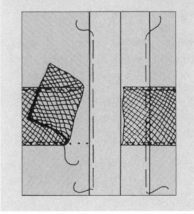

General Information

● For accurate placement, be sure to mark necessary foldlines or stitching lines.

● To keep elastic from getting stuck in the seam allowances as it's inserted, use fusible web or machine basting to anchor them to the garment within the casing area. Do this before you create the casing.

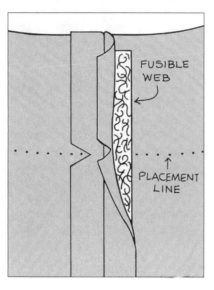

● Purchase elastic that is ⅛" to ¼" (3mm to 6mm) narrower than the casing or you'll have trouble inserting it.

● For a drawstring opening that occurs at a seamline, reinforce the opening with small pieces of lightweight fusible interfacing or by adding small squares of seam binding when backstitching.

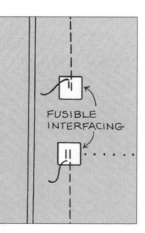

tips

● *Before applying a bias casing, use steam to preshape the tape into a curve that matches the garment edge.*

● *If your fabric is too bulky, too scratchy or too loosely woven for a folded casing, make an applied facing instead. Use the casing foldline as your seamline.*

Inserting Elastic

● Cut the elastic 1" (2.5cm) larger that the body measurement or according to the pattern guides.

● Fasten a safety pin or bodkin to one end of the elastic and thread it through the casing opening. To prevent accidentally pulling the elastic all of the way through the casing, before inserting one end of the elastic into the casing opening, use a safety pin to anchor the other end of the elastic to the garment just below the casing.

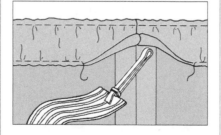

tip

If you're making a one-piece garment, you may want to change the design slightly to add waistline definition. To do this, make a bias casing, centering it over the waistline marking on your pattern and then insert elastic through the casing.

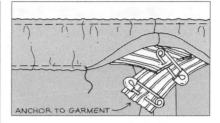

● Overlap the ends of the elastic ½" (1.3cm), and stitch together in a square or with parallel rows of stitches. (*Note:* If you have any doubt about the fit, try the garment on and pin-fit the elastic before permanently securing it.) Stitch the casing opening closed.

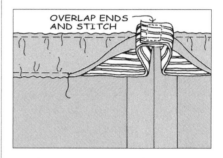

● To keep the elastic from rolling and twisting during wear, stitch in the ditch (the groove) formed by each seam.

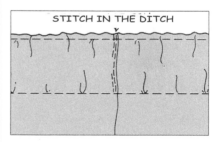

DIRECT APPLICATION METHODS

With these methods, you stitch through the elastic so there's no chance of the elastic twisting or curling.

tip

Many of these elastic application methods suggest dividing and marking the elastic and the garment edge into quarters. However, if you're a beginning sewer, or if you're working on a long edge, you'll have an easier time if you divide and mark into eighths.

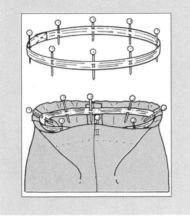

Hidden Elastic, The Conventional Method

Use this quick technique to create a casing at the edge of a garment and apply the elastic at the same time. It's a no-twist method suitable for knits or wovens that won't ravel and for aerobic wear, swimwear and lingerie.

● Cut the elastic the required length, generally 3" (7.5cm) smaller than the body measurement. Overlap the ends ½" (1.3cm) and stitch.

● Trim the seam allowance on the garment edge to equal the width of the elastic.

● Divide the elastic and the garment edge into quarters or eighths and mark.

Pin the elastic to the wrong side of the garment, matching the markings and keeping the edge of the elastic even with the edge of the garment. Zigzag, overcast or straight stitch the elastic to the edge of the garment. Be sure to stretch the elastic to fit as you sew.

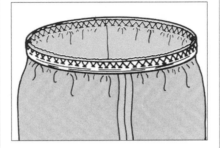

● Fold the elastic to the inside of the garment. Stitch close to the raw edge of the fabric, through all of the layers, with a straight or a zigzag stitch. Again, stretch the elastic to fit as you sew. For increased stretch and recovery, use a straight stitch with elastic thread in the bobbin (see TIP, page 125) or a zigzag stitch with nylon thread in the top and the bobbin.

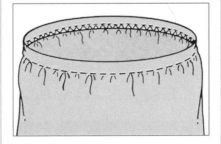

Hidden Elastic, ⑤The Serger Method

Here's where your serger really shines!

● Adjust your serger to the appropriate settings (see chart, page 125).

tip

⑤ *When applying elastic with the serger, you'll find it easier to serge it on straight if there's a wide margin of fabric for the serger's blade to trim away. Before you cut out your pattern, check the distance between the foldline and the cut edge of the garment. It should be at least ½" (1.3cm) wider than the width of the elastic. For ¼" (6mm) wide elastic, you should have at least a ¾" (2cm) wide seam allowance; for ⅜" (1cm) wide elastic, at least a ⅞" (2.2cm) wide seam allowance. If necessary, adjust the seam allowances before you cut out the garment.*

● Leave one seam open. Divide and mark the elastic into quarters or eighths.

● Divide and mark the garment edge into quarters or eighths.

● Pin the elastic to the wrong side of the garment, placing the inside edge along the foldline and matching the markings.

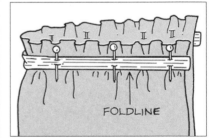

FOLDLINE

● With the elastic side up, position the outer edge of the elastic next to the blade. Serge, holding the elastic next to the blade. Serge a couple of stitches to anchor the elastic. Be careful—don't cut the elastic! Continue serging, holding

Hidden Elastic Application			
TYPE OF SERGER STITCH:	**3**	**4**	**MINE**
Stitch length:	4mm-5mm	4mm-5mm	
Stitch width:	Widest	Widest	
Tensions—Needle:	Tight	Tight	
Right needle:	N/A	N/A	
Upper looper:	Normal*	Normal*	
Lower looper:	Normal	Normal	
*Can use woolly nylon thread.			

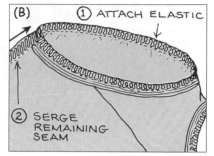

the elastic up slightly off the fabric against the toe of the presser foot and stretching the elastic to fit between the pins. *Remember to remove the pins before the presser foot reaches them* (A).

• Adjust your serger to a balanced stitch setting and serge the remaining seam all of the way up through the elastic (B).

• Fold the elastic to the inside of the garment. Using your conventional machine, stitch close to the edge of the fabric, through all of the layers. To keep this row of stitches from popping when you wear the garment, use elastic

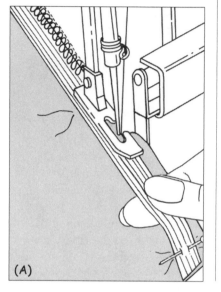

thread in the bobbin or use a zigzag stitch and nylon thread in the top and bobbin (C).

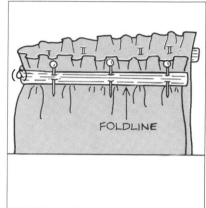

tip

Here's a technique borrowed directly from ready-to-wear swimwear and aerobic wear:

For your final row of stitches, put elastic thread in the bobbin and stitch with the right side of the garment facing you. For best results, use nylon thread in the needle.

• *How you wind the bobbin threads depends on how your conventional machine is designed. If it has a self-winding bobbin, wind the elastic thread by hand, stretching it slightly. If you must remove the bobbin case to wind it, guide the elastic thread onto the bobbin while it's turning on the bobbin winder, being careful not to stretch it.*

• *If your bobbin case has a tension bypass hole, insert the elastic thread through it, replace the bobbin case and bring the thread up through the hole in the throat plate. This gives you a lighter bobbin tension (see illustration at right.)*

• *Set your machine for a straight stitch, 3mm long or 8 stitches per inch.*

• *Working on the right side of the garment, topstitch close to the inner edge of the elastic, through all the layers.*

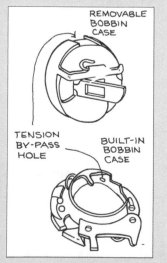

Flatlock Elastic Application			
TYPE OF SERGER STITCH:	3	4	MINE
Stitch length:	3mm-4mm	3mm-4mm	
Stitch width:	Widest	Widest	
Tensions-Needle:	Very loose	Very loose	
Right Needle:	N\A	N\A	
Upper Looper:	N/A	Loose	
Lower Looper:	Normal	Very tight	

S Flatlock or Exposed Application

This professional one-step application makes for fast sewing and comfortable wearing. Because the elastic is exposed, this technique is most frequently used for lingerie. For the most attractive results, use lingerie elastic, a soft, stretchy elastic with one picot or decorative edge.

- Adjust your serger to the appropriate setting (see chart above.)

- Leave one garment seam open. Divide and mark the elastic into quarters or eighths.

- Divide and mark the garment edge into quarters or eighths.

- Position the elastic so that the straight edge is along the foldline. If you want the seam to be flat against the body, with the ladder stitches on the outside, pin the elastic to the right side of the fabric. If you want the seam on the outside, with the ladder stitches against the body, pin the elastic to the wrong side of the fabric.

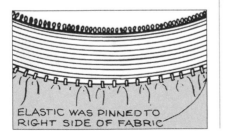

ELASTIC WAS PINNED TO RIGHT SIDE OF FABRIC

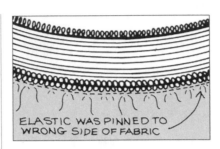

ELASTIC WAS PINNED TO WRONG SIDE OF FABRIC

- With the elastic side up, position the straight edge of the elastic next to the blade. Serge a couple of stitches to anchor the elastic. Be careful—don't cut the elastic! Continue serging, holding the elastic up slightly off the fabric, against the toe of the foot. As you do this, stretch the elastic to fit between the pins. Remember to remove the pins as you come to them.

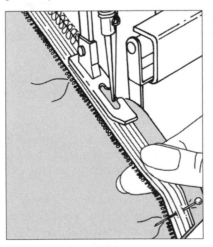

- Pull on the elastic until the picot edge is up and the seam is flat.

- Adjust your serger for a balanced

stitch setting and serge the remaining seam all the way up through the elastic.

tip

S *Get some practice on your serger and make yourself a quick present, 1-2-3. Using an old half-slip as a guide, cut a piece of tricot the desired width and length. Allow 1½" (3.2cm) for side seams and ½" (1.3cm) for the waistline seam.*

1. Flatlock a piece of the flat lace to one end of the slip. (See "Trims," page 185.)

2. Attach elastic to the other end using the flatlock method.

3. Adjust your serger for a balanced stitch setting and serge the side seam. For a bit of custom comfort, cover the seam in the elastic with a piece of ribbon. Use a dot of glue stick to hold it in place and then stitch it on your machine. That's it!

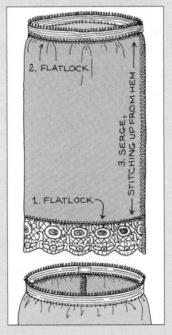

2. FLATLOCK

3. SERGE, STITCHING UP FROM HEM

1. FLATLOCK

CLOSURES

When you make a garment, you—not the pattern company—are the ultimate designer. This means that you can make the closures as subtle or as obvious as you wish. Buttons can match or contrast… or be replaced by snaps, toggles, frogs, ties or self-gripping hook and loop fasteners, such as Velcro®.

Other than the quickie serger technique for making ties that appears at the end of this section, closures are sewn on by hand or on the conventional sewing machine. Here's where your serger gets a rest!

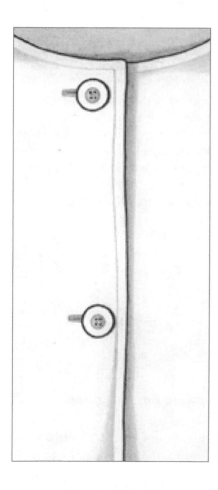

BUTTONS AND BUTTONHOLES

Once upon a time, anyone who learned to sew had to struggle with learning how to make bound buttonholes. Not so in today's machine age! Look around you at some of the most expensive ready-to-wear garments. Even their buttonholes are made by machine.

In Chapter 5, we talked about the importance of making friends with your sewing machine. Here's one place it really pays off. Take a rainy weekend afternoon to practice making buttonholes in a variety of fabrics. Read your sewing machine manual and learn what, if any, tension or pressure adjustments are required.

If you're not satisfied with the buttonholes your machine makes, do one of the following:

● Take it to the dealer and get it cleaned and overhauled. Bring your sample buttonholes with you so the dealer can see where you are having problems.

● Find someone else to make them for you. Ask at your local fabric store and check out the Yellow Pages.

● Consider substituting with a closure that doesn't require buttonholes. Sometimes the substitute is a better choice. For example, small children who are learning to dress themselves will find Velcro® closures easier to maneuver than buttons and buttonholes.

Some Button and Buttonhole Basics:

● Stick to the button size recommended on the pattern envelope. If you can't find a button you like in the right size, don't go more than ⅛" (3mm) larger or smaller. Otherwise, either the buttons will look out of proportion on the garment, or the buttonholes will have to be respaced.

● Always make a test buttonhole first on a scrap of fabric. Use the same number of layers (fashion fabric, interfacing, facing, etc.) as the garment will have.

● To make sure your buttonholes are accurately placed, begin stitching horizontal buttonholes at the marking closest to the garment edge; begin stitching vertical buttonholes at the marking closest to the upper edge of the garment.

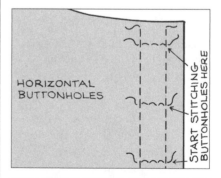

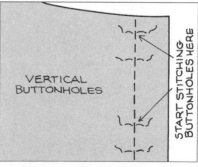

tip

If your fabric doesn't feed evenly through the machine when making buttonholes, try using a piece of nonwoven stabilizer such as Trace Erase™ or Stitch-n-Tear™ underneath all the layers. If your fabric is very sheer or very fragile, try putting the stabilizer both on the bottom and on the top. It's easy to tear it away once the buttonholes are completed.

Transferring the Markings

Buttonhole placement should be marked on the right side of your fabric. You can do this during the cutting and marking stage, when you transfer all of the other markings, or you can wait until just before you're ready to stitch.

Even if you carefully marked the placement lines when you cut out the garment, it's a good idea to re-check them when you're ready to make the buttonholes. Here's how:

● Place the pattern tissue on top of the garment, aligning the pattern seamline with the garment opening edge.

● Stick pins straight through the tissue and the fabric at both ends of each marking; then carefully remove the pattern without disturbing the pins.

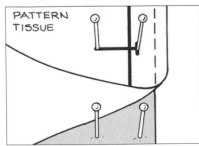

PATTERN TISSUE

● If appropriate for your fabric, mark between the pins with a water-soluble or evaporating marking pen. If these are not suitable, place a strip of ½" (1.3cm) wide transparent tape or masking tape alongside, but a scant ⅛" (3mm) away from, the pins. Mark the position of each pin on the tape. When you make the buttonhole, stitch next to the tape, being careful not to stitch through it. Caution: Tape mars some fabrics. Test first on a scrap of the fabric, experimenting with cellophane tape and masking tape.

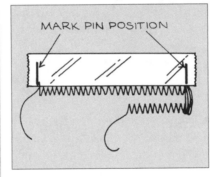

MARK PIN POSITION

Determining Buttonhole Size

The buttonhole markings on the pattern tissue indicate the placement, not the size, of the buttonhole. Buttons are sized according to their diameter. However, it is a button's circumference that determines how large the buttonhole needs to be. For example, a ⅝" (1.5cm) flat button will require a smaller buttonhole than a ⅝" (1.5cm) domed button.

● To determine the circumference, wrap a piece of narrow ribbon, seam binding or twill tape around the widest part of the button and pin the ends together.

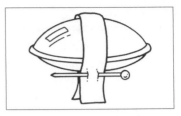

● The length of your test buttonhole should be equal to half the circumference plus ⅛" (3mm). If your button is very thick, you may need to increase the size a little bit more. Test the size before making any buttonholes on your garment.

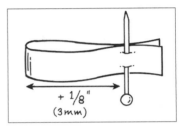

+ ⅛" (3mm)

Cutting the Buttonhole Open

Once all of the buttonholes are stitched, cut them open using a razor blade, X-acto® knife and a cutting board, buttonhole cutter, seam ripper or a pair of small, sharp scissors. Start at the center and cut toward each end. To prevent cutting too far, put a straight pin at each end of the buttonhole opening.

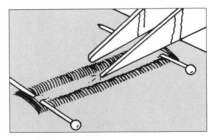

Sewing on the Button

Buttons come in two styles: Sew-through and shank. The shank is designed to compensate for the

tip

A liquid seam sealant, such as Fray Check™, is a great remedy for buttonhole bloopers.

- *If you cut into the stitches, repair the damage with a dot of the seam sealant.*
- *If fabric "whiskers" develop along the cut edges of your buttonhole, trim off all of the loose threads and then treat the edges with a thin beading of Fray Check™. If the Fray Check comes out of the bottle too fast, apply it with a very fine paintbrush. Wipe off the bristles immediately or the brush will be too stiff to use again.*

thickness of the garment layers. On sew-through buttons, you'll need to use thread to create a shank. You do this at the same time as you sew on the button.

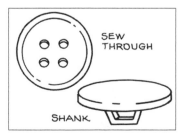

- ● *To locate the button position:*

After making the buttonholes and cutting them open, lap the gar-

ment edges, matching centers, so the garment looks buttoned.

- For a horizontal buttonhole, stick a pin through at the center front or back marking, ⅛" (3mm) in from the end of the buttonhole.

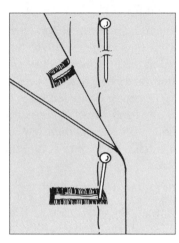

- For a vertical buttonhole, insert the pin ⅛" (3mm) below the top of the buttonhole.

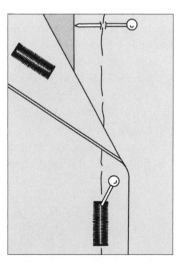

- ● *To attach the button by hand:*

- Thread the needle with a double thread. Take a few small backstitches to lock the thread at the point of the pin marking.

tip

To sew on buttons super quickly, double your thread before passing it through the needle's eye. You'll be sewing with four strands instead of two, so you'll need to take only half as many stitches!

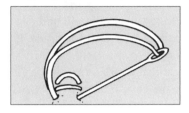

- Bring the needle through the button and back into the fabric. Repeat several times. To create a thread shank on a sew-through button, place a toothpick or wooden match on top of the button and sew over it. Sew back and forth several times; then remove the toothpick and wind the thread round and round the extra thread under the button. Stitch back into the fabric.

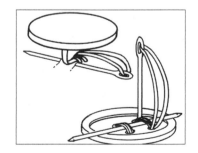

- Instead of making an ugly knot on the underside of your garment, do this:

1. Draw the needle to the underside of the garment and fasten the thread with several small, tight backstitches.

2. Insert the needle into the fabric and tunnel it between the garment layers for about 1" (2.5cm).

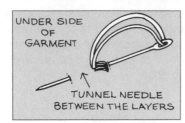

3. Bring the needle out and clip the thread close to the fabric. If your garment is only one layer thick or if your fabric is sheer, clip the thread close to the back-stitches instead of tunneling it.

tip

To add a shank to a button that is attached by machine, place a pin or a toothpick on top of the buttonhole foot before you begin to stitch. (Note: Check your manual. Some machines have a small accessory plate that will raise the button so there's no need for the tooth-pick.) When you are finished stitching, leave a 10" (25.5cm) tail. Bring the needle thread down through one of the but-ton's holes and wrap it around the shank several times. Using a hand-sewing needle, draw the needle thread to the wrong side of the fabric. Tie the needle and bobbin threads together in a knot.

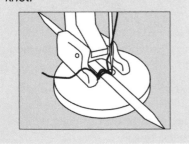

● *To attach the button by machine:*

If your sewing machine makes a zigzag stitch, you can probably use it to attach sew-through buttons by machine. It's a wonderful feature that many people overlook.

●Attach the buttonhole foot. Set the machine's stitch width to "0." Position the button and fabric under the foot so that the needle is in the center of the left hole. Turn the hand wheel to check the needle position, and then sew several stitches in place to secure the threads.

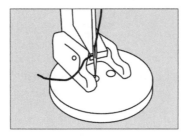

● Adjust the stitch width so that the needle will swing from the left hole to the right hole. (Check your manual for information. If you have a mechanical machine, it will recommend a stitch width setting. If you have a computerized machine, the setting, the number of stitches and the lockstitches will

be programmed into the machine.) Sew 8-10 stitches. To lock the stitches (unless this fea-ture is programmed into your machine), set the stitch width to "0," reposition the needle over the right hole and sew a few stitches.

● Remove fabric and button from the machine and clip the threads.

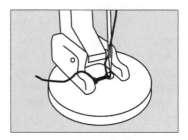

FROGS AND TOGGLES

Your pattern may recommend these two-part closures…or you can choose them as a substitute for buttons and buttonholes. In gen-eral, toggles add a sporty touch, while frogs are more decorative.

● Lap the garment edges so that the center fronts match, or make the edges meet if there is no overlap.

● Position the toggle or ball part of the closure on the left side of the garment and the loop part on the right, so that they close directly

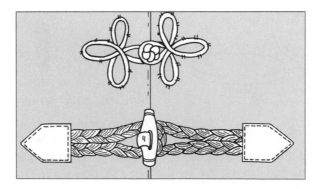

over the center front, as shown. (For men's clothes, the toggle part goes on the right and the loop part goes on the left.) Hold them in place with pins, double-faced basting tape or glue stick.

● Machine-stitch or hand-tack them in place, as appropriate (see illustration on previous page).

HOOKS AND EYES

Hooks and eyes may be used alone or in combination with another fastener, such as at the top of a zipper. They range in size from 0 to 4, for light- to heavyweight fabrics. Most hooks come with both loop eyes and straight eyes. Which eye you use depends on where the hook and eye fastener is placed on your garment.

For edges that meet, use a hook and loop eye:

● On the inside, sew the hook ⅛" (3mm) from the right-hand edge of the garment by making a few tacking stitches through the holes. Then sew across the end, under the curve of the hook.

● Position the eye opposite the hook, letting it extend slightly beyond the garment edge. Make a few tacking stitches through the holes. Take a few stitches along the sides of the loop to hold it flat.

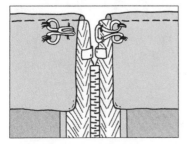

For edges that overlap, use a hook and straight eye. For a waistband, use two sets of regular hooks and eyes or one set of the heavy-duty-hooks and eyes especially designed for waistbands.

● Sew the hook(s) to the inside of the garment on the overlap, ⅛" (3mm) from the edge. Hand-tack in place, sewing through the holes, and then across the end, under the curve of the hook. Don't let the stitches for the hook(s) show on the outside of the garment.

● Close the zipper or other closures and then mark the eye position(s) with pins.

● Position the eyes on the outside of the underlap. Make a few tacking stitches through the holes.

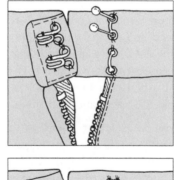

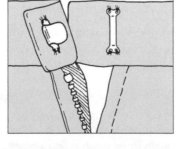

tip

When attaching hooks and eyes, your stitches should never show on the outside of the garment.

No-sew Hooks and Eyes

This type of waistband hook and eye requires no sewing—just hammer them or clamp them on. Use them on sturdy or firmly woven fabrics only. No-sew hooks and eyes should be applied before the waistband is finished, following the manufacturer's instructions.

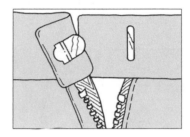

SNAPS

Snaps are used when a garment edge needs to be held flat but where there is no strain. Decorative snaps can be used as a substitute for buttons on loose-fitting, casual garments.

Snaps, like hooks and eyes, come in many sizes, for light- to heavyweight fabrics, and in sew-on and no-sew versions.

Sew-on Snaps

● Sew the ball half to the inside of the garment on the overlap. Positioning it approximately ⅛" (3mm) from the edge, make several tacking stitches through each hole. To keep the stitches from showing on the outside, pick up only one or two threads of fabric with each stitch and tunnel the needle between the layers of fabric as you go from hole to hole.

● To mark the socket position, close the garment and stick a pin

tip

Baste the snap sections in place with a dot of glue stick. Let them dry thoroughly before you sew.

through the center of the ball to underlap.

- Sew the socket half in place the same way as you did the ball half.

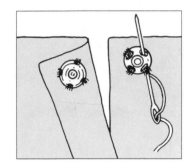

No-sew Snaps

These sturdy, hammer-on snaps are a fast substitute for buttons and buttonholes on children's garments and sportswear. Follow the package instructions to hammer them in place, or purchase a pliers-like tool which also comes with instructions.

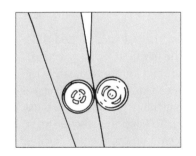

Snap Tape

Available in a range of colors, this tape comes with the snaps already attached. To apply, preshrink the tape first in hot water. Then, using a zipper foot, edgestitch the tape in place, turning the raw ends under. Sew the ball strip to the underlap and the socket strip to the overlap.

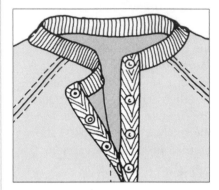

SELF-GRIPPING HOOK-AND-LOOP FASTENERS

These flexible, two-part fasteners (e.g., Velcro®) have tiny, stiff hooks and soft loops that interlock when you press them together. They're an easy substitute for buttons or snaps and are available in precut dots and squares or in strips. The light adhesive backing holds them in place for permanent stitching.

- Position each part at least ¼" (6mm) from the garment edge. The loop part goes on the overlap, the hook part on the underlap.

- To attach by machine, stitch the dots in a triangular pattern; edgestitch the squares and the strips.

tip

Ribbon is a quick and easy substitute for fabric ties. Pick matching or contrasting ribbon. To prevent raveling, notch the ends or cut diagonally. If necessary, apply a little bit of Fray Check™

If you don't want the stitching to show on the outside of the garment, hand-sew in place all around the edges.

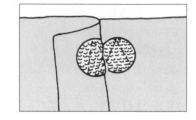

TIES

If your pattern calls for self-fabric ties, here's a quick way to make them. The method varies slightly, depending on whether you're using a conventional machine or a serger. But, either way, the result is a neat, narrow tube of fabric that can be used for ties, belt loops, button loops or spaghetti straps.

The Conventional Method

• Cut a piece of string twice the length of the finished tie, plus 5" (12.5cm).

• With right sides together, fold the tie in half lengthwise, placing the string inside the fold, as shown.

• Sew back and forth across the top of the tie to secure the end of the string. Stitch along the length of the tie, being careful not to catch the string in the stitching. This will be easier to do if you use your machine's zipper foot.

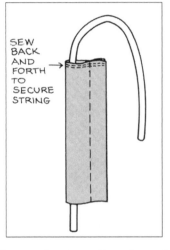

SEW BACK AND FORTH TO SECURE STRING

• To turn the tie, pull on the string.

• To remove the string, trim off the end where it is attached.

S The Serger Method

• Serge a chain the length of the tie, plus 2" (5cm). *Do not cut the chain*. Pull the chain around to the front of the foot.

• With right sides together, fold the tie in half lengthwise, placing the thread chain inside the fold.

• Serge the length of the tie, being careful not to catch the thread chains in the stitching.

• To turn the tie, pull on the inside chain (see below).

If you need to finish the ends, tie them in a knot or tuck them into the "tube" and slipstitch the openings closed.

COLLARS

In sewing terminology, a collar has two visible layers: The top layer, called the collar or upper collar, and the bottom layer, called the undercollar or facing. Almost every collar has a third, unseen layer of interfacing. Some collars, called one piece collars, are designed so

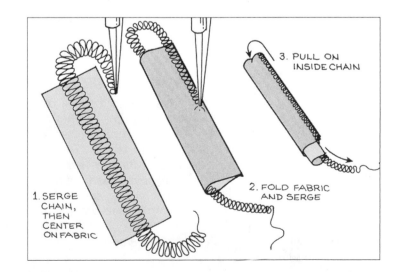

1. SERGE CHAIN, THEN CENTER ON FABRIC

2. FOLD FABRIC AND SERGE

3. PULL ON INSIDE CHAIN

that the undercollar is an extension of the upper collar. As a result, the outer edge is a fold rather than a seam.

Although there are many different fashion terms that describe collars, they all fall into three basic categories:

● A *flat collar* lies flat against the neck edge of the garment. If you compared the neckline seam of the collar with the neckline seam of the garment, you would find that the curves are almost identical.

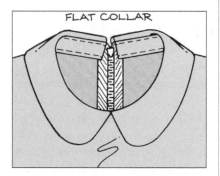

FLAT COLLAR

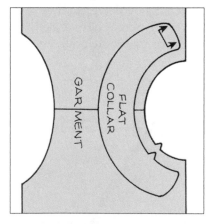

GARMENT / FLAT COLLAR

● A *rolled collar* rises straight up from the neck edge for a short distance and then rolls down to rest on the garment. The part that rolls down is called the fall. On a rolled collar, the collar neckline seam

has a shallower curve than the garment neckline seam.

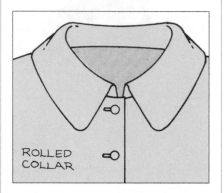

ROLLED COLLAR

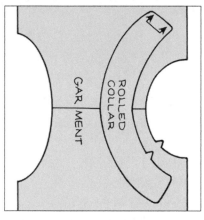

GARMENT / ROLLED COLLAR

● A *standing collar* is a band that rises straight up from the neckline seam. It can be a narrow, single-layer band or a double-layer band that folds back onto itself. On a standing collar, the collar neckline

tip

When using fusibles on light- to medium-weight fabrics, forget about pre-trimming the interfacing. The amount of bulk these interfacings add is almost imperceptible. Once the collar is stitched, careful trimming and grading, as well as good pressing will take care of any bulk.

seam is very straight in comparison to the garment neckline seam.

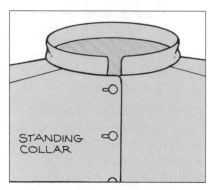

STANDING COLLAR

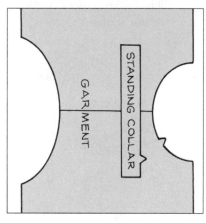

GARMENT / STANDING COLLAR

COLLAR BASICS

Regardless of the style of collar, the techniques for professional results are basically the same.

Interfacing

Most collars have a layer of interfacing sandwiched between the collar and undercollar. Your pattern instructions will tell you what pattern piece(s) to use and where to apply the interfacing. In most cases, the interfacing is fused or machine-basted to the upper collar. This way it acts as a cushion against all of the seam allowances.

To reduce bulk, it's a good idea to trim ½" (1.3cm) off the interfac-

tip

If your collar has corners or sharp curves, remember to use a smaller stitch for about 1" (2.5cm) on either side. For a sharper corner, take one stitch across the point.

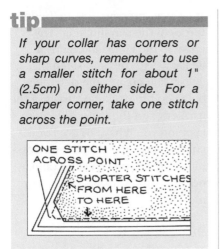

ing's seam allowances. For sew-in interfacings, trim the seam allowances after the interfacing is machine-basted in place. For fusibles, trim the seam allowances first and then fuse the interfacing. To reduce bulk at the corners, trim the interfacing diagonally, and just inside the seamline.

Stitching It Together

Instead of starting at one edge of the collar and stitching all of the way around to the other edge, you'll get a more symmetrical collar if you stitch in two steps.

Step 1: Begin at the center back and stitch to one edge of the collar.

Step 2: Begin again at the center-back, overlapping several stitches, and stitch to the other edge of the collar (see below).

Trimming and Grading

Trim the seam allowances and the corners. On medium and heavyweight fabrics, grade the seam allowances so that the undercollar seam allowance is narrower than the upper collar seam allowance. Remember to notch your curved collars.

Pressing

- Before turning the collar right side out, press it flat on both the collar side and the undercollar side. This blends the stitches.

- To ensure a sharp edge once the collar is turned, do one of the following:

 Press the seam allowance open over a point presser.

Or

Place the collar flat on the ironing board with the undercollar side facing up. Press the undercollar seam allowance toward the collar (see above).

- Turn the collar right side out. If the collar has points, gently coax them out from the inside with the eraser end of a pencil or the tip of a point turner. Resist the temptation to use the tip of your scissors—it's all too easy to poke them right through the fabric.

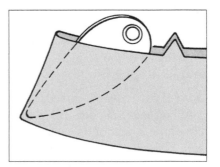

- Press the collar. As you press, roll the seamline slightly underneath to the undercollar side.

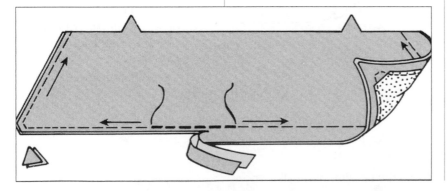

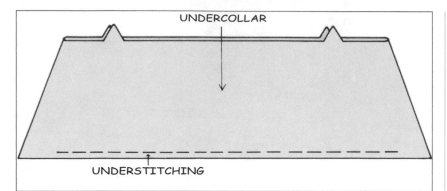

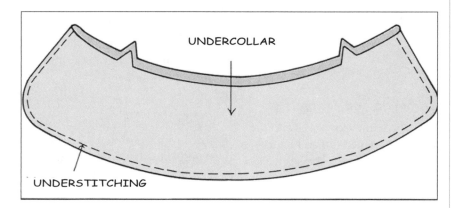

Understitching

Understitching is that extra bit of security that keeps the undercollar from rolling to the outside.

● Turn the collar inside out again and slip it under your presser foot so that the right side of the under-collar is facing you. Stitch on the undercollar, next to the seamline, catching all of the seam allowances in your stitching.

Note: If your collar is curved, you'll be able to understitch along the entire length of the collar. If your collar is pointed, understitch along the back edge, between, and almost to, the points.

● Turn the collar right side out and press again (shown above.)

Preparing the Garment

The finished collar won't look smooth and neat unless you've done some preliminary work on your garment.

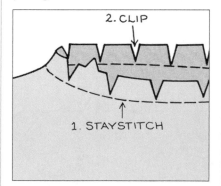

● Staystitch the garment's neckline edge to keep it from stretching out of shape as you sew.

● Clip the neckline seam allowance

at regular intervals, just to, but not through, the staystitching. This releases the fabric and helps it to lie flat as you pin and stitch the collar. The greater the difference between the neckline curves of the garment and the collar, the more clipping you'll have to do. For flat collars, very little clipping is necessary. For standing collars, you may need to clip every ½" (1.3cm) or more.

Attaching the Collar

There are many different methods of attaching the collar. Sometimes it is attached at the same time as the neckline facing, so that the facing hides the neckline seam allowances. Sometimes there is no facing. Instead, the collar is attached so that the garment neckline seam allowance is sandwiched between the collar and the undercollar. Follow your pattern directions, making sure that you trim, grade and clip the neckline seam; then press the seam allowances as indicated.

CUFFS

Buttoned and snug, or turned up and loose, cuffs are a popular detail on sleeves and pants.

As you read your pattern instructions, keep in mind that most cuffs, like most collars, are made up of three layers. The top layer is called the cuff; the underneath layer is called the facing. In between is the interfacing.

will include a pattern piece for the facing and complete instructions.

Two other common openings are the **hemmed opening** and the **continuous lap opening**. A fifth opening, **the tailored placket**, is similar to the conventional neckline placket band. If you're making this type of placket, review the information on "Placket Band," pages 110–112.

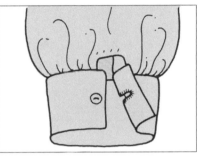

HEMMED OPENING

THE ATTACHED CUFF

Sewing an attached cuff is very similar to sewing a collar. In fact, the basics of assembling—interfacing, stitching, trimming and grading, and pressing—are exactly the same. Before you make a cuff, reread the previous sections on collars, pages 133–136.

An attached cuff can be a continuous band cuff or it can have a cuff opening. If the cuff opens, there is a corresponding sleeve opening, or placket, that can be finished in a variety of ways.

The easiest "placket" is an **opening in the sleeve seam**. To create this placket, stitch the seam to the mark and backstitch; then press the entire seam open.

The **faced opening** is another style of placket. If your pattern calls for this type of opening, it

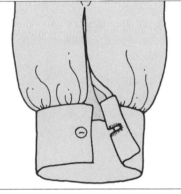

SEAM OPENING

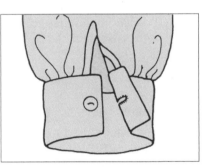

CONTINUOUS LAP

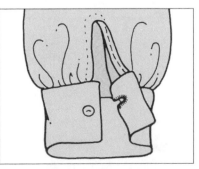

FACED PLACKET

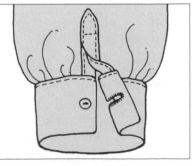

TAILORED PLACKET

Hemmed Opening

Some patterns have a small sleeve opening that's formed by turning up part of the seam allowance.

- Reinforce along the seamline, as indicated on your pattern, extending the stitching ½" (1.3cm) beyond the mark.

- Clip to the stitching at the mark.

- Fold the flap up and press. Turn the raw edge of the flap in to meet the stitching line and press again.

- To secure the flap to the sleeve, use fusible web or slipstitch it in place across the top of the fold.

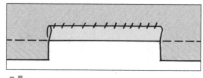

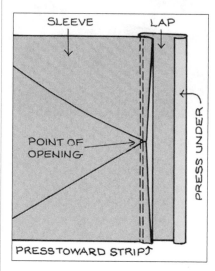

tip

If your fabric has a tendency to fray, treat the cut edges of the flap with a liquid sealant. Test first to make sure it isn't visible on your fabric when dry.

Continuous Lap

A cuff on a tailored shirt may have an opening that is bound with a strip of fabric. This is done before the underarm seam is stitched. Your pattern either includes a pattern piece for this strip or tells you how to measure and cut it.

The Conventional Method

The following method may be slightly different from the one in your pattern instructions. Continuous laps can be tricky but with this method even your first attempt will be successful.

First, create the opening at the lower edge of the sleeve:

- Mark the slash stitching lines.

- Stitch along these lines, using reinforcement-length stitches for 1" (2.5cm) on either side of the point and taking one stitch across the point.

- Cut an opening between the stitching lines, being careful not to slash through the stitch at the point.

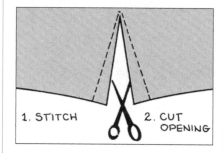

1. STITCH   2. CUT OPENING

Next, attach the lap:

- Spread the edges of the opening apart so that they almost form a straight line.

- With right sides together, pin the fabric strip to the slashed edge so that the stitching line on the opening is ¼" (6mm) from the edge of the strip.

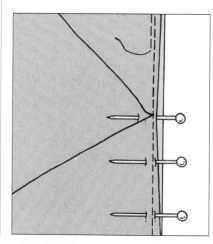

- Working with the sleeve on top, machine-stitch, stitching just to the left of the previous stitching. As you come to the point of the opening, fold the extra sleeve fabric out of the way.

- Press the seam allowance toward the strip.

- Press under ¼" (6mm) on the remaining long edge of the strip. Pin this edge over the seam on the inside of the sleeve and slipstitch in place. (See TIP on next page).

SLEEVE   LAP

POINT OF OPENING

PRESS UNDER

PRESS TOWARD STRIP

- Press the front portion of the lap to the inside and baste it in place across the lower edge of the sleeve.

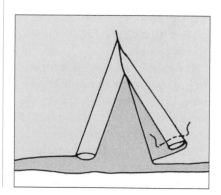

tip

To reduce bulk, cut the strip from the selvage edge of the fabric, so that you eliminate one of the $1/2$" (6mm) seam allowances. Then there's no need to press this edge under before slipstitching it in place.

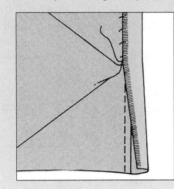

S *The Serger Method*

• Measure the length of the placket opening on your pattern tissue. Cut a 1" (2.5cm) wide bias strip of fabric that is twice the length of the placket opening.

• Reinforce and slash the placket opening as for the conventional machine technique.

• With right sides together, pin the bias strip to the slashed edge so that the stitching line of the opening is $1/4$" (6mm) from the edge of the strip.

• Working with the sleeve on top, serge until the blade reaches the point of the slash. Be sure to keep the fabric in front of the blade clear. Rearrange the sleeve folds and continue serging. *Note:* As you stitch, guide the bias strip under the needle with your right hand, while holding the placket edge straight with your left hand.

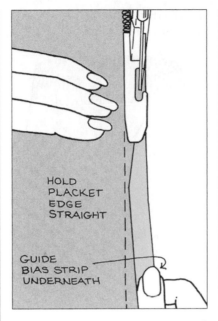

HOLD
PLACKET
EDGE
STRAIGHT

GUIDE
BIAS STRIP
UNDERNEATH

• Serge the remaining raw edge of the bias strip, trimming away about $1/8$" (3mm) as you serge.

• Press the seam allowance toward the bias strip.

• Fold the bias strip to the wrong side of the garment so the edge of the strip extends $1/8$" (3mm) over the line of the reinforcement stitching. Press and then stitch in the ditch, using your conventional machine.

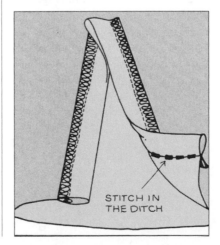

STITCH IN
THE DITCH

• Press the front portion of the lap to the inside and baste it in place across the lower edge of the sleeve.

Attaching the Cuff

Once the cuff is assembled and the sleeve opening is finished, you're ready to attach the cuff.

The Conventional Method

Your pattern will probably tell you to attach the cuff in one of the following conventional ways.

Technique 1: Stitch the cuff to the lower edge of the sleeve. Working on the inside, slipstitch the facing in place over the seam allowances.

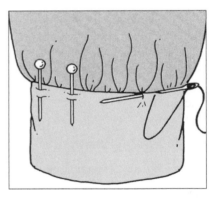

tip

When you are attaching the cuff to the sleeve, the pattern directions usually tell you to trim and grade the seam allowances. However, if you are using a sheer or loosely woven fabric, do not trim and grade. If you do, you may find that the first time you bend your elbow and rest it on a table, the strain may cause the trimmed seam allowance to pull away along the stitching line.

Technique 2: Stitch the cuff facing to the lower edge of the sleeve. Working on the outside, edgestitch the cuff in place over the seam allowances.

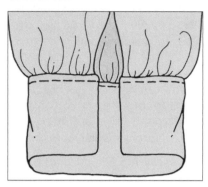

Although Technique 2 sounds much easier (and has a sportier look), you may find it more difficult to get neat results, particularly if this technique is new to you. Feel free to substitute Technique 1 for Technique 2 and then, to achieve the sportier look, you can go back and edgestitch the cuff on the outside.

⑤ *The Serger Method*

Note: This serged technique is successful *only* if your "placket" is an opening in the sleeve seam. On sleeves with a faced opening, a hemmed opening, a continuous lap or tailored placket, the cuff should be attached using a conventional machine.

● With right sides together, pin the cuff to the lower edge of the sleeve, matching markings.

● Roll the edge of the opening over the ends of the cuff and pin. Trim the corners diagonally before serging. This eliminates bulk at the corner once the seam is serged.

● Serge the cuff to the sleeve and secure the thread ends.

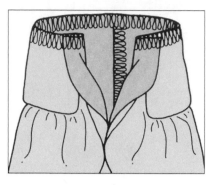

● Turn the lap edges of the opening to the inside. Press the seam allowance toward the sleeve.

RIB-KNIT CUFFS

These cuffs are a good way to finish the legs or sleeves of a sporty garment. For more information on this and other types of continuous bands, see "Bands and Ribbing," pages 109–114.

FOLD-UP CUFF

This type of cuff is often found on pants, particularly trouser styles, and short sleeves. Patterns styled this way include the extra length that's needed to form cuffs.

The traditional fold-up cuff includes some hand sewing. However, a shortcut machine method will save you time. If your machine

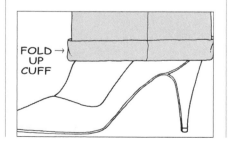

has a free arm, it's even easier. Be sure you have marked the hem and cuff foldlines.

● Turn the leg or sleeve inside out and press the hem up.

● If necessary, finish the raw edge. Machine-stitch the hem in place. (These hem stitches won't show on the outside of the finished cuff.)

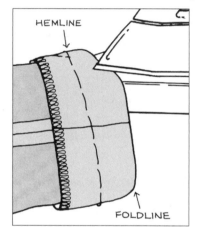

● Turn the leg or sleeve right side out. Fold the lower edge up along the cuff foldline and press.

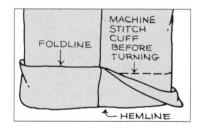

● To keep the cuff in place, stitch in the ditch at the seams, through all of the layers.

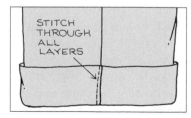

MOCK FOLD-UP CUFF

If your pattern has straight, unta-
pered sleeves or legs, and you want
to add cuffs, here are two easy
ways to fake it.

The Conventional Method

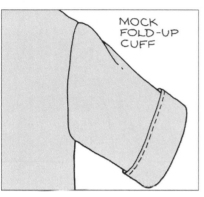

• Before you cut out your garment,
you'll need to alter the pattern.
Cut the pattern apart along the
hemline, spread it ½" (1.3cm),
and pin or tape it to paper.

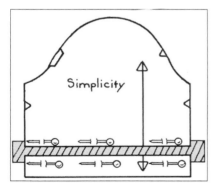

• When you're ready to hem the garment, fold the edge to the inside
along the hemline and press (A).

• Fold the edge up again the same
amount and press.

• Stitch ¼" (6mm) from the second
fold. This will create a tuck and encase the raw edge of the hem (B).

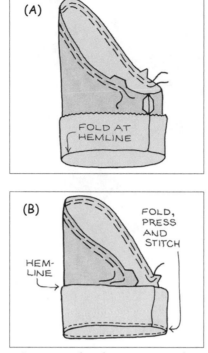

(A) FOLD AT HEMLINE

(B) HEM-LINE → FOLD, PRESS AND STITCH

• Open out the sleeve or pants leg
so that you can press the tuck up
and the "cuff" down.

🅂 *The Serger Method*

It's easier to make this type of cuff
before serging the underarm seam
(on sleeves) or the inner leg seam
(on pants).

• Before you cut out your pattern
make sure that the cuff allowance
is twice the width of the finished
cuff, plus ¾" (2cm). If necessary,

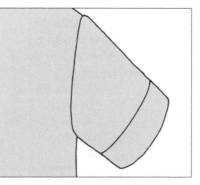

lengthen the pattern at the lower
edge.

• Measure up from the lower edge
of the sleeve or pants a distance
equal to the width of the finished
cuff, plus ¼" (6mm). Fold the lower
edge of the garment section to the
wrong side along this line; press.

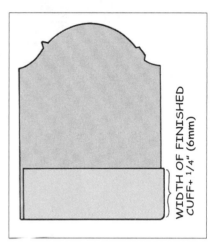

WIDTH OF FINISHED CUFF + ¼" (6mm)

• Now turn the folded portion of
the garment back to the right side;
press.

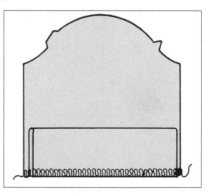

• Serge along this second fold,
being careful not to cut the fabric.

• Press the cuff down.

• Beginning at the lower edge of
the garment, serge the underarm
or inner leg seams.

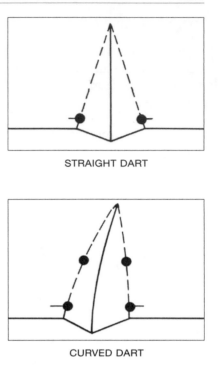

STRAIGHT DART

CURVED DART

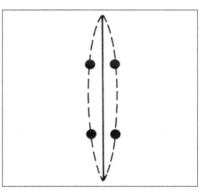

DOUBLE-POINTED DART

DARTS

Darts are one of the ways that fabric is molded to conform to the curves of the body.

Darts can be straight (for an easy fit) or curved (for a closer-to-the-body fit). A dart usually starts at a seamline, tapering to nothing at its tip. However, a double-pointed dart, found on one-piece dresses and closely fitted shirts, blouses and jackets, is actually two darts combined into one. The result is a long dart with the widest part occurring at the waist. It tapers to nothing near the bust (or shoulder blade on the back of a garment) and near the hip.

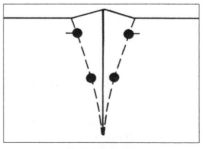

CURVED DART

MARKING

Examine the shape of your dart. If the stitching line is straight, all you need to do is mark the ●'s. If the stitching line is curved, it's a better idea to mark the entire stitching line. That way, you'll be sure you've stitched the curve exactly right.

STITCHING

● With right sides together, fold the fabric through the center of the dart, matching the markings and the stitching lines. Place pins at right angles to the stitching lines.

● Stitch the dart from the wide end to the point. To prevent a bubble at the point, make the last few stitches right at the fold and leave the thread ends long enough to tie a knot. *Do not* backstitch at the point.

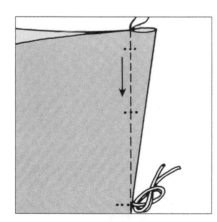

● If it is a double-pointed dart, pin and stitch as above, working from the middle to one end; then, overlapping several stitches, work from the middle to the other end. Carefully clip the dart at its widest point so that it will lie flat.

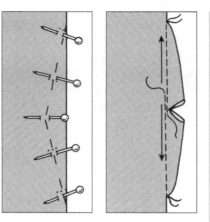

PRESSING

Press the darts flat and then open or to one side, as indicated on your pattern instructions. As a rule, vertical darts are pressed toward the center of the garment and horizontal ones are pressed downward. Occasionally, your pattern instructions will tell you to slash the dart along the fold line and press it open.

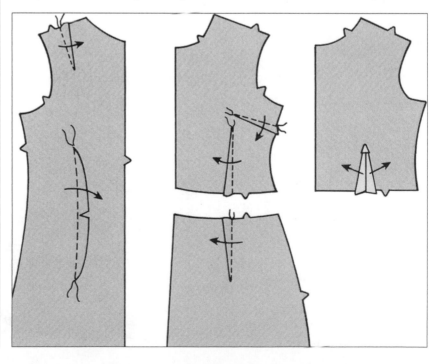

FACINGS

FACING BASICS

A facing is a piece of fabric that finishes a garment edge. Facings are most frequently found at necklines, armholes, front and back openings and, occasionally, at the waistline or the lower edge of a sleeve.

Most facings are created by attaching a separate piece of fabric to the garment edge. However, a garment that opens at the center front or back often has a special facing, called a self-facing, that is cut in one piece with the garment. When this extension is folded back, it serves as the facing for both the opening edges and part of the neckline. To finish off the rest of the neckline, the garment will also have a back neck facing and/or a collar.

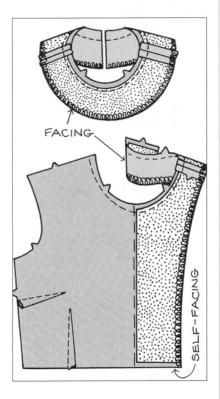

Although the shape and the location can vary, the basics for creating a facing that lies flat and looks professional remain the same.

Staystitch

If the facing is located at the neckline or the waistline, staystitch the neck/waist edges on both the garment and the facing. For armhole facings and front and back edges, staystitching is not necessary.

Interface

Apply interfacing to either the facing section or the garment section, as recommended in your pattern instructions. As a general rule, fusible interfacing is applied to the facing section.

Finish the Edge

Stitch the facing sections together at the shoulder or side seams; then finish the outer edge. If appropriate, the stitched-and-pinked or the zigzag/overcast finish (see page 81) will add the least amount of bulk. If your fabric is very bulky and/or ravels a great deal, use the tricot-bound finish (see page 81).

Attach the Facing

Stitch the facing to the garment, as indicated on your pattern instructions. If there are any corners, remember to shorten your stitch length for about 1" (2.5cm) on either side of each corner.

Trim and Grade

To prevent ridges from showing on the outside, remove bulk from the seams by trimming the seam

allowances to ¼" (6mm). On thick fabrics, also trim the facing seam allowance to ⅛" (3mm) so that the layers are graded. To ensure a smooth edge when the facing is turned to the inside, clip or notch curved seam allowances.

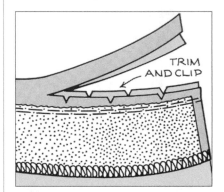

Press

Press the seam allowances flat to blend the stitches. Next, press them open; then press them toward the facing.

Understitch

Open the facing out. With the facing on top, stitch through the facing and both seam allowances very close to the seam.

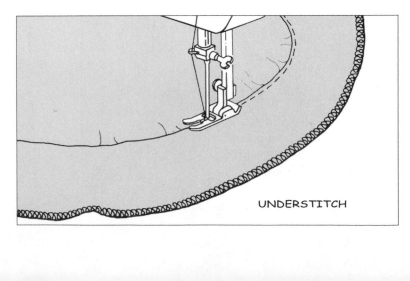

Simply the Best
Patternless Projects

Whether your goal is to try out some new techniques or polish up some rusty sewing skills, these patternless projects are sure to whet your sewing appetite.

Change the fabric and your project has a whole new personality.

Easy-to-follow instructions include options for conventional and serger sewing.

Simple shapes.
Timeless styles.
Versatile silhouettes.

Simply Smart Separates

When a polished look is on the fashion agenda, the kimono jacket, T-top and skirt provide a stylish mix-and-match ensemble.

Best Dressed

It's the perfect partnership! Skirt and T-top in matching fabric take center stage in dress mode, or spin off to form alliances with other pieces in your wardrobe.

Costume Capers

A change of fabric, plus some appropriate accessories, transform the versatile kimono into a fast and fabulous Halloween costume.

Take-Along Tote

Generous proportions and practical pockets make this tote
a welcome companion on any excursion. And if you're looking
for a great teach-someone-to-sew project, this is it!

Bedtime Beauty

Cuddle up in comfort with soft-to-the-touch fabrics, such as terrycloth or velour, and the basic kimono pattern customized to your favorite bathrobe length.

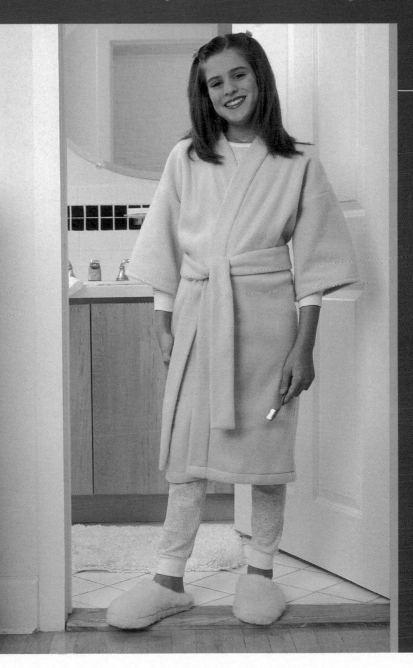

Painless Ponchos

Easy to make, easy to fit and easy to wear, this poncho can be translated into a multitude of sizes, making it a terrific cover-up for all ages.

Sensational Shawl

A sweep of fabric, graced with a roomy catch-all pocket, is great for around-the-town shopping as well as a wonderful addition to a travel wardrobe.

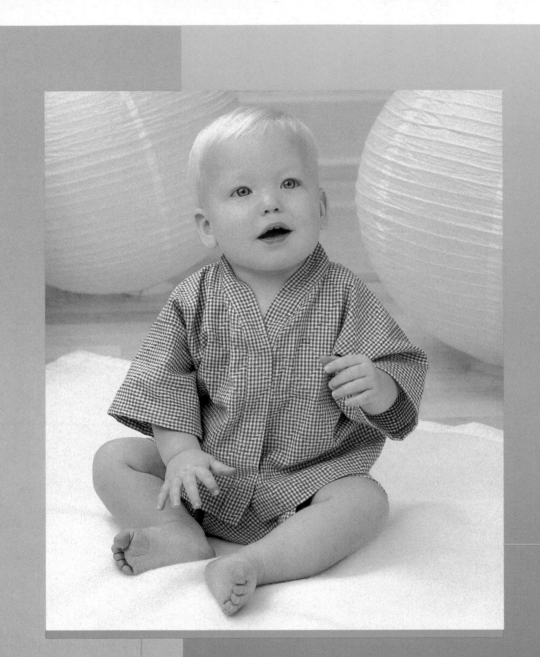

Just for Baby

Baby looks dapper all day long in an easy-to-make diaper cover and scaled-down version of the patternless kimono.

Press Again

Fold the facing to the inside of the garment along the seamline and press.

Tack

To keep the facing from rolling to the outside, secure it at the seam allowances by tacking it by hand, stitching in the ditch, or applying a small piece of fusible web.

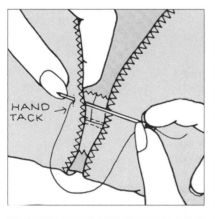

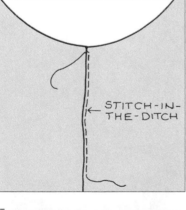

tip

If your fabric is loosely woven or tends to fray, apply fusible interfacing to the facing. It will reinforce the fabric and seal the yarns, making it possible for you to use the easy stitched-and-pinked finish.

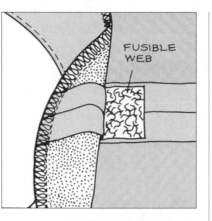

tips

● *If you've clipped the curves, understitch carefully, checking frequently to make sure those small wedges of seam allowance don't get caught in the stitching.*

● *If the garment edge ultimately will be topstitched, there's no need to tack the facing in place.*

S THE SERGER METHOD

When it comes to facings, your serger can save you a lot of time. Use it first to finish the edges of the facing. Then, if the edge to be faced is a straight edge or a gradual curve, you can use your serger to attach the facing to the garment. Because the serger automatically gives you very narrow seam allowances, trimming, grading, notching and clipping won't be necessary.

● Serge the facing pieces together. Press the seams to one side.

● Finish the facing by serging around the outside edges.

● Pin the facing to the garment edge. If the faced edge has an opening, fold the garment and facing to the inside along the opening edge and pin as shown.

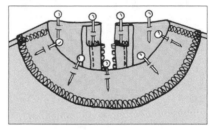

● Serge along the ⅝" (1.5cm) seamline, through all of the layers.

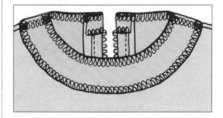

● Press the seam allowances toward the facing; then understitch on your conventional machine.

tip

S *To reduce bulk, make sure the facing seam allowances and the corresponding garment seam allowances are pressed in opposite directions before serging the facing to the garment.*

BIAS TAPE FACING

As an alternative to a regular facing, you can substitute single-fold bias tape. It's a quick and easy technique that's particularly popular for children's clothes. Because the tape is made from bias strips of fabric, it will fit smoothly around curves of neckline and armhole edges.

Purchase either ½" (1.3cm) or ⅞" (2.2cm) wide single-fold bias tape.

● Trim the garment seam allowance to ½" (6mm).

● Open out one fold of the tape. If you're facing a curved edge, steam-press the tape and pre-shape it to match the garment curve.

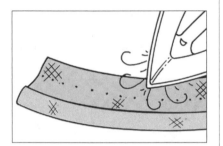

● With right sides together and raw edges even, pin the tape to the garment. To join the ends of the tape, turn under ½" (1.3cm) on the first end; lap the other end over it. Straight-stitch or serge a ¼"(6mm) seam.

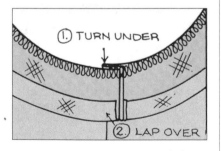

● Turn the tape to the inside and press. As you press, roll the tape slightly to the inside of the garment so it will not show on the outside.

● On the outside, edgestitch close to the garment edge and then top-stitch about ⅜" to ¾" (1cm to 2cm) from the edge.

Serged Neckline			
TYPE OF SERGER STITCH:	3	4	MINE
Stitch length:	3mm	3mm	
Stitch width:	Widest	Widest	
Tensions—Needle:	Tight	Tight	
Right needle:	N\A	N/A	
Upper looper:	Normal	Normal	
Lower looper:	Normal	Normal	

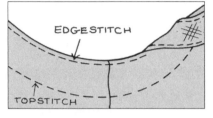

⑤ SERGED NECKLINE

Instead of facing a collarless neckline, serge it! The serger stitches create a decorative, finished edge.

This is a great technique for firmly woven fabrics and knits that don't curl.

Always test first to be sure you like the results before serging your garment's neckline. To test stitching and thread tension, cut the test swatch so that it duplicates the curve of the garment's neckline.

● Adjust your serger to the appropriate setting (see chart above).

tip

If your fabric is sheer, you may wish to eliminate the facings and finish the edge with a bias binding cut from your fashion fabric. For more information, see "Bindings," page 117.

tip

S *This technique for a serged neckline can also be used to replace the facing in other parts of a garment, such as an armhole, a hemline or the opening edges of a jacket.*

- Serge one shoulder seam (1).

- Serge around the neckline along the ⅝" (1.5cm) seamline (2).

- Serge the remaining shoulder seam, beginning at the armhole and chaining off 3" to 4" (7.5cm to 10cm) at the neckline edge (3).

- To secure the stitches at the neckline edge, thread the chain onto a tapestry needle and weave it back through the shoulder seam stitches, as shown below.

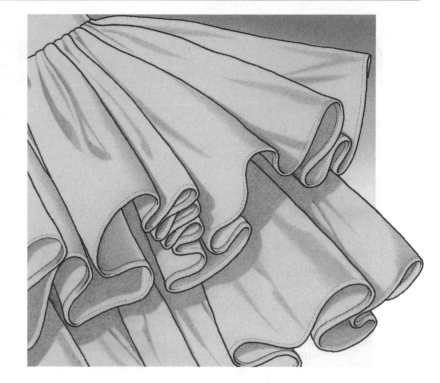

① SERGE ONE SEAM

② SERGE NECKLINE

③ SERGE REMAINING SEAM

GATHERS

Gathers are used to control fullness in just about any part of the garment. You'll find them at the waistline, at a yoke seam, at the cuff of a full sleeve or on the cap of a puffed sleeve. Gathers are also used to create ruffles.

The fabric you choose will affect the appearance of your gathers.

The softer the fabric, the more the gathers will drape and cling to the body. Crisper fabrics create billowy, stand-away-from-the-body gathers.

STRAIGHT STITCH GATHERING

The most common way to create gathers is to use a long, straight machine stitch.

- Loosen the needle thread tension slightly. This will make it easier to pull up the bobbin thread later.

- Set the stitch length for a long stitch; the heavier the fabric, the longer the stitch.

- Working on the right side of the fabric, stitch along the seamline of the area to be gathered. Stitch again, ¼" (6mm) away, within the seam allowance. Be sure to leave long thread tails—and do not backstitch!

- With right sides together, pin the section to be gathered to the shorter one, matching notches, seams and markings.

- Gently pull the bobbin threads at each end, sliding the fabric along until it fits the shorter section. At both ends, wrap the excess bobbin

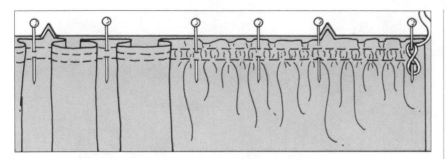

thread around the pins in figure 8s. Distribute the gathers evenly and pin as shown above.

● Before stitching the seam, make sure you have readjusted the needle thread tension on your machine. Working with the gathered side up, stitch on the seamline, just next to the first row of gathers. To keep tucks from forming along the seamline, use the tips of your fingers to hold the fabric on either side of the presser foot.

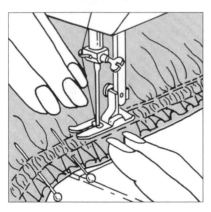

Gathering Long Sections

The longer the area you're working on, the greater the chances of having a thread break while you are forming the gathers. To avoid this:

● Divide the edges of both the short and long sections into four or eight equal parts and mark with safety pins or straight pins.

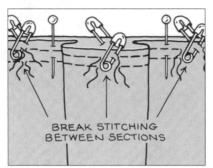

● On the edge to be gathered, make separate rows of gathering stitches for each section.

● Pin the edges together, distribute the fullness and stitch as for straight stitch gathering.

GATHERING OVER A CORD

This fast method for gathering a long section eliminates any worries about threads breaking.

● Cut a piece of strong, thin cord, such as pearl cotton, button and carpet thread or lightweight packing string that is slightly longer than the edge to be gathered.

● Set your machine for a zigzag stitch wide enough to stitch over the cord without catching it in the stitches. Position the cord within the seam allowance so that the left swing of the needle falls just short of the seamline. Stitch.

tip

If the gathers will intersect a previous seam:

● **On light- and medium-weight fabrics,** *trim the ends of the seam allowances diagonally before stitching the gathers.*

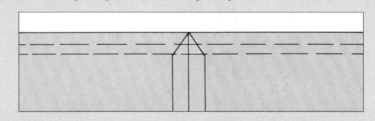

● **On bulky fabrics,** *trim ends of seams and stitch up to the seams, keeping the seam allowances free.*

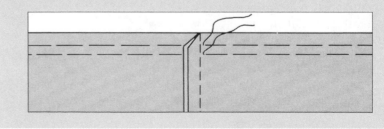

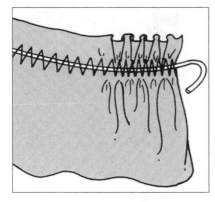

- Wrap one end of the cord around a pin in a figure 8 to secure it.

- Pin the sections together, matching notches, seamlines and markings. To distribute the gathers, hold the cord taut and slide the fabric along it.

- Working with the gathered side up, stitch along the seamline, being careful not to catch the cord. Depending on the weight of your fabric and the thickness of your cord, you may find it easier to use your machine's zipper foot.

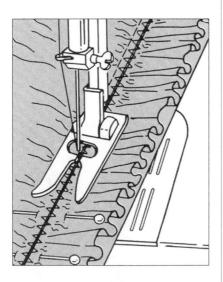

- When you're finished stitching, just pull out the cord.

Basic Gathering			
TYPE OF SERGER STITCH:	3	4	MINE
Stitch length:	3mm—5mm	3mm—5mm	
Stitch width:	Widest	Widest	
Tensions—Needle:	Very tight	Very tight	
Right needle:	N\A	Tight	
Upper looper:	Normal	Normal	
Lower looper:	Normal	Normal	

S GATHERING ON THE SERGER

One of the most frustrating things about gathering is that just when you think you have everything adjusted, you give one last yank, the gathering stitches break, and the whole thing explodes in your lap. You can zigzag over a cord on your conventional machine or you can put your serger to work. Here are two serger techniques. If you use them, remember that the serger will trim your seam allowances to ¼" (6mm) which isn't always an advantage on a gathered edge.

S *The Basic Technique*

- Adjust your serger to the appropriate setting (see chart, above).

- Make a test sample. Light- to medium-weight fabrics will gather automatically. For more gathers, tighten the needle thread tension(s). For fewer gathers, loosen the needle thread tension(s).

- Place the garment edge wrong side up and serge along the ⅝" (1.5cm) seamline.

- Remove the fabric from the machine and adjust the density of the gathers by pulling the needle thread(s) along gently.

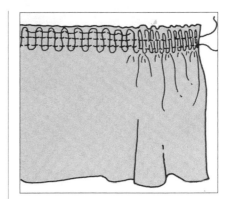

S *Over a Cord*

For heavier fabrics, you may want to gather over a cord for extra reinforcement.

- Adjust your serger to the appropriate setting (see chart, page 150).

- On some sergers, the foot has a hole in front. If so, thread a strand of cord, pearl cotton, crochet cotton or topstitching thread through the hole. Work from the front, bringing the thread under the foot toward the back.

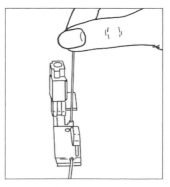

• If your serger does not have a hole in the front of the foot, guide the cord over the toe of the foot, over the finger guard and between the stitch fingers. Then bring the cord under the back of the foot.

• Place the fabric wrong side up and serge along the ⅝" (1.5cm) seamline. The stitches will form over the cord.

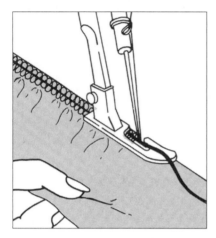

• To create the gathers, hold the cord taut while sliding the fabric along it.

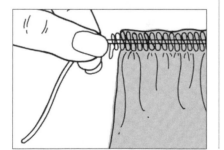

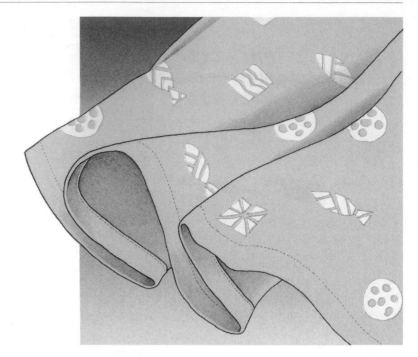

HEMS

Hems can be done by hand or by machine. The choice is up to you. If you decide to hem by hand, the stitches should be invisible on the outside of the garment. If you decide to hem by machine, some stitching will appear on the right side. That's why you want to match the thread perfectly to the fashion fabric. Make sure your choice is visually compatible with the other design details on your garment. For example, a topstitched hem may look out of place if there is no other topstitching on the garment.

Occasionally, you might decide to forget about your needle and thread, and simply fuse the hem in place.

HEM BASICS

Regardless of which technique you choose, the basics of preparing the hem are almost the same. However, since some of these procedures vary slightly depending on the type of hems, read through this section and decide on your technique before you begin. For hemming pleats, see "Pleats," page 162.

Marking

When your garment is at the "almost finished" stage, when there's not much left to do but sew on the buttons and put up the hem, it's a good idea to let it hang for 24 hours. This gives the fabric grain time to "settle in" before you mark the hem. This rest period is

Gathering Over a Cord			
TYPE OF SERGER STITCH:	3	4	MINE
Stitch length:	2mm-3mm	2mm-3mm	
Stitch width:	Widest	Widest	
Tensions—Needle:	Normal	Normal	
Right needle:	N\A	Normal	
Upper looper:	Normal	Normal	
Lower looper:	Normal	Normal	

tip

If your fabric is bulky, trim the seam allowances that occur within the hem allowance. Trim them to ¼" (6mm) between the edge of the garment and the hemline.

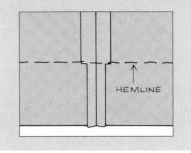

particularly important for knit garments or for garments with a bias or circular hem. If you skip this step, your finished garment may develop mysterious hemline dips and sags after a couple of wearings.

Once your garment has rested, try it on. Wear suitable undergarments and, if possible, the shoes, belt, etc. that you plan to wear with it. These accessories will affect how the garment hangs as well as influence the visual proportions. With them on, it will be easier to determine the most flattering hem length.

The best, and easiest, way to mark a hemline is to enlist the help of a friend. For even results, you stand in one spot, with your feet together; the friend moves around you, using a yardstick or pin-type skirt marker to establish the hem length. Pins should be placed parallel to the floor about 2" to 3" (5cm to 7.5cm) apart.

Trimming

Take the garment off, turn it wrong side out and place it over the iron-ing board or on a table. Turn the hem up along the pin-marked line. Matching the seamlines first, insert pins at right angles to the hemline, through both layers of fabric; then remove the pins that indicate the hemline. Once the hem is pinned up, it's a good idea to try on the garment to check length and evenness.

Hand-baste the hem about ¼" (6mm) from the folded edge, removing the pins as you go. *Note:* If you're making a machine-rolled hem or a narrow topstitched hem, you should skip this step.

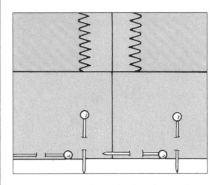

Measure and mark the desired hem allowance plus ¼" (6mm) for finishing. Trim away the excess. The type of hem you choose, as well as the shape of the hemline, will determine the depth of the hem allowance. On a straight garment, the hem allowance should be no more than 3" (7.5cm). On

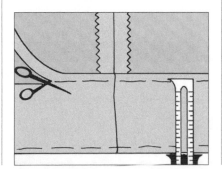

an A-line or flared garment, the hem allowance is usually between 1¼" to 2" (3.8cm to 5cm).

Press the hem. If necessary, put strips of brown paper or adding machine tape between the hem allowance and the garment to prevent ridges as you press. Use a press cloth to protect your fabric.

Easing

If the garment edge is slightly curved, the hem allowance will have extra fullness. Unless this fullness is eased so that the hem allowance lies flat against the garment, your finished hem will have ripples and ridges.

The Conventional Method

Easing is done after the hem allowance is trimmed but before the raw edge is finished.

- Ease-stitch ¼" (6mm) from the edge, remembering to loosen the needle tension slightly.

- Working on a flat surface, use a pin to draw up the bobbin thread wherever there is extra fullness. Pin to control the distribution of the fullness.

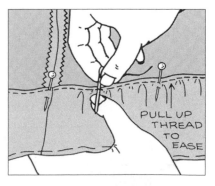

- Steam-press to shrink out some of the fullness.

⑤ *The Serger Method*

This technique can be used to ease the fullness in the hem allowance on full, circular and A-line skirts and shirttail hems.

- Adjust your serger to the appropriate setting (see chart below).

- On the right side of the fabric, serge 3" to 4" (7.5cm to 10cm) along the edge of the hem allowance. As you do, hold your forefinger behind the foot so that the fabric piles up. Release the fabric.

- Repeat, serging all around the raw edge. The hem allowance will automatically roll toward the garment.

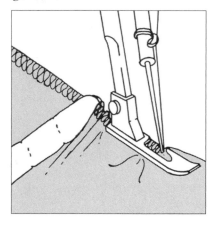

- Working on a flat surface, pin to control the distribution of the fullness.

- Steam-press to shrink out some of the fullness.

Note: Some fabrics may not ease up enough using this technique. For heavier fabrics, tighten the needle tension even more so that the fabric curls. This will enable you to adjust the gathers.

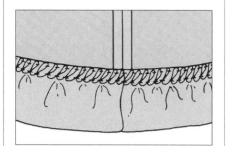

HAND-SEWN HEMS

Finishing the Edge

If your fabric doesn't ravel, you don't need to finish the edge. However, if a finish is necessary, the stitched-and-pinked, the zigzag/overcast and the bound seam finishes described under "Seam Finishes," page 81, are all excellent choices…or use the serger technique on page 94.

Other good hem finishes include adding seam binding or stretch lace. Both these products are applied exactly the same way. However, seam binding is suitable for straight hems only. Stretch lace,

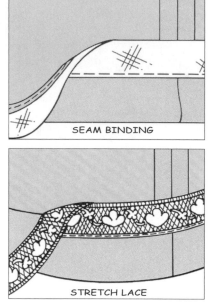

SEAM BINDING

STRETCH LACE

because of its flexible properties, is a better choice for knits and for curved hems. To apply, lap the lace or binding ¼" (6mm) over the edge of the hem allowance and edgestitch it in place.

Sewing the Hem

Depending on your fabric, choose the ***blindstitch***, the ***catchstitch*** or the ***hemming stitch*** (see "Hand Sewing," page 103). Use a thread that is the same color or one shade darker than your fabric. (Thread looks lighter when sewn.) To make sure the finished hem is invisible, pick up only one or two garment threads with each stitch.

MACHINE-MADE HEMS

Hems done by machine are a quick and easy alternative to hand sewing. Just be sure the machine technique you choose is suitable for your fabric.

Easing			
TYPE OF SERGER STITCH:	3	4	MINE
Stitch length:	2mm-3mm	2mm-3mm	
Stitch width:	Normal	Normal	
Tensions—Needle:	Tight	Tight	
Right needle:	N\A	Tight	
Upper looper:	Normal	Normal	
Lower looper:	Normal	Normal	

If your fabric is very bulky or if you're letting down a child's garment and you don't have enough fabric for a hem allowance, a faced hem is a good idea. Purchase packaged bias hem facing tape or make your own wide bias strips (see "Bindings," page 117). Trim the hem allowance to ½" (1.3cm). With right sides together and raw edges even, pin the facing to the hem allowance, lapping the cut edges as shown. Stitch a ½" (6mm) seam. Press the seam allowances toward the facing. Turn the hem up ¼" (6mm) below the facing seam. Sew the hem in place and slipstitch the ends of the facing closed.

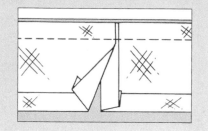

Machine Blindstitch

Many machines have a built-in stitch that can be used for straight or nearly straight hems on medium-weight wovens and stable knits. It is particularly popular for children's playclothes and home decorating. A special foot is usually required. Check your sewing machine manual for details.

• Turn up the finished edge of the garment to the desired hem depth.

• Turn the garment over so that the hem allowance is underneath. Fold the fabric back, exposing ¼" (6mm) of the hem allowance.

• Place the garment under the foot with the folded-back edge along the hem guide. Adjust the foot, as indicated for your machine, so that the fabric fold is against the guide and the needle barely catches the fold as you sew.

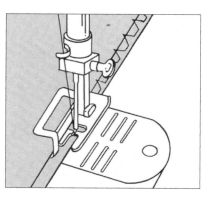

Narrow Topstitched Hem

This finish is suitable for sheer, lightweight or medium weight fabrics.

• **For knits:** Press under along the hemline and then trim the hem allowance to ⅝" (1.5cm).

tip

A decorative thread, such as buttonhole twist, can turn a topstitched hem into a design feature. For balance, repeat the stitching elsewhere on your garment.

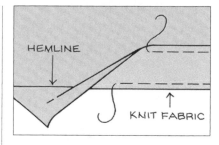

• **For wovens:**

• Press under along the hemline and then trim the hem allowance to 1" (2.5cm). Fold the raw edge in to meet the first crease and press again.

• Working on the right side, topstitch close to the edge of the hem allowance.

• If you wish, topstitch again, close to the edge of the garment.

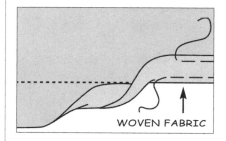

Wide Topstitched Hem

This technique can be used on all fabrics and styles, except for very curved hems. If the hem is slightly curved, be sure to easestitch it before topstitching.

For the most attractive proportions, the hem allowance should be 1½" to 2" (3.8cm to 5cm) wide.

• Press the hem up along the hemline. Ease in the fullness on any curves.

• For woven fabrics only, press the raw edge under ½" (1.3cm). For knit fabrics, eliminate this step.

- Working on the wrong side, stitch close to the edge of the hem allowance.
- Stitch again, ¼" (6mm) away from the first row of stitching, within the hem allowance.

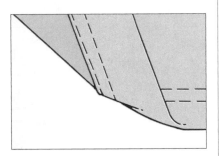

Machine-Rolled Hem

This is a quick and easy way to achieve the narrow rolled hem look that is particularly attractive on sheers, lightweight silk and synthetic fabrics, and for hemming ruffles.

Note: To do this hem, your garment must have at least a ⅝" (1.5cm) hem allowance.

- Mark the hemline ⅛" (3mm) longer than desired. Fold the garment up along this hemline and then stitch as close as you can to, but not more than ⅛" (3mm) from, the fold. Do not press before you stitch. If the hemline is not on straight of grain, pressing first will distort the hem.

tip

When making the machine-rolled hem on sheers, use long basting stitches for the first row of stitches and then remove them when the hem is completed.

- Using embroidery scissors, carefully trim away the hem allowance above the stitching.

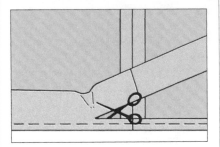

- Fold the hem allowance up along the stitching line, rolling the stitching line just slightly to the inside of the garment; press.

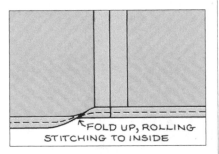

- Stitch again, close to the inner fold; press.

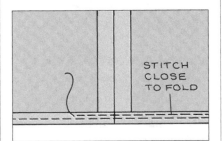

HEMMING ON THE SERGER

Your serger provides you with an array of hemming techniques.

⑤ *Overcast Hem*

Overcasting on the serger is an easy way to finish the raw edges of your hem allowance.

Plan your hem allowance so there's at least 1/16" (2mm) extra that you can trim off as you serge. This ensures that your fabric "fills" the stitches and that, in time, the stitching won't pull away from the raw edge.

- Adjust your serger to the appropriate setting (see chart below).
- Serge along the raw edge for the hem allowance.

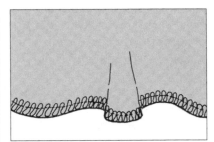

- Secure the thread chains.
- Complete your hem, folding up the hem allowance and using the appropriate hand stitches or top-stitching on the conventional machine.

Overcast Hem				
TYPE OF SERGER STITCH:	**2**	**3**	**4**	**MINE**
Stitch length:	2mm-3mm	2mm-3mm	2mm-3mm	
Stitch width:	Normal	Normal	Normal	
Tensions—Needle:	Very loose	Normal	Normal	
Right needle:	N/A	N\A	Normal	
Upper looper:	N/A	Normal	Normal	
Lower looper:	Normal	Normal	Normal	

S *The overcast technique can be used to create a finished hem. Using topstitching thread in both the upper and lower loopers, serge along the hemline.*

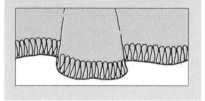

S Blind Hem

Because the stitches will show a little bit on the outside of the garment, this type of hem is more appropriate for children's wear, casual garments and home decorating. The serger finishes and secures the hem in one operation.

● Adjust your serger to the appropriate setting (see chart above right).

● Prepare the hem allowance as for a hand-sewn hem; then fold the garment back ¼" (6mm) from the raw edge of the hem allowance. Baste or pin in place. Press.

● Serge along the raw edge so that the needle just catches the fold of the fabric.

SERGE, JUST CATCHING THE FOLD

● Remove the pins or the basting stitches. Open out the garment until the stitches lie flat and then press on the wrong side to set the stitches and ease out the fullness.

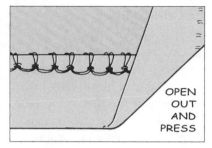

OPEN OUT AND PRESS

Blind Hem			
TYPE OF SERGER STITCH:	2	3	MINE
Stitch length:	Longest	Longest	
Stitch width:	Widest	Widest	
Tension—Needle:	Loose	Very loose	
Upper looper:	N/A	Normal	
Lower looper:	Normal	Tight	

S Rolled Hem

The rolled hem, sometimes referred to as a handkerchief hem, is the beautiful and durable finish found on the edges of scarves, napkins, tablecloths and ruffles. Until you bought your serger, there was almost no way you could duplicate the rolled hem at home.

The best fabric choices for a rolled hem are silk or polyester crepe de chine, georgette, lightweight tissue faille and soft cottons. If you use a washable fabric, you'll get better results if you preshrink it to remove the sizing.

What gives the hem its finished appearance is the serger's ability to roll the fabric to the underside as the edge is stitched and finished. The thread you see in a rolled hem is the upper looper thread; the lower looper and needle threads are hidden inside the roll. As a first choice, use silk or woolly nylon thread in the upper looper. These threads have the stretch and recovery necessary to help the fabric roll,

S *A special blind hemming foot is available for some sergers. Check your machine's instruction manual. Generally, only the right needle is used when the blind hem foot is attached.*

will lay smooth along the finished edge, and have a beautiful sheen. Use polyester serger thread in the lower looper and the needle. If you can't find the right color silk or woolly nylon thread, use the same polyester thread in the upper looper.

● To make a rolled hem, you should have at least a ½" (1.3cm) hem allowance.

● Adjust the serger to the appropriate setting (see chart, page 156).

● Place a test swatch, right side up, under the presser foot and serge. Fine-tune the tension settings until the hem rolls properly.

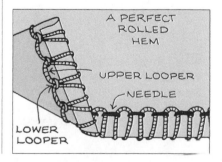

A PERFECT ROLLED HEM

UPPER LOOPER

NEEDLE

LOWER LOOPER

● If the lower looper thread forms large loops on the underside, loosen the upper looper and tighten the lower looper.

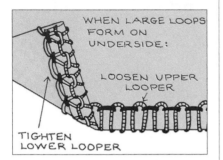

● If the needle thread is visible on the underside, tighten the needle tension.

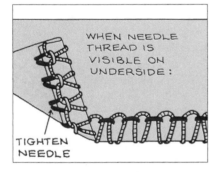

tips

S *If you can't get the proper look to the stitch, and your lower looper needs to be set higher than the tightest tension setting, wrap the thread around the tension dial twice. Just remember what you've done and rethread the lower looper before doing any regular serging.*

S *When you record your serger setting for a rolled hem, keep the information with a swatch of the fabric. Rolled hem settings often differ slightly from fabric to fabric.*

S Lettuce Edge

This delicate edge finish works best on very stretchy knits, such as interlocks, tricots and knit ribbing, that are cut and serged across the grain or "with the stretch." You can also achieve good results on light-weight wovens if they are cut on the bias. The lettuce edge looks great on ruffles and lingerie hems, as well as neck and sleeve ribbings.

● Use the same serger settings as for a rolled hem (see chart below). Test the settings on a swatch of fabric cut "with the stretch."

● Place the fabric under the presser foot, right side up, ¼" (1.3cm) from the raw edge. Begin serging so that the machine grabs the fabric for a couple of stitches.

● Continue serging, holding the fabric firmly in front of the foot so that it's stretched before it's serged. The finished edge will curl just like the edge of a lettuce leaf.

Note: If your knit runs, don't stretch the fabric before you serge. Instead, stretch it after the serging is finished.

S Picot or Shell Hem

When you want a softer treatment, the picot or shell hem is a variation of the rolled hem that will provide a scalloped, decorative application. The more supple look is achieved by using a longer stitch length for less thread coverage. It is particularly beautiful on lingerie, as well as along the edges of silks, crepe de chines and soft, scarf-like fabrics.

● Adjust your serger for the appropriate setting (see chart, next page). For best results, use polyester thread.

● Follow the instructions for the rolled hem on page 155.

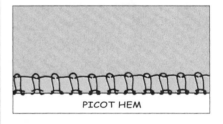

PICOT HEM

S Narrow Hem

Because the narrow hem is flat rather than rolled, it's better for heavier fabrics when a soft treatment is desired.

● Adjust your serger for the appropriate setting (see chart, next page).

● Follow the instructions for the rolled hem on page 155.

Rolled Hem and Lettuce Edge Hem		
TYPE OF SERGER STITCH:	3	MINE
Stitch length:	1mm	
Stitch width:	2mm*	
Tensions—Right needle:	Normal	
Upper looper:	Tight	
Lower looper:	Very tight	

*Narrow the stitch width to 2mm or use the presser foot and needle plate especially designed for a rolled hem. Consult your serger manual for specific information about your machine.

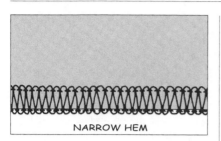

NARROW HEM

S Cover Hem

The cover hem resembles a twin or triple needle straight stitch on one side of the fabric; on the reverse side, it looks like a serger stitch. It is up to you whether the needle threads or the looper threads appear on the outside of your garment. Consult your serger's manual for the settings for the cover stitch.

- Stitch around the hem, overlapping at the original starting point for about 2" (5cm).

- Follow your manual for declutching the chain looper and pulling off the threads.

- Cut the threads, leaving a long tail. Pull the threads to the underside; tie them in a knot. Apply a

drop of seam sealant to the knot. Clip the tails close to the knot.

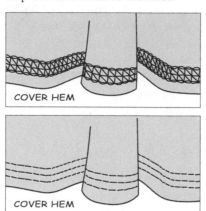

COVER HEM

COVER HEM

FUSED HEMS

This no-sew method of hemming is suitable for all but very sheer or lightweight fabrics. Use packaged strips of fusible web or cut your own from web purchased by the yard.

The strip of web should be narrower than your hem allowance. Sandwich the strip between the hem allowance and the garment, just below the finished edge. Fuse in place following the manufacturer's directions.

tip

S *When using the cover hem, you may experience skipped stitches as you serge over bulky seams. If this occurs, reduce the foot pressure when you reach the seam. Once you've serged past the seam, readjust the pressure to its previous setting.*

To make sure that no ridges appear on the right side of your garment, test the fusible web on scraps first. If ridges show, pink the edges of the web before applying and try not to rest the iron on the finished edge of the hem allowance.

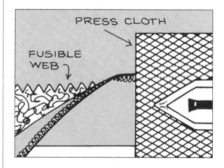

PRESS CLOTH

FUSIBLE WEB

ALTERING A HEMLINE

Fashions change, children grow… and hemlines need to altered.

Shortening a hem is no problem. Just remove the old stitches and proceed as if you were hemming the garment for the first time.

Lengthening can create a few problems.

- If you don't have a deep enough hem allowance once you let the garment down, add seam binding or stretch lace, or make a faced hem. To do the latter, cut 2½" (6.3cm) wide bias strips of a firmly

Picot Hem		
TYPE OF SERGER STITCH:	3	MINE
Stitch length:	3mm-4mm	
Stitch width:	Narrowest	
Tensions—Right needle:	Normal	
Upper looper:	Tight	
Lower looper:	Very tight	

Narrow Hem		
TYPE OF SERGER STITCH:	3	MINE
Stitch length:	1mm—2mm	
Stitch width:	Narrowest	
Tensions—Needle:	Normal	
Right needle:	N/A	
Upper looper:	Normal	
Lower looper:	Normal	

woven, lightweight fabric (see "Making Custom Binding," page 117) or purchase bias hem facing tape. To apply, follow the directions for "Bias Tape Facing," page 145 and see TIP on page 153.

● If a good steam pressing doesn't remove the old crease, make a solution of equal parts white vinegar and water. Apply it along the crease line using a small brush or an eyedropper, and then press. To be sure the vinegar won't affect the color of the garment, test this technique first on an inside seam allowance.

● If the crease still remains or the color has faded along the former hemline, consider covering the mark with a trim that is compatible with your garment. On children's garments, you might want to forego the vinegar treatment altogether and add some colorful trim.

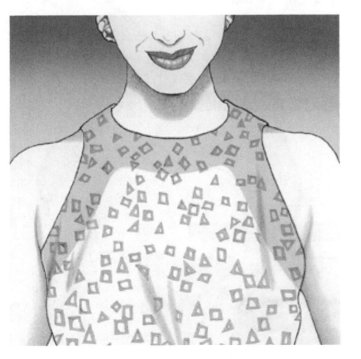

INTERFACING

Interfacing is an extra layer of fabric that provides shape and support in detail areas of the garment. Interfacing is frequently used in collars, cuffs, lapels, necklines, pockets, waistbands and along opening edges.

TYPES OF INTERFACING

The two basic types of interfacings are sew-in and fusible. Both are available in woven, knitted and nonwoven versions, and in a variety of weights, ranging from heavy to sheer weight. In addition to these specially developed interfacing fabrics, batiste, organza and organdy can be used as interfacings on sheer to lightweight fabrics.

The rule of thumb is that the interfacing should always be slightly lighter in weight than the fashion fabric.

Choosing between a fusible and a sew-in interfacing is really a matter of personal preference. In general, fusibles provide slightly crisper results. Because fusibles "set" the yarns, they're an excellent choice for fabrics that fray. However, some fabrics do not react well to fusibles. These include metallic, beaded, sequined or re-embroidered fabrics, rayon and acetate velvets, most brocades, fake furs, leather, vinyl and openwork fabrics, such as lace and mesh. Always test fusible interfacing on a scrap of the fashion fabric before you begin to be sure it works and that you like the results. Use the chart on page 161 to match fabric type with suggested interfacings.

Most people think of fusibles as easier to use and they are—as long as you take the time to follow the manufacturer's fusing directions carefully. The key to successful results is the prescribed combination of heat, steam and pressure. In addition, even if the directions do not suggest it, take the time to go through the entire fusing process twice, first on the wrong side and then on the right side of the garment section. This extra step will ensure a strong, even bond.

WHERE TO INTERFACE

Your pattern will tell you which pieces require interfacing and the back of your pattern envelope will tell you how much to buy. If you want to add it to certain areas of your garment, even if the pattern doesn't suggest it, go right ahead.

For example, you might want to add a little bit of crispness to a patch pocket.

Don't think that you have to use the same weight interfacing throughout the entire garment. For example, you might decide that the collar should have softer shaping than the cuffs. If you find this confusing, take a look at some of the better ready-to-wear garments. Note how some detail areas in the same garment feel crisper than others. You can certainly reproduce this concept in the garments that you sew.

Interfacing is usually applied to the wrong side of what will ultimately be the outermost layer of fabric. For example, apply to the upper collar rather than the undercollar, to the cuff rather than to the cuff facing. Since there are exceptions, be sure to follow your pattern instructions.

CUTTING AND MARKING

Woven and knitted interfacings have lengthwise, crosswise and bias grains. The interfacing pieces should be cut out so that the pieces are on-grain as indicated in the pattern layouts.

tip

Don't buy exactly the amount of interfacing the pattern calls for. Buy several yards. That way, you can experiment with it on other fabrics. To keep your stash of interfacing neat, store the leftovers in a Ziploc® or similar self-sealing plastic bag. If it's a fusible, be sure to keep a copy of the fusing directions with the interfacing.

Technically, nonwoven interfacings do not have a grain. However, this doesn't mean that you can cut out your pieces any old way. Some of these interfacings are stable in all directions, others stretch in the crosswise direction, and still others are all bias. Read the instructions that come with the interfacing and follow their recommendations for how to position the pattern pieces.

Transfer the pattern markings to the interfacing sections rather than to the fabric. Buttonhole markings are the exception to this rule. That's because you must be able to see them on the outside of your almost-finished garment.

APPLICATION

● *Sew-in type:* To minimize bulk, trim the outside corners of the interfacing diagonally, just inside the point where the seamlines meet. Pin- or glue-baste the interfacing to the wrong side of the garment section, and machine-baste ½" (1.3cm) from the edges. Trim the interfacing seam allowances close to the stitching and trim off any hem allowances.

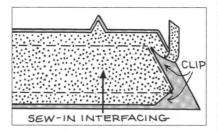

SEW-IN INTERFACING

CLIP

● *Fusible type:* Trim the corners diagonally, the same way as for sew-in interfacings and trim off any hem allowances. Most sewing books will also tell you to trim ½"

tips

● *Sometimes one edge of the interfacing does not extend all the way to a seamline, for example, on a collarless neckline or on the front of a jacket. With a fusible interfacing, a ridge may be visible on the outside of the garment. To find out, test-fuse a piece of the interfacing to a scrap of the fashion fabric. If a ridge forms, try cutting the edge of the interfacing with pinking shears. If this doesn't help, apply the interfacing to the facing rather than to the body of garment.*

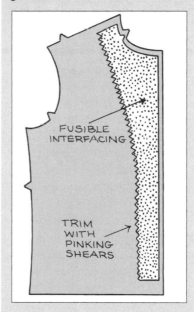

FUSIBLE INTERFACING

TRIM WITH PINKING SHEARS

● *For small detail areas, such as pockets, pocket flaps, collars or cuffs, fuse the interfacing to the fashion fabric before cutting out the garment section. Pin the pattern in place on the interfacing/fabric and cut as one.*

(1.3cm) from the seam allowances to reduce bulk. However, on all but the heaviest fabrics, you can eliminate this step. It's just too difficult to get the interfacing positioned correctly on the garment section once it's trimmed. Besides that, the amount of bulk it adds is minimal. Fuse the interfacing in place, following the manufacturer's directions.

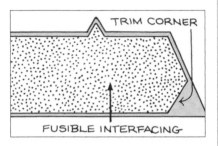

MITERING

Mitering—creating a corner by joining a vertical and a horizontal edge—is one technique that pattern instructions usually assume everyone knows how to do. However, doing it is one thing.... doing it so that the corners come out crisp and square is quite another.

Knowing how to make a professional-looking miter comes in handy when you're turning under a corner in places like a patch pocket (a folded miter), the hem/facing edge of a skirt slit (a stitched miter) or when you're applying trim.

Bindings, because they encase the edge of the fabrics, require slightly different techniques for mitering. For more information, see "Bindings," pages 119–121.

FOLDED MITER

This method works on patch pockets and slit hems.

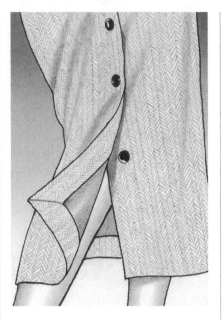

● Stitch along the pocket seamlines; then press the seam allowances to the inside along the stitching.
● Open out the seam allowances at the corners. Fold the corner up diagonally and press; then trim this seam allowance to ¼" (6mm).
● Fold all of the seam allowances back to the inside. The folded edges will just meet forming a neat corner miter.
● To make sure the corners stay neat as you edgestitch or topstitch the pocket to the garment, slipstitch the edges together, or secure them with glue stick or fusible

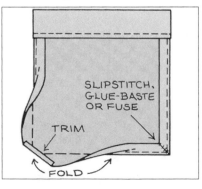

web. If your folded miter is at the corner of a hem, use slipstitching.

STITCHED MITER

This method is most frequently used at the corner of a turned-up hem.

● Turn the garment edges to the inside along the seamlines or fold lines; press.
● Open out the pressed edges. Fold the corner diagonally across the point so that the pressed lines meet; press.

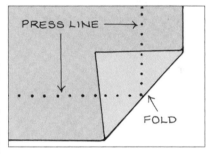

● Open out the corner and, with right sides together, fold the garment diagonally through the corner so those creases meet, as shown. Stitch on the diagonal crease line. Trim the corner seam allowance, trimming diagonally at the point.

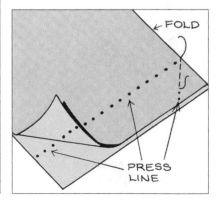

Fabric and Use	Interfacing	
	FOR A SOFT EFFECT	**FOR A CRISP EFFECT**
Very light to lightweight fabrics (voile, gauze, crepe, challis, calico, chambray, interlock knit, jersey, single knit, batiste) **Use:** Blouses, shirts and dresses	Batiste; organza; sew-in sheer, regular or stretch very lightweight nonwoven; self-fabric.	Organdy; sew-in or fusible lightweight or sheer (nonwoven or woven); fusible knit
	Do not use fusibles on chiffon or seersucker.	
Medium-weight fabrics (linen, denim, poplin, flannel, gabardine, satin, duck, chino, velour, stretch terry, double knit, sweater knit) **Use:** Dresses, lightweight suits, active sportswear	Sew-in or fusible medium-weight woven; regular or stretch light- to medium-weight nonwoven; fusible knit	Sew-in or fusible lightweight hair canvas; sew-in or fusible medium-weight (woven or nonwoven)
	Do not use fusibles on rainwear fabrics.	
Heavyweight fabrics (corduroy, tweed, worsted, camel hair, melton, sailcloth, canvas, gabardine, coatings) **Use:** Jackets, suits, coats	Soft, lightweight canvas; sew–in or fusible medium-weight nonwoven	Sew-in or fusible medium- or heavyweight woven; crisp medium- or heavyweight hair canvas; fusible heavyweight nonwoven
Leather types (suede, suede cloth) Do not use fusibles on real leather.	Crisp or soft canvas; fusible or sew-in medium-weight nonwoven or woven	
Waistbands	Fusible nonwoven precut strips; woven stiffener sold by the width; sew-in or fusible medium- to heavyweight (woven or nonwoven)	
Crafts **Use:** Belts, hats, bags, camping gear, home decorating items	Sew-in nonwovens in all weights; fusible medium- to heavyweight (woven or nonwoven)	

● Press the corner seam open.

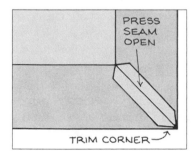

● Turn the seam allowances or the hem facing to the inside and press.

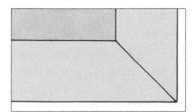

MITERING FLAT TRIMS

Flat trims require mitering any time they turn a corner. No matter where the trim is positioned on the garment, the technique is the same. It's the style of the trim—for example, whether it has two straight edges or one straight edge—that determines the mitering technique.

If you're applying the trim any place except along the edge of the garment, mark the trim placement line so that it is visible on the outside of the garment. Use a disappearing marking pen, disappearing tracing paper or a line of machine basting—whichever is appropriate for your fabric.

For Trims with Two Straight Edges

Note: With this technique, the right edge of the trim is aligned with the garment edge or the placement line.

● Pin the trim to the garment edge or along the placement line. Topstitch both edges, ending the stitching when you reach the corner.

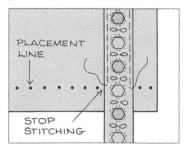

- Working at your ironing board, fold the trim back up on itself and press. Fold the trim diagonally so that it meets the intersecting garment edge or placement line; press again.

- Refold the trim back up on itself and stitch along the diagonal crease through all of the layers.

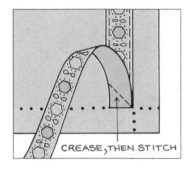

CREASE, THEN STITCH

- Fold the trim back down along the diagonal line of stitching and press. Continue topstitching along both edges of the trim.

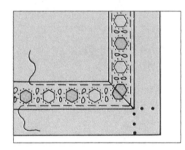

For Trims with One Straight Edge and One Decorative Edge

Note: With this technique, the left (straight) edge of the trim is aligned with the garment edge or placement line.

- Pin the straight edge of the trim to the garment edge or along the placement line. Topstitch all the way to the corner.

- Working at your ironing board, fold the trim back up on itself, positioning the fold slightly below the garment edge or placement line. Fold the trim back down so that it meets the intersecting garment edge or placement line. Secure the trim to your ironing board with a few straight pins; press the corner.

Note: You may have to refold the trim several times until you get it "just right" and are ready to press.

- Open out the trim and stitch along the diagonal crease through all of the layers.

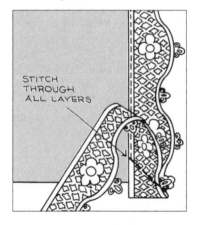

STITCH THROUGH ALL LAYERS

- Fold the trim back down, press again, and continue stitching the trim to the garment.

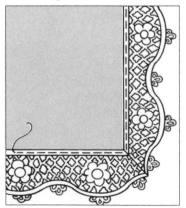

PLEATS

Pleats are folds of fabric that control fullness. They can be soft or crisp, depending on the fabric you choose and whether they're pressed or unpressed.

If you're new to sewing, or your sewing skills are rusty, wait until you've got a little more experience at your machine before you attempt pleats. It's not that pleats are difficult to sew, but they do require accurate cutting, marking and stitching...perhaps even more than most other details. Think about it: Pleats usually occur in multiples. Suppose you were making a pleated skirt with eight box pleats. If you were "off" ⅛" (3mm) on each pleat, the skirt would be 1" (2.5mm) too large or too small at the waistline.

Pleats can be formed by working on either the right or the wrong side of a garment. Your pattern instructions will tell you what to do. Mark the pleats on the wrong side of the fabric; then transfer the markings to the right side, if necessary. Mark both the fold lines and the placement lines. If you're using tracing paper or thread basting, use a different color paper or thread so you can quickly distinguish between the two types of lines.

BASIC PLEAT FORMATIONS

Knife or Straight Pleats

These pleats all face in the same direction. To make them, fold the fabric on the solid line and bring the fold to the broken line, following the arrows printed on the pattern piece. Hand-baste or pin the pleats along the folded edges; then baste across the top of all of the pleats. If the pleats are to be pressed, do it before the pleated section is attached to the rest of the garment.

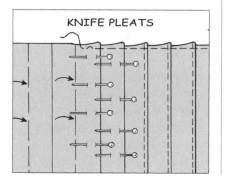

KNIFE PLEATS

Box Pleats

Each pleat consists of two straight pleats facing in opposite directions. Following your pattern instructions, fold, baste and press as for straight pleats.

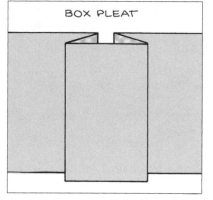

BOX PLEAT

Inverted Pleats

Often used at center front or back, an inverted pleat looks like two straight pleats that face each other, with their folds meeting at the center. An inverted pleat has a pleat underlay. It can be a separate underlay section that is seamed to the garment, or it can be formed by basting and then folding and pressing the garment section itself. Your pattern instructions will tell you how to do this.

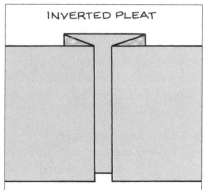

INVERTED PLEAT

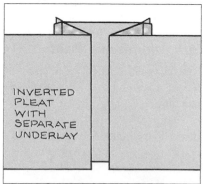

INVERTED PLEAT WITH SEPARATE UNDERLAY

tip

Here's a shortcut method for marking and making straight pleats:
- *Use your scissors to snip-mark the pleat lines within the seam allowance.*
- *Use straight pins to mark the rest of each pleat line. If you have pins with regular, flat heads and pins with rounded heads, use one style to mark the solid lines and the other to mark the broken lines.*
- *Crease the fabric along the solid line, press gently and remove the pins. Bring this pressed edge to meet the broken line and pin it in place.*
- *Continue until all of the pleats are formed. Machine-baste across the top of the pleats; then press the inside folds.*

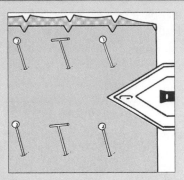

PRESSING

The best looking pleats are those that have been carefully—and properly—pressed.

Once the pleats are formed, you'll be pressing over several thicknesses of fabric. Since you don't want these layers to create ridges on the outside of your garment, here are a few suggestions:

● Always use a press cloth. If you haven't got one, use a scrap of your fashion fabric instead.

● Put strips of brown paper between the garment and the unbasted fold of each pleat as you press.

Soft (Unpressed) Pleats

Use a dry press cloth. Hold the iron 2" to 3" (5cm to 7.5cm) above the fabric and apply just a little bit of steam. Don't rest the iron directly on the fabric.

Crisp (Pressed) Pleats

Use a damp press cloth, lots of steam and the full pressure of your iron. Since the garment still has to be hemmed, press lightly when you get to within 8" (20.5cm) of the hemline. Once the hem is put in, thoroughly re-press this area.

● Once you have pressed the pleats, be sure your garment is thoroughly dry before handling it.

TOPSTITCHING AND EDGESTITCHING

Pleats are often topstitched and/or edgestitched to hold them in place. The topstitching, which starts at the waistline and extends into the hip area, is done through all of the layers.

If the fabric does not hold a crease well, it's also a good idea to edgestitch below the hip, catching only the fold of the pleat in your stitching. Do this, too, if you're going to wash your garment rather than have it dry-cleaned. The pleats

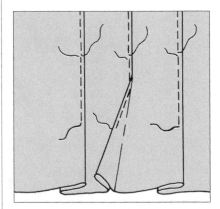

will be much easier to re-press if they're edgestitched.

To make the topstitching above and the edgestitching below the hip look like one continuous line, edgestitch the pleat fold below the hipline first. Edgestitch to within about 8" (20.5cm) of the hemline. Starting at the waistline edge, topstitch between the waist and the hip, overlapping the stitches at the hipline. Once the garment is hemmed, go back and complete the edgestitching.

HEMMING

If a seam falls at the inside fold of a pleat, you'll need to perform a little magic with your scissors to make sure everything lies flat.

- Clip the seam allowance to the line of stitching at the top of the hem allowance.

- Press the seams open below the clip and trim them to ¼" (6mm).

- Finish the raw edge of the hem allowance and hem the garment.

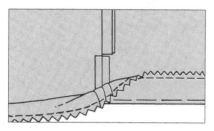

- Working on the inside of the garment, edgestitch the pleat folds within the hem allowance to keep it flat.

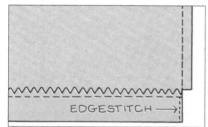

Once your garment is hemmed, you'll need to go back and re-press the lower edges of the pleats.

POCKETS

Pockets should be more than just an attractive design feature. In order to be functional they should be constructed so that they can withstand the wear and tear of frequent use!

PATCH POCKETS

Patch pockets come in an assortment of sizes and shapes, creating

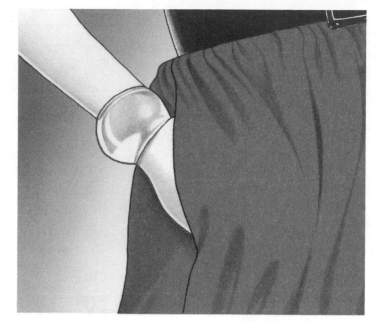

design interest on skirts, blouses, pants and jackets. Patch pockets can be lined, unlined or self-lined. Although your pattern will include only one of these techniques, you can easily convert any patch pocket to the treatment you prefer.

Unlined Pockets

Unlined pockets are the easiest to make. They're particularly popular on casual clothes and children's garments in light- to medium-weight fabrics.

To create the facing:

- Press under ¼" (6mm) on the upper edge of the pocket and edgestitch…or finish the upper edge on your serger.

- To create the pocket facing, fold the upper edge to the right side along the fold line; press.

- Starting at the fold, stitch along the seamline, backstitching at the beginning and the end.

- Trim the seam allowances in the facing area only to ¼" (6mm). If your fabric is bulky, diagonally trim the corners.

How you complete the patch pocket depends on how it is shaped.

For a curved patch pocket on your conventional machine:

- Make a row of machine gathering stitches around the curved edges. Put them ¼"(6mm) away from the first stitching, within the seam allowance.

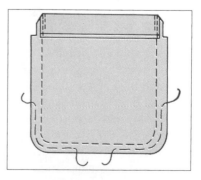

- If you own a point presser, use it when pressing the seams open in the facing area.

- Turn the facing to the wrong side pushing the upper corners out with a pin or a point turner.

- Pull up the gathering threads to shape the curve; then press under along the seamline, rolling the stitching to the wrong side. Press the facing seams and the fold.

- To eliminate bulk, notch out the fullness in the seam allowance at the curves as far as the machine basting stitches.

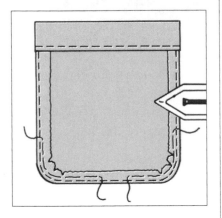

S *For a curved patch pocket on your serger:*

- Adjust your serger to the appropriate setting (see chart, right).

- Working on the right side of the pocket, serge around the pocket on the ⅝" (1.5cm) seamline, tightening the needle tension when you reach the curved areas. This will make the seam allowances curl to the inside, easing in the fullness. When you are past the curved area, loosen your needle tension to the normal setting.

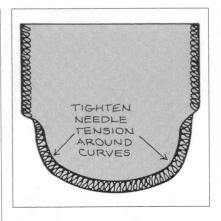

TIGHTEN NEEDLE TENSION AROUND CURVES

- Press the seam allowances to the wrong side along the stitching line.

Curved Patch Pocket			
TYPE OF SERGER STITCH:	3	4	MINE
Stitch length:	3mm	3mm	
Stitch width:	Widest	Widest	
Tensions—Needle:	Normal to very tight	Normal to tight	
Right needle:	N/A	Very tight	
Upper looper:	Slightly tight	Slightly tight	
Lower looper:	Slightly loose	Slightly loose	

For a square or rectangular pocket:

Miter the lower corners, as described in "Mitering," page 160.

To finish the patch pocket:

Edgestitch or topstitch the facing in place or secure it to the pocket with a strip of fusible web.

Lined Pockets

There are times when a pocket lining makes a nice finish. You can add this touch even if your pattern doesn't include it.

- Once the pocket is cut out, fold

tip

Another way to ensure a perfectly-shaped pocket is to use a template. You can make your own by tracing the shape of the pocket, minus seam allowances and facing, onto a piece of cardboard. Cut out the cardboard template. After the facing is turned and pressed, slip the cardboard under the facing; pull up the gathering threads and press the seam allowances over the cardboard. Or invest in a pocket curve template. This notion is a metal template with four different corner shapes and a clip to help the fabric conform to the appropriate curve for your pocket.

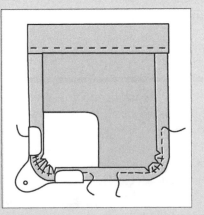

the pocket pattern piece along the fold line to omit the facing. Use this new shape to cut the lining.

- Fold under along the upper edge of the lining. The width of this fold should be equal to half the depth of the original pocket facing. Press.

- With right sides together, pin the lining to the pocket, matching sides and lower edge. Turn the pocket facing down over the lining so that all of the raw edges match; pin.

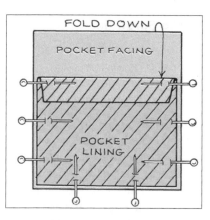

- Starting at the fold, stitch along the seamline, backstitching at the ends.

- Trim the seam allowances and corners; notch any curves.

- Press the lining seam allowance toward the lining.

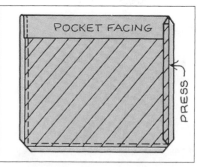

tip

Interface the pocket with a light-weight fusible interfacing. Cut the interfacing from the pocket pattern piece, eliminating the seam allowances and the facing. This will provide you with an accurate guide for shaping the curves or mitering the corners. In addition, it will help the finished pocket retain its shape.

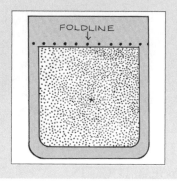

- Turn the pocket right side out and press, rolling the seam slightly to the lining side.

- Slipstitch the opening in the lining to the facing.

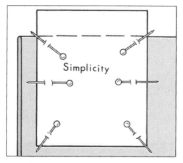

Self-lined Pockets

This super-simple way to line a pocket works best on lightweight fabrics. If your pattern does not utilize this technique, you can easily convert it.

tip

Trim ⅛" (3mm) off the sides and lower edge of the pocket lining. Pin the lining to the pocket, matching the raw edges, and proceed as for a lined pocket. The smaller lining will automatically cause the seams to roll slightly to the inside.

- When you cut out your pocket, place the pattern piece so that the foldline is on a crosswise fold of the fabric. (The facing part of the pattern will extend beyond the fold and will not be cut.)

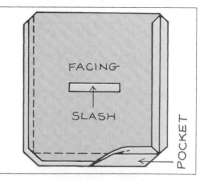

- To make the pocket, fold it in half with right sides together. Stitch, trim, clip and notch as for the lined pocket.

- Press one seam allowance toward whichever side you wish to designate as the pocket facing.

- Cut a 1½" (3.8cm) slash near the lower edge of the pocket facing.

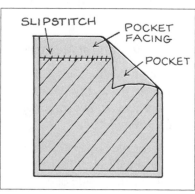

- Turn the pocket right side out through the slash. Press, rolling the seam toward the pocket facing.
- Fuse a strip of interfacing or mending tape over the slash.

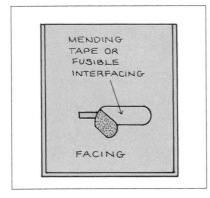

Applying the Pocket

The easiest way to apply the pocket is to topstitch or edgestitch it to the garment.

- Pin or baste the pocket in place.

tip

On delicate or hard-to-handle fabrics, such as velvet, it is easier to apply the pocket by hand. To do this, pin or hand-baste the pocket in place. Turn back the pocket edge slightly and slipstitch it to the garment. To secure, take several small stitches at the upper corners of the pocket.

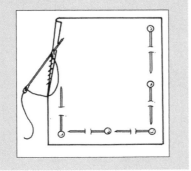

Glue stick or double-faced basting tape also work well.

- Edgestitch and/or topstitch ¼" to ⅜" (6mm to 1cm) from the edge.
- To reinforce the upper corners, backstitch or stitch a small triangle.

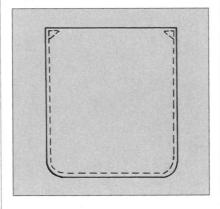

IN-SEAM POCKETS

In-seam pockets can be found at the side seams of dresses, skirts and pants. Often these pockets are created from a separate pattern piece so that the pocket can, if you wish, be cut from a lining fabric.

The Conventional Method

Your pattern instructions will tell you how to make this type of pocket. There are two important things to remember:

- Reinforce the corners by shortening your stitch length for about 1" (2.5cm) on either side of each corner.
- Clip the garment/pocket back seam allowance only so that you can press the side seams open and the pocket toward the front of the garment.

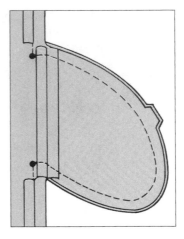

ⓢ The Serger Method

Use this technique for in-seam pockets on a skirt or pants.

If the pockets are separate sections, serge them to the garment front and back along the seamline.

- With right sides together, pin the pocket/garment sections together at the side seams. On your conventional machine, and beginning at the waistline edge, stitch along the side seam to the first marking; backstitch. Machine baste to just below the next marking. Switch back to a regular length stitch, backstitch to the marking and then stitch forward for about 3" to 4" (7.5cm to 10 cm).
- Machine-baste or glue-baste the pocket sections together along the outside edges.

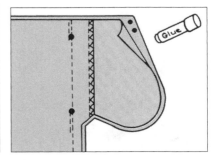

• Serge the side seams, beginning at the hemline. This is important! If you begin serging from the waistline, it is very difficult to serge around the lower edge of the pocket without cutting into the garment.

• As you approach the lower edge of the pocket, pull the pocket forward with your right hand to form as straight a line as possible. At the same time, use your left hand to guide the stitches around the curve so they remain on the garment.

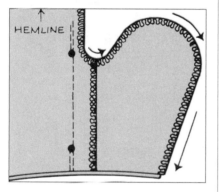

• Press the pocket toward the center front, and then remove the basting stitches from between the markings.

Cut-in-one Pockets

Some patterns have the pocket shape built into the front and back pattern pieces. This saves time because you don't have to cut out the pockets separately or stitch them to the garment. If your pattern wasn't designed this way, you can adapt it to use this method—as long as your fabric is wide enough to accommodate the expanded pattern piece.

• Lap the pocket pattern piece over the garment front pattern piece, matching the seamlines and markings. Pin or tape together. Repeat for the garment back.

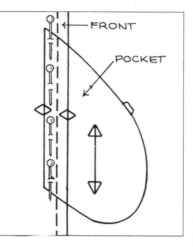

• Cut out the front and back garment sections.

• Sew the garment together on either your conventional machine or your serger, following the guidelines for in-seam pockets.

FRONT HIP POCKETS

Many pants and skirts feature partially hidden hipline pockets, sometimes called slant pockets. The slanted opening may be straight or curved.

Front hip pockets consist of two different-shaped pieces: The pocket, which also becomes part of the main section of the garment at the waistline, and the pocket facing, which finishes the opening edge.

If your pattern features this style of pocket, the pattern instructions will tell you how to construct it. However, there are a few extra things you might want to do, depending on your fabric:

• If your fashion fabric is heavy or bulky, cut the pocket facing from lightweight lining fabric in a matching color.

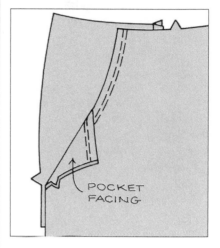

• If your fabric is very stretchy or very delicate—or if the pocket is going to get lots of use—you might want to reinforce it against the wear and tear it will endure. Cut a strip of interfacing 2" (5cm) wide and shaped to follow the opening edge of the pocket. Baste or fuse it on the inside, along the opening edge of the pocket.

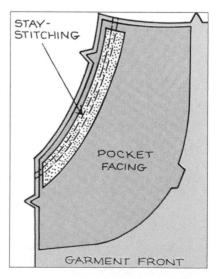

tip

S *Regardless of your choice of fabric, a front hip pocket will retain its shape better if the opening edge has a pocket stay. If you use your serger to create the stay, you'll also eliminate the need to interface the edge of the opening:*

- *With right sides together, pin the pocket facing to the garment front along the pocket opening.*
- *Serge the seam. As you do this, thread pearl cotton through the hole in the front of your presser foot or guide it over the finger guard of the presser foot so that it's caught in the stitching and acts as a stay in the seam. This technique is the same as the one used for gathering over a cord on page 148.*

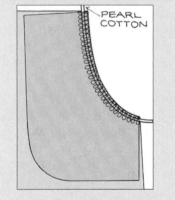

- *In place of the pearl cotton, you can also feed twill tape under the presser foot as you serge.*

RUFFLES

The two most common types of ruffles are single ruffles and double ruffles.

Single ruffles have one hemmed edge; the other edge is gathered

and then incorporated into a seam or attached to an edge.

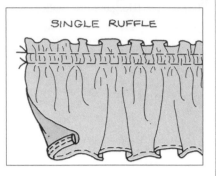

Double ruffles have two hemmed edges. The gathers can be placed along the center of the ruffle or near one edge. Then the ruffle is topstitched in place on the garment.

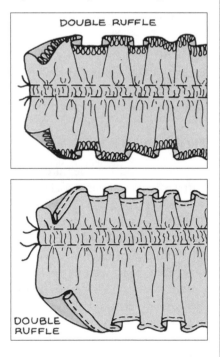

HEMMING

Since ruffles are usually made from very long strips of fabric, you'll want to use a hemming method that's fast and easy. The *narrow*

topstitched hem, the *machine-rolled hem* on your conventional machine, or the *rolled hem* or *lettuce edge hem* on your serger are all particularly good choices. See pages 150–158 for information on how to do these hems.

GATHERING

Hem the ruffle first and then gather it. Gathers in ruffles are handled the same way as gathers in any other part of a garment. (See "Gathers," page 147.) For double ruffles, put the gathering stitches along the lines indicated on your pattern pieces.

If you're making a double ruffle, do not use the technique for gathering over a cord. If you do, those zigzag stitches will be visible on the outside of your garment.

ATTACHING THE RUFFLE

Single Ruffle in a Seam

- With right sides together, pin the ruffle to one garment edge, matching notches and markings. Adjust the gathers and machine baste in place.

tip

If you're making a single ruffle from a lightweight fabric, you can eliminate the need to do any hemming. Cut the strips twice the desired depth, plus 1½" (3.8cm). Fold the strip in half lengthwise with wrong sides together and gather the raw edges with two rows of stitches.

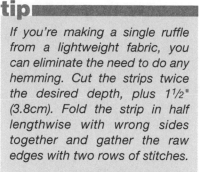

- With right sides together, pin the ruffled section to the remaining garment section. With the ruffled section on top, stitch along the seamline, just to the left of the basting.

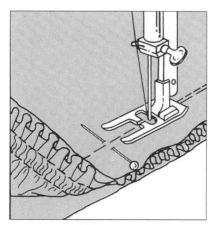

- Press the seam allowances flat and then press them in the direction indicated on the pattern instructions.

Single Ruffle at an Edge

If you're customizing your pattern by adding a ruffle, begin by trimming the garment hem allowance to ⅝" (1.5cm).

The Conventional Method

- Press under along the hemline or seamline.

- Working with right sides up, lap the pressed edge of the garment over the raw edge of the ruffle so that the raw edges meet underneath. Pin, adjusting the gathers to fit and allowing for extra fullness if you're going around any corners.

- Edgestitch close to the fold through all of the layers.

- Finish the raw edges of the ruffle by zigzagging, machine overcasting or serging the edges together.

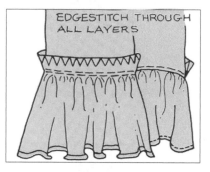

S *The Serger Method*

- With right sides together, pin the ruffle to the garment edge, adjusting the gathers to fit.

- Serge the seam and then press the seam allowances toward the garment.

- Working on the right side, and using your conventional machine, edgestitch close to the seamline, through all the layers.

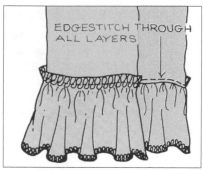

Double Ruffle

- Pin the wrong side of the ruffle to the right side of the garment, matching all of the markings. Adjust the gathers to fit.

- Topstitch over the gathering stitches.

- Remove the gathering stitches or hide them with a trim, such as ribbon or rickrack.

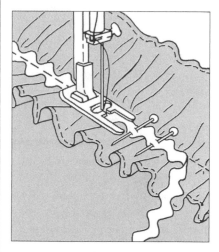

ADDING YOUR OWN RUFFLES

You can add ruffles to your garment even if the pattern does not include them.

Ruffles can be cut on the straight grain or the bias. If the ruffle is very long, you'll probably have to piece it.

tips

● *Adding a single ruffle to the hem edge is a good way to lengthen a child's dress, particularly when there isn't enough hem allowance to let down. If the old hemline leaves permanent marks, cover it with ribbon or trim.*

● *Use ribbon as a substitute for a ruffle. Because the long edges are already finished, there's no need to hem the edge. For best results, the ribbon must be at least 1½" (3.8cm) wide.*

As a rule of thumb, the ruffle section should be two to three times the length of the area to which it will be attached. In general, the wider the ruffle or the more sheer the fabric, the longer the ruffle should be. This will result in a fuller, more attractive ruffle. Cut your ruffle the desired finished width plus 1½" (3.8cm) for hem allowances and seam allowances.

SHOULDER PADS

Shoulder pads are an integral part of the stylish silhouette but, depending on the prevailing whims of fashion, their role may be very subtle or dramatically prominent.

AS A FITTING TOOL

In addition to enhancing the fashion look, shoulder pads can be a quick and easy way to enhance the fit of a garment.

Narrow or Hollow Shoulders

Shoulder pads can fill the natural hollow that occurs just below the shoulder. They can also add width to narrow shoulders.

Uneven Shoulders

This is a common fitting problem that's easily corrected with different size shoulder pads. The shoulder that's lower gets the thicker pad. Don't try to get away with just one pad for the lower shoulder.

The result will be a bumpy, lop-sided appearance.

Large Bust

Try adding small shoulder pads to your garments. By adding balance to the upper body, shoulder pads can minimize the appearance of a large bust.

AS A FASHION TOOL

Shoulder pads are available in the traditional style for set-in sleeves,

NARROW SHOULDERS

BEFORE

AFTER

UNEVEN SHOULDERS

BEFORE

AFTER

LARGE BUST

BEFORE

AFTER

TRADITIONAL
JACKET
PAD

TRADITIONAL
DRESS
PAD

EXTENDED
JACKET
PAD

EXTENDED
DRESS
PAD

as well as in an extended shoulder style for kimono or raglan sleeves or dropped shoulders.

The type of garment you're making determines the size pad you'll need:

- Use ¼" to ½" (6mm to 1.3cm) pads for blouses and dresses. This size is occasionally used for jackets when a small pad is desired.

- Use ½" to 1" (1.3cm to 2.5cm) pads for jackets and coats. This size is occasionally used for dresses when an oversized look is the fashion focus.

ATTACHING THE SHOULDER PAD

On Set-in Sleeves

- Pin the shoulder pad to the inside of the garment so that the largest layer of the pad is against the garment. The shoulder line of the pad should match the shoulder seam of the garment and the straightest edge of the pad should extend ½" (1.3cm) beyond the armhole seam.

- Try the garment on to check the pad placement.

- Remove the garment. On the inside, loosely hand-tack the pad in place at the shoulder seam allowance and along the armhole seam allowance.

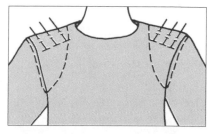

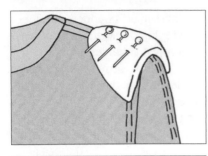

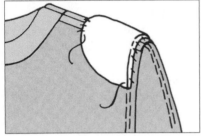

On Drop Shoulders, Kimono or Raglan Sleeves

● Try on the garment and slip the shoulder pad inside. Shift the pad over the shoulder until it looks right and feels comfortable. Pin it in place from the outside of the garment.

● Remove the garment. On the inside, loosely hand tack the pad to the shoulder seam allowance.

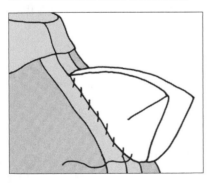

Removable Shoulder Pads

Permanently attaching the shoulder pads may not be the most efficient idea. Suppose they need to

be removed when the garment is washed or dry-cleaned…or suppose you don't want to invest in multiple sets of pads. The solution? Use self-gripping hook-and-loop fasteners to make them easy to remove.

● Using the hook side of the fastener, hand-sew three dots or one strip to the garment along the shoulder line or seam.

Try on the garment. Adjust the position of the pad until it looks right and feels comfortable. Pin it in place from the outside of the garment.

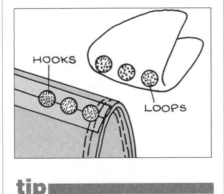

● Remove the garment. On the pad, mark the corresponding position(s) of the loop section(s) of the fastener. Hand-tack them in place.

SHOULDER PAD COVERS

Sometimes, particularly in the case of unlined jackets and coats, you'll want your shoulder pads to be the same color as your garment. Shoulder pad covers are easy to make.

● Cut a rectangle of lining fabric large enough to cover both sides of the pad, plus ⅝" (1.5cm) all around.

● Position the shoulder pad so that the straight edge of the pad is on the bias grainline.

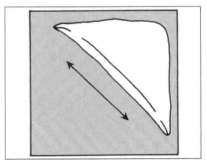

● Fold the lining over the pad.

● Straight-stitch along the edge of the pad, trim the seam allowances to ½" (6mm) and zigzag over the raw edge *or* serge the edges.

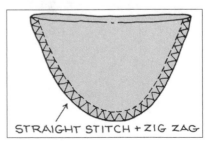

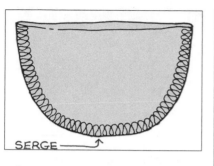

SERGE

tip

If you're using covered shoulder pads on a dress or blouse, don't even bother attaching them to your garment. Instead, use ½" (1.3cm) wide strips of hook-and-loop fasteners. Hand-sew the hook side to the top of the pad, along the shoulder line. Position the loop side on top of the hook side and hand-sew the two sections together at the end nearest the neck edge. To wear the pads, open the fastener, position the pad on your shoulder under your bra strap, and close the fastener.

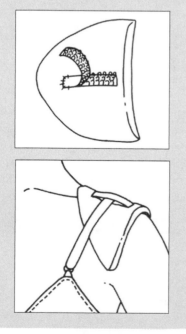

SLEEVES

There are three basic styles of sleeves: Set-in, kimono and raglan. Because they're easy to sew and easy to fit, raglan and kimono styles are usually the best choices when you are just learning to sew. However, sooner or later, a garment with a set-in sleeve will be at the top of your sewing list. The result you'll want is a smooth fitting sleeve, one that doesn't have any dimples or tucks along the seam of the sleeve cap.

KIMONO SLEEVES

Kimono sleeves are cut as part of the garment front and garment back. Since there's nothing to deal with but an underarm seam, they're the easiest style to sew.

- Pin the garment front and back together at the side/underarm seams, matching raw edges, notches and markings.

- Beginning at the lower edge of the garment, stitch along the ⅝" (1.5cm) seamline.

- Reinforce the underarm area by stitching at the curve…or center a 4" to 5" (10cm to12.5cm) piece of seam binding or twill tape over the curved area before the seam is stitched and baste it in place. When you stitch the seam, shorten the stitch slightly along the length of the tape (A).

- Clip the curves and press the seam open. *Do not* clip the seam binding (B).

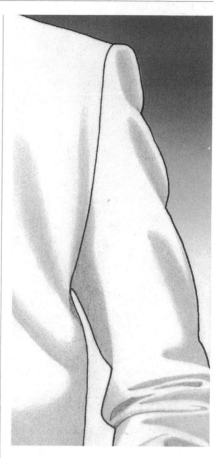

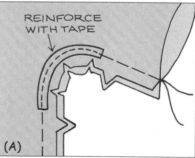

REINFORCE WITH TAPE

(A)

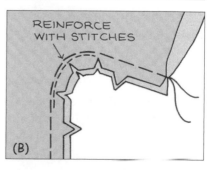

REINFORCE WITH STITCHES

(B)

RAGLAN SLEEVES

Raglan sleeves are joined to the garment front and garment back by diagonal seams that run from the underarm to the neckline. In addition, there may be a shoulder dart or a shoulder seam. To insert the sleeve on your conventional machine, follow your pattern instructions, reinforcing the diagonal seams by stitching again over the first stitching.

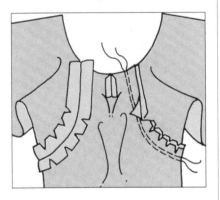

S *The Serger Method*

The flatlock or trellis seam is an easy technique that lends a decorative, ready-to-wear look to any item. Because it's a strong seam that can withstand many washings, it's a good choice for raglan sleeve sweatshirts and children's garments. Consider it, too, if you want to make your raglan sleeve garment reversible.

S The Two-thread True Flatlock Seam

• Adjust your serger to the appropriate settings (see chart above).

• With wrong sides together, serge the seams; then, working from the right side of the fabric, pull the two layers apart until the seam lies flat.

True Flatlock Seam		
TYPE OF SERGER STITCH:	2	MINE
Stitch length:	2mm-3mm	
Stitch width:	Widest	
Tensions—Needle:	Very loose	
Right needle:	N/A	
Upper looper:	N/A	
Lower looper:	Normal	

S The Three-thread Mock Flatlock Seam

If your serger does not have two-thread capabilities, here's how to create the same effect with a three-thread stitch. Don't limit its use to raglan sleeves. It's great anyplace else you want a flatlock effect.

• Adjust your serger to the appropriate settings (see chart below).

• Trim the seam allowances to ¼" (6mm).

• With the wrong sides together, place the seam under the presser foot so that the raw edge will not be trimmed and the fabric fills up only half of the stitch. Note: Filling up only half of the stitch ensures that the flatlock seam will lie perfectly flat. Serge a test seam to determine exactly where the raw edge needs to be positioned on your serger.

Mock Flatlock Seam		
TYPE OF SERGER STITCH:	3	MINE
Stitch length:	2mm-3mm	
Stitch width:	Widest	
Tensions—Needle:	Very loose	
Upper looper:	Normal to loose	
Lower looper:	Very tight	

• Serge the seam; then, working from the right side of the fabric, pull the two layers apart until the seam lies flat.

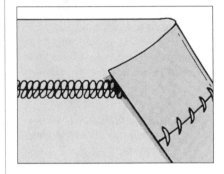

Set-in Sleeves

One of the things that distinguishes a set-in sleeve from a kimono or raglan style is the fact that the sleeve itself is slightly larger than the armhole of the garment. The excess fabric occurs in the area between the notches, called the sleeve cap. If the sleeve didn't have this extra fabric, there wouldn't be enough "play" for you to raise your arm. The mark of a professional-looking garment is a set-in sleeve that's properly eased

tip

For your first set-in sleeve, consider one with a tucked or gathered sleeve cap. Then you won't have to bother about carefully easing in the fullness. Once you've had the experience of setting in a sleeve, go on to a second project that has an eased sleeve cap.

into the armhole, creating a smooth seam and a rounded shape for your shoulder.

Easing the Sleeve Cap— Three Methods

For best results, ease the sleeve cap before stitching the sleeve underarm seam.

The Traditional Easing Method

Working on the right side of the fabric, ease-stitch the sleeve cap twice. Ease-stitch first along the seamline between the notches; then stitch ¼" (6mm) away, within the seam allowance. Be sure to leave the threads long enough to pull them up to create the sleeve cap.

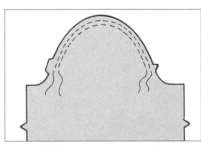

The Ease-stitch-plus Method

If you are working with a pliable, woven fabric, try this method.

- Stitch along the seamline between the notches with a regular stitch. As you stitch, place one forefinger on each side of the seamline just in front of the needle and pull the fabric horizontally so it's stretched off-grain. While you're doing this, push the fabric back and under the presser foot for four or five stitches.

- Stop stitching, relax the fabric and then repeat, pulling and pushing the fabric back as you sew. The sleeve will automatically shape itself into a cap.

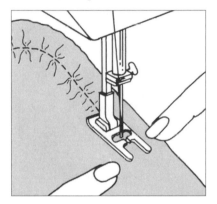

⬛ The Serger Easing Method

Easing a sleeve cap on the serger is simply a matter of tightening the needle tension until the fabric starts to pull up behind the foot. However, once stitched, these gathers can be adjusted only

slightly. Test on a scrap of fabric…and save this technique until you and your serger are good friends.

Note: Because this technique will cut off the notches, be sure to mark their location with a fabric marking pen or dressmaker's carbon.

- Adjust your serger to the appropriate setting (see chart below).

- There are two ways to serge your easing stitches:

Technique 1: Working on the wrong side, serge the easing stitches on the ⅝" (1.5cm) seamline. This leaves you with a ¼" (6mm) seam allowance when you sew the sleeve to the garment.

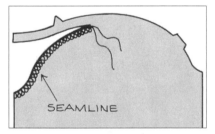

SEAMLINE

Technique 2: Working on the wrong side, serge the easing stitches, keeping the raw edge of the sleeve cap even with the blade so you don't trim off any of the seam allowance. Later on, when you stitch the sleeve to the garment on your conventional

Serger Easing Method			
TYPE OF SERGER STITCH:	**3**	**4**	**MINE**
Stitch length:	Normal	Normal	
Stitch width:	Normal	Normal	
Tensions—Needle:	Tight	Tight	
Right needle:	N/A	Very tight	
Upper looper:	Normal	Normal	
Lower looper:	Normal	Normal	
Note: If the fabric is heavy or more easing is required, tighten the needle tension(s) even more. If you need to remove the stitches and start again, see page 98 for the fastest way to rip.			

machine, place one forefinger on either side of the presser foot and pull the fabric horizontally so that the sleeve cap is stretched off grain. It's just like ease-stitching plus, but without pushing the fabric.

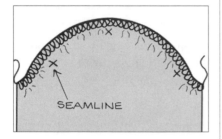

SEAMLINE

Preparing the Sleeve

Stitch the sleeve seam and press it open. Finish the lower edge of the sleeve according to the pattern instructions and/or the information provided in "Cuffs," page 136. Now you're ready to pin baste the sleeve to the garment.

- Turn the sleeve right side out; turn the garment inside out. Slip the sleeve inside the armhole and pin together at the sleeve and garment underarm seams, the shoulder markings and notches.

- Now match and pin the remaining markings.

- Draw up the ease stitching at each end, sliding the fabric along

tip

If you're working with a knit that stretches, forget about ease stitching. Working with the garment side up, pin the sleeve to the armhole edge, matching markings. As you stitch, ease in the fullness by stretching the armhole to fit the sleeve.

to distribute the fullness evenly in the area between the notches. Your goal is to get the sleeve to fit smoothly in the armhole. Pin closely all around the eased area and then pin the underarm area between the notches.

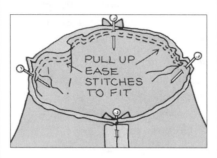

PULL UP EASE STITCHES TO FIT

Stitching the Sleeve

- With the sleeve side up, begin at the underarm seam and stitch along the seamline, just to the left of the first row of ease stitches. As you stitch, place your forefingers on either side of the presser foot, as shown, to keep the eased area from puckering under the needle (see illustration below).

- When you reach the underarm seam, overlap the stitches.

- Stitch a second row ⅛" (3mm) away from the first, within the seam allowance.

- Trim the seam allowance close to the stitching in the underarm area between the notches.

- To strengthen and reinforce the underarm area, it's wise to finish the seam allowances between the notches by machine zigzagging, overcasting or serging the edges. If your fabric ravels, finish the entire armhole.

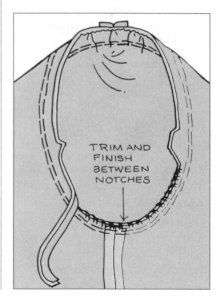

TRIM AND FINISH BETWEEN NOTCHES

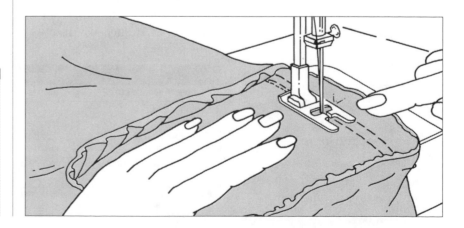

tips

● *If you haven't had much experience setting in a sleeve...or if your machine doesn't stitch over pins...or if you want to try the garment on to check the fit of the sleeve, hand-baste close to the seamline and remove the pins.*

● *The shallower the curve of the sleeve cap, the less ease the sleeve has. If your sleeve has very little ease, you may find it easier to attach it to the garment before the underarm seam is stitched. Once the sleeve is attached, sew the garment side seam and the sleeve seam in one continuous stitching operation.*

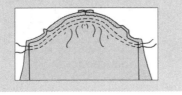

Pressing the Sleeve

● With the sleeve side up, place the upper portion of the armhole seam (the area between the notches) over the end of a sleeve board, tailor's ham or ironing board.

● With the point of the iron, press only the seam allowances. Use steam if appropriate for your fabrics. This blends the stitching and shrinks out some of the fullness. No further pressing is needed because the seam allowances will naturally turn toward the sleeve.

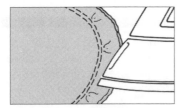

TAILORING THE SPEED WAY

Tailoring a jacket has never been easier. Today, speed tailoring techniques are synonymous with quality tailoring techniques. The reason: Fusible interfacings that can replace padstitching and other tedious handwork.

APPLYING THE INTERFACING

The following guidelines are for a woman's lined classic blazer.

Although the style of your jacket, as well as the shape of the interfacing sections, may vary, the general principles will remain the same.

Take a close look at the accompanying sketches of the collar, undercollar, jacket front, jacket back and facing sections of a classic blazer. You can clearly see the areas where the interfacing should go. For a softer look, you may want to eliminate the interfacing on the facing and the upper collar.

Since most jackets are made from medium- to heavyweight fabrics, you'll need to keep the bulk in the seam allowances to a minimum. To do this, trim ½" (1.3cm) from the seam allowances of all of the interfacing sections before fusing them in place.

If the jacket front or back has darts, trim the interfacing away along the dart stitching lines before fusing.

Note that an extra layer of interfacing has been added to the undercollar and the jacket front. The undercollar stand and the lapel reinforcement sections shape and stabilize these critical areas, eliminating the need for padstitching.

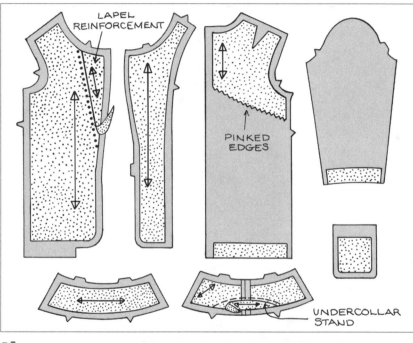

tips

● *If it's your first tailoring project, speed tailoring begins with the right fabric. Choose one that is easy to work with. Because it can be easily steamed and molded into shape, your best bet is either 100 percent wool or a blend with a high percentage of wool. To hide any less-than-perfect stitching, choose a wool with a slight texture, such as tweed or double knit, or one with a brushed surface or slubbed yarns. Since most jackets are made from medium– to heavyweight fabrics, you'll need to keep the bulk in the seam allowances to a minimum. To do this, trim ½" (1.3cm) from the seam allowances of all of the interfacing sections before fusing them in place.*

● *You may not want to use the same weight interfacing throughout the entire jacket. For example, you might use a fusible knit interfacing for the jacket back and a firmer woven or nonwoven interfacing in the rest of the jacket. If you wanted a soft look at the edges, you might choose a lighter weight interfacing for the hems.*

Undercollar Stand

For this technique, you'll have to create a pattern piece:

● Trace the shape between the roll line and the neck edge on the undercollar pattern piece, eliminating the ⅝" (1.5cm) neckline seam allowance.

● Change the center back seamline to a "place on the fold" line, eliminating the center back seam allowance.

● Draw a grainline that is perpendicular to the foldline.

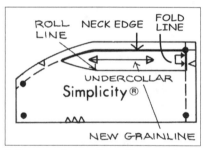

● Cut out the undercollar stand. Position it on the wrong side of the (already interfaced) undercollar, a scant ⅛" (3mm) below the roll line, and fuse in place.

Lapel Reinforcement

For this technique, you'll have to create a pattern piece:

● Using the jacket front pattern piece, trace the shape formed between the roll line and the outer edge of the lapel, eliminating the ⅝" (1.5cm) seam allowances.

tip

To prevent a ridge across the back of the jacket, pink the lower edge of the back interfacing before fusing it in place.

• Draw a new grainline that's parallel to the roll line. Fuse the front interfacing to the jacket front. Then place the lapel reinforcement over the first layer of interfacing, positioning it a scant ⅛" (3mm) from the roll line. Fuse in place.

PRESSING TO ADD SHAPE

Once your interfacings are fused in place, but before sewing any of the garment sections together, use your steam iron to build in some additional shape.

The Undercollar

Fold the undercollar down along the roll line. Using straight pins, fasten it to a tailor's ham the way it would rest on your body. Holding the iron several inches away, apply

a generous amount of steam. Be sure the undercollar is thoroughly dry before you remove it from the ham.

The Lapels

Put the jacket front, right side up, on the ironing board. Fold a hand towel lengthwise into several thicknesses and insert it under the curve of the lapel. Holding your iron several inches above the lapel, apply a generous amount of steam. Repeat for the other lapel. Be sure each section is thoroughly dry before you remove it from the ironing board.

To continue assembling the jacket, consult your pattern instructions.

Speed Linings

The traditional way to insert a lining in a jacket is by hand; the modern, speed method is by machine.

To put the lining in by machine, follow these steps:

Step 1. Assemble the body of the jacket, but do not attach the upper

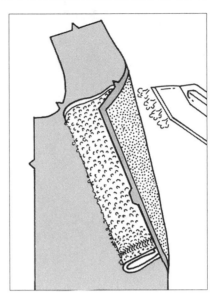

collar or the facings or construct the hem.

Step 2. Sew the body of the lining together, including setting in the sleeves.

Step 3. Sew the jacket facings and upper collar together.

Step 4. Sew the facings/upper collar to the lining, beginning and ending the seam approximately 5"(12.5cm) from the lower edge of the lining.

SPEED LININGS

STEP 1

UNDER COLLAR

FACING

LINING

LEAVE SEAM OPEN AT BOTTOM

STEPS 2,3 & 4

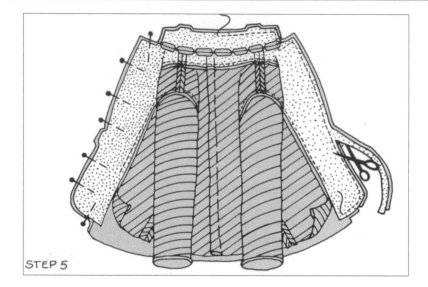

STEP 5

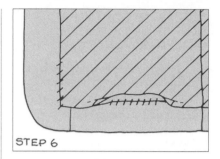

STEP 6

Step 5. With right sides together, pin the facings/upper collar to the body of the jacket, matching all of the markings; stitch. Trim, grade and press the seam allowances. Then turn the garment right side out and give it a thorough pressing. (To learn the secret of crisp, neat notches where the collar meets the lapel, see the TIP below).

Step 6. Hem the jacket and then hem the lining by slipstitching it in place over the raw edge of the jacket hem allowance and the lower edge of the front facing.

TRIMS

Trims are the finishing touches that give your garment its personality. Go tailored, sportive or feminine with trims that you purchase by the yard or trims that you create yourself on the serger.

You don't have to be limited by the trim recommendations on your pattern envelope. Feel free, as the fashion mood strikes you, to add trims to any garment. Use them to highlight a seam or detail and bring it into focus.

tip

The first secret to crisp, neat notches is to make sure that the dot that indicates the notch is clearly marked on all of the sections—the collar, undercollar, jacket front and front facing. The second secret is in the stitching procedure:

• *With right sides together, pin the facings/undercollar to the body of the jacket.*

• *Take one small hand basting stitch through only the jacket and the jacket facing at the notch marking. This will keep the layers from shifting during machine stitching. Don't catch the seam allowances, the undercollar or the upper collar in the basting stitch. Tie the ends of the thread in a square knot.*

• *Keeping the seam allowances free, and beginning at the notch marking on the collar/undercollar, machine-stitch from the dot to the center back of the collar.*

• *Beginning at the notch marking on the jacket front/front facing, stitch from the dot to the lower edge of the jacket, keeping the seam allowances free at the notch marking. Tie the thread ends at the notch in a knot.*

• *Repeat for the other side of the jacket, overlapping the stitches at the center back collar.*

• *If you look carefully, you'll see that you have a small hole at the lapel notch where you started your stitching. Without it, there wouldn't be enough room for all of the layers of fabric that converge at the notch when the jacket is turned and pressed. The hole will magically disappear on your finished jacket.*

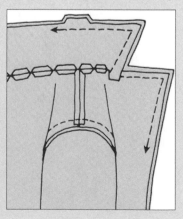

TRIMMING HINTS

Here are some practical tips to follow when using purchased trim:

● If you're adding trim to a pattern that does not already call for it, you'll need to determine how much to buy. Measure the areas to be trimmed and then add at least ½ yd.(.5m) so you'll have enough extra to join the ends and go around corners and curves.

● Be sure the trim requires the same care as your garment. Don't put a dry-clean-only trim on a garment you intend to wash.

● For curves, choose a flexible trim, such as rickrack, bias tape, foldover braid or knitted bands.

● Use pins, double-faced basting tape, strips of fusible web or fabric glue to hold the trim in place for

Gathering Lace			
TYPE OF SERGER STITCH:	3	4	MINE
Stitch length:	Longest	Longest	
Stitch width:	Widest	Widest	
Tensions—Needle:	Tight*	Tight*	
Right needle:	N/A	Tight	
Upper looper:	Normal	Normal	
Lower looper:	Normal	Normal	

For denser gathers, tighten the needle tension.

stitching. As you do this, keep the trim relaxed, not taut, so there won't be any puckering once the trim is permanently stitched in place.

● Stitch trims in place with a slightly loose thread tension.

● If the trim needs to be stitched along two edges, for example, when you're applying a ribbon or a band, or if you're stitching parallel rows of trim, always stitch in the same direction. This prevents ripples or puckering.

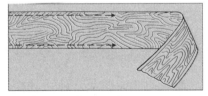

● When applying a flat trim at a corner, make sure your corners are neat and sharp. Review the section on "Mitering," pages 160–162.

Ⓢ GATHERING LACE

Occasionally, you may want to use a coordinating straight lace and ruffled lace trim in the same garment. Since it's not always easy to find matching lace, use your serger to transform a piece of straight lace trim into a ruffled trim.

Note: Because lace has a delicate,

open weave, this technique differs slightly from the ones described in "Gathers," pages 147–150.

● Adjust your serger to the appropriate setting (see chart, above).

● With the right side up, place the straight edge of the lace just to the left of the blade so that you won't cut the lace as you serge.

● Holding your finger firmly against the back of the foot, begin serging. As you stitch, the lace will pile up behind the foot. Keep serging until you can't hold the lace any longer.

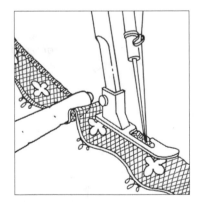

● Repeat, until you've serged the entire length of the lace.

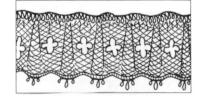

EDGINGS

Trims with at least one decorative edge, such as fringe, piping and pre-gathered ruffles, can be applied

tip

If you are applying a heavy trim to a lighter-weight fabric, machine stitching may mean lots of undesirable puckers. As an alternative, consider fusing the trim in place, using strips of paper-backed fusible web. (See "Iron-ons, Fusibles and Fusible Webs," page 101.)

tip

Pre-gathered trims require some special handling if they are inserted in a seam.
• To get the trim to lie flat at a corner, some extra fullness is needed. To get it, take a tiny tuck in the trim at the corner before basting it in place.
• If the trimmed edge will be intersected by another garment edge, such as on a collar or a cuff, taper the ends into the seam allowance, clearing the edge that will be stitched to the garment.

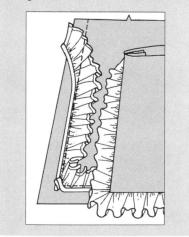

in several different ways, depending on where they are located on the garment.

Inserted in a Seam

• With the wrong side of the trim to the right side of the fabric, place the trim along the seamline so that the decorative edge is toward the garment and the raw edge is inside the seam allowance. For pre-gathered ruffles or piping, place the binding edge just over the seamline; for rickrack, center it over the seamline.

• Machine-baste the trim in place along the seamline. Use a zipper foot when stitching bulky trims, such as piping or bound ruffles.

• Pin the garment sections right sides together. Then, using your conventional machine or your serger, stitch just to the left of the basting.

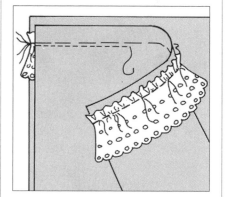

• Press the seam allowances to one side.

Along an Edge

Topstitched method: Use this technique on a finished garment edge or on a raw edge that has been folded under and pressed.

• Lap the finished edge or the pressed edge of the garment over the straight edge of the trim and topstitch it in place. For rickrack, lap the garment edge so that only one set of points is visible.

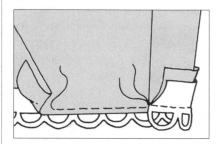

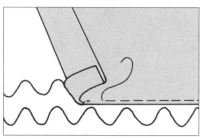

• Trims with two decorative edges, such as scalloped braid or rickrack, can be positioned on the outside of the garment and topstitched in place.

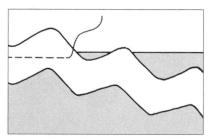

S *Three/Four Thread Method:*

Use this method to apply lace trim with one straight edge to the raw edge of a garment. This technique also can be used with other straight-edge trims. However, always make a test sample first to make sure the finished effect is not too bulky.

- If necessary, trim the raw edge of the garment so that there is a ⅝" (1.5cm) seam or hem allowance.

- Adjust your serger to the appropriate setting (see chart below).

- Place the lace and the fabric right sides together, with the straight edge of the lace parallel to and ½" (1.3cm) from the raw edge of the fabric. Use glue sticks or pins to hold the lace in place.

- Lift the presser foot and place the garment, lace side up, so that the straight edge of the trim is aligned slightly to the lcft of the blade; serge, trimming off the excess garment fabric.

- Press the seam allowance toward the garment.

- If desired, topstitch on your conventional machine.

Flatlock Method			
TYPE OF SERGER STITCH:	3	4	MINE
Stitch length:	2mm-3mm	2mm-3mm	
Stitch width:	Widest	Widest	
Tensions—Needle:	Very loose	Very loose	
Right needle:	N/A	N/A	
Upper looper:	N/A	Loose	
Lower looper:	Normal	Very tight	

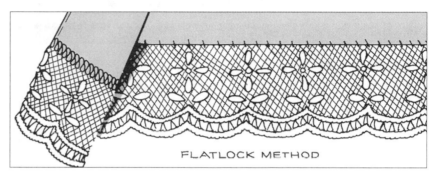

FLATLOCK METHOD

Flatlock method: This technique can be used to apply lace with one straight edge to a raw edge or to a finished garment edge.

- Adjust your serger to the appropriate setting (see chart above).

- Place the lace and the fabric right sides together, with the straight edge of the lace parallel to and ½" (1.3cm) from the raw edge of the fabric. Use a glue stick or pins to hold the lace in place.

- Lift the presser foot and place the garment, lace side up, so that the straight edge of the trim is aligned slightly to the left of the blade; serge, trimming off the excess garment fabric.

- Gently pull on the lace and the fabric until the stitches are flat; press.

Rolled Hem Method: This technique can be used to apply lace with one straight edge to the raw edge of a garment.

- Adjust your serger to the appropriate setting (see chart, page 186).

- Place the lace and the fabric right sides together, with the straight edge of the lace parallel to and ½" (1.3cm) from the raw edge of the

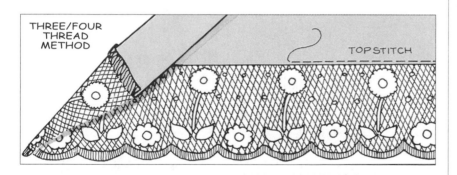

THREE/FOUR THREAD METHOD

TOPSTITCH

Three/Four Thread Method			
TYPE OF SERGER STITCH:	3	4	MINE
Stitch length:	2mm-3mm	2mm-3mm	
Stitch width:	Widest	Widest	
Tensions—Needle:	Normal	Normal	
Right needle:	N/A	Normal	
Upper looper:	Normal	Normal	
Lower looper:	Normal	Normal	

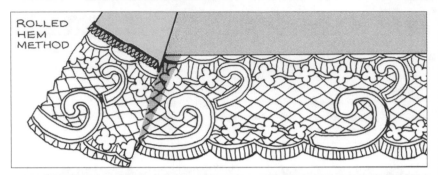

ROLLED
HEM
METHOD

Rolled Hem Method		
TYPE OF SERGER STITCH:	3	MINE

Stitch length:
Stitch width:
Tension—Needle:
     Upper looper:
     Lower looper:
	1mm
	Narrowest
	Normal
	Tight*
	Very tight	

*Use woolly nylon or silk thread		

fabric. Use a glue stick or pins to hold the lace in place.

● Lift the presser foot and place the garment, lace side up, so that the straight edge of the trim is aligned slightly to the left of the blade; serge, trimming off the excess garment fabric.

● Gently pull on the lace and the fabric until the stitches are flat; press.

APPLIED TRIMS

Bands or any other trim with two finished edges can be applied almost anywhere on the outside of the garment. Create borders by applying the trims in parallel rows. Create a checkered or woven effect by crisscrossing them on a bodice, yoke or cuff. Use narrow, flat trims, such as braid or yarn, to create intricate, curved designs.

For a wide trim: Apply it before stitching the garment sections together. That way the trim ends will be caught in the seams. Topstitch along both trim edges.

For a narrow trim: Stitch through the center of the trim or along both edges, depending on the trim's width. For very narrow braid or yarn, use a special braid foot that has a groove to make the application easier.

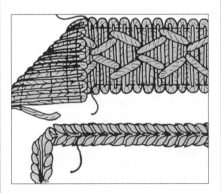

INSERTIONS

See-through trims with two finished edges, such as lace or eyelet, are perfect for insertions on flat garments where there are no darts or curved seams.

Apply the insertions to the garment sections before seaming so that the ends of the trim can be included in the seam.

The Conventional Method

● Pin the trim in place and topstitch close to both edges. For scalloped edges, stitch just inside the points, leaving the decorative edges free.

● Working on the wrong side of the garment, cut the fabric only between the two rows of topstitching. Press the seam allowances away from the trim.

● Working on the right side of the garment, edgestitch close to pressed edges, through all of the layers.

● Working on the wrong side of the garment and using your embroidery scissors, trim the seam allowances close to the stitching, as shown at the top of the following page.

⑤ The Serger Method

If your lace has two straight edges, you can insert it using either the Flatlock Method or the Rolled Hem Method described under "Edgings," page 184.

Before you begin, use a fabric marker, dressmaker carbon or other appropriate method to mark two parallel trim placement lines. The distance between these lines should be ½" (1.3cm) less than the width of your trim.

To apply the lace:

● Position one finished edge of the lace between the placement lines

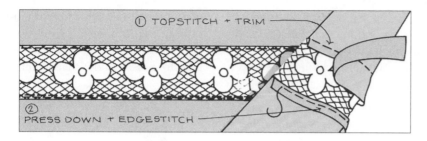

so that it overlaps the marking ⅛" (3mm).

● Adjust your serger and serge, following the directions for either the Flatlock Method (see chart, page 185, top right) or the Rolled Hem Method (see chart, page 186).

● Match the other finished edge of the lace with the other placement line and serge.

● Open out the garment section so the lace lies flat; press.

⑤ CREATING CUSTOM TRIM ON THE SERGER

Decorative threads (see Chapter 5, page 89) can be used to create special effects with your serger. Consider threading knitting ribbon (silk or rayon, but not 100 percent polyester) or pearl cotton through the upper looper and then serging around the edges of a wool cape or jacket. Imagine variegated pearl cotton used to serge the neckline,

hem and sleeve edges of a dress or tunic. No need for linings, facings, or hems!

When working with any decorative thread, use the following procedure:

● Thread the needle with all-purpose thread.

● Thread the decorative thread through the thread guides and the upper looper and/or the lower looper. (You may wish to use all-purpose thread in one of the loopers.)

● Adjust your serger to the appropriate settings (see chart, below left).

● Serge a test swatch of the garment fabric, feeding the fabric so that the seam/hem allowance is trimmed off. Adjust the tensions as necessary so that the decorative thread forms an even stitch. If you get an uneven stitch—or your stitches form an S or a zigzag pattern—loosen the tensions even more or bypass the tension assemblies. If the thread still doesn't feed smoothly (a special problem with knitting ribbon), try bypassing the top thread guide of the upper looper.

● If you're serging in a circle, stop stitching when the stitches meet and then overlap two stitches. Pull on the needle thread just above the needle so that there's about 3" (7.5cm) of slack. Lift the presser foot and pull the garment out from under the foot. Cut the threads. To secure the thread ends use a craft or yarn needle with a large eye and tunnel the threads back under the stitching on the wrong side of the garment.

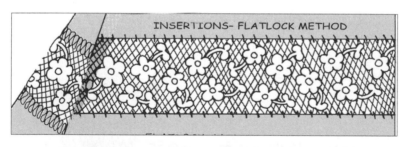

Custom Trim			
TYPE OF SERGER STITCH:	**2**	**3**	**MINE**
Stitch length:	2mm-4mm	2mm-4mm	
Stitch width:	Widest	Widest	
Tensions—Needle:	Very loose	Tight	
Upper looper:	N/A	"0"	
Lower looper:	"0"	Normal	

tips

● **S** *To determine how much decorative thread you will need, measure the length of the project edge to be finished. Multiply this by 7 and add 6 yds. (5.5m) for testing. You will need this amount for each looper through which you are using decorative thread.*

● **S** *If you're using decorative three-thread stitching on a garment where both sides of the stitches will show, for example, a cape, poncho or reversible garment, consider using topstitching thread in the needle and the lower looper. The stitches will have a more polished look.*

S Shirring

For a smocked, decorative treatment at the waistline or wrist, or on the bodice of a child's dress, use your serger, pearl cotton and narrow elastic cord. This is a quick and easy substitute for conventional smocking or shirring, as well as an attractive substitute for an elasticized casing.

● Adjust your serger to the appropriate setting (see chart, below).

● With wrong sides together, fold the garment along one smocking line.

● Thread pearl cotton, knitting ribbon or other decorative thread through the upper looper for three-thread stitching or the lower looper for two-thread stitching.

● Place the garment section under the presser foot, positioning the fold slightly to the left of the blade so that the fabric fills only half of the stitch. Serge, being careful not to cut the fabric.

● Repeat, flatlocking as many rows as desired. The shirring will look best if the folds are spaced about ¾" (2cm) apart.

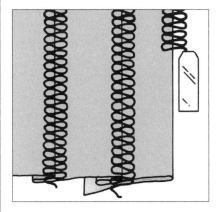

● If you own a long, thin loop turner, tunnel it under the stitches on the back of the fabric. Knot one end of a length of ⅛" (3mm) elastic cord, attach the other end to the loop turner and pull it through the stitches. If you don't own a loop turner, thread the knotted

end of the elastic onto a blunt tapestry needle and, working on the back of the fabric, gently work the tapestry needle under the stitching.

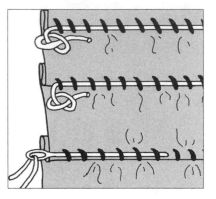

● Once the elastic is pulled through, adjust the shirring until the garment section is the desired width; then knot the other end of the elastic.

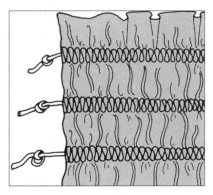

S Fagotting

Fagotting is a method of joining two pieces of fabric with visible decorative stitching while leaving a space between the fabric sections. Use it as a delicate, decorative way to join sections of the garment or to add a fine trim to dresses and blouses. If the fagotting is purely decorative, you may find it easier to fagot the fabric first and then cut out the garment, rather than

Shirring			
TYPE OF SERGER STITCH:	2	3	MINE
Stitch length:	2mm-3mm	2mm-3mm	
Stitch width:	Widest	Widest	
Tensions—Needle:	Very loose	Very loose	
Upper looper:	N/A	"0"	
Lower looper:	"0"	Very tight	

attempting to adjust your pattern to accommodate the fagotting.

• Press under ½" (1.3cm) on the fabric edges that will be fagotted together. (*Note:* If your fabric ravels, serge-finish the raw edges before pressing them under.)

• Adjust your serger to the appropriate setting (see chart at left).

• Place the fabric right sides together so that the folded edges are even. Insert the fabric under the presser foot to the left of the blade so that the needle just catches the fabric; serge.

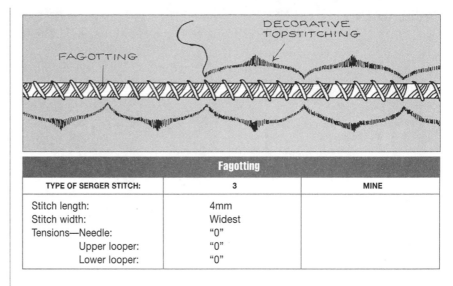

Fagotting		
TYPE OF SERGER STITCH:	3	MINE
Stitch length:	4mm	
Stitch width:	Widest	
Tensions—Needle:	"0"	
Upper looper:	"0"	
Lower looper:	"0"	

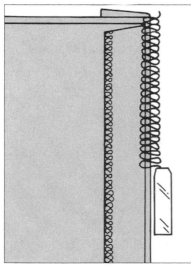

• Gently pull the fabric apart. There will be a ⅛" (3mm) space between the folded edges that is filled with thread. Press.

• If you want to further embellish your garment, use your conventional machine to topstitch on either side of the fagotting. Use a straight stitch or a decorative stitch. For a rich, custom look, do all of your stitching in a thread that matches the fabric.

TUCKS

A tuck is a stitched fold of fabric that controls fullness and/or adds a decorative touch to a garment. Alone or in groups, tucks can be found just about any place—at shoulders, waistline or hipline, or adorning a yoke, pocket, cuff or hemline. A special type of tuck, called a growth tuck, can be incorporated into children's garments so that they can be quickly and easily lengthened.

MARKING AND STITCHING

Depending on the design of your pattern, tucks can appear on the outside or be hidden on the inside of your garment. If the tucks will be folded and stitched on the inside of the garment, transfer the markings to the wrong side of the fabric. If the tucks will be folded and stitched on the outside, transfer the markings to the right side of the fabric. Choose a method that won't leave permanent marks on the fabric.

If the tucks are straight and parallel to each other, they'll be easier to stitch if you press in the foldlines first. Then be sure to stitch all of the tucks in the same direction. Press them in the direction indicated in the pattern instructions. Vertical tucks are usually pressed away from the center front or center back; horizontal tucks are usually pressed down.

NARROW OR PIN TUCKS

These are usually indicated on the pattern tissue by a series of solid

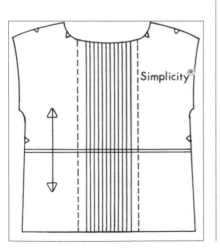

lines. Because pin tucks are narrow, the stitching lines are not indicated. Fold the fabric along the solid line and stitch the specified distance from the fold.

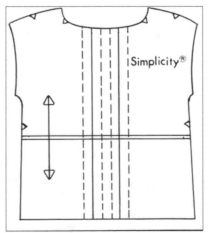

WIDE TUCKS

Wide tucks are indicated on the pattern tissue by a series of solid and broken lines. To create the tuck, fold the fabric on the solid line, matching the broken lines to each other. Then stitch along the broken lines.

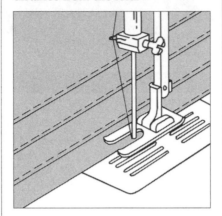

To save time, transfer only the solid lines to the fabric. Fold the fabric on the solid line; then use a stitching guide, such as the mark-

ings on the throat plate, a strip of tape placed on the throat plate, or a seam guide, to evenly stitch the specified distance from the fold.

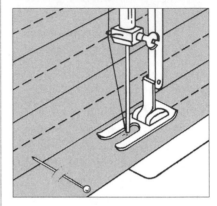

DECORATIVE PIN TUCKS

The Conventional Method

If your sewing machine does decorative stitching with regular thread, you can add pretty shell tucks or tucks with fancy stitches to lingerie, dainty blouses or children's dress-up clothes. On lightweight knits or sheers, create a shell tuck by using a machine blindstitch along the folded edge. On crisper fabrics, choose an appropriate machine embroidery stitch. Position the stitching so that the design falls within the tuck.

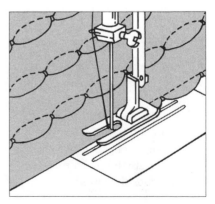

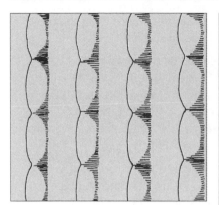

If thread build-up is a problem with a decorative stitch, put a strip of water-soluble or heat-disintegrating stabilizer underneath your stitching. (See "Stabilizers," page 217, for more information.)

S *The Serger Method*

For colorful, decorative tucks, thread the upper looper with pearl cotton, embroidery floss, variegated crochet yarn, knitting ribbon or metallic thread.

- Adjust your serger to the appropriate setting (see chart at right).

- Mark and press on the tuck foldline as for conventional tucks.

- Serge, keeping the fold slightly to the left of the blade so that the fabric isn't cut. Repeat for as many tucks as desired.

- Press the tucks to one side.

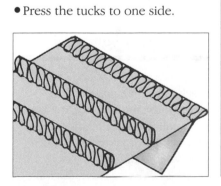

tip

S *To add another interesting dimension to your serger tucks, use decorative thread in the upper and lower loopers. Then use your conventional machine to straight stitch horizontally across the serged tucks. Stitch the rows ¾" to 1" (2cm to 2.5cm) apart, alternating the stitching direction. This makes the tucks appear wavy.*

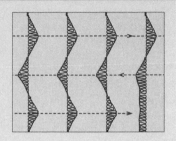

GROWTH TUCKS

Children often grow taller faster than they grow wider. As a result, garments may be too short long before they're too tight. To solve this problem, you can incorporate a growth tuck into the garment.

Plan on doing this before the pattern is cut out so you can alter the pattern pieces to allow for extra length.

Growth tucks can be incorporated into any straight hemline. The most obvious place to allow for growth is in the skirt hem.

Pin Tucks		
TYPE OF SERGER STITCH:	**3**	**MINE**
Stitch length:	3mm-5mm	
Stitch width:	Widest	
Tensions—Needle:	Normal	
Upper looper:	Loose*	
Lower looper:	Normal	
Use decorative thread in the upper looper.		

tips

- *On light- and medium-weight fabrics, you can create a tucked effect without actually making tucks. Use a twin needle and two matching spools of thread in the top of your machine. The two needle threads combine with one bobbin thread to create raised rows that look like narrow pin tucks. If your sewing machine doesn't have an extra spool holder, put the second spool of thread in a glass placed behind, and to the right of, the machine. It will unwind smoothly without rolling away!*

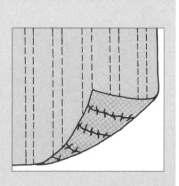

- **S** *The narrow rolled hemstitch can also be used to make lovely pin tucks. Adjust your machine for its three-thread narrow rolled hem function. Fold the fabric wrong sides together along the tuck line and then serge over the fold. For a satiny appearance, use silk or 100 percent rayon thread in the upper looper.*

However, this technique can also be used on long- or short-sleeve shirts, blouses and pants for both boys and girls.

• Before you cut out the garment, add 3" (7.5cm) to the hem allowance.

• Construct the garment and finish the hem allowance edge.

• Using a machine basting stitch, form a 1½" (3.8cm) tuck on the right side of the fabric, within the hem allowance. Press the tuck toward the hemline (see at right.)

• When you need to lengthen the garment, remove the basting and

tip

If you're adding tucks to a pattern that doesn't include them, tuck the fabric first and then cut out the garment. Be sure to purchase extra fabric to accommodate the tucks.

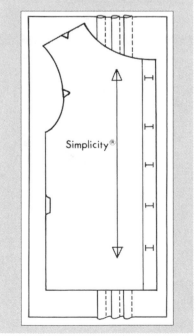

press, creating a new hemline. If necessary, stitch ribbon or trim over the old hem crease to disguise it.

On a dress with a waistline seam, you can incorporate the growth tuck in the bodice area.

• Before you cut out the garment, lengthen the front and back bodice 1" to 3" (2.5cm to 7.5cm).

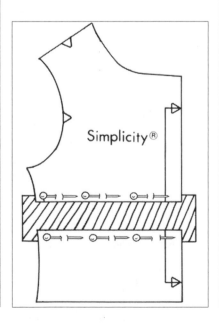

• Sew the bodice together at the side seams.

• On the inside of the bodice, baste a tuck half as wide as the amount you lengthened the bodice. Position the tuck so it is about ¼" (6mm) above the waistline seam.

• Press the tuck up; then join bodice to skirt and complete the garment.

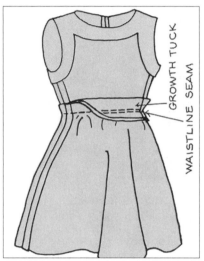

• When the garment needs to be lengthened, simply release the tuck. If there is a zipper, rip out the lower part, release the tuck and re-stitch the zipper and the seam. If necessary, cover fade marks with a contrasting ribbon or sash.

WAISTBANDS

There are several different methods for applying and finishing waistbands. Your pattern instructions will include a method appropriate for your garment. You can follow those directions exactly… or use one of our easy variations.

INTERFACING

Regardless of the construction method you choose, the waistband must be interfaced so that it retains its shape. For best results, interface the entire waistband, eliminating the seam allowances as described under "Interfacings," page 158. If you're using a sew-in interfacing, add a row of basting on the facing side of the waistband, near the foldline. This will keep the interfacing from shifting.

THE NO-BULK WAISTBAND METHODS

For most sewers, the biggest stumbling block to a smooth waistband is learning how to deal with all of the layers of fabric that converge at the waistline seam. Both of the following methods solve this problem by eliminating the seam allowance on the waistband facing. These methods are suitable for all fabrics, but are especially good for heavyweight or bulky fabrics. It's up to you whether you prefer machine stitching or hand stitching as your final step.

Stitch-in-the-ditch Machine Method

Prepare your waistband one of the following ways:

• Cut out the waistband, placing

> **tip**
>
> *Mark the stitching lines on your waistband pattern piece so it can serve as an accurate, see-through template for positioning the interfacing.*

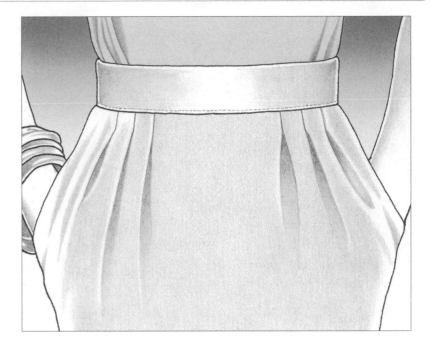

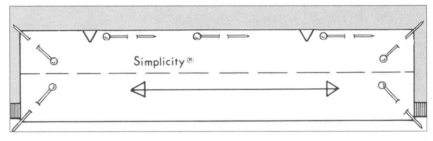

the long, unnotched edge along a selvage, and eliminating ¼" (6mm) from the seam allowance. Fuse the interfacing in place.

Or

• Cut out the waistband. Apply fusible or sew-in interfacing. To finish the long, unnotched edge, serge, trimming off ¼" (6mm) as you stitch. If you don't own a serger, trim off ¼" (6mm) and then overcast the edge on your conventional machine.

CUT, INTERFACE AND SERGE, OR OVERCAST WAISTBAND.

To attach the waistband:

● With right sides together, pin or baste the notched waistband edge to the garment, matching notches, centers and markings; stitch (a).

● Press the seam allowances toward the waistband; trim the seam to ⅜" (1cm) (b).

● With right sides together, fold the waistband along the foldline and stitch the overlap end (c).

● On the underlap, turn the waistband seam allowance down. Beginning at the fold, stitch the end to ⅜" (1cm) from the lower edge; pivot and continue stitching to the small dot marking. Backstitch to secure. Clip the seam allowances to the dot marking and trim the seams (d).

● Turn the waistband right side out so that the finished or selvage edge extends ⅜" (1cm) below the waistband seam on the inside of the garment; press.

● On the inside, fold the finished or selvage edge under diagonally at the zipper; pin. On the outside, pin the waistband layers together along the waistband seam (e).

● On the outside, stitch in the ditch or groove of the waistband seam, catching the finished edge of the waistband and the diagonal turn-under. Remove the pins as you stitch (f).

Hand Sewing Method

Prepare the waistband using one of the following methods:

● Cut out the waistband, placing

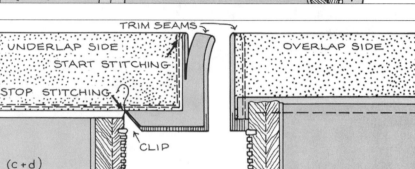

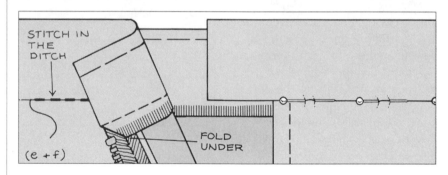

the long, unnotched edge along a selvage, eliminating the ⅝" (1.5cm) seam allowance. Fuse the interfacing in place.

Or

● Cut out the waistband. Apply fusible or sew-in interfacing. To finish the long, unnotched edge, serge, trimming off the ⅝" (1.5cm) seam allowance as you stitch. If you don't own a serger, trim off the ⅝" (1.5cm) and then overcast the edge on your conventional machine.

To apply the waistband:

● With right sides together, pin the notched waistband edge to the garment, matching notches, centers and markings; stitch.

● Press the seam allowances toward the waistband; trim the seam to ⅜" (1cm).

● With right sides together, fold the waistband along the foldline. Stitch the seams at both ends of the waistband; trim. *Note:* When stitching the underlap end, open out the fold that was created when you pressed the seam allowances toward the waistband (a).

• Turn the waistband right side out so that the finished or selvage edge meets the waistband seam on the inside of the garment and pin; press (b).

• On the inside, slipstitch the serged or selvage edge in place along the entire length of the waistband seams, including the underlap (c).

S *Serger Method*

This is a quick way to attach a waistband and finish the raw edges in one step. It's an excellent choice for knits and light- to medium-weight fabrics.

• With right sides together, fold the waistband in half lengthwise. Using your conventional machine, stitch across the ends. At the underlap end, pivot and stitch along the waistline seam, ending at the small dot. Backstitch to secure. Clip to the stitching at the dot and then trim the seams (d).

• Turn the waistband right side out and press.

• Pin both cut edges of the waistband to the outside of the garment, matching notches, centers and markings.

• With the garment side up, and beginning at the underlap edge, serge along the waistline seams (e).

• Press the seam toward the garment and the waistband away from the garment. Hand-tack the seam allowance in place at the inside edges of the garment opening.

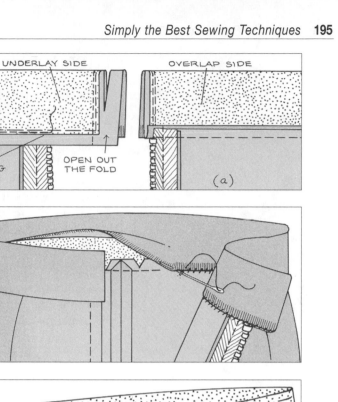

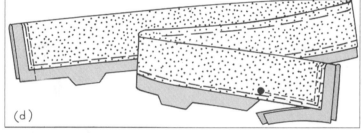

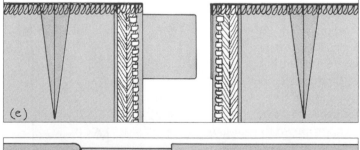

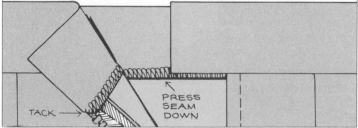

ZIPPERS

Because zippers have a reputation for being difficult to install, many sewers—especially new or returning ones—unnecessarily avoid patterns that feature zippers. Don't be caught up in that type of thinking! The little tricks that guarantee a perfect zipper are so simple that anyone can learn them.

There are four basic zipper applications: Centered, lapped, fly-front and separating. Your pattern will give you instructions for the method appropriate to your garment.

In order to easily follow those instructions, as well as the hints given, check the accompanying diagram so you're familiar with the names of the parts of a zipper.

BEFORE YOU BEGIN

● Check the back of your pattern envelope for the necessary length and type of zipper. If it says "separating zipper," be sure that's what you get. This is a special type of zipper, most frequently used for coats and jackets. It splits open into two separate sections so you don't have to put the garment on over your head.

● Unless the zipper tape is 100 percent polyester, pre-shrink the tape by plunging the zipper into hot water for a few minutes.

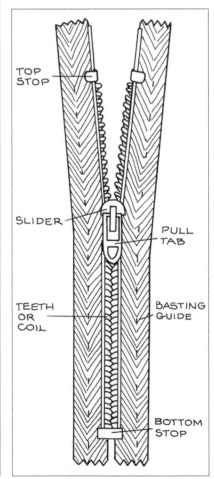

● Working on the wrong side, press the zipper tape to remove any packaging folds. Don't rest the iron on the teeth or the coils.

INSTALLATION TIPS

Consult your pattern instructions for when and how to put in the zipper. As you follow those directions, keep these tips in mind:

● Always use a zipper foot when machine basting and permanently stitching the zipper. It can be positioned either to the right or the left of your needle, making the installation easier and your stitching straighter.

● To keep ripples out of your finished product, always stitch in the same direction—from the bottom of the zipper to the top. This rule holds true for both machine basting and permanent stitching.

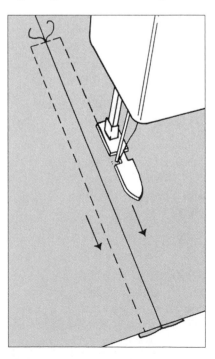

When Basting

● If the garment seam is basted closed before the zipper is installed, use a long machine basting stitch. Then, before pressing the seam open, clip the basting stitches at the bottom of the zipper opening, as well as every 2" (5cm). This will make the basting easier to remove once the zipper is installed. At that point, if you have trouble grabbing the thread ends, use pointed tweezers.

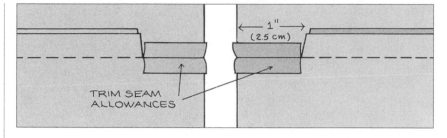

TRIM SEAM ALLOWANCES

allowances within the clipped section to ⅜" (1cm) and press them open.

● Although machine basting is usually the suggested method for holding a zipper in place for permanent stitching, you may get better results with double-faced basting tape or glue stick. Put the basting tape along the outside edge of the zipper tape so you don't stitch through it. You can stitch through glue stick as long as you let it dry for a few minutes first. Otherwise, it will gum up your needle. If you don't have either of these products on hand, use masking tape, positioning the tape along the edge of the zipper tape so that you absolutely do not stitch through it.

● As you baste the zipper in place, keep the pull tab flipped up. Later

on, this will make it easier to permanently stitch around the pull tab and the slider.

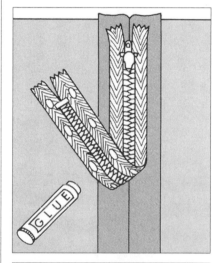

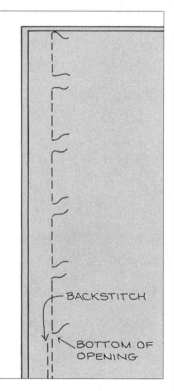

BACKSTITCH

BOTTOM OF OPENING

● If the zipper is going to cross a seam (for example, a center back zipper on a dress with a waistline seam), you may need to reduce some of the bulk before basting the seam closed. To do this, make a clip in the intersecting seam allowances, 1" (2.5cm) in from each opening edge. Trim the seam

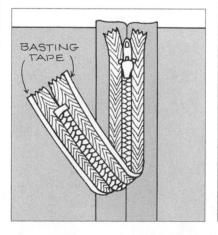

BASTING TAPE

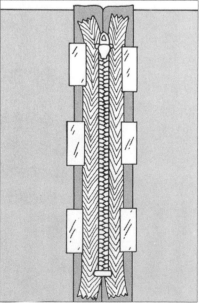

When Topstitching

For a professional-looking zipper installation, the topstitching should be smooth, straight, and a consistently even distance from the edge(s) of the garment all along the length of the zipper. If you can't do it "by eye," try one of the following:

● Use a ruler and a water-soluble or evaporating fabric marking pen to draw stitching guidelines on the right side of your fabric. Test first to make sure the ink is removable.

● Use topstitching or stick-on sewing tape. This tape is perforated so that you can separate it into different widths. Stitch next to the edge of the tape and then pull it off.

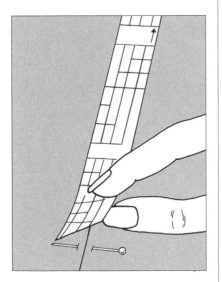

● If you're inserting a lapped zipper, ½" (1.3cm) wide transparent tape makes a great topstitching guide.

● To avoid bumpy topstitching around the tab and slider, stop topstitching just before you get to

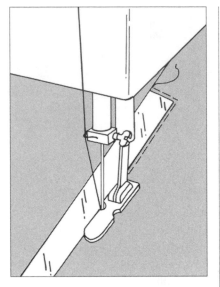

the slider. Leaving the needle in the fabric, raise the presser foot and pull the slider down below the needle. (If you can't work it down gently with your finger, you may have to remove some of the basting that is holding the garment seam closed.) Lower the presser foot and continue topstitching.

THE HAND-SEWN ZIPPER

If your fabric is delicate or requires special handling (for example, chiffon, velvet or lace), consider doing the final row of stitching by hand. In addition, many people prefer the couture look of a hand-sewn zipper for tailored suits and dresses.

The final row of stitching is done with the pickstitch. (See Chapter 5, page 103.) To keep the stitches straight, use a row of hand basting or any of the topstitching guidelines mentioned above.

THE INVISIBLE ZIPPER

This type of zipper is so named because after it is installed, it looks like a plain seam with a small pull tab at the top. Generally, if your pattern calls for a zipper, you can choose a conventional or an invisible zipper.

---

tip

Another way to avoid stitching around the slider "bump" is to purchase a zipper that's longer than the pattern calls for. When you install the zipper, position it so that the pull tab and slider extend above the edge of the garment. Once the zipper is installed, slide the pull tab down and cut off the excess zipper tape at the raw edge of the garment. The intersecting waistband, seam, facing, etc. will act as the top stop for the zipper.

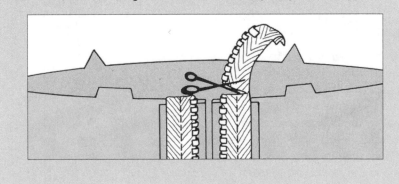

A perfect installation requires a special invisible zipper foot. It is available in the notions department where you purchase your invisible zippers. This inexpensive plastic accessory comes in pieces—one foot for zippers with polyester coils, one foot for zippers with metal teeth and a choice of shanks. Following the instructions that come with the foot, you choose the shank that is suitable for your sewing machine and then snap the appropriate foot and shank together. The foot is designed to hold the coil upright while positioning the needle so that the stitching crowds up close to the coil. The result is a "tight"—i.e. invisible—installation.

There are two important differences between installing an invisible zipper and a conventional zipper.

● The invisible zipper is installed first, before the seam is stitched.

● All stitching is done from top to bottom. (Conventional zippers are stitched from bottom to top.)

Installation

● Open the zipper and press the tape flat. Do not press the coils.

● Place the open zipper face down on the right side of the fabric so that the coil is along the seamline and the tape is within the seam allowance. Pin or glue-baste in place.

● Position the foot at the top of the zipper with the right-hand groove over the coil and the needle aligned with the hole in the center of the foot. Stitch to the slider, backstitch for a few stitches and knot the thread tails.

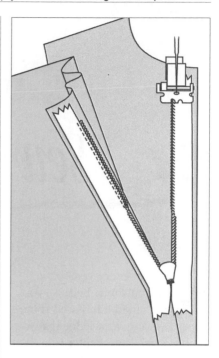

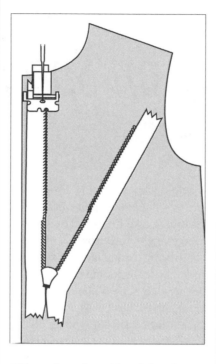

● Place the other side of the zipper face down on the right side of the adjacent garment section so that the coil is along the seamline and the tape is within the seam allowance. Pin or glue-baste in place. Position the foot at the top of the zipper with the left-hand groove over the coil. Stitch to the slider, backstitch for a few stitches and knot the thread tails.

● Close the zipper. Pin the seam together below the zipper. Using your machine's regular zipper foot, finish stitching the seam, overlapping the stitches at the bottom of the zipper.

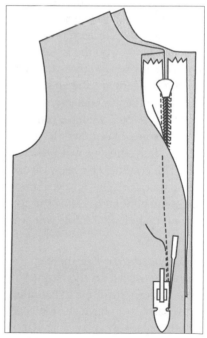

chapter 7
Sewing on Special Fabrics

Have you ever bypassed a beautiful fabric because you were afraid it required some special sewing knowledge that you didn't have? This chapter is designed to give you the confidence you need to experiment— and to achieve successful results.

Always begin with the standards— good quality sewing thread, a new sewing machine needle and a well-maintained sewing machine.

In this chapter, we have gathered tips for some of our favorite special fabrics. But, since we want you to have the confidence to sew on any fabric that catches your eye, here are some general guidelines to follow no matter what fabric you are considering.

● *Compatibility.* Use the suggested fabric list on the back of your pattern envelope as a guide. If the fabric you have chosen is not listed, make sure it has a similar "hand" (body and weight) to those recommended.

● *Cutting Layout.* When it comes to the cutting layout, your fabric may require special attention. A single thickness cutting layout is preferred for most pile fabrics, including fake fur, velvet and heavyweight corduroy. Use the "with nap" cutting layout for one-way fabrics, including those that are shaded, have a pile or a directional motif. Review Chapter 5 "The Cutting Layout" (pages 60-66), for layout options. If you have any doubt, use a "with nap" layout.

● *Needle.* Start each new project with a new needle. Sometimes problems such as skipped stitches or puckered seams need more help than just a new needle. Be sure the needle is the right size for your fabric. You might need a special type of sewing machine needle.

Machine needles come in European sizes 60 to 125 (for lightweight to heavyweight fabrics) and American sizes 6 to 20 (for lightweight to heavyweight fabrics). Schmetz®, the most widely available European brand, lists the European sizes first, followed by a slash and the corresponding American size. This is then fol-

lowed by a letter or letters that indicate the style of the needle. "H" indicates a universal point needle; "HS" indicates a ballpoint tip for stretch fabrics; and "HJ" indicates the sharp point tip and stronger shank required for fabrics such as heavyweight denim. Singer®, the most common American brand, uses a color band to indicate the needle style. For example, a yellow band indicates a ballpoint tip; a violet band indicates an extra sharp point. Keep a collection of needles in assorted types and sizes on hand. See Chapter 3, "Needles," (page 31) for more information.

● *Machine Settings.* In addition to a special purpose needle, an "out of the ordinary" setting on your sewing machine may solve a problem. Sometimes, a tighter or looser hold on the fabric is necessary. To accomplish this, you may need to increase or decrease the pressure on the presser foot, use a different foot or change the throat plate. Consult your sewing machine manual for assistance.

● *Marking.* You want to be sure that the marking method you choose provides accurate, visible markings…and that these markings will disappear once the garment is completed. Review Chapter 5, "Marking" (page 66). In addition to those marking techniques, the pages that follow suggest one more—tailor's tacks. These thread markings are useful for fabrics that have a particularly deep texture or that are delicate and may be marred by any other technique. The tacks are made while the pattern is still pinned to the (single or double thickness) fabric.

To make tailor's tacks, start with a long double strand of unknotted thread.

● Leaving a 3" to 4" (7.5cm to 10cm) tail, take a small running stitch at the pattern symbol.

● Take a second stitch that crosses the first, leaving a 3" to 4" (7.5cm to 10cm) loop between the two.

● Continue to the next symbol, leaving a generous loop of thread in between, and make two more crossed stitches.

● Clip the loops and the long threads between each marking.

● Unpin the pattern tissue and gently remove it.

● For a double thickness layout, carefully pull the two layers of fabric apart. Clip the threads between them, leaving small tufts of thread for each marking. See illustrations (A) and (B).

● *Interfacing.* Some fabrics are fusible-friendly; others are not. Review Chapter 6, "Interfacings,"

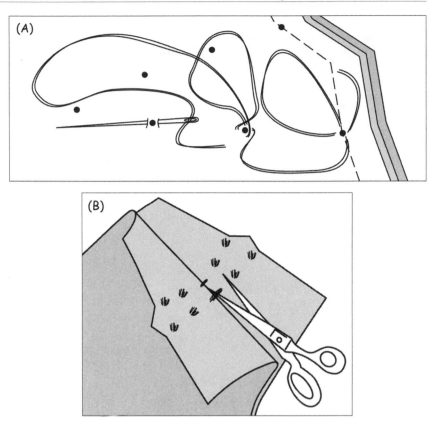

(pages 158-160) and consult the chart on page 161. Then experiment on scraps of your fashion fabric before making a final decision regarding the type and weight of interfacing.

● *Pressing.* The "Press-As-You-Sew Guide" on page 101 will give you pressing guidelines. Experiment on scraps of your fabric before putting an iron to your garment sections.

● *Stabilizers.* The last few pages of this chapter contain some general information about stabilizers. These "helpers" add temporary firmness to fabrics. A stabilizer may be just the magic ingredient that helps you achieve smooth machine-made buttonholes, pro-

fessional-looking appliqués, or pucker-free stitching, or adds support to a lightweight or openwork fabric.

● *Keep Records.* Start a notebook or an index card system for special fabrics. Along with a swatch of the fabric, record the pattern number and information regarding interfacings, machine needle, machine settings, marking technique, etc. This record will be a real timesaver the next time similar fabric catches your eye.

Finally, if you are searching for pattern suggestions, start by considering the patternless projects in Chapter 8. These simple shapes lend themselves to a variety of special fabrics.

DENIM

LAYOUT

● A double thickness cutting layout is fine, but take care to align the grainline arrows exactly. If they are not aligned, the fabric will twist when the garment is on the body. This characteristic is a result of the twill weave.

● Use a "with nap" cutting layout for brushed denim; a "without nap" layout for all others.

● Use a single thickness cutting layout for heavy denim.

MARKING

Use dressmaker's chalk, tracing paper or water-soluble fabric marking pens.

CUTTING

Use very sharp scissors or a rotary cutter. For very heavy denim, cut single thickness.

NEEDLE

Use a needle with a sharp point for densely woven fabrics; a heavy-duty shank to resist bending or breaking.

Choose a medium- to heavyweight size: 90/14 HJ to 100/16 HJ (Schmetz) or 14 to 16 Red Band (Singer).

INTERFACING

Sew-ins or fusibles, wovens or non-wovens are suitable.

SEAMS AND SEAM FINISHES

● Seam Options: Almost any type of seam is suitable for this fabric. However, it must be finished

tip

To help prevent the presser foot from rocking (which can cause uneven stitches and jammed threads) when hemming over bulky flat-fell seams (or anywhere you encounter multiple layers), use a shim to keep the foot level. This shim can be as simple as a scrap of denim folded several times to the necessary thickness. Use the shim in front, in back or to the side of the presser foot, as necessary to keep it level. Stop stitching as often as necessary to reposition the shim. The Jean-a-ma-jig™ is a 1/8" (3mm) thick plastic notion that performs a similar task. Another choice is the Hump Jumper®, available in 1/8" (3mm) and 1/16" (1.5mm) thicknesses.

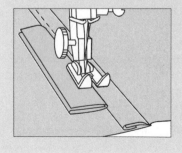

securely to prevent raveling. The serged seam and the Flat Fell Seam (page 79) are popular choices.

● Because of denim's raveling properties, avoid clipping and notching seams.

TOPSTITCHING

Use a medium length stitch and heavy-duty thread, polyester thread or jeans topstitching thread.

HEMS

Options: The Wide Topstitched Hem (page 153), the Fused Hem (page 157), the Cover Hem (page 157) and the Narrow Topstitched Hem for Wovens (page 153).

PRESSING

Medium to high temperature; steam setting.

FAKE FUR

LAYOUT

● Use a single thickness cutting layout, wrong side up.

● Always use a "with nap" cutting layout. Generally, the pile runs down. However, you might want to run a short pile up to add color depth.

● Use long pins (quilting pins) with large round heads or to avoid pins altogether, use fabric weights and/or trace the pattern onto the fur backing.

MARKING

Mark on the wrong side, using dressmaker's chalk or colored pencils.

Or

Mark on the right side, using tailor's tacks.

CUTTING

● If the backing fabric is firm, trim the seam allowances on the pattern tissue to ¹/₄" (6mm) before cutting. This will help reduce bulk.

● When cutting, use only the tip of the blades so that you cut through the backing only, separating the fur as you cut.

NEEDLE

Use a standard universal point needle for fake fur with a woven backing; a ballpoint needle for fake fur with a knit backing.

● For short pile fur with a medium-weight woven backing to long pile fur with a heavyweight backing: 80/12 H to 100/16 H (Schmetz).

● For a medium- to heavyweight knit backing: 80/12 HS to 100/16 HS (Schmetz) or 12 to 16 Yellow Band (Singer).

INTERFACING

The backing on most fake furs provides enough support to eliminate the need for interfacing. However,

for collars or other areas that need extra support, use a woven interfacing secured to the backing with pad stitches. Pad stitching consists of rows of blindstitches placed ½" (13mm) apart. Cover the entire surface so that the interfacing is attached to the fur backing without disturbing the fur. Do not use fusible interfacing.

SEAMS AND SEAM FINISHES

● Before pinning and stitching a seam, brush long pile furs towards the center of the pattern section. This will prevent the ends of the fur from getting caught in the seam and will allow the fur to appear less "interrupted" on the right side.

● Use a roller foot attachment for long pile furs.

● Seam Options: Plain Seam or Double-Stitched Seam (page 78). Disregard all references to pressing.

HEMS

The Hand Sewn Hem (page 152) is the best choice. Ease the hem, as necessary. If desired, finish the edge with seam binding.

PRESSING

Avoid pressing. Many fake furs are made from fibers that are extremely heat sensitive and will become damaged when pressed.

FLEECE

LAYOUT

● Use a double thickness cutting layout. For heavyweight fleece, use a single thickness layout.

● Always use a "with nap" cutting layout.

● If you can't see a difference between the right and wrong side of the fabric, pick one side and

tip

To determine the right side of the fleece (or which grain is which), see how it curls. On the crosswise grain, fleece will curl to the wrong side. On the lengthwise grain or along the selvage edge, fleece will curl to the right side.

stick with it. To help keep track as you sew, mark the side you choose.

MARKING

Use dressmaker's chalk or fabric marking pens.

CUTTING

Use sharp scissors or a rotary cutter.

NEEDLE

Use a standard universal point needle in a medium-weight size: 70/10 H to 80/12 H (Schmetz).

Or

Ballpoint or stretch needle in a medium-weight size: 75/11 HS to 90/14 HS (Schmetz) or 11 to 14 Yellow Band (Singer).

Or

For windbreaker-style fleece, very sharp Microtex point needle: 70/10 HM to 80/12 HM (Schmetz).

MACHINE SETTINGS

● Use a slightly longer than average straight stitch (3mm or 9-12 stitches per inch).

● Decrease the pressure slightly on the presser foot.

Interfacing

Avoid fusible interfacing as it tends to flatten the fabric. Use a nonwoven, sew-in interfacing with a slight amount of stretch as support for collars and cuffs, as well as behind buttonholes and zippers.

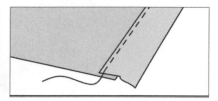

tip

When stitching fleece to another fabric (such as a lining), stitch with the fleece against the feed dog. This will help keep the bulk and the stretch under control.

Seams and Seam Finishes

● Seam Options: Double-Stitched Seam (page 78), Stretch Knit Seam (page 79) or a serged seam.

● If the seam allowances tend to curl, use the Topstitched Seam (page 86).

HEMS

● Use a single hem with a slightly wider than usual hem allowance. If necessary, edgestitch or topstitch the hem to hold it flat.

● A hem allowance that is finished on the serger will keep the edge of the fabric from becoming wavy but still provide some stretch.

● Instead of traditional hems and facings, consider self-binding or contrast binding. Review Chapter 6, "Bindings" (pages 117-121). Because fleece does not ravel, single-layer binding made from matching or contrasting fleece is an option.

● Cut crosswise strips of fabric that are twice the desired finished width of the binding.

● With wrong sides together, center the binding over the garment edge. Edgestitch the binding in place using a straight stitch.

● Turn the garment over. Wrap the binding around the raw edge. Edgestitch in place, using a straight stitch or a zigzag stitch and stitching through the garment and both layers of binding. *Note:* If you want only one row of edgestitching to be visible on your finished garment, use water-soluble thread in the top of your machine for the first row of edgestitching.

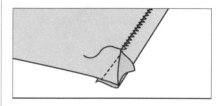

PRESSING

Avoid pressing. If it is absolutely necessary, use a press cloth. Often finger pressing will do just as good a job.

KNITS

LAYOUT

● Use a double thickness cutting layout, except for sweater knits which require a single thickness layout.

● Use a "with nap" cutting layout. Knits frequently have one-way shading that may not be discernible until the garment is

finished. Sweater knits have motifs or cable designs that are usually directional.

● If the fabric has been folded on the bolt or for storage, the crease may not be easy to remove. Try steam. If this isn't successful, refold the fabric or cut around the crease.

● Always position the pattern pieces on the fabric so that the greatest amount of stretch goes around the body.

● Use pattern weights for sweater knits.

MARKING

Use dressmaker's chalk or fabric marking pens; tailor's tack or small safety pins on sweater knits.

CUTTING

Use scissors or a rotary cutter for lightweight knits.

NEEDLE

Use a ballpoint or stretch needle in a medium-weight size: 75/11 HS to 90/14 HS (Schmetz) or 11 to 14 Yellow Band (Singer).

MACHINE SETTINGS

● Narrow zigzag stitch (0.5mm width, 2.5mm length) or a stretch stitch.

● Decrease pressure on presser foot for heavy sweater knits; increase pressure for lingerie knits.

INTERFACING

Choose a lightweight nonwoven or stretch interfacing. Avoid fusibles. Apply interfacing to the facings rather than to the body of the garment.

SEAMS AND SEAM FINISHES

● Seam Options: Stretch Knit Seam (page 79). Because they build in stretch, clean-finish the edges and prevent curling, serged seams are ideal for knits.

● When appropriate, stabilize the seam (see page 79).

HEMS

Many different hems, including the Narrow Topstitched Hem, the Wide Topstitched Hem and the Serger Rolled Hem, are suitable, depending on the weight of the knit and the look you want to achieve. Review Chapter 6, "Hems" (pages 150-158).

PRESSING

Use steam or a damp press cloth and a temperature appropriate for the fabric's fiber content. Do not over press.

LACE

LAYOUT

● Use a single thickness "with nap" cutting layout.

● A cutting surface with a contrasting color will help you get the best view of your lace.

● Plan the layout so that large motifs fall attractively on the figure.

● Consider using a decorative edge of the lace as a finished (straight) edge of the garment. This way you can eliminate hem allowances and/or facings.

● Pattern weights are a good alternative if pins prove difficult to use.

MARKING

Use tailor's tacks or fabric marking pens.

tip

If a pattern marking falls at a hole in the lace, put a piece of transparent tape over the hole, then mark the symbol with a pencil.

CUTTING

Use scissors or rotary cutter.

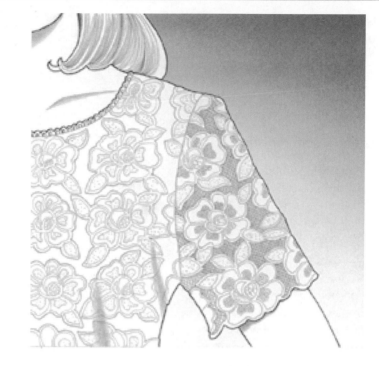

NEEDLE

Use a standard universal point needle, usually in a light- to medium-weight size: 70/10 H to 90/14 H (Schmetz) or 10 to 14 (Singer).

THREAD

Very lightweight lace may require an extra-fine polyester or cotton-covered polyester thread.

MACHINE SETTINGS

● Straight stitch, slightly shorter than average (1.75 to 2mm or 12 to 25 stitches per inch); or short, narrow zigzag stitch (0.5mm width, 1.5mm length).

● On some lightweight laces, increasing the pressure on the presser foot may be helpful.

● On lightweight lace, use a small, single-hole throat plate when sewing a straight stitch. This will prevent the fabric from being "swallowed" into the machine. A narrow straight stitch foot and/or flat bottomed presser foot may also be helpful. If you do not have these machine attachments, consider moving the needle to the far left to provide support on three sides of the fabric.

INTERFACING

● Eliminate interfacing whenever possible. If additional body is needed, use tulle or netting to maintain the open quality of the fabric. For a semi-opaque look, consider a sheer voile, organza or organdy instead of commercial interfacing.

● An underlining (a layer of lining fabric basted to the main garment sections and sewn as one with the lace) in a skin tone can be used to maintain the open look while eliminating the see-through qualities and provide an anchor for attaching the interfacing.

Seams and Seam Finishes

● Seam Options: Double Stitched Seam (page 78); Stretch Knit Seam (page 79), using a very narrow zigzag stitch (0.5mm width, 1.5mm length); a narrow serged seam.

● The overlapped seam is useful when you don't want to break up the flow of the motifs at prominent seams, such as center front, center back or shoulder seams. Preliminaries for this type of seam begin when you are cutting out your garment.

● Draw in the seamlines on your pattern pieces.

● Position the first pattern piece so that the dominant lace motifs are balanced within the seamlines. Thread-trace along the seamlines. Using a different color thread, thread-trace around the motif outline as it extends beyond the seamline. Carefully cut out the garment section along this second traced line.

● Remove the pattern tissue. Lap the pattern piece for the adjacent garment section over the cut-out section, matching the seamlines. Trace the overlapping motif onto the pattern tissue. Pin this pattern piece to the fabric, matching the traced motif to the fabric underneath. Thread-trace the seamlines. Cut out the garment section.

● To construct the seam, overlap the first garment section onto the second one, matching the thread-traced seamlines. Stitch along the edge of the overlapping motifs, using small slipstitches (see page 104) or a short, narrow machine zigzag stitch. For the latter, a stabilizer may be required (see page 217).

● Once the seam is stitched, use embroidery scissors to carefully cut away the excess underlap.

HEMS

● If the hemline is on the straight grain and the lace has a decorative edge, you can eliminate the hem allowance and use the decorative edge as the finished edge of the garment.

● If the lace fabric does not have its own decorative edge, hand or machine stitch a strip of coordinating lace trim to the right side of the fabric along the hemline. Cut away the excess lace underneath.
  This step is illustrated at the top of page 209.

● For a conventional approach, use the Hand Sewn Hem (page 153).

PRESSING

Always use a press cloth. To prevent flattening lace with raised motifs, place the fabric face down on a terrycloth towel and press lightly.

tip

Sheer tricot seam binding can substitute for a facing at both straight and curved edges of a garment.

MICROFIBERS

LAYOUT

● Use a double thickness cutting layout with right sides together.

● Use a "with nap" cutting layout. These fabrics shade differently in each direction.

● On lightweight microfibers, shift the pattern pieces slightly "off grain" (not more than 10 percent). This will prevent puckering on lengthwise seams.

MARKING

Use dressmaker's chalk or fabric marking pens.

CUTTING

● Use scissors with serrated blades or a rotary cutter.

● Use fine pins only within the seam allowance. Regular pins may leave permanent pinholes. Pattern weights are another good choice.

NEEDLE

Use a microtex needle with a very sharp point and a slender shaft in a light- to medium-weight size: 60/8 HM to 80/12 HM (Schmetz) or 8 to 12 Violet Bands (Singer).

THREAD

Use very fine cotton-covered polyester thread or lingerie thread.

MACHINE SETTINGS

● Straight stitch, slightly shorter than average (1.75 to 2mm or 12 to 25 stitches per inch).

● On some lightweight microfibers, increasing the pres-

sure on the presser foot may help prevent puckers.

● For lightweight microfibers, use a small, single-hole throat plate when sewing a straight stitch. This will prevent the fabric from being "swallowed" into the machine. A narrow straight stitch foot and/or flat-bottom presser foot may also be helpful.

INTERFACING

Avoid high temperature fusibles. Lightweight sew-in wovens or non-wovens are best. Organdy or organza fabrics are also an option.

SEAMS AND SEAM FINISHES

● Seam Options: Plain Seam (page 78); Topstitched or Welt Seam (page 80). Choose carefully—top-stitching may cause puckers.

● If you finish the seam allowances on a serger, use lightweight thread or woolly nylon thread. This will prevent thread imprint on the right side of the garment.

HEMS

Hand stitched hems are difficult to keep invisible on the right side. Avoid narrow machine rolled hems. Fused hems will be the least conspicuous. Experiment with different fusing products and be careful not to use too much heat. A Topstitched Hem (page 153) is a good possibility. Experiment on scraps to determine the best hem allowance width before hemming your garment.

PRESSING

● Use moderate heat, preferably on the wrong side of the fabric. Use a press cloth on the right side of fabric to avoid shine. Avoid steam.

● Cover the holes in the iron's sole plate with a Teflon shoe so that they won't make an impression in the fabric.

● Press seams flat first, then open. Press over a seam roll or a seam stick so that the seam allowances won't create ridges on the outside of the garment.

PLAIDS AND STRIPES

LAYOUT

Note: Review Chapter 5, "Designs That Must Be Matched" (pages 65 and 66), before cutting out your garment.

● Before deciding on a cutting layout, it is important to determine whether you have an even or uneven plaid or stripe. In an even plaid or stripe, the arrangement of bars (stripes) is the same on both sides of the main bar. In an uneven plaid or stripe, the arrangement of bars is different on either side of the main bar. To see what your fabric is, fold it on the center of a main lengthwise bar. See if the design and colors repeat evenly on either side of it. Do the same for the main crosswise bar. If all the bars on both fabric layers match, the fabric is even; if not, it's uneven.

● For even plaids or stripes you may use a "without nap" cutting layout unless the fabric surface is brushed or napped. You may fold and cut through a double layer of fabric if you align and pin the bars together first.

● For uneven plaids and stripes, use a "with nap" cutting layout and cut a single layer at a time. An uneven plaid can be made to pro-

tip

To eliminate some of the matching—and add visual interest to your garment—cut small detail sections, such as collars, cuffs, pockets and yokes, on the bias.

before they are cut again. Place center seams or center front lines along the center of a main bar or group of bars. Position the center of the sleeve along a main bar and cut it out. Then, to cut out the second sleeve, reverse and turn the pattern piece. Match the direction of the plaid on the right sleeve to the right side of the bodice front; on the left sleeve to the left side of the bodice front.

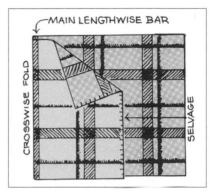

UNEVEN PLAID

ceed around the figure in one direction or in opposite (mirror-image) directions from the center.

To lay out the plaid so it goes around the figure: Fold fabric at the center of a main bar or group of bars. Position the pattern pieces that must be cut on the fold. Then cut the remaining pieces from a single layer of fabric. For fly-front openings, place the foldline on the center of a main bar. Be sure to place sleeves so that the plaid moves in the same direction on both sleeves.

For a mirror image effect: The pattern must have a center front and back seam or closure. Work with a single layer of fabric. The main pieces (garment front and back) must be cut once, then reversed and turned upside down

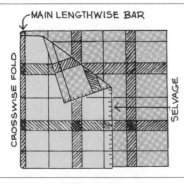

EVEN PLAID

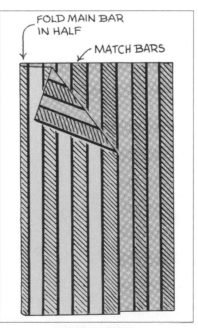

EVEN STRIPE

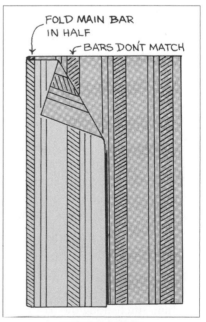

UNEVEN STRIPE

MACHINE SETTINGS

● Average length straight stitch (2.5mm or 15 stitches per inch).

● Decrease presser foot pressure slightly.

● When sewing two layers together, consider using a roller foot or even-feed foot to minimize shifting.

SEAMS AND SEAM FINISHES

● Seam Options: Choose a seam and seam finish appropriate to the fiber content and fabric weight and construction.

● No matter what type of seam you use, it is important to match the color bars and keep them from shifting as you sew. Basting tape or glue stick are two excellent options. Hand slip basting is another option. To slip baste:

● Press one seam allowance under along the seamline. Lap it over the adjoining section, matching seamlines and fabric design. Pin at right angles. Bring the needle and thread through to the right side at the folded edge, through all three layers.

● Insert the needle just opposite the fold, through the single layer of fabric, and bring it back up through the fold, about ⅜" (1 cm) to the left of the previous stitch.

● Continue to slip baste the seam in place.

● To sew the seam, remove the pins, open out the fabric, and machine stitch along the basting line.

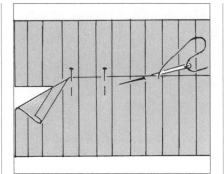

● The serger is a great choice when sewing seams in plaids. Because the serger sews without feed dogs, the fabric won't shift or crawl as you serge, helping you to keep the bars aligned. The trick is in the pinning.

● Pin the fabric layers, right sides together with pins at right angles to the seam line and matching the bars as you go. Alternate each pin so that the one above the dominant bar or repeat is pinned from right to left and the pin below the repeat is pinned from left to right.

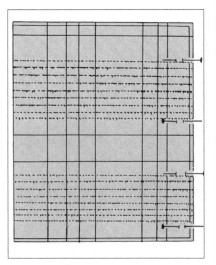

● Serge slowly, remembering to remove the pins before they reach the serger knives.

SATIN

LAYOUT

● Use a double thickness cutting layout, right sides together.

● Use a "with nap" cutting layout as satins tend to shade in different directions.

● Use fine pins, pinning within the seam allowances.

MARKING

Use dressmaker's chalk. Avoid fabric marking pens as they run and bleed into the fabric. Avoid wax dressmaker's carbon as it may leave spots.

CUTTING

Use scissors with serrated blades or a rotary cutter.

NEEDLE

● Use a standard universal point needle, usually in lightweight size: 70/10 H (Schmetz) or 10 (Singer).

● If runs or pulls occur, try a Microtex needle with sharp point in lighter weight size: 70/10 HM (Schmetz) or 10 Violet Band (Singer).

THREAD

Use standard or fine cotton-covered polyester thread or lingerie thread.

MACHINE SETTINGS

● Straight stitch, average length to slightly shorter than average (2mm to 2.5mm or 10 to 15 stitches per inch).

● On some lightweight satins, increasing the pressure on the presser foot may be helpful.

● For lightweight satin, use a small, single-hole throat plate when sewing a straight stitch. This will prevent the fabric from being "swallowed" into the machine. A narrow straight stitch foot and/or flat-bottom presser foot may also be helpful. If you do not have these machine attachments, consider moving the needle to the far left to provide support on three sides of the fabric.

INTERFACING

Sew-in woven or nonwoven. Consider organdy or organza on lightweight satin. Avoid fusibles.

SEAMS AND SEAM FINISHES

● Seam Options: Plain Seam (page 78); French Seam (page 79) on lightweight satins. *Note:* French Seams are not suitable on curved seams.

● When finishing seam allowances with a serger, use lightweight thread or woolly nylon thread. This will prevent thread imprint on right side.

HEMS

● Avoid hand sewn hems unless the garment is underlined (see TIP). Without an underlining, the hem stitches will show on the right side.

tip

Underlining is a layer of fabric that is sewn as one with the fashion fabric. Use the main pattern pieces to cut out the underlining sections, then carefully pin the underlining to the fashion fabric sections, wrong sides together. Hand-baste together along the center front and center back lines and just inside the seamlines. This underlining will serve as a buffer so that details like interfacings and hand-sewn hems can be attached to the underlining, rather than to the fashion fabric. For satins, silk organza is a great underlining. It has a soft hand but will support the weight of a hem.

● On lightweight satins, use the Machine Rolled Hem (page 154).

● Topstitched hems may pucker. However, by interfacing the hem and topstitching several rows spaced ¼" to ½" (6mm to 1.3cm) apart, you can create a design feature.

PRESSING

● Press with a warm dry iron, preferably on the wrong side of the fabric.

● When pressing on the right side, use a press cloth to avoid shine.

● Avoid steam. Satins tend to water spot.

● Press seams open over a seam roll or seam stick, or use strips of paper underneath the seam allowances. This will prevent ridges from forming on the outside of the garment.

SHEERS

LAYOUT

● Use a single or double thickness cutting layout with right sides together.

● Use a "without nap" cutting layout.

● A cutting surface with a contrasting color will help you get the best view of your sheer.

● Soft sheers will easily slip off grain. Use pushpins to anchor the fabric to a padded cutting surface. Insert the pins along the selvage

and across the cut edge along the crosswise grain.

● Pin only within the seam allowances, especially on crisp sheers. Extra fine pins are suitable on crisp sheers but may easily fall out of soft sheers. Insert pins at more frequent intervals than usual.

MARKING

Use tailor's tacks or an evaporating fabric marking pen. Avoid dressmaker's chalk and wax dressmaker's carbon.

CUTTING

Use scissors with serrated blades or a rotary cutter.

NEEDLE

Use a standard universal point needle in a light- to medium-weight size: 70/10 H to 80/12 H (Schmetz) or 10 to 12 (Singer).

THREAD

Standard or fine cotton-covered polyester thread or lingerie thread.

MACHINE SETTINGS

● Straight stitch, average length to slightly shorter than average (2mm to 2.5mm or 10 to 15 stitches per inch).

● On some lightweight sheers, increasing the pressure on the presser foot may be helpful.

● Use a small, single-hole throat plate when sewing a straight stitch. This will prevent the fabric from being "swallowed" into the machine. A narrow straight stitch foot and/or flat-bottom presser foot may also be helpful. If you do not have these machine attachments, consider moving the needle to the far left to provide support on three sides of the fabric.

INTERFACING

● Eliminate interfacing whenever possible.

● In place of a commercial interfacing, choose organza for soft sheers and organdy for crisp sheers. These fabrics are compatible with the transparent qualities of a sheer.

● Never use a fusible interfacing.

SEAMS AND SEAM FINISHES

● Seam Options: Double Stitched Seam (page 78); French Seam (page 79) (for straight seams, but not for curved ones); the three-thread or four-thread serger seam. The Narrow Seam (see TIP on page 215) is a variation of the narrow hem that works well as a seam technique for sheers.

● Sheers can be seamed quite successfully on the serger. Test first to be sure you are happy with the

tip

On faced edges, consider substituting bias binding for both the facing and interfacing.

amount of thread that shows through.

HEMS

● Choose the narrow Machine Rolled Hem (page 154) or the Narrow Rolled Hem (page 155). If you are using the latter, test first. If the serger stitches are too dense, the hem may pull away from the fabric.

● On crisp sheers, the Narrow Topstitched Hem or the Wide Topstitched Hem (page 153) are also good choices, particularly if the hemline is on the straight grain of the fabric.

tip

When making a collar from sheer fabric, seams should be as inconspicuous as possible. Use one of the following seam techniques. Note that clipping, grading and understitching are not necessary.

The Conventional Method

● *Stitch along the seamline over a filler cord of pearl cotton or crochet thread, using a fine zigzag stitch. Trim the seam allowance close to the stitching; then turn and press the collar.*

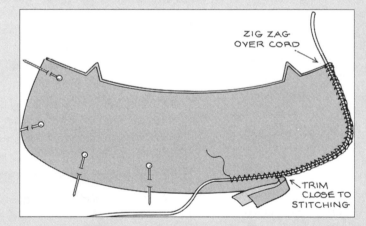

ZIG ZAG OVER CORD

TRIM CLOSE TO STITCHING

S The Serger Method

● *Set the machine to make a narrow seam.*
● *Serge along the seamline; then turn and press the collar.*

Narrow Seam		
TYPE OF SERGER STITCH:	3	MINE
Stitch length:	2-3	
Stitch width:	Narrowest	
Tensions—Needle:	Normal	
Upper looper:	Normal	
Lower looper:	Normal	

Note: These two techniques work equally well for cuffs.

PRESSING

Press with a warm, dry iron.

VELVET

Layout

● Use a single thickness cutting layout with the wrong side of the fabric facing up.

● Use a "with nap" cutting layout.

● Do not allow the fabric to hang off the cutting table. The weight may distort the fabric, pulling it off grain.

● Pin within the seam allowances. Use extra–fine pins.

MARKING

Use dressmaker's chalk or fabric marking pens on the wrong side of the fabric only. If it is absolutely necessary to mark on the right side, make tailor's tacks using silk thread.

CUTTING

Use sharp scissors.

NEEDLE

For woven velvets: Use a standard universal point needle in a medium-weight size: 70/10 H to 80/12 H (Schmetz) or 10 to 12 (Singer).

For stretch velvets: Use a ballpoint or stretch needle in a medium-weight size: 70/10 HS to 80/12 HS (Schmetz) or 10 to 12 Yellow Band (Singer).

SEAMS AND SEAM FINISHES

● Seam Options: Plain Seam (page 78) with a Pinked, Zigzagged or Tricot Bound Seam Finish (page 81).

● The serger is also a good choice for seams or to finish the edges of a plain seam.

HEMS

Choose a Hand Sewn Hem (page 152), finishing the edge of the hem allowance with seam binding, stretch lace, or by overcasting it on the serger.

PRESSING

● Press with the velvet face down on a needle board, a thick terrycloth towel or a piece of scrap velvet positioned face up.

● Press velvet from the wrong side, keeping the weight of the iron off the surface of the fabric.

THREAD

Cotton, polyester or cotton-covered polyester thread for general sewing; silk thread for tailor's tacks and hand basting.

MACHINE SETTINGS

● Average length straight stitch (2.5mm or 15 stitches per inch) or narrow zigzag stitch with average length (0.75mm wide and 2.5mm long).

● Reduce presser foot pressure slightly.

● When sewing two layers together, a roller foot or even-feed foot will minimize velvet's tendency to "creep."

● Use silk thread to hand-baste each seam before stitching it by machine.

INTERFACING

● Use sew-in woven interfacing. Nonwoven interfacing may be used with stretch velvets.

● Avoid fusibles.

tip

As two layers are joined together, velvet tends to "creep" so that one layer ends up longer than the other. To avoid this, use silk thread to hand-baste each seam before stitching. Then, when you are stitching at the machine, stop stitching every 3" to 4" (7.5cm to 10cm). With the needle in the fabric, raise the presser foot, allowing the fabric to relax. Lower the presser foot and continue stitching. Repeat, stopping and starting, until you reach the end of the seam.

● Check the fiber content of the fabric. Acetate or rayon velvets may scorch or shine under heat and steam. Cotton velvets can withstand a slightly higher temperature and some steam.

● When pressing, put strips of paper underneath the seam allowances to avoid leaving an impression on the right side of the fabric.

STABILIZERS

Technological developments and increased consumer interest in embellishments have spawned a whole new category of sewing aids. These "helpers," called stabilizers, do just what their name implies: Supply a firm, secure base for the fabric so that the result is smooth and pucker-free.

Stabilizers are the secret behind professional looking results for just about any embellishment technique that utilizes thread and a sewing machine—computerized embroidery, free motion embroidery, heirloom sewing, appliqué, quilting, monogramming, etc. And, on the utilitarian side, a bit of stabilizer underneath machine-made buttonholes can vastly improve their appearance. Stabilizer can also provide a smooth, temporary cover that can be valuable when sewing "loopy" fabrics such as mohair and terrycloth.

Some stabilizers are designed to function exclusively as a base—i.e., placed underneath the project, between the feed dog and the fabric. Some see-through versions can also be used as a cover, either to protect the fabric or as a stitch-through template for the design. And some stabilizers are temporary backings, while others are permanent.

THE BASIC CATEGORIES

The easiest way to categorize stabilizers is by how they are removed.

● *Tear-off:* This type of stabilizer offers temporary support. Once the stitching is completed, the stabilizer is gently torn away. This category is generally recommended for stable fabrics. Most tear-offs are nonwovens. However, there are also several clear plastic tear-off films on the market.

● *Cut-off:* These are woven products that provide permanent support during stitching and throughout the life of the garment. They are suitable for most fabrics, but are particularly good for knits and stretch wovens, in areas such as under machine-made buttonholes or satin-stitched appliqués. After stitching, the excess stabilizer is carefully cut off close to the stitches. Sometimes the choice between a cut-off and a tear-off is merely a matter of personal preference. However since cut-offs are usually softer than tear-offs, comfort may be a factor if the stabilizer cannot be easily removed from all areas of the design.

Note: Tear-offs and cut-offs come in different weights. When a heavier foundation is required, many sewing experts recommend two or more layers of a lightweight stabilizer. Each layer is removed individually, putting less strain on the stitches.

● *Wash-away:* This category includes water-soluble films, liquids or sprays designed to be used as temporary support in washable fabrics. They are desirable when you do not want any traces of stabilizer left in the finished project. Liquids and sprays are generally more suited to lightweight fabrics. They also require drying time before stitching. This type of stabilizer can be a great help when you are trying to hem a washable knit fabric that has a tendency to curl.

● *Heat-disintegrating:* These stabilizers disappear when they are treated with a hot, dry iron. These are used in place of a cut-off when you don't want any stabilizer showing, or in place of a wash-away, particularly on dry-clean-only fabrics.

Water-soluble films and heat-disintegrating stabilizers are preferred any time the stabilizer must be completely removed. They should be stored in Ziplock® bags. Unfinished projects should be similarly stored until the stabilizer is removed.

SECURING THE STABILIZER

It's not enough to simply place a stabilizer underneath the fabric. It must also be secured so that the stabilizer and fabric act as one during stitching. While pinning or basting often suffices, more secure methods will eliminate slippage or the possibility of an off-register motif when used for techniques such as machine embroidery or monogramming.

A few stabilizers come with a variety of self-securing backings.

Some can be temporarily ironed onto the fabric. Some have a pressure-sensitive backing, somewhat like Post-it® notes. If these stabilizers are removed carefully, they can often be used again. There are also temporary spray adhesives that can be used to transform cut-off, tear-off and water soluble stabilizers into self-adhesive versions. Self-adhesion is particularly desirable if you need a cover stabilizer and you are working with velvet or some other fabric that cannot handle pins or ironing.

ADDING A COVER

Under some circumstances, the surface quality of the fabric needs to be changed in order to achieve professional-looking results. Here the solution is to add a cover layer of stabilizer.

This cover can be a tear-off, wash-away or heat-disintegrating stabilizer. If it is a tear-off, it should be one that pulls cleanly away from the stitching and does not leave any whiskers behind. If two stabilizers are needed, the cover and the backing stabilizers can be the same or they can be different products.

Use a stabilizer cover:

● To hold down the loops (as in terrycloth or mohair) or the pile (as in velour or velvet).

● To work together with a stabilizer backing to bridge the openings when embellishing on an open weave fabric such as mesh, netting or lace.

● To smooth out the surface of a textured fabric such as piqué or corduroy, particularly in the case of machine-made buttonholes.

● To provide a transfer surface for an embellishment design. If the design can be traced onto the stabilizer, there is no need to mark the fabric.

● To provide extra protection against hoop burn. "Hoop burn" refers to the marks caused by friction when the inner and outer rings of a machine embroidery hoop rub up against the fabric.

Water-soluble and clear tear-off film stabilizers are generally preferred for these cover tasks. However, when the thread is dark, the stitches are dense and the fabric is light, such as an appliqué outlined with black satin stitches on white terry cloth, look for a stabilizer that is available in a color that will help camouflage the fabric behind the stitching.

chapter 8
Simply the Best Patternless Projects

Why on earth would a sewing book produced by a pattern company include a whole chapter of "patternless" projects?

The answer is simple. We wanted your sewing adventure to get off to the best possible start.

● For the novice sewer, the instructions are organized in an easy-to-follow sequence, from Supplies to Cutting Directions to Sewing Directions. You can concentrate on becoming familiar with your sewing machine and developing your basic sewing skills before moving on to a commercial pattern.

● For those new to serger sewing, these projects offer the opportunity to integrate serger techniques with conventional techniques.

● For the experimental sewer, these projects are simply styled so that they are suitable for a wide variety of fabrics. General fabric recommendations are included in each project's description, but you need not be limited by this list. For example, velvet is not included because it requires special handling. However, the kimono, the T-top, the skirt and the shawl would all be stunning in this luxurious fabric. Consult Chapter 7, "Sewing With Special Fabrics," for fabric ideas and sewing support.

● For the more experienced sewer, these versatile silhouettes provide a wonderful canvas for embellishment. Add appliqués, trims or machine embroidery. Use your serger to create decorative edges. Let your imagination soar and set your creativity loose.

● For the fashion conscious sewer, these timeless silhouettes will look up-to-the-minute for many seasons.

This chapter includes mix-and-match separates—kimono, T-top and skirt—plus shawl and poncho in Misses' sizes. The adaptable kimono, which is also sized for Girls and Boys, can become a wonderful terrycloth bathrobe, a great karate jacket or a terrific Halloween costume. The poncho, which has also been sized for Misses, Girls and Children, is a practical, fashionable protection against wind or rain. The roomy tote bag can hold everything, from portable sewing projects to beach supplies. And for the fashionable baby, we've even included a mini-kimono and diaper cover in Infant Size Six to Nine Months. Everything is sized to Simplicity standards.

Check out the color section between pages 144 and 145 and you'll see just a sampling of the exciting results you can achieve by following the easy, self-contained instructions for the projects in this chapter.

KIMONO

(Misses', Girl's and Boy's sizes)

This versatile kimono can be made in a Misses' hip-length or dress-length version, or for a girl or a boy. As sized for the Misses' figure, it fits up to a 42" (107cm) bust; for Girls, sizes 7-14; and for Boys, sizes 7-12. A baby-sized version appears on page 250.

Change the length and/or the fabric and the kimono silhouette translates into a coat, a topper, a robe, a karate jacket or a geisha costume. Suitable light- to medium-weight fabrics include silk, linen, terrycloth, broadcloth, chino, poplin, chambray, cotton sateen, shantung, wool flannel, jersey and double knit.

Note: Except for the Cutting Diagrams and the measurement differences indicated in Steps 3 and 4 of the Sewing Directions, the procedures for making the Misses' and the Girl's/Boy's versions are exactly the same.

SUPPLIES

Fabric

Note: Select fabric without a nap or one-way design.

For the Misses' hip-length jacket:

- 2½ yds. (2.3m) of 44"/45" (115cm) or 54" (138cm) fabric

For the Misses' dress-length robe or coat:

- 3 yds. (2.8m) of 44"/45" (115cm) or 54" (138cm) fabric

For the Girl's or Boy's hip-length karate jacket:

- 2 yds. (2m) of 44"/45" (115cm) or 54" (138cm) fabric

For the Girl's or Boy's knee-length robe:

- 2½ yds. (2.3m) of 44"/45" (115cm) or 54" (138cm) fabric

For the Girl's ankle-length geisha costume:

- 3 yds. (2.8m) of 44"/45" (115cm) or 54" (138cm) fabric

Note: For contrasting color tie belt as shown with the geisha costume and karate jacket, you will need ⅜ yd. (0.4m) of contrasting fabric.

Additional Supplies

- Thread
- Chalk marking pencil or fabric marking pen
- Yardstick or T-square
- Glue stick (optional)

CUTTING DIRECTIONS

Place your fabric, single thickness and right side up, on a large, flat surface or cutting board. Using the appropriate Cutting Diagram [Diagram A for Misses' hip-length, Diagram B for Misses' dress-length (page 222) and Diagram C for Girl's or Boy's versions (page 222) in all lengths], plot out and cut the following sections of the kimono:

- One BODY
- Two BELTS
- Two SLEEVES
- One NECKBAND

Notes:

● If you prefer a contrasting belt, eliminate the two belt sections shown on the diagram. Instead, cut them from contrasting fabric, following the crosswise grain.

● For 54" (138cm) wide fabric, follow the same cutting diagram as for 44"/45" (115cm) fabric. You will have some fabric left over along one selvage edge.

The measurements for each section are indicated on the appropriate Cutting Diagram. Use the yardstick or T-square to draw cutting lines that are straight, even and parallel.

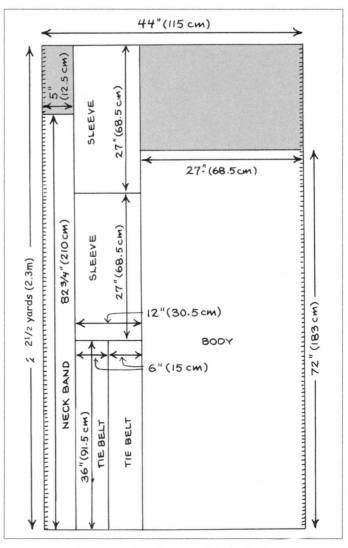

DIAGRAM A — MISSES' HIP LENGTH

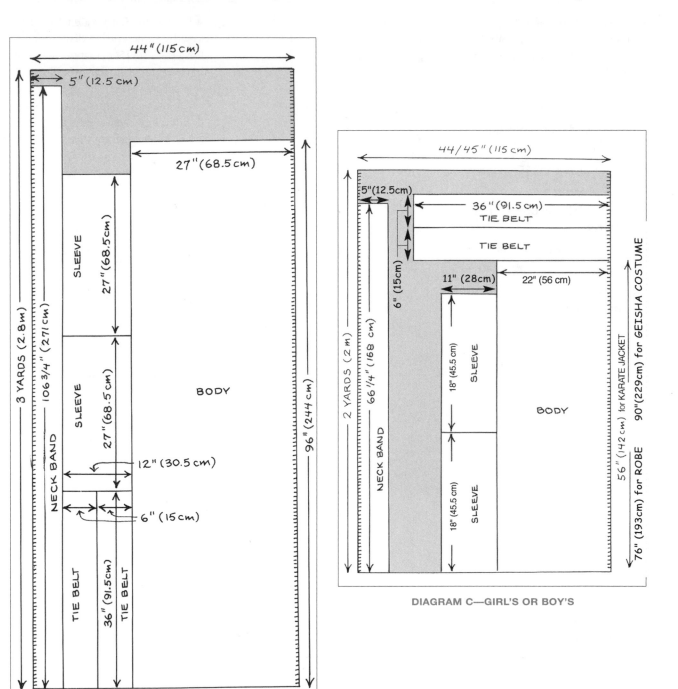

DIAGRAM B — MISSES' DRESS LENGTH

44" (115 cm)

5" (12.5 cm)

27" (68.5 cm)

3 YARDS (2.8 m)

106 3/4" (271 cm)

96" (244 cm)

SLEEVE

27" (68.5 cm)

SLEEVE

27" (68.5 cm)

BODY

NECK BAND

12" (30.5 cm)

6" (15 cm)

TIE BELT

36" (91.5 cm)

TIE BELT

DIAGRAM C—GIRL'S OR BOY'S

44/45" (115 cm)

5" (12.5 cm)

36" (91.5 cm)

TIE BELT

TIE BELT

6" (15 cm)

11" (28 cm)

22" (56 cm)

18" (45.5 cm)

SLEEVE

18" (45.5 cm)

SLEEVE

BODY

2 YARDS (2 m)

66 1/4" (168 cm)

NECK BAND

56" (142 cm) for ROBE

76" (193cm) for ROBE

90" (229cm) for GEISHA COSTUME

for KARATE JACKET

SEWING DIRECTIONS

Note: All seam allowances are ⅝" (1.5cm). The hem allowance is 1" (2.5cm) at lower edge.

Establish the Neckline and Center Front Opening

1. With right sides together, fold the BODY in half lengthwise and mark the fold. This is the Center Front/Center Back line.

2. Unfold the BODY and refold it in half crosswise, right sides together; mark the fold. This is the Shoulder Line.

3. The point where the Center Front/Center Back Line and the Shoulder Line intersect is the starting point for establishing the neckline curve.

For the Misses' kimonos only:

- On the Center Back Line, put a mark ¾" (2cm) from the intersection point.

- On the Center Front Line, put a mark 10" (25.5cm) from the intersection point. See Misses' neckband illustration below.

- On both sides of the Shoulder Line, put a mark 3" (7.5cm) from the intersection point.

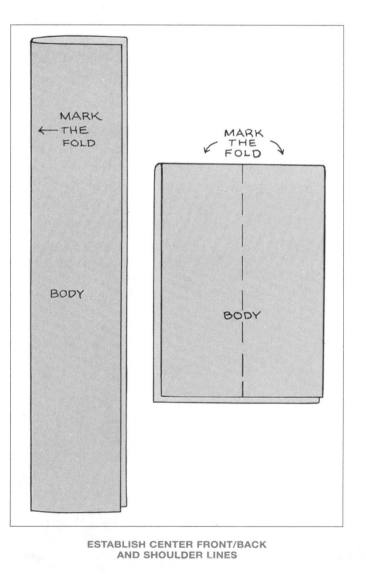

ESTABLISH CENTER FRONT/BACK AND SHOULDER LINES

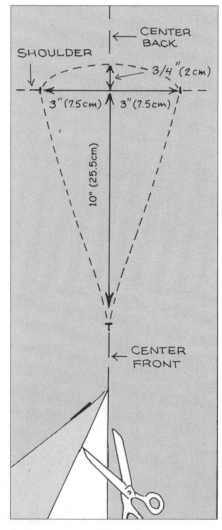

MISSES' NECKLINE

For the Girl's or Boy's kimonos only:

● On the Center Back Line, put a mark ¾" (2cm) from the intersection point.

● On the Center Front Line, put a mark 9" (23cm) from the intersection point.

● On both sides of the Shoulder Line, put a mark 2¾" (7cm) from the intersection point.

tip

Draw one side of the curve, then fold the BODY along the Center Front/Center Back Line and use dressmaker's carbon and a tracing wheel to transfer the curve to the other side.

For all versions:

● To create the neckline, draw a line, as shown, connecting these four marks. Gently curve the line to get rid of the corner at the point where the neckline meets the Shoulder Line. Be sure that the left side of the neckline matches the right side.

● Beginning at the lower edge of the Center Front Line, cut the BODY apart until you reach the 10" (25.5cm) mark of the Misses' BODY or the 9" (23cm) mark of the Girl's or Boy's BODY, then cut around the neckline.

Attach the Neckband

4. To establish the Center Back and Shoulders on the NECKBAND, fold it in half crosswise and mark at the raw edges. This is the CB marking.

For the Misses' kimono only:

● Mark along the raw edges 4⅜" (11.2cm) from the Center Back on each side .

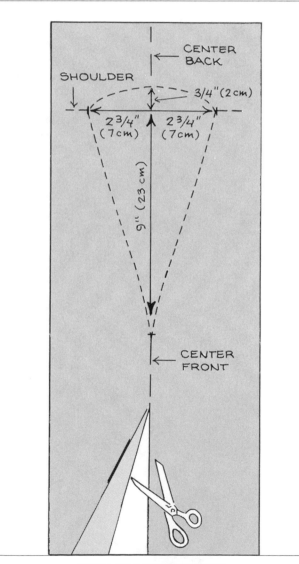

GIRL'S OR BOY'S NECKLINE

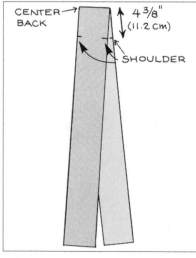

MISSES' NECKBAND

For the Girl's or Boy's kimono only:

• Mark along the raw edges 4⅛" (10.5cm) from the Center Back on each side.

These are the Shoulder markings.

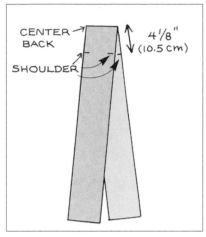

GIRL'S OR BOY'S NECKBAND

5. Staystitch the BODY neckline. Clip the seam allowances just to, but not through, the staystitching all around the neckline, as shown.

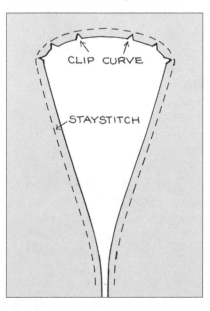

6. With right sides together, pin the NECKBAND to the BODY, matching the CB and Shoulder markings. Be careful not to stretch the band; instead, ease it carefully around the curves. Stitch, trim and clip the seam, or serge the seam on the serger.

Note: Depending on your fabric and how much easing you have to do, the NECKBAND may extend beyond the lower edges of the BODY. Trim off the excess before hemming the kimono (Step 13).

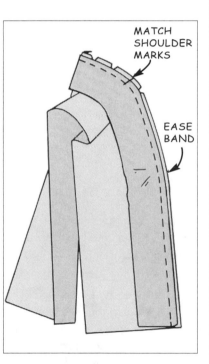

7. Press the long raw edge of the NECKBAND under ⅝" (1.5cm). Then fold the band to the inside of the kimono so that the folded edge just covers the seamline. Hand-baste or glue-baste in place, easing it carefully around the curves. Slipstitch in place.

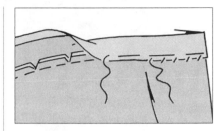

8. Working on the outside of the kimono, edgestitch the NECK-BAND close to the seamline, through all thicknesses.

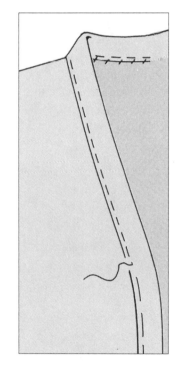

Attach the Sleeves

9. To find the Shoulder Line, fold each sleeve in half crosswise and mark. Then, along one 27" (68.5cm) edge of each Misses' SLEEVE or one 25" (63.5cm) edge of the Girl's or Boy's SLEEVE, mark ⅝" (1.5cm) in from each outer edge.

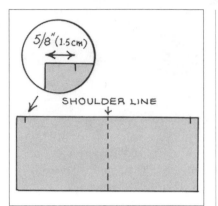

10. With right sides together, pin the SLEEVE to the BODY, matching shoulder lines and raw edges. Stitch the seam, beginning and ending the stitching at the ⅝" (1.5cm) marks. Repeat for the other sleeve; then press both sleeve seams open.

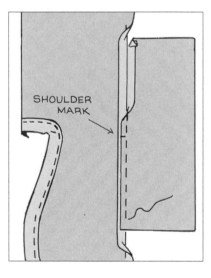

tip

S *Both the sleeves and the lower edge of the kimono can be finished on the serger, then turned up and topstitched in place.*

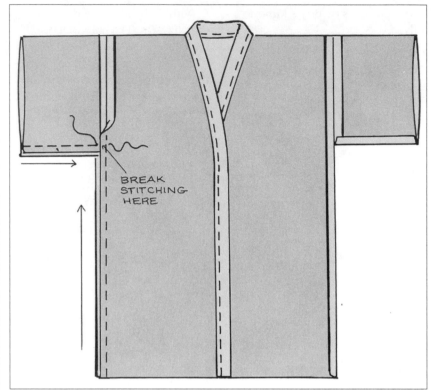

STITCH THE SIDE SEAMS

Stitch the Side Seams

11. With right sides together, pin the BODY front and back together at the side seams and underarm seamlines.

● Beginning at the lower edge of the BODY, stitch the side seam. End the stitching when you reach the sleeve seam, keeping the sleeve seam allowances free.

● Beginning at the lower edge of the SLEEVE, stitch the underarm seam. End the stitching when you reach the ⅝" (1.5cm) markings, keeping the sleeve seam allowances free. This "break" in the stitching at the underarm is what makes this seam smooth on the finished kimono.

● Press the side/underarm seams open.

Hem the Kimono

12. Make a narrow hem on the lower edge of the sleeves, following the directions for the Narrow Topstitched Hem, page 153, and changing the hem allowance from 1" (2.5cm) to ⅝" (1.5cm).

13. Mark the hem at the lower edge of the kimono, then press up along the hemline. Trim the hem allowance to 1" (2.5cm). Finish, following the directions for the Narrow Topstitched Hem, page 153, or serge-finish the edge and topstitch, as shown.

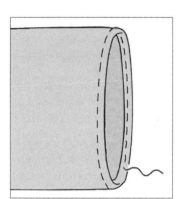

HEM SLEEVES

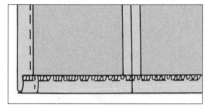

HEM LOWER EDGE

Construct the Belt

14. With right sides together, serge or stitch the two BELT sections together along one 6" (15cm) end. Then finish the belt on the conventional machine or serger, following the directions for Soft Belts in Chapter 6, page 114.

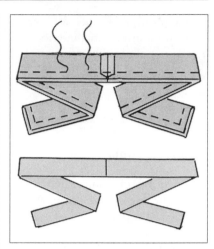

T-TOP

(Misses' Sizes)

This comfortable, contemporary "T" is a beautiful and easy-to-sew top. The simple lines and wide range of suitable fabrics make it the perfect choice for either casual or evening wear. Choose a soft or crisp, light- to medium-weight woven. Think silk, linen, cotton, challis, crepe de chine or lightweight wool.

SUPPLIES

- 1⅜ yds. (1.2m) of 44"/45" (115cm) wide fabric without a nap or one-way design

- Thread

- One ⅜" (1cm) button

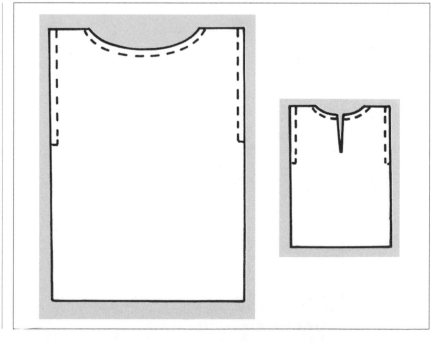

• One package of single-fold bias tape (for conventional method only)

• Chalk marking pencil or fabric marking pen

• Yardstick or T-square

CUTTING DIRECTIONS

Place your fabric, single thickness and right side up, on a large, flat surface. Using the Cutting Diagram as your guide, plot out and cut the one BODY section of the T-top. The measurements for the section are indicated on the Cutting Diagram. Use the yardstick or T-square to draw cutting lines that are straight, even and parallel.

SEWING DIRECTIONS

Note: The neckline has a ¼" (6mm) seam allowance. All other seam and hem allowances are ⅝" (1.5cm).

Establish the Neckline, Center Back and Armhole Openings

1. Fold the BODY in half crosswise, right sides together, and mark the fold. This is the Shoulder Line.

MARK THE FOLD

2. Unfold the BODY and refold it in half lengthwise, right sides together; mark the fold. This is the Center Front/Center Back Line.

3. The point where the Center Front/Center Back Lines and the Shoulder Line intersect is the

starting point for establishing the neckline curve, armhole opening, and the center back opening.

Create the Neckline Curve

4. On the Center Back Line, put a mark 1¼" (3.2cm) from the intersection point as shown on the next page.

• On the Center Front Line, put a mark 3" (7.5cm) from the intersection point.

• On both sides of the Shoulder Line, put a mark 4¼" (11cm) from the intersection point.

• To create the neckline, draw a curved line, as shown, connecting these four marks. Be sure that the curve on the left side of the Center Front/Center Back Line matches the curve on the right side.

• Cut out the neck opening along this line.

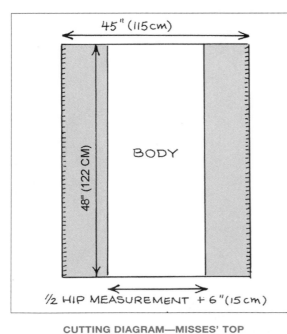

45" (115CM)

48" (122 CM)

BODY

½ HIP MEASUREMENT + 6" (15cm)

MARK THE FOLD

CUTTING DIAGRAM—MISSES' TOP

Mark the Armhole Opening

5. Put four marks at the side seams, each 7½" (18cm) from the Shoulder Line, as shown below.

Create the Center Back Opening

6. Put a mark on the Center Back Line, 5" (12.5cm) down from the back neck edge. Now put two marks at the back neck edge, each

tip

You might want to draw one side of the neckline curve, then fold the BODY along the Center Front/Center Back Line and use dressmaker's carbon and a tracing wheel to transfer the curve to the other side.

¼" (6mm) from the Center Back Line. Draw two lines, connecting these three marks into a V. Do not cut along these lines. They are stitching lines.

● Staystitch the neckline opening ⅛" (3mm) from the raw edge.

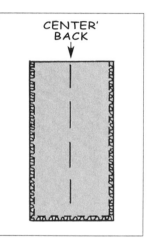

Face the Back Opening

7. For the facing section, cut a 3" x 6" (7.5cm x 15cm) rectangle from your leftover fabric.

● To locate the Center Back Line, fold the FACING in half lengthwise, right sides together; mark along the fold.

● To finish the sides and lower edge of the facing, serge around the edges or trim off ¼" (6mm) and overcast on your conventional machine.

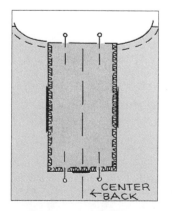

8. With right sides together, pin the facing to the back, matching the Center Back Lines and the raw edges at the neckline.

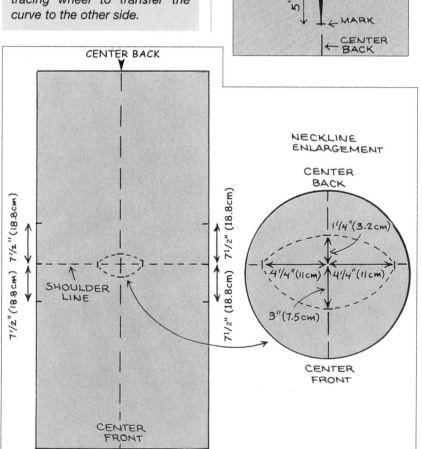

9. With the BODY facing up, stitch along the stitching lines, shortening the stitch for 1" (2.5cm) on either side of the point. Slash along the Center Back Line, between, and just up to, the stitching.

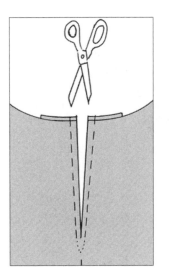

10. Turn the facing to the inside and press.

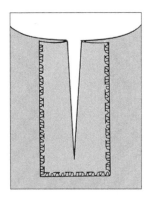

Finish the Neckline
The Conventional Method

11-A. With right sides together and raw edges even, open out the bias tape and pin it to the neck edge, beginning and ending ⅝" (1.5cm)

from the back opening, keeping the FACING free, as shown. Stitch a ¼" (6mm) seam.

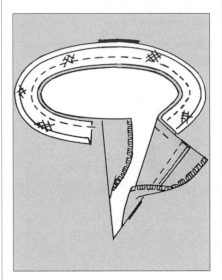

11-B. Press the bias tape up, away from the neckline, then fold it to the inside along the stitching line, clipping where necessary, and press again; baste. See below.

11-C. Fold the upper edge of the FACING and the remaining neckline edge under ¼" (6mm). Slipstitch the FACING to the neckline edge.

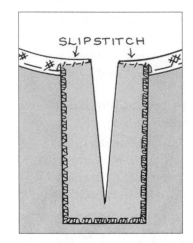

11-D. Topstitch the neckline ¼" (6mm) from the edge. Edgestitch around the back opening.

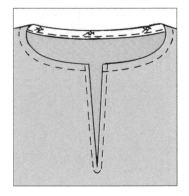

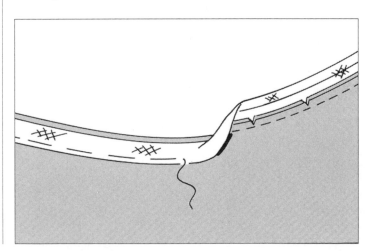

S *The Serger Method*

11-A. Baste the FACING to the neckline edge.

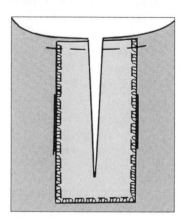

11-B. Serge along the neckline edge, trimming ¼" as you stitch. Edge-stitch around the back opening.

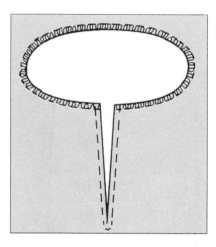

Finish the Armholes and Stitch the Side Seams

The Conventional Method

12-A. With right sides together, pin the BODY front and back together at the side seams, matching the armhole markings. Starting at the lower edge, stitch the side seam,

between the lower edge and the armhole marking to reinforce. Press the seam open.

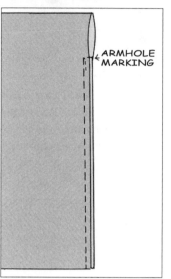

12-B. Finish the armhole edges, following the directions for the Narrow Topstitched Hem, page 153, changing the hem allowance from 1" (2.5cm) to ⅝" (1.5cm) and squaring the stitching at the underarm, as shown.

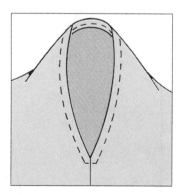

S *The Serger Method*

12-A. Serge the armhole edges between the markings, angling the stitches on and off the fabric for approximately 1½" (1.5cm) as you stitch.

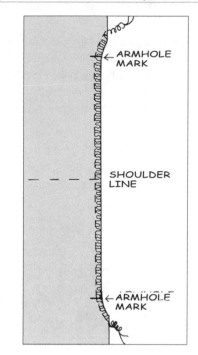

12-B. With right sides together, pin the BODY front and back together at the side seams. Starting at the lower edge, serge a ⅝" (1.5cm) seam, angling off the fabric at the armhole markings.

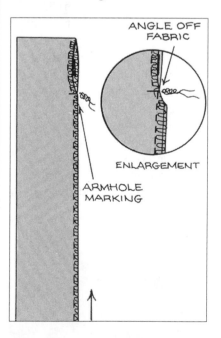

Finish the Top

13. Make a thread loop at the left back neck opening. (See Chapter 6, Machine Thread Loops, page 116.) Sew a button to the right back neck opening, opposite the loop.

Or

Sew a hook and loop eye at the top of the back opening. (See Chapter 6, Hooks and Eyes, page 130.)

14. Try on the top to determine

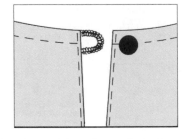

the desired length. Mark the hemline. Before hemming the lower edge, review Chapter 6, Hems, and choose the hand or machine hem-

ming method you prefer. Good choices on your conventional machine include the Narrow Top-stitched Hem, page 153, or the Machine Rolled Hem, page 154. If you prefer to use your serger, options include the Narrow Hem, page 156, the Rolled Hem, page 155 or the Cover Hem, page 157. Another option is to serge-finish the lower edge and topstitch, as shown for the kimono on page 227.

SKIRT

(For hip measurements up to 50" or 127cm)

This straight skirt with elastic waistline casing has several variations. We've provided two length options—a short version with a 24" (61cm) finished length or a long version with a 34" (86.5cm) finished length —but you can adapt these instructions to any length you desire. The skirt can also be made with one or two side slits (for walking ease). However, if you choose the short length, you can eliminate the slits entirely.

Fabric recommendations include cotton and cotton blends, rayon, silk, lightweight synthetics, lightweight cotton knits and crepe. If you choose a fabric with a nap or one-way design, see the TIP on page 233.

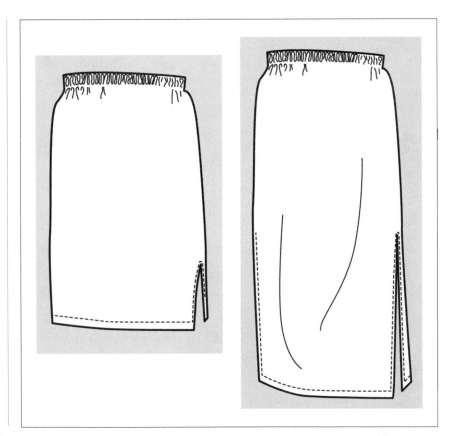

SUPPLIES

Fabric

For the short version with a 24" (61cm) finished length:

- 1½ yds. (1.4m) of 44"/45" (115cm) fabric

Or

- ⅞ yd. (0.8m) of 58"/60" (150cm) wide fabric

For the long version with a 34" (86.5cm) finished length:

- 2⅛ yds. (1.9m) of 44"/45" (115cm) fabric

Or

- 1⅛ yds. (1m) of 58"/60" (150cm) wide fabric

Additional Supplies

- ¾" (2cm) wide elastic*
- Thread
- Tape measure
- Chalk marking pencil or fabric marking pen
- Yardstick or T-square

*Purchase an amount of elastic equal to your waist measurement plus 1" (2.5cm).

CUTTING DIRECTIONS

Determine the Cutting Width

1. Measure the fullest part of your hip. Divide this measurement by four. Add 2" (5cm) to this number for seam allowances and ease. This total is your cutting width for each SKIRT section. On the cutting diagrams, it is indicated by a "W."

(*Note:* The SKIRT sections are cut on the fold. When unfolded, the width of each section will be equal to one-half of your hip measurement plus some extra for seam allowances and ease.)

Cutting and Marking

2-A. For 44"/45" (115cm) wide fabric:

Place the fabric, folded lengthwise in half with right sides together and selvages matching, on a large, flat surface or cutting board. Using Cutting Diagram A as your guide, plot out and cut one SKIRT section. Choose the short or long version. With the remaining fabric, repeat the measuring process and cut a second SKIRT section that is identical to the first. Use the yardstick or T-square to draw cutting lines that are straight, even and parallel. Diagram A is shown on page 234.

2-B. For 58"/60" (150cm) wide fabric:

Place the fabric, folded lengthwise in half with right sides together and selvages matching, on a large, flat surface or cutting board. Mark the fold with a few pins. Unfold the fabric, then re-fold it, keeping it right sides together, so that the selvages meet at the center pin line. Using Cutting Diagram B as your guide, plot out and cut two SKIRT sections, as shown. Choose the short or long version. Use the yardstick or T-square to draw cutting lines that are straight, even and parallel. Diagram B is shown on page 234.

3. For the slits, measure 21" (53.5cm) down from the upper edge of one SKIRT and ⅝" (1.4cm) in from the cut edge and place a mark on the wrong side of the fabric. Do this on both SKIRT sections.

tip

If you wish to make the skirt in a length other than the ones we have provided, use the following formulas to figure out how much fabric is required.

When you are ready to cut out the skirt, use the finished length plus 2½" (6.3cm) for your cutting length.

● *For 44"/45" (115cm) wide fabric:*

● *Determine the desired finished length of your skirt, add 2½" (6.3cm) and then multiply by 2.*

● *Divide this total by 36" (100cm)—that's how many yards (meters) of fabric you will need.*

● *For 58"/60" (150cm) wide fabric:*

● *Determine the desired finished length of your skirt and add 2½" (6.3cm).*

● *Divide this total by 36" (100cm)—that's how many yards (meters) of fabric you will need.*

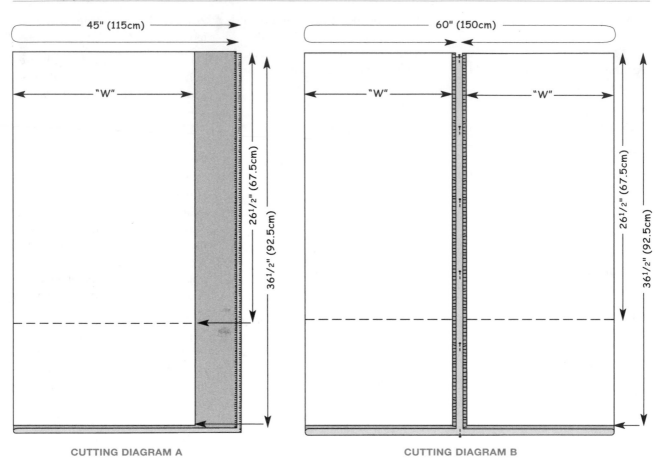

CUTTING DIAGRAM A   CUTTING DIAGRAM B

SEWING DIRECTIONS

Note: All seam allowances are ⅝"
(1.5cm). The hem allowance is 1¾"
(3.2cm) at the lower edge.

Sew the Side Seams

1. With right sides together, stitch
the SKIRT side seams, starting
at the upper edge and stitching
to the slit marks. Backstitch at the
marks to reinforce the slit openings. Press the seams open. See
illustrations for both the one and
two slit skirts on page 232.

Hem the Skirt

2. Press the lower edge of the
SKIRT up 1¼" (3.2cm) to the
wrong side, forming the hem
allowance. Press the raw edge
of the hem allowance under ¼"
(6mm). Topstitch the hem in place,
keeping the stitches close to the
second fold.

Finish the Slits (Optional for Short Version)

3. Press under ⅝" (1.5cm) along
the slit opening edges. Press under
¼" (6mm) on each raw edge.

Starting at the bottom of the skirt,
stitch close to the folded raw edge,
finishing one side of the slit. Repeat
for the other side of the slit opening.

4. Repeat Step 3 to finish the
second slit.

tip

S *If you are making the short
version of the skirt and are eliminating the side slits, use your
serger to sew the SKIRT side
seams (Step 1) and to finish the
raw edge of the hem allowance
instead of pressing it under ¼"
(6mm) as in Step 2.*

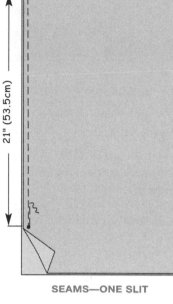

21" (53.5cm)

SEAMS—ONE SLIT

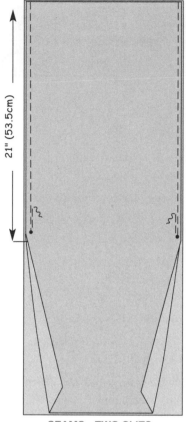

21" (53.5cm)

SEAMS—TWO SLITS

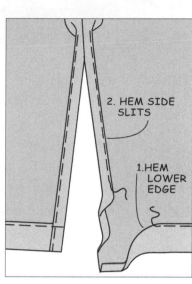

2. HEM SIDE SLITS

1.HEM LOWER EDGE

HEM THE SKIRT

Make the Casing

5. Machine-baste the side seam allowances to the SKIRT for about 2½" (6.3cm) from the upper edge of the SKIRT. This will help keep the elastic from getting stuck in the seam allowances as it is inserted.

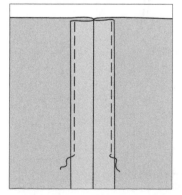

6. Finish the upper edge of the SKIRT.

The Conventional Method
Press the raw edge under ¼" (6mm).

S *The Serger Method*
Serge-finish the raw edge, trimming off ¼" (6mm) as you serge.

7. Press the finished edge of the skirt down 1" (2.5cm) to the wrong side, forming the casing. Stitch close to the lower edge of the casing, leaving a 2" (5cm) opening at the center back for inserting the elastic.

8. To insert the elastic, review Chapter 6, Casings and Elastic, and follow the directions for "Inserting Elastic" on page 123.

9. Remove the machine basting at the side seams.

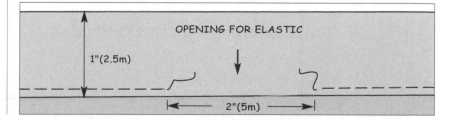

OPENING FOR ELASTIC

1"(2.5m)

2"(5m)

PONCHO

(One-size-fits-all in Misses', Girl's and Children's sizes)

This easy-fit poncho features a V-neck opening and a generous front pocket with slanted side openings.

Approximate finished length measured from the shoulder:

- Misses' version—35" (89cm) long

- Girl's version—25" (63.5cm) long

- Children's version—21" (53.5cm) long

Suitable medium- to heavy-weight knit or woven fabrics include fleece, wool and wool blends. Choose a 58"/60" (150cm) wide fabric without a nap or one-way design. For the Girl's and Children's version, 44"/45" (115cm) wide fabric can also be used.

SUPPLIES

Fabric

Note: Select fabric without a nap or one-way design.

For the Misses' version:

- 2½ yds. (2.3m) of 58"/60" (150cm) wide fabric

- ½ yd. (0.5m) of 22"/25" (55cm/64cm) wide lightweight fusible interfacing

For the Girl's version:

- 1⅞ yds. (1.7m) of 58"/60" (150cm) wide fabric

- ½ yd. (0.4m) of 22"/25" (55cm-64cm) wide lightweight fusible interfacing

For the Children's version:

- 1¾ yds. (1.6m) of 58"/60" (150cm) wide fabric

- ⅜ yd. (0.4m) of 22"/25" (55cm-64cm) wide lightweight fusible interfacing

Additional Supplies

- Thread

- Chalk marking pencil or fabric marking pen

- Yardstick or T-square

- Small ruler

- French Curve ruler (optional)

- Brown paper or tissue paper, approximately 24" x 10" (61cm x 25.5cm)

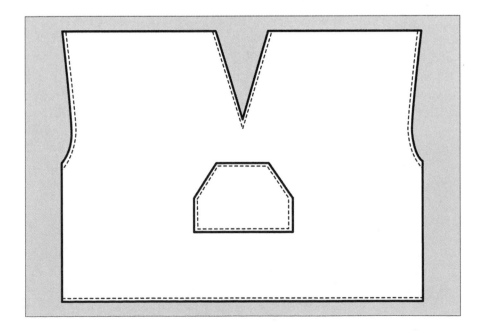

CUTTING AND MARKING DIRECTIONS

Cut Out the Poncho.

1. Fold your fabric lengthwise in half with right sides together and selvages matching and place it on a large, flat surface. Using the Cutting Diagram as your guide, plot out and cut one PONCHO section in the desired size. Use the yardstick or T-square to draw cutting lines that are straight, even and parallel.

2. Measure and mark along the folded edge of the PONCHO for the neck opening. Mark along the folded edge of the PONCHO for the center back (CB), the center front (CF) and the pocket placement, as shown in the Cutting Diagram. Do not unfold the PONCHO.

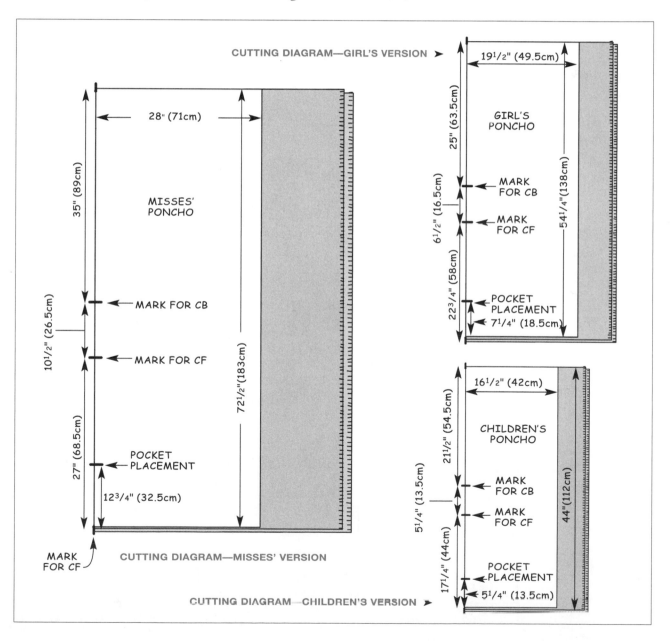

CUTTING DIAGRAM—GIRL'S VERSION ➤

19¹/₂" (49.5cm)

GIRL'S PONCHO

25" (63.5cm)

54¹/₄" (138cm)

6¹/₂" (16.5cm) — MARK FOR CB

— MARK FOR CF

22³/₄" (58cm)

POCKET PLACEMENT

7¹/₄" (18.5cm)

28" (71cm)

35" (89cm)

MISSES' PONCHO

72¹/₂" (183cm)

10¹/₂" (26.5cm) — MARK FOR CB

— MARK FOR CF

27" (68.5cm)

POCKET PLACEMENT

12³/₄" (32.5cm)

MARK FOR CF

CUTTING DIAGRAM—MISSES' VERSION

16¹/₂" (42cm)

CHILDREN'S PONCHO

21¹/₂" (54.5cm)

44" (112cm)

5¹/₄" (13.5cm) — MARK FOR CB

— MARK FOR CF

17¹/₄" (44cm)

POCKET PLACEMENT

5¹/₄" (13.5cm)

CUTTING DIAGRAM—CHILDREN'S VERSION ➤

Create the Neck Facing Pattern

1. Use the T-square or yardstick to make a straight edge along one long edge of the brown paper. This straight edge will be the foldline on the finished neck facing pattern. Mark on the foldline 6" (15cm) down from the top of the paper. This mark is your starting point.

2. Using the Neck Facing Pattern Diagram as a guide, mark out from the starting point, as shown. Connect the marks, creating the curve for the back neckline and tapering to form a V at the center of front neckline. *Note:* If you own a French Curve ruler, use it to draw a smooth back neckline curve.

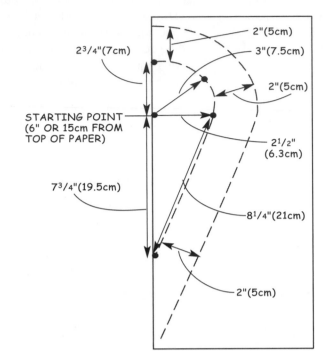

MISSES' NECK FACING PATTERN

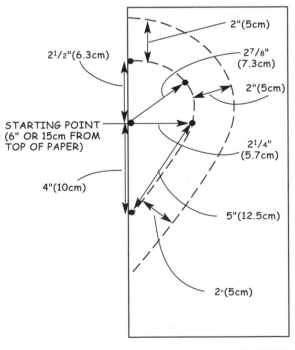

GIRL'S NECK FACING PATTERN

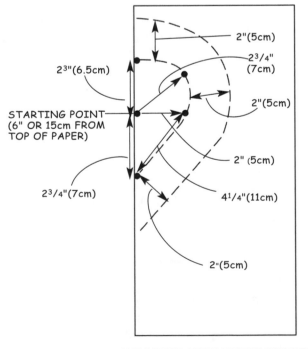

CHILDREN'S NECK FACING PATTERN

3. Measure and mark 2" (5cm) out from the neckline all around. Connect the marks, creating the outer edge of the neck facing. Note that the width of the facing will measure more than 2"(5cm) below the **V**.

Mark the Poncho Neckline

1. Cut out the Neck Facing pattern.

2. Pin the Neck Facing pattern to the PONCHO, matching the fold-lines and the markings for the neck opening. Trace the neckline opening onto the PONCHO. Cut the PONCHO along the neckline opening. Remove the Neck Facing pattern. Set the PONCHO aside.

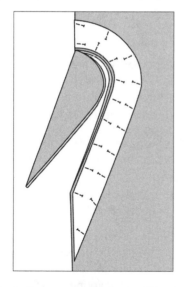

Cut Out and Mark the Neck Facing and the Pockets

Follow the cutting diagram shown at the top of the next column.

1. Refold the remaining fabric so that the selvages meet in the middle. Pin the Neck Facing pattern along one fold of the fabric. Cut out the NECK FACING.

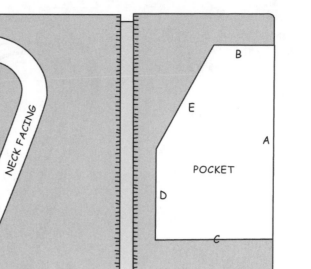

2. Measuring from the other fold, plot out and cut the POCKET section using the measurements in the chart below for the appropriate size. At the fold, mark the center at the upper and lower edges.

Pocket Measurements			
	MISSES'	GIRL'S	CHILDREN'S
SIDE A	11¼" (28.5cm)	8½" (21.5cm)	8" (20.5cm)
SIDE B	4½" (11.5cm)	4" (10cm)	3¼" (8.3cm)
SIDE C	8¼" (21cm)	7" (18cm)	6½" (16.5cm)
SIDE D	5¾" (14.5cm)	4" (10cm)	4" (10cm)
SIDE E	6¾" (17cm)	6½" (16.5cm)	5¾" (14.5cm)

Cut Out and Apply the Interfacing

1. Fold the interfacing fabric lengthwise in half with right sides together. Pin the Neck Facing pattern in place along the foldline and cut out the NECK INTERFACING. On the right side, mark along the folded edge for the center back (CB) and the center front (CF).

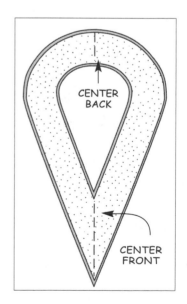

2. Fuse the NECK INTERFACING to the wrong side of the NECK FACING, following the fusible interfacing manufacturer's directions.

SEWING DIRECTIONS

Note: All seam allowances are ⅝" (1.5cm) unless otherwise noted. The hem allowance is ¾" (2cm) at the edges of the poncho.

Finish the Neck Facing Edges

Note: If you are using fleece, wool melton or a similar non-raveling fabric, you can omit this step.

The Conventional Method

1. Stitch ¼" (6mm) from the outer edge of the NECK FACING. Turn under along the stitching line and straight stitch close to the fold.

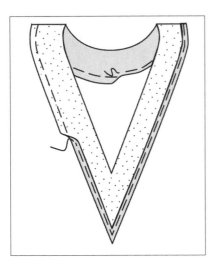

S The Serger Method

1. Serge along the outside edge of the NECK FACING, trimming off ¼".

Apply the Neck Facing

2. Working on the interfaced side of the NECK FACING, mark a ⅝" (1.5cm) seamline around the neck edge. Mark with a dot where the lines cross at the **V**.

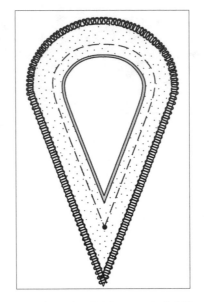

3. On the PONCHO, staystitch ¼" (1.3cm) from the neck edge, starting at the center front and stitching in the direction of the arrows.

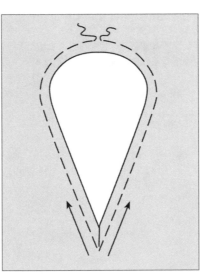

4. With right sides together, pin the NECK FACING to the PONCHO, matching the neckline edges and the CF and CB markings. Working with the NECK FACING on top and starting at the back neck edge,

stitch along the marked seamline. When you come to the **V** mark, stop stitching with the needle in the fabric. Lift the presser foot and pivot the fabric. Lower the foot and continue stitching up the other side of the neckline. To reinforce the seam at the center front, stitch over the first stitching for about 1" (2.5cm) on either side of the **V** mark. Trim the seam. Clip the curves and clip to the stitching at the center point.

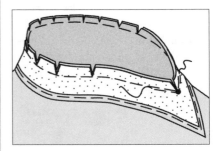

5. Turn the NECK FACING to the inside of the PONCHO and press.

Topstitch the Neckline

6. Working on the right side of the PONCHO and using a chalk pencil, mark a topstitching line by measuring and marking ½" (1.3cm) from the neck edge. Cross the lines at the **V**.

7. Starting at the back neck edge, topstitch over the marked topstitching line, pivoting the PONCHO when you reach the tip of the **V**.

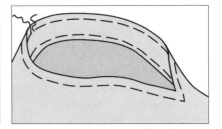

Hem the Poncho

The Conventional Method

8. Hem the front and back edges of the PONCHO, then hem the side edges, following the directions for the Narrow Topstitched Hem, page 153, and changing the hem allowance from 1" (2.5cm) to ¾" (2cm).

Note: If your fabric does not ravel, follow the directions for the Narrow Topstitched Hem for Knits, page 153, trimming the hem allowance to ⅜" (1cm).

⑤ The Serger Method

8. Serge and topstitch the front and back edges of the PONCHO, then repeat on the side edges, following the directions for the Overcast Hem on the Serger, page 154, and changing the hem allowance from 1" (2.5cm) to ¾" (2cm).

Finish the Pocket

9. Finish the slanted edges of the POCKET, using the same hemming technique as for the edges of the PONCHO.

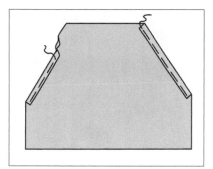

10. Stitch ⅝" (1.5cm) from the unfinished edges of the POCKET. Trim to ⅜" (1cm). Press under along the stitching, favoring the stitching line slightly to the wrong side of the POCKET.

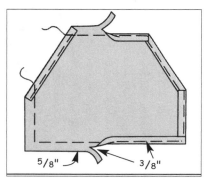

5/8"   3/8"

Apply the Pocket

11. On the right side of the PONCHO front, pin the POCKET in place, matching the center mark-

ings and keeping the lower edge of the POCKET parallel to the lower edge of the PONCHO.

- For the Misses' size, the lower edge of the POCKET should be 12" (30.5cm) from the lower edge of the PONCHO.

- For the Girls' size, the lower edge of the POCKET should be 6½" (16.5cm) from the lower edge of the PONCHO.

- For the Children's size, the lower edge of the POCKET should be 4½" (11.5cm) from the lower edge of the PONCHO.

  If desired, try on the PONCHO. If necessary, move the POCKET up or down for personal comfort.

12. Topstitch the POCKET to the PONCHO, stitching ¼" (6mm) from the upper, lower and side edges.

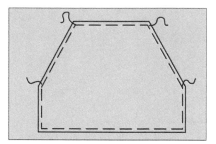

SHAWL

(Approximately 30" wide x 83" long or 76.5cm x 21.2cm long)

This large, rectangular shawl can serve as a great summer cover-up or as an extra layer of warmth over a winter coat or suit jacket.

Large pockets, cleverly positioned at each end, are always at-the-ready to keep hands warm when a cool breeze kicks up. Select any

medium-weight woven or knit fabric such as wool, wool types, fleece or double knit.

Note: This shawl can be cut from

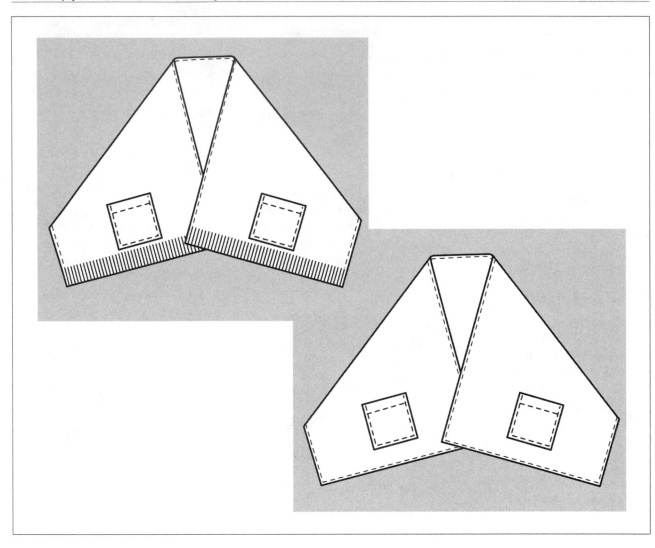

any suitable fabric that is at least 44"/45" (115cm) wide. If your fabric is more than 44"/45" (115cm) wide, you have the option of making your shawl wider.

SUPPLIES

• 2⅜ yds. (2.2m) of 44"/45" (115cm) fabric without a nap or one-way design

• Thread

• Chalk marking pencil or fabric marking pen

• Yardstick or T-square

CUTTING DIRECTIONS

Place your fabric, single thickness and right side up, on a large flat surface. Using the Cutting Diagram as your guide, plot out and cut the following sections of the shawl:

• One SHAWL

• Two POCKETS

The measurements for each section are indicated on the Cutting Diagram, shown on page 243. Use the yardstick or T-square to draw cutting lines that are straight, even and parallel.

SEWING DIRECTIONS

Note: The seam allowances on the pockets and the hem allowance on the shawl are ⅝" (1.5cm).

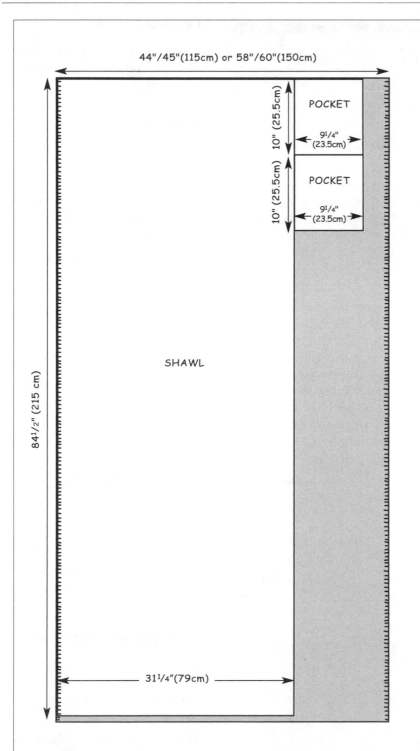

44"/45"(115cm) or 58"/60"(150cm)

POCKET

10" (25.5cm)

9¼"
(23.5cm)

POCKET

10" (25.5cm)

9¼"
(23.5cm)

SHAWL

84½" (215 cm)

31¼"(79cm)

Finish the Edges

The Conventional Method

1. Hem the long edges of the SHAWL first, then hem the short ends, following the directions for the Narrow Topstitched Hem, page 153, changing the hem allowance from 1" (2.5cm) to ⅝" (1.5cm).

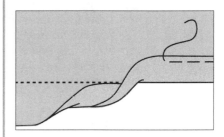

S The Serger Method

1. Serge and topstitch the long edges of the SHAWL first, then repeat on the short ends, following the directions for the Overcast Hem on the Serger, page 154, and changing the hem allowance from 1" (2.5cm) to ⅝" (1.5cm).

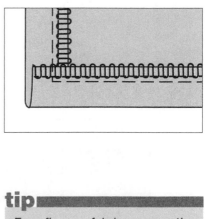

tip

For fleece fabrics, use the Narrow Topstitched Hem, page 153, following the recommendations for knit fabrics.

tip

For fabrics that truly do not ravel, such as fleece, consider this "fringed" alternative for hemming the ends of the shawl. Narrow hem the long edges of the shawl following a conventional method. On the ends of the shawl, using chalk or a fabric marking pen with

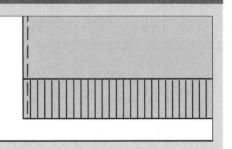

disappearing ink, measure and mark a line 3"(7.5cm) from the cut edge...or stitch a row of machine basting 3" (7.5cm) from the cut edge. With sharp dressmaker's shears, cut 3" (7.5) long slashes, approximately ³⁄₄" (2cm) apart across the entire width. Repeat at the other end of the shawl. For best results, test this technique on a fabric scrap before cutting into your shawl.

Establish the Pocket Placement Line

2. With wrong sides together, fold the SHAWL in half lengthwise. Mark the fold at each end.

3. Working along the fold, measure in 4" (10cm) from each end and mark. See (A).

4. Open up the shawl. Beginning at the inner mark at one end, draw a line that extends 4" (10cm) out from each side of the center fold and is parallel to the lower edge of the SHAWL. The total length of this pocket placement line is 8" (20.5cm). Repeat, drawing a pocket placement line at the other end of the SHAWL. See (B).

Construct the Pockets

5. Press under ¼" (6mm) on one 9¼" (23.5cm) pocket edge and edgestitch...or finish the upper edge on your serger.

6. To form the pocket facing, fold the finished edge 1½" (3.8cm) to the right side; press.

7. Starting at the fold, stitch ⅝" (1.5cm) from the raw edges of the pocket, backstitching at the beginning and the end.

8. Trim the seam allowances in the facing area only to ¼" (6mm). If your fabric is bulky, diagonally trim the corners.

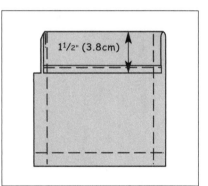

9. Turn the facing to the wrong side, using a pin or point turner to push out the upper corners.

10. Repeat Steps 5 to 9 for the other pocket.

Finish and Apply the Pockets

11. Miter the lower corners of the pocket, as shown at the top of the next column. (See Mitering, page 160.)

12. On the right side of the shawl, match the lower edge of one pocket to one pocket placement

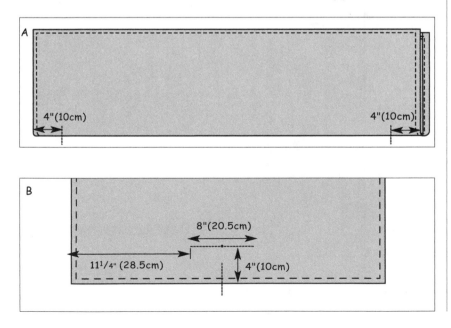

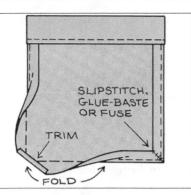

line. Pin or baste the pocket in place. Edgestitch ¼" to ⅜" (6mm to 1cm) from the sides and lower edge of the pocket, stitching through all layers, as shown in the illustration at the right.

13. Repeat Steps 11 and 12 for the other pocket.

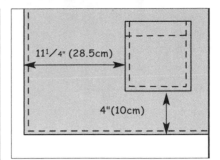

TOTE BAG

(9¼" x 17¾" x 21¼" deep or 23.5cm x 45cm x 54cm deep)

This handy tote is the perfect carryall for shopping, office or beach gear. Use a sturdy, medium- to heavyweight fabric, such as denim, canvas, sailcloth, synthetic suede or quilted fabric.

SUPPLIES

- 1¼ yds. (1.2m) of 44"/45" (115cm) fabric without a nap or one-way design
- Thread
- Chalk marking pencil or fabric marking pen
- Iron-on monogram letters (optional)
- Liquid seam sealant (optional)
- Glue stick (optional)

CUTTING DIRECTIONS

Place your fabric, single thickness and right side up, on a large, flat surface. Using the Cutting Diagram

as your guide, plot out and cut the following sections of your tote bag:

- One BAG
- One BOTTOM

- Two POCKETS
- Two HANDLES

The measurements for each section are indicated on the Cutting

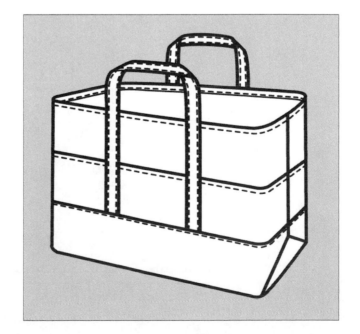

Diagram. Use the yardstick or T-square to draw cutting lines that are straight, even and parallel.

SEWING DIRECTIONS

Note: All seam allowances are ⅝" (1.5cm).

Note: Since you will be sewing through four or more layers of heavy fabrics, the right size sewing machine needle is essential. Use a size 16/100 or 18/110. You may find it easier if you choose a wedge-point needle (the type designed for leather or vinyl) rather than a general purpose needle.

Prepare the Pockets

1. Using chalk or a fabric marking pen, mark 6¾" (17cm) in from each end on both long edges of each POCKET. Connect each set of marks, as shown. These are the Handle Placement Lines.

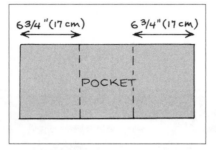

Create the Pocket Facings

2. Finish one long edge of one POCKET.

The Conventional Method

Turn the edge under ¼" (6mm) and topstitch close to the fold.

🅢 The Serger Method

Serge along the edge, trimming off ¼" (6mm).

3. Fold the finished edge 1" (2.5cm) to the inside and press.

4. Topstitch ¾" (2cm) from the fold.

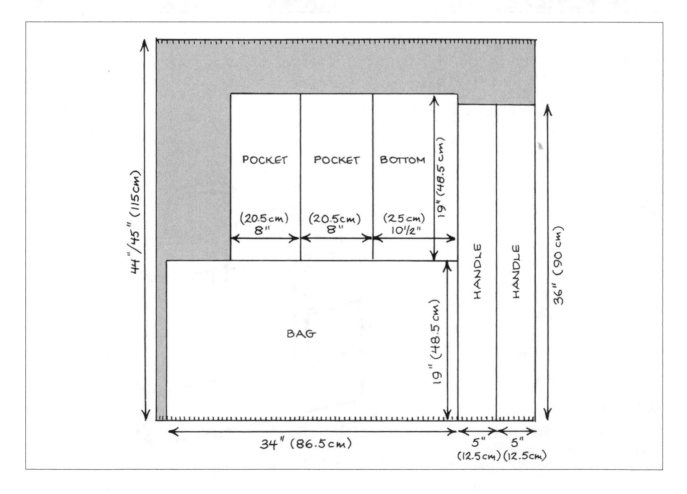

5. Repeat Steps 2 to 4 to create the facing on the other POCKET.

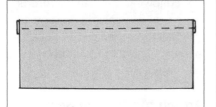

Mark the Pocket Placement Lines

6. Mark 12½" (32cm) in from each end on both long edges of the BAG. Connect each set of marks, as shown below.

Finish the Edges of the Bag

7. Finish the 19" (48.5cm) edges of the BAG.

The Conventional Method

Turn the edges under ¼" (6mm) and topstitch close to the fold.

S The Serger Method

Serge along the edges, trimming off ¼" (6mm).

Baste the Pockets

8. With the wrong side of one POCKET to the right side of the BAG, position the POCKET so that its long raw edge extends ⅝" (1.5cm) beyond the Pocket Placement Line; pin.

9. Baste the POCKET to the BAG along the sides and lower edge of the POCKET, then along the Handle Placement Lines.

10. Repeat Steps 8 and 9 for the other POCKET.

Make the Handles

11. Fold each HANDLE in half lengthwise, wrong sides together; press.

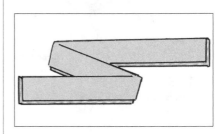

12. Unfold one HANDLE and turn in each long edge so that the raw

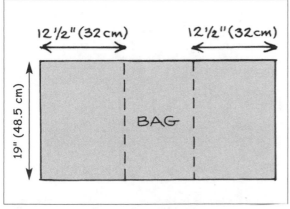

POCKET PLACEMENT

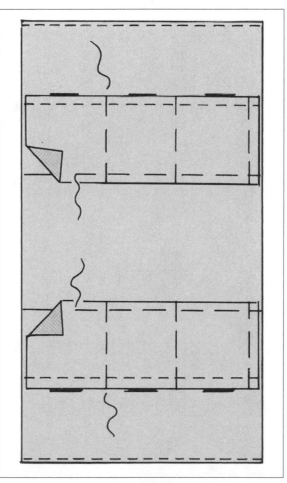

BASTE POCKETS

edge meets the fold; refold and press again. Edgestitch along both outer edges, through all four layers of fabric. Repeat for the other HANDLE.

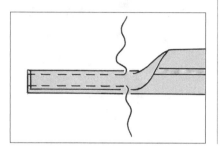

Attach the Handles

13. Position the HANDLES on the outside of the BAG over the Handle Placement Lines so that the raw edges of the HANDLES and the POCKETS are even. Pin or glue-baste in place. Topstitch each handle to the POCKET and BAG, as shown, over the edgestitching. End the topstitching at the upper edge of the POCKET; backstitch to reinforce.

Optional: Apply the Monogram

14. Following the manufacturer's instructions, apply the iron-on monogram to one center pocket between handles. (See photo in color section.)

Attach the Bottom Section

15. Press under ⅝" (1.5cm) on both long edges of the BOTTOM.

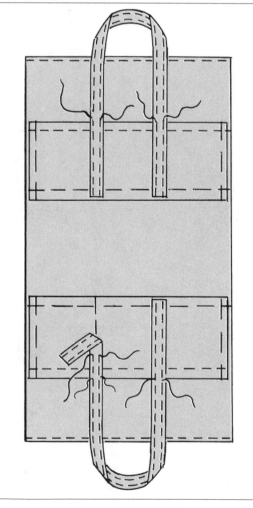

ATTACH HANDLES

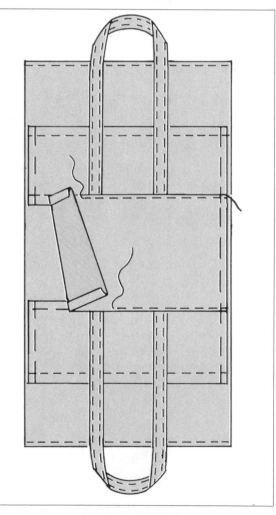

ATTACH BOTTOM

With the wrong side of the BOT-TOM to the right side of the BAG, position the BOTTOM so that the sides are even and the folded edges just cover the Pocket Placement Lines; pin or glue-baste in place.

16. Topstitch close to the folded edges of the BOTTOM, catching the POCKETS and HANDLES in the stitching.

17. Baste the BOTTOM and BAG together along the remaining edges.

Stitch the Side Seams

18. Fold the bag in half, right sides together, so that the edges match.

The Conventional Method

Stitch the side seams. Stitch again ¼" (6mm) from the first stitching, within the seam allowance. Trim close to the second row of stitching. If the raw edges have a tendency to fray, treat them with liquid seam sealant.

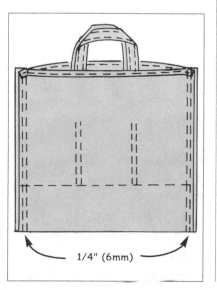

1/4" (6mm)

S The Serger Method

Serge the side seams.

Finish the Bag

19. To form the BAG facing, fold the finished edge of the BAG 1½" (3.8cm) to the inside and press. Folding the handles out of the way, topstitch the facing to the BAG 1¼" (3.2cm) from the fold.

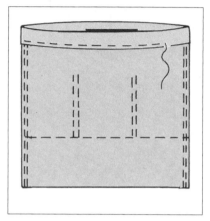

20. On the outside of the BAG, topstitch the HANDLES to the rest of the BAG. To keep the stitching lines smooth and connected, start stitching about 1" (2.5cm) below the top of the pocket, directly over the previous stitching. To reinforce the handles, backstitch at the upper edge of the bag, as shown at top of next column.

21. If you want your tote to have a flat bottom, fold the bottom corners up 1¾" (3.2cm), as shown in next column, and slipstitch in place.

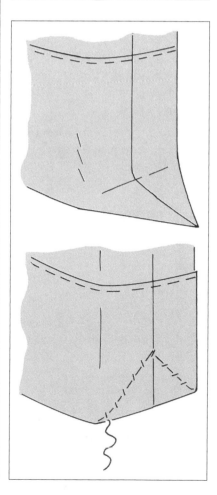

BABY KIMONO

(Fits Infants' Sizes Six to Nine Months)

Keep baby chic and cozy in this wonderful wrap. Moms will love it too because the clever hook and loop closures make it super simple to dress and undress baby.

BABY KIMONO

SUPPLIES

- ½ yd. (0.5m) of 42"/43" (107-110cm) wide fabric without a nap or one-way design

Note: For children's sleepwear, use fabrics and trims that meet the flammability standards set by the U.S. government.

- Three sets of ½" (2cm) diameter self-gripping hook-and-loop fasteners, such as Velcro®

- Thread

- Chalk marking pencil or fabric marking pen

- Yardstick or T-square

CUTTING DIRECTIONS

Place your fabric, single thickness and right side up, on a large, flat surface. Using the Cutting Diagram as your guide, plot out and cut the following sections of the baby kimono:

- One BODY

- Two SLEEVES

- One NECKBAND

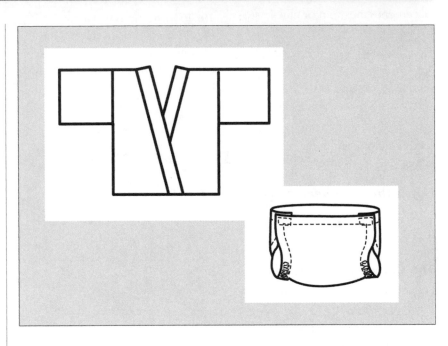

The measurements for each section are indicated on the Cutting Diagram. Use the yardstick or T-square to draw cutting lines that are straight, even and parallel. See diagram on opposite page.

SEWING DIRECTIONS

Note: The seam allowances at the neckline and center front opening on the BODY and the seam allowances on the NECKBAND are ¼" (6mm). All other seam allowances are ⅝" (1.5cm).

Establish the Neckline and Center Front Opening

1. With right sides together, fold the BODY in half lengthwise and mark the fold. This is the Center Front/Center Back Line.

2. Unfold the BODY and refold it in half crosswise, right sides together; mark the fold. This is the Shoulder Line.

3. The point where the Center Front/Center Back Line and the Shoulder Line intersect is the starting point for establishing the neckline curve.

- On the Center Back Line, put a mark ⅝" (1.5cm) from the intersection point.

- On the Center Front Line, put a mark 3½" (9cm) from the intersection point.

- On both sides of the Shoulder

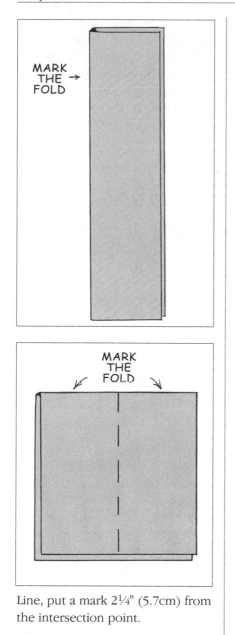

MARK
THE →
FOLD

MARK
THE
FOLD

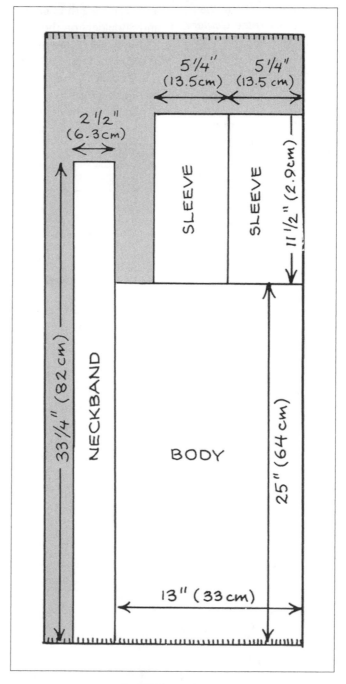

5¼"   5¼"
(13.5cm)   (13.5 cm)

2½"
(6.3cm)

SLEEVE

SLEEVE

11½" (2.9cm)

33¼" (82cm)

NECKBAND

BODY

25" (64cm)

13" (33 cm)

CUTTING DIAGRAM

Line, put a mark 2¼" (5.7cm) from the intersection point.

• To create the neckline, draw a line as shown, connecting these four marks. Gently curve the line to get rid of the corner at the point where the neckline meets the Shoulder Line (refer to the illustration on page 252.) Be sure that the left side of the neckline matches the right side.

tip

Draw one side of the curve, then fold the BODY along the Center Front/Center Back Line and use dressmaker's carbon and a tracing wheel to transfer the curve to the other side

• Beginning at the lower edge of the Center Front Line, cut the BODY apart until you reach the 3½" (9cm) mark, then cut around the neckline.

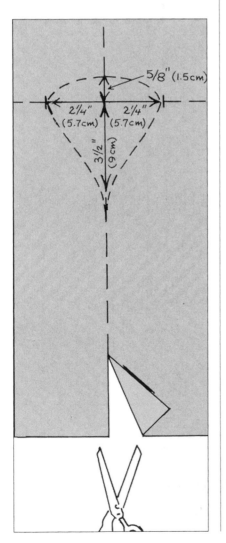

Attach the Neckband

4. To establish the Center Back and Shoulders on the NECKBAND, fold it in half crosswise and mark at the raw edges. This is the Center Back (CB) marking. Then mark along the raw edges 3" (7.5cm) from the center back on each side. These are the Shoulder markings.

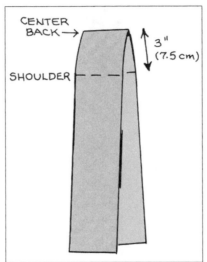

5. Staystitch the BODY neckline a scant ¼" (6mm) from the raw edge. Clip the seam allowances just to, but not through, the staystitching all around the neckline, as shown.

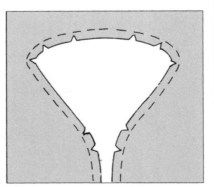

6. With right sides together, pin the NECKBAND to the BODY, matching the CB and Shoulder markings. Be careful not to stretch the band; instead, ease it carefully around the curves. Stitch, trim and clip the seam, or serge it on the serger.

7. Press the long raw edge of the NECKBAND under ¼" (6mm). Then fold the band to the inside of the kimono so that the folded edge just covers the seamline. Hand-baste or glue-baste in place, easing it gently around the curves. Slipstitch in place.

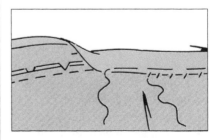

8. Working on the outside of the kimono, edgestitch the NECK-BAND close to the seamline, through all thicknesses.

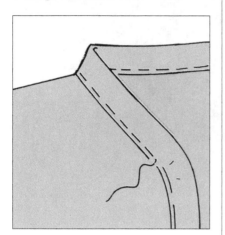

Attach the Sleeves

9. To find the Shoulder Line, fold each sleeve in half crosswise and mark. Then, along one 11½" (29cm) edge of each SLEEVE, mark ⅝" (1.5cm) in from each outer edge.

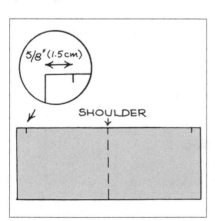

10. With right sides together, pin the SLEEVE to the BODY, matching shoulder lines and raw edges. Stitch the seam, beginning and ending the stitching at the ⅝"

(1.5cm) marks. Repeat for the other sleeve; then press both sleeve seams open.

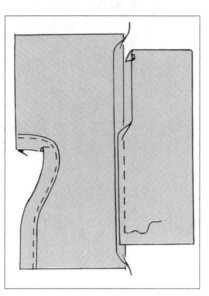

Stitch the Side Seams

11. With right sides together, pin the BODY front and back together at the side seams and underarm seamlines.

12. Beginning at the lower edge of the BODY, stitch the side seam. End the stitching when you reach the sleeve seam, keeping the sleeve seam allowances free.

13. Beginning at the lower edge of the SLEEVE, stitch the underarm seam. End the stitching when you reach the ⅝" (1.5cm) markings, keeping the sleeve seam allowances free. This "break" in the stitching at the underarm is what makes the seam smooth on the finished kimono.

14. Press the side/underarm seams open. See illustration below.

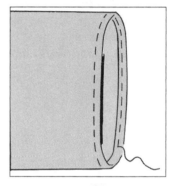

Finish the Edges

15. Make a narrow hem on the lower edge of the sleeves and the kimono, following the directions for the Narrow Topstitched Hem, page 153, and changing the hem allowance from 1" (2.5cm) to ⅝" (1.5cm).

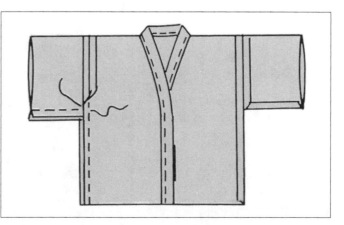

Construct the Closures

16. On the outside of the right front band, measure up 3½", 5½" and 7½" (9cm, 14cm and 19cm) from the lower edge and mark. Repeat on the inside of the left front band.

17. Center the hook sections of the fasteners over the markings on the right front band; hand- or machine-stitch in place.

18. Center the loop sections of the fasteners over the markings on the left front band; hand- or machine-stitch in place.

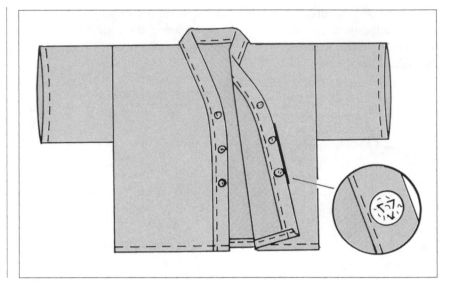

DIAPER COVER

(Fits Infant's Sizes Six to Nine Months)

For the fashionable little one, make the diaper cover to match the baby kimono. As a beginner's sewing project, this one's a breeze.

SUPPLIES

• ¾ yd. (.7m) of 42"/43" (107cm-110cm) wide fabric

Note: For children's sleepwear, use fabrics and trims that meet the flammability standards set by the U.S. government.

• ⅜ yd. (34.5cm) of ½" (1.3cm) elastic

• 4" (10cm) of ¾" (2cm) self-grip-ping hook-and-loop tape, such as Velcro®

• Thread

• Chalk marking pencil or fabric marking pen

• Yardstick or T-square

CUTTING DIRECTIONS

Place your fabric, single thickness and right side up, on a large, flat surface. Using the Cutting Diagram as your guide, plot out and cut a 13½" x 21½" (33.5cm x 54cm) rectangle.

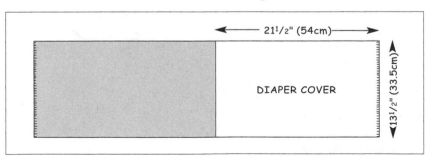

21¹/₂" (54cm)

DIAPER COVER

13¹/₂" (33.5cm)

SEWING DIRECTIONS

Finishing the Edges

The Conventional Method

1-A. Machine-stitch 1¼" (3.2cm) from the raw edges, crossing the stitching at the corners.

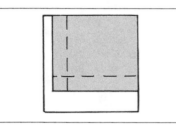

1-B. Where the stitches cross, fold the corners diagonally to the wrong side; press. Trim these corner seam allowances to ½" (13mm).

1-C. Fold the raw edges to the wrong side so they just meet the stitching line; press.

1-D. Fold up along the stitching line and press again.

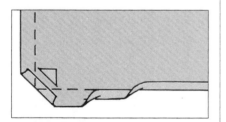

1-E. Edgestitch all around the diaper cover, close to the inner fold. See top of next column.

S The Serger Method

1. Narrow hem the edges following the directions for the Narrow Topstitched Hem for Knits or Wovens, page 153, changing the hem allowance from 1" (2.5cm) to 1¼" (3.2cm).

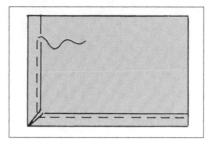

Apply the Elastic

2. Cut the elastic into two pieces, each 6" (15cm) long. Fold each piece of elastic in half and mark the center.

3. Locate and mark the center of each long edge of the COVER. Measure and mark 4" (10cm) above and below each center mark.

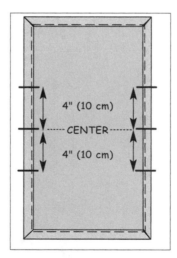

4. On the wrong side of the COVER, center one piece of elastic over the hem allowance, matching the center markings of elastic and COVER; pin in place. Match each end of the elastic to the corresponding 4" (10cm) marks; pin in place. Using the machine zigzag stitch, stitch the elastic to the COVER, stretching the elastic to fit between the markings. Repeat,

stitching the other piece of elastic to the other long edge of the COVER.

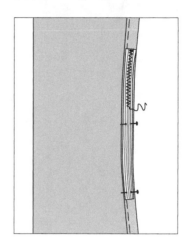

Attach the Hook-and-Loop Tape

5. Cut the hook-and-loop tape into two pieces, each 2" (5cm) long.

6. On the wrong side, position the loop sections of the tape to the corners at one end of the COVER. Machine-stitch around the edges of the tape, stitching through all of the layers. Repeat, attaching the hook sections of the tape to the opposite corners on the right side of the COVER.

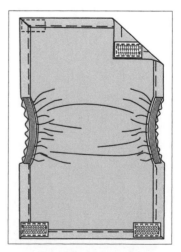

index

notes